THE ASSASSINATION OF PARIS

THE
ASSASSINATION
OF PARIS

LOUIS CHEVALIER

Translated by
DAVID P. JORDAN

With a Foreword by
JOHN MERRIMAN

THE UNIVERSITY OF CHICAGO PRESS
Chicago & London

Louis Chevalier has taught political science at the Collège de France and the Institute d'études politiques. His many publications include *Les paysans, Le problème démographique nord-africain, Classes laborieuses et classes dangereuses,* and *Les Parisiens.*

The University of Chicago Press, Chicago 60637
The University of Chicago Press, Ltd., London
© 1994 by The University of Chicago
All rights reserved. Published 1994
Printed in the United States of America
03 02 01 00 99 98 97 96 95 94   1 2 3 4 5
ISBN: 0-226-10360-9 (cloth)

Originally published under the title *L'Assassinat de Paris,*
© 1977 Calmann–Lévy. The English edition has been published
with the support of the French Ministry of Culture.

Library of Congress Cataloging-in-Publication Data
Chevalier, Louis, 1911–
    [Assassinat de Paris. English]
    The assassination of Paris / Louis Chevalier ; translated by David
P. Jordan ; with a foreword by John Merriman.
        p.   cm.
    Includes bibliographical references.
    1. Historic buildings—France—Paris—Conservation and
restoration.   2. Historic sites—France—Paris—Conservation and
restoration.   3. City planning—France—Paris.   4. Urban renewal—
France—Paris.   5. Paris (France)—Buildings, structures, etc.—
Conservation and restoration.   I. Title.
DC771.C4713   1994
363.6'9—dc20   93-13565

⊚ The paper used in this publication meets the minimum
requirements of the American National Standard for Information
Sciences—Permanence of Paper for Printed Library Materials,
ANSI Z39.48-1984.

CONTENTS

PART THREE: POWER AND CHOICES
141

A section of photos follows p. 154

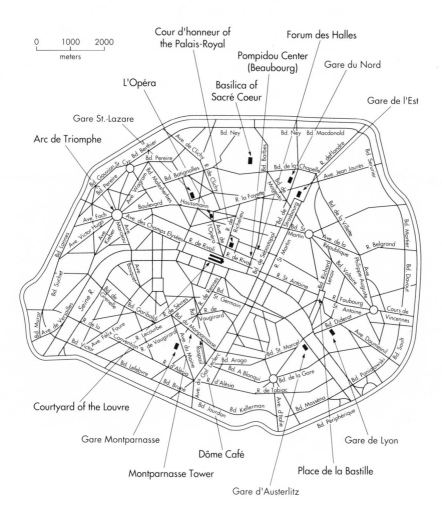

Cour d'honneur of
the Palais-Royal

Forum des Halles

Pompidou Center
(Beaubourg)

Gare du Nord

L'Opéra

Basilica of
Sacré Coeur

Gare de l'Est

Gare St.-Lazare

Arc de Triomphe

0   1000   2000
meters

Bd. Ney

Bd. Ney   Bd. Macdonald

Bd. Gouvion St. Cyr

Bd. Berthier

Ave. de Clichy

R. de Clichy

Bd. Barbès

Bd. de la Chapelle

R. de/lande

Ave. Jean Jaurès

Bd. Sérurier

Bd. Pereire

Ave. Wagram

Bd. Malesherbes

Bd. Batignolles

Bd. de Magenta

Bd. Pereire

Boulevard   Haussmann

R. la Fayette

Bd. de la Villette

Ave. Foch

Ave. des Champs Elysées

Ave. Victor Hugo

Bd. Lannes

Ave. Kléber

Ave. Marceau

R. de Rivoli

R. de Richelieu

R. de Sébastopol

R. St. Martin

Strasbourg

Bd. St.
Martin

Ave. de la
République

R. Belgrand

Bd. Mortier

Bd. Suchet

Bosquet

Ave.

R. de Rivoli

R. St. Antoine

Bd. Richard Lenoir

Ave. Philippe Auguste

Bd. Voltaire

Bd. Davout

Seine R.

Bd. de
Grenelle

Bd. Garibaldi

R. de Sèvres

St. Germain

R. de
Vaugirard

R.
Faubourg
St. Antoine

Cours de
Vincennes

Ave. de Versailles

R. de la

Ave. Félix Faure

R. Lecourbe

R. de Vaugirard

R. de Rennes

Bd. du Montparnasse

Raspail

Bd. Diderot

Ave. Daumesnil

Bd. Soult

Bd. Mirabel

Bd. Victor

Convention

Ave. du Maine

Bd. Arago

Bd. A Blanqui

Bd. St. Marcel

Bd. Poniatowski

Bd. Lefebvre

R. d'Alésia

Ave. du Gal. Leclerc

R. d'Alésia

Bd. de la Gare

Bd. Brune

Bd. Jourdan

Bd. Kellerman

R. de Tobiac

Bd. Masséna

Ave. d'Italie

Bd. Périphérique

Courtyard of the Louvre

Gare Montparnasse

Dôme Café

Gare de Lyon

Montparnasse Tower

Place de la Bastille

Gare d'Austerlitz

FOREWORD

L OUIS Chevalier loves Paris and almost certainly knows more about it than anyone else. Professor at the Collège de France, he is the city's most eminent historian. In *The Assassination of Paris,* David Jordan's elegant translation of *L'Assassinat de Paris,* published in 1977, he proclaims the death of Paris. He wants us to understand how Paris "was put to an end." It is the autopsy of a loved one, the story of how "the capital of the kingdom was given to the highest bidder under the reign of its last king," Charles de Gaulle, and that of his Gaullist successor, Georges Pompidou.

Louis Chevalier, witness to "these final years of Parisian history," some of them observed from an office in the Hôtel de Ville (town hall) quotes Daniel Halévy: "Je voulais parler de Paris et voilà que je raconte ma vie." Exuding outrage and a sense of betrayal, this is a deeply personal history, full of nostalgia, a litany of disillusionment. Chevalier writes that "Anecdotes are not, as Voltaire insisted, 'this small field where one gleans what is left from the vast harvest of history,' but rather lovely bouquets of history, at least when it concerns Paris, where the anecdote is at a premium."[1]

T HIS is an angry book, full of scathing sarcasm and denunciations, the emotions of which have been faithfully rendered in translation. It is far more than merely pessimistic, written by someone "persuaded . . . that the worst will happen. . . ."[2] There will be times as you read this learned polemic that you will wonder if he likes anyone. Cer-

---

1. This approach characterizes his other books, including *Les Parisiens* (Paris, 1967), *Montmartre, du plaisir et crime* (Paris, 1980), and *Histoires de la nuit parisienne* (Paris, 1982). My thanks to Carol Merriman, Peter Gay, and David Bell for reading a draft of this foreword and for their suggestions.
2. More than even Lewis Mumford in his classic *The City in History* (New York, 1964).

tainly not existentialists, in the regulation outfit of "a ponytail, dirty fingernails," and, under one arm, "a thick volume of Sartre." Nor American
universities—"Inspiration is not found on the American campus either,
where you can't escape the students." Sometimes, he does not seem to
like Parisians very much, either (Chevalier himself was born in the fishing
village of Aiguillon-sur-Mer in the Vendée),[3] viewing them as more than
occasionally proving themselves unworthy of their city. Parisians love
automobiles, but "do not love trees." To Chevalier, trees are the city, and
they have fallen before the onslaught of the automobile.

I first met Louis Chevalier in, of all places, Malibu, California. The occasion, in 1972, was a conference on comparative urban development,
sponsored by UCLA. Having recently completed my dissertation, I was
there as a replacement, a long-haired pinch hitter, because my mentor,
Charles Tilly, could not attend. Several days of meetings were held in an
"inn" near the corner of Sunset Boulevard and the Pacific Coast Highway
(the place is now the "Capital of the Age of Enlightenment of California,"
run by the World Plan Executive Council, an enterprise of the Maharishi,
and is complete with a "flying room").

Louis Chevalier's appearance was the highlight of the conference.
Amid ghastly architecture, he looked something like an ill-at-ease Breton
curé who has by accident ended up on vacation on one of the nudist
beaches outside Saint-Tropez. Because I spoke French (though at the
time not very well), it was my pleasure to escort him during part of
the conference. At one point, we went for a walk. The only possible
direction led to the fast-food restaurant next to the inn, where, in response to his question, I explained to him the intricacies of stuffing a
taco, while bikers roared in and out of the parking lot. It was the meeting
of two cultures.

Now, in California, he addressed an audience that included many
social scientists, a number of whom were devoted to accumulating
"hard facts" on urban growth. Professor Chevalier defended "qualita-
tive" sources, especially contemporary literature.[4] Balzac, Hugo, and

3. His *Les relais de mer* (Paris, 1983) is the engaging story of Aiguillon from World
War I into the Fifth Republic.
4. "Malgré tout le labeur le mérite des historiens, je ne crois guère à la résurrection des
temps qu'on n'a pas vécus, à moins que la littérature ne vienne leur donner un sérieux coup
de main, leur apportant ce qui est absent des textes: les sensations, les passions, la vie"
(Chevalier, *Les relais de mer*, p. 40).

even the seventeenth-century teller of fables, La Fontaine, pop up frequently, perceptive interpreters of the past summoned to comment on the present. (What about Zola, I asked him. "No, not Zola," came the reply. "He was a socialist.") Similarly, in *The Assassination of Paris* he returns to "involuntary and spontaneous literary testimony" as unassailable sources for history.

Some years later, in response to the generous gift of his personal archives and papers to Yale University's Sterling Memorial Library, I had the pleasure of visiting him in his apartment near the Pantheon. It was the day of a metro strike—there are a good many such days in Paris. As I live in the Marais not far across the Seine, my walk to his apartment had not been long. But he apologized for the strike: "There are good Parisians and bad Parisians and, my poor fellow, you have the bad fortune of coming to see me on a day when the bad Parisians are out in force." He separates people into two groups, those who love Paris and those who do not.

Professor Chevalier's first book had been a demographic study of the formation of the Parisian population during the first half of the nineteenth century.[5] In 1958 Professor Chevalier had published *Laboring Classes and Dangerous Classes in Paris during the First Half of the Nineteenth Century.*[6] The book, for all of its excellent marshalling of quantitative evidence on the fundamental inequality of rich and poor in the face of disease and mortality (for example, during the cholera epidemic of 1832), reflects Chevalier's insistence that only contemporary opinion—above all, the novel—reflects historical reality. To Chevalier, nineteenth-century Paris was a "sick city" itself, overwhelmed by migration. It is the classic restatement of the uprooting hypothesis, that rapid migration leads to individual anomie and a collective pathology marked by the criminality of "the dangerous classes," whom he identifies, as did much of contemporary middle-class opinion, with the "laboring classes." His implication that the nineteenth-century revolutions were the result of "uprooting" has not stood up, in view of considerable research on the composition of "revolutionary" crowds in 1830 and 1848, whose members turn out to have been, above all, artisans. But Chevalier presents a brilliant view of middle-class attitudes toward Paris and the lower classes

5. *La formation de la population parisienne au XIXe siècle* (Paris, 1949).
6. *Classes laborieuses et classes dangereuses à Paris pendant la première moitié du XIXe siècle* (Paris, 1958).

(who made up more than three-quarters of the population). His depiction of contemporary bourgeois opinion remains fundamental to our understanding of the nineteenth-century urban world.

FOR Louis Chevalier, one of the fundamental problems of Paris has been its inability to adapt to massive immigration. This was the dominant theme of his *Laboring Classes and Dangerous Classes;* it views Paris, which doubled in population between 1800 and 1846, as being overwhelmed by newcomers. After the Revolution of 1848, which Chevalier implies was the result of unchecked migration to the capital, the provisional government tried, through local authorities, to discourage provincials from coming to the capital. A prefectorial circular in 1955 had exactly the same intention.

Over the past thirty years, to be sure, the population of Paris has declined, from 2.9 million in 1911 to 2.1 in the early 1980s. But the Paris region has increased in population dramatically. In 1976, only 2.3 million of the region's 9.9 million people lived in Paris and today even more people in the Paris region live outside the city than in it. Most cannot afford to live in Paris, but many of them pour into the capital each day to work. Paris itself, in any case, continued to be overcrowded. Adequate housing has almost always been difficult to find, and in the first two decades after the war, many neighborhoods, particularly in the center and eastern quarters of the Right Bank, were dilapidated and unhealthy. Now there is more housing, but it is too expensive for most families. Traffic makes automobile access into the center of Paris extremely difficult. Of course, traffic jams are nothing new to the city. Henry IV met death from an assassin's knife in 1610 because the royal carriage became caught in a traffic jam on the rue de la Ferronnerie on the central Right Bank. His guards had jumped out to move carriages to one side, allowing the mad monk *manqué* Ravaillac—he had been rejected by both the Feuillants and Jesuits—to jump in and plant his knife in the king's ribs.

Planners since the beginning of this century turned their attention to accommodating Paris to the automobile. Some were willing to sacrifice historic Paris in the interest of "modernizing" the city. Eugène Hénard, employed in the first decade of this century by the office of public works, wanted to plan for the increasing volume of traffic brought by the automobile, which had already begun to compound the crowding caused by carriages and wagons. Hénard came up with a plan to build wide streets that would radiate from the center of Paris. His proposed *grande croissée* (formed by the intersection connecting the rue de Rivoli and the boulevard Sébastopol) would have plowed through the narrow historic streets of the Left Bank, as well as what had been for centuries the longest street in Paris, the rue Mouffetard. It also would have entailed the extension of the rue de Rennes to the Seine, which would have obliterated the rue Bonaparte, one of the Left Bank's most beautiful streets.[7]

The scale of change imagined by Hénard seems small indeed when compared with Le Corbusier's frightening vision of the capital. In 1925, his Voisin plan proposed a large grid formed by expressways and other streets that would tear through the heart of Paris, eliminating the market of les Halles and reorganizing a good chunk of the center of the Right Bank districts. Le Corbusier projected the construction of sixteen skyscrapers to stand like Frederick the Great's troop of giants under review, the front row just north of the rue de Rivoli, paralleling the Seine.[8]

D URING the two decades following World War II, automobiles poured into Paris in ever greater numbers. The capital was inundated, as if the Sorcerer's Apprentice had been turned loose. Chewing gum was just the first step in the advent of consumer society, much of it imported from the United States: "Suddenly a new supermarket springs up to gobble up all the shops in a neighborhood—the grocery store, the bakery, the butcher shop, from the first to the last; that is to say it devours the joy, the life, the expected and the unexpected, the particular structure of the place, the variegated colors of the streets which, henceforth, are sterile, fatally boring, ruined commercially." The French attraction to consumer society reached its apogee, Chevalier contends, between 1965 and 1970.

Most of the damage was done to the French capital during this period. The wine market near the Seine on the eastern edge of the Left Bank became a victim of "rethinking," so that the university could be expanded. The Jussieu tower went up—I once sat through a doctoral thesis defense in a horrible room with not a single window, because the *salle* is

---

7. On these plans and on the entire question of planning in and around Paris, see Norma Evenson's excellent *Paris: A Century of Change, 1878–1978* (New Haven, 1979), pp. 24–36. Evenson quotes Pierre Lavedan: "the extension of the Rue de Rennes has been the mania of all the Parisian prefects since Haussmann" (p. 68).

8. See ibid., pp. 51–54, 173–74. Here is Richard Cobb on Le Corbusier: "The implacable Helvetian is tireless in his assault on Paris, doggedly determined to line both banks of the river with an aligned barrier of dragon's teeth. What is the secret of his hatred of the place? . . . What distinguishes Le Corbusier is the sheer persistence of his war against the French capital" ("The Assassination of Paris," a review of Evenson's *Paris: A Century of Change, 1878–1978*, in Cobb's *People and Places* [Oxford, 1985], p. 188).

underground. What is above ground is nothing but windows, but is hideous. Plans were readied for the destruction of les Halles and the construction of the Montparnasse tower and La Défense, the cluster of skyscrapers two miles beyond the Arc de Triomphe.

Who is to blame? In Chevalier's view, Paris has been violated by indifferent bureaucrats, arrogant technocrats and "planners," modern architects—the "know-it-all's" of modern civilization, who turned Paris over to greedy developers. He traces the crisis of real estate after World War II, as rent increases drove out many of the real Parisians. Developers destroyed neighborhoods. Banks and architects then got into the act with the connivance of municipal officials, allowing all rules to be skirted.

In particular, he is the sworn enemy of technocrats; after holding "shadow power" before 1958, their power became overt in the Fifth Republic. Revered by the press, these "énarques," pompous graduates of the ENA (École nationale de l'administration), all drawn from virtually the same social milieu, became "the popes of technocracy," their aura of infallibility deriving from the imperialism of statistics.

Chevalier traces the postwar history of the commissions which drew up plans to "modernize" Paris. In 1962 the planning office for the Paris region came forward with a "Plan d'Urbanisme Directeur de Paris." Approved by the municipal council, it underlined the importance of balancing "forces of all kinds—intellectual, aesthetic, economic, industrial."[9] They achieved no such balance, as the redevelopment of fully a quarter of the city went on. With France's entry into the European Economic Community and General Charles de Gaulle's obsession with national grandeur, the intellectual and aesthetic considerations began to lose out.[10] The revised plan, the "Schéma Directeur d'Aménagement et d'Urbanisme," promulgated with Gaullist pomposity in 1968, began the process by which five new satellite cities would be planned: Cergy-Pontoise, Evry, St. Quentin-en-Yvelines, Melun-Sénart, and, to the east, Marne-la-Vallée. It is in this latter town that the French Disneyland is to be found, what someone from the French Cultural Ministry referred to as "a cultural Chernobyl." It is the only one where Mickey, Minnie, Goofy, and swarms of visitors (far fewer to date than anticipated) frolic under almost perpetually gray skies.

Planners, polytechnicians, and the like, Chevalier insists, do not know

9. See John Ardagh, *France in the 1980s* (New York, 1982), p. 262.

10. Evenson, *Paris*, pp. 281, 310: between 1954 and 1974, 1,200 hectares, almost a quarter of the buildable surface of the city, was redeveloped.

Paris. The prefect of the Seine—"he is the power"—in the tradition of
Baron Haussmann, the Second Empire prefect of the Seine who, under
Napoleon III's direction, forged the *grands boulevards,* arrives with his
own staff, drawn from the provinces. He does not care about Paris and
its history. One of them said, "Paris cannot, without irremediably impov-
erishing itself, dwell in a morose contemplation of the past."[11] Like developers, the prefect operates from the principle of self-interest. Chevalier
is outraged that officials and technocrats should be arrogant enough to
think that they could "rethink" Paris.

Richard Cobb, the English historian of the French Revolution and of
Paris, and an inveterate Haussmann hater, dedicated a book to Chevalier.[12] Cobb has written that "what virtually all architects and urbanists
since Haussmann have had in common is a loathing for the past and an
overriding desire to erase its visible presence . . . they have little time for
individuals and their trying, quirky, and unpredictable ways, tending to
think only in terms of human destiny; so many units in the formation of
a Grand Design (or a *Grand Ensemble,* to use a modish French expression), as if people, in rectangular blocks of a thousand, or ten thousand,
were to be assimilated to a gigantic set of Lego."[13]

Interestingly enough, Chevalier's attack on the planners echoes that of
the left, which condemned the scheme for being "far too grandiose and
technocratic, 'a pipe-dream of polytechnicians'."[14] This alliance between
conservatives like Chevalier and the left against the center is not uncommon in the history of French *urbanisme.* Chevalier is no friend of the
soixante-huitards, but seems to join them in offering the same critique of
capitalism and consumerism. As they destroyed trees along the boulevard
St. Michel by using them for barricades, they seemed, at least in part, to
be rebelling against being "manipulated and lumped together precisely as
the social critics of 1968 described."

As in Daniel Defoe's account of eighteenth-century London, the market is the center of Chevalier's account. Another of his books, *Les nuits
parisiennes,* takes place nearby, at Strasbourg-St. Denis ("All of Paris was

---

11. Ibid., p. 295.
12. Chevalier's understanding of space and his evocative writing remind me of Cobb. *A
Second Identity: Essays on France and French History* is dedicated by Cobb to Chevalier
(London, 1969). Among Cobb's many essays, see particularly his extraordinary *Paris and
Its Provinces 1792–1802* (London, 1975); "Paris Xme" in his *Promenades* (Oxford,
1980), and "Preamble Danton 71, 48 [his old phone number]," in *Tour de France* (London,
1976).
13. Cobb, *People and Places,* p. 187.
14. Ardagh, *France in the 1980s,* p. 263.

at Strasbourg-St. Denis, except the high society, of course, who were not missed."). The destruction of les Halles was, above all, what Louis Chevalier means by the "assassination" of Paris—"with les Halles gone, Paris is gone." The fateful decision was taken in 1963 during the de Gaulle régime.

As a young student in June 1967, I was lucky enough, on the very first day I arrived in Paris, to have a friend with the good sense to take me there in the middle of the night to see it before it was too late. The meat market was to be moved to La Villette on the northern edge of Paris, vegetables, fruits, and everything else to Rungis, not far from Orly airport south of the city. The choice to move the market out of Paris seemed justified by the fact that the region served by the market (one-fifth of all of the meat, vegetables, and fruit sold in France went through les Halles) had expanded too rapidly for the market, which had, with the surrounding streets, become extraordinarily congested.

There were protests against the demolition of les Halles. It was absolutely barbaric that the government did not leave a single one of Victor Baltard's pavilions of glass and iron standing, so people could see what it had been like. A few people chained themselves to Baltard's magnificent structures. The old restaurant Au pied de cochon, where elegant diners could eat near the bar populated by butchers in their bloody smocks, has lost its originality. What is left above ground is no better than the sub-basements of shops below ground. The account of the market's fall reads like a death watch, complete with stays of execution, in this case a public execution (such as occurred in France into the mid-1930s), and, finally, the last night of les Halles, February 27, 1969.

The Assassination of Paris traces the protracted debate between business interests and advocates for Paris's history, over what was to be built where les Halles and its surrounding neighborhoods had once stood. In 1979, the Forum opened on three levels below ground, a fourth containing the metro and R.E.R. station. To Chevalier, the Forum has "no other purpose than to concentrate in a deep, fetid underground all that Paris has to show and offer as high-class merchandise, all that one found in the shops along the great boulevards and elsewhere. . . ." Perhaps we should be grateful that Pompidou or, later, Jacques Chirac (who in 1977 became first mayor of Paris in over a hundred years because one government after another had feared the competition a popular mayor might provide) did not make a deal with the Disney people to let Goofy and Donald romp where les Halles had once stood. It could not be much worse.

T HE Tour Montparnasse, standing fifty-six stories tall at the top of
the rue de Rennes, and the cluster of skyscrapers of La Défense,
beyond the Avenue de la Grande Armée, the extension of the Champs-
Elysées, represent technocratic "rethinking." Chevalier views them as
the coup de grace delivered to Paris. To Pompidou, La Défense was part
of "a general effort to make France a great economic power and Paris a
great center of business," permitting "the conception of a thoroughly exceptional ensemble of modern architecture." [15]

These two projects, reflecting "Cartesianism gone mad" through the
attempt to "balance" the Tour Montparnasse with La Défense, unleashed
"an army of bulldozers." There were towers "suddenly thrusting up on
the horizon, all at once, in a few months . . . like those monsters of
Japanese films who rouse themselves from a millennial sleep, get up on
their haunches and destroy cities with their horrible appendages."

Georges Pompidou, who succeeded de Gaulle as president following
the latter's resignation in 1969, acquiesced in the planning of the Tour.
Chevalier describes his sense of personal betrayal. The French president
had been Louis Chevalier's friend in school, and they still ate lunch together at the same brasserie from time to time. Chevalier describes how
these lunches became more difficult. They simply did not talk about Paris.

Pompidou, who once proclaimed "we must renounce forever the out-
moded aesthetic," authorized the Right Bank freeway that tears along the
quais. He presided with a detached Gaullist indifference over the destruction of Louis Chevalier's Paris, following the "law of profit," the "aegis
of good business." Explanations were brief: "France has chosen to compete on an international level and has therefore accepted the risks and
laws involved." The risks for old Paris were enormous. Certainly things
had changed since 1964, when the minister of communications referred
to the telephone as "a gimmick." As Brussels put up one ugly hotel and
office building after another in anticipation of its new status as capital of
the new Europe, Paris would be a world capital of business, "not a museum to maintain." [16]

Louis Chevalier particularly hates Beaubourg. From the study of his
Left Bank apartment, crammed with books and pamphlets, he overlooks
Paris. He cannot avoid seeing Beaubourg ("it's *blue*, and Paris is gray!"),
the Georges Pompidou National Center of Art and Culture, dedicated in

15. Evenson, *Paris,* pp. 188–89.
16. Ibid., p. 190.

1976, its blue pipes sticking up on the edge of the Marais. Richard Cobb pointed out the irony of naming a cultural center after Georges Pompidou (who, it must be said, did not choose, nor necessarily approve of, the architectural design). It seems rather like inaugurating an "Attila the Hun Reading Room."

Beaubourg also entailed the destruction of a neighborhood that, however run down, had been there for centuries, near the heart of the revolutionary Paris. In the Second Empire, Haussmann had taken care to eliminate the rue Transnonain, which lay not far north of the future site of the Pompidou Center.[17] It was the site of a massacre of several working-class families by the bourgeois national guard and troops in 1832, captured by one of Honoré Daumier's most haunting lithographs. Much of the neighborhood had lived on, however.

Beaubourg has become the second most visited tourist attraction in the world. Each day more than 20,000 visitors arrive, more than visit the Louvre and the Eiffel Tower combined.[18] To be fair, the Pompidou Center does offer Parisians, as well as tourists, something that Paris did not really have (despite the admirable Bibliothèque historique de la ville de Paris in the Marais): a library where ordinary people can actually go and read, as well as learn languages, watch films, and do other things. It has, to be sure, attracted too many people, including an inordinate number of clochards, whom Chevalier calls "the last lovers of Paris . . . they loved unselfishly and with peculiar preferences, private tastes, a wholly secret sense of discovery, without repugnance for the hidden corners of the city. . . ."

Chevalier notes that Beaubourg has also attracted many pickpockets, drug dealers, and *voyous,* descendants of the infamous *apaches* of the fin-de-siècle, who came from the impoverished suburbs into Paris to raise some hell. He suggests that the Forum has been marked by a return of the "dangerous classes," who "descended in droves on these once forbidden places, with all their belongings, with their musical instruments, their accoutrements, their strange haircuts, with their work and their diver-

17. Haussmann, to be sure, had many contemporary critics. See, among others, Pierre Lavedan, *Histoire de l'urbanisme (Epoque contemporaine)* (Paris, 1952); Jeanne Gaillard, *Paris, la ville, 1852–70* (Paris, 1979); *Histoire de la France urbaine,* vol. 4, Maurice Agulhon, ed., *La ville de l'âge industriel: le cycle haussmannien (1840–1940)* (Paris, 1983); David H. Pinkney, *Napoleon III and the Rebuilding of Paris* (Princeton, 1958); Anthony Sutcliffe, *The Autumn of Central Paris* (Paris, 1970); and Howard Saalman, *Haussmann: Paris Transformed* (New York, 1971).

18. Ardagh, *France in the 1980s,* p. 277.

sions, with their innocent amusements and those that are not innocent—
drug addicts in corners and their suppliers observing them from the
shadows." He solemnly notes that the first suicide at Beaubourg occurred
on August 19, 1977, not long after it opened.

Pompidou died in 1974. Valéry Giscard d'Estaing, his successor as
president, annulled the plan to build a Left Bank expressway. He did so
by refusing to allocate funds for it, and threw more support toward public transportation. He also vetoed proposals to build more glass skyscrapers on the southern edge of Paris at the Porte d'Italie, a project begun in
1966, and more high-rises that were planned for La Défense.[19] Many
Parisians had had enough of "Manhattanization." It helped that the
president of France was among them. (My copy of L'Assassinat de Paris
may be a collector's item. There is an inscription inside it to Valéry Giscard d'Estaing, with a poem by Boileau. But Professor Chevalier had inadvertently smudged it, so he crossed out the inscription, and kindly gave
the copy to me.) One can take some measure of satisfaction knowing that
a plaque put up in honor of Pompidou can be seen only from a car caught
in a traffic jam on the Right Bank expressway.

C HEVALIER'S epilogue, written fifteen years after the original publication of L'Assassinat de Paris, leaves us with a sense of optimism.
In 1977, Chevalier argued that it was already too late to save Paris, that
it was dead. If anything, the automobile problem in Paris has become
even worse, compounded by tour busses, the exhaust fumes of which are
ravaging Cité and Montmartre, among other places. Still, Jacques Chirac,
between snipes at immigrants in the hope of keeping the anti-immigrant
vote for his Gaullist party instead of benefiting the National Front, has
made a number of agreeable improvements, including the beautification
of the square in front of the Hôtel de Ville.

Paris continues to gentrify, in the Marais, above all, as almost all of the
old hôtels particuliers have been restored. They have been sandblasted,
and attract tourists and provincial and foreign apartment-buyers. But
such renovation has transformed the old neighborhoods, making them,
in many ways, unrecognizable. I remember in the late 1970s when two
very elderly sisters were evicted from their apartment on the rue Pont
Louis-Philippe in the Marais so that the building could be transformed
into upscale apartments. They were expelled in August, that very sneaky
month when many French families are on vacation. A placard posted on

19. Evenson, Paris, p. 63.

the doorway by a neighbor called attention to the injustice. But there was hardly anyone around to read it. The old Parisians disappear. Developers now are taking on the eleventh and twelfth arrondissements beyond the Place de la Bastille and the gare de Lyon. Waves of newcomers continue to change Paris: North Africans, black Africans and Turks (settling particularly around Strasbourg-St. Denis), and Asians. Because of the arrival of thousands of Asian immigrants, the thirteenth was the only one of Paris's arrondissements not to decline in population between 1975 and 1982. Migrants to Paris in the nineteenth century enriched the city while transforming it. One cannot imagine nineteenth-century Paris without its Auvergnats on and around the rue de Lappe, its Bretons living near the gare Montparnasse, where they arrived.

In 1976, Louis Chevalier wrote that, in fifteen years, "No one will have any idea of what Paris was." He still hates Beaubourg, and now has the controversial Bastille Opera and the columns in the courtyard of the Palais Royal, and the glass pyramid in the courtyard of the Louvre, to hate as well. Not all people, Parisians and otherwise, would agree. Professor Chevalier's epilogue itself suggests that he still enjoys the incredible discoveries, experiences, and small daily joys of Paris, " 'the enchantment of finding spared from all manner of destroyers, as if by a miracle, the old-fashioned bakery, the fountain in the center of a courtyard. . . .' This is the secret that one might discover from the many remnants of old Paris that have miraculously escaped the demolishers; this is the attraction, or rather the fascination, they still hold for so many."

I remember once going to a very modest restaurant which stood where Beaubourg now looms. I went there with a friend, a Parisian lawyer, who was dressed in a suit and tie. The *serveuse* had her regular clients, and thus her own agenda, which obviously did not include us, at least for the foreseeable future. My friend tried again and again to catch her attention, first with an eye, and then with calm gestures, and finally with frantic, even angry ones. Finally she gave in, coming over to our table and, eyeing with some condescension my friend and his very fancy suit, said with a smirk, "Je suis à toi comme l'huile est à la sardine." It was a saucy gesture of rejection, but, at the same time, of acceptance, because we had come there. The restaurant, of course, is gone. Other such places are rapidly disappearing. But there are many that still remain to be discovered and enjoyed. The task is to protect what is left.

John Merriman

Translator's Note

There is no need here to reiterate all that has been said over the centuries about the difficulties, even the impossibilities, of translation, about the incompatible genius of languages. Anyone who has done this kind of work knows its pains and pleasures, knows that in place of the author's text the translator makes one of his own which, at best, approximates the original.

This is a deeply felt, polemical, autobiographical work, filled with anger and affection. It is as much about Louis Chevalier, who has spent a long and productive life studying and writing about Paris, as it is about the city itself between 1955 and 1968. It is written in a style both dense and lucid, ironic and flamboyant, filled with literary and cultural allusions. I have tried to capture this tone in English—or rather American, a distinction M. Chevalier always carefully makes—to give some flavor of this style. I have often had to break his sentences into shorter ones; and when I had to choose between a literal rendering of a word or phrase and an impressionistic or emotional one which I thought closer to the writer's feelings or intentions, I have chosen the latter.

I have had the pleasure and instruction of M. Chevalier's friendship and encouragement, both epistolary and personal, throughout this project. He has answered my questions with a promptness and politeness that may date from an earlier generation. When in Paris I have visited him on the rue du Cardinal Lemoine to enjoy his company and his stunning view of the city. I shall always remember looking out over Paris and listening to him talk about the city he has so loved for so long. The two of us together chose the photographs that illustrate this translation.

I have been immeasurably helped by Sophie Vige, who saved me from many imprecisions and some howlers. All the misconstruings that remain are my own.

Because Chevalier was addressing a French audience, he assumed not only considerable familiarity with Parisian history and geography but with French literature and French institutions. I have tried to guess which references and allusions would be unfamiliar to an American reader and provide some guidance. All the notes—unless identified as the author's— are my own. Here and there I have silently intruded into the text an explanatory clause about a book title or an author's first name, or some similar small elucidation. Where a familiar American designation of a Parisian monument or institution exists—as the Eiffel Tower—I have used it; where such a designation does not exist I have retained the French—as the rue d'Ulm. Here and there I have indicated that one of Chevalier's many puns cannot be translated into English, more to remind the reader that this is a rich and brilliant text than to advertise my failures.

David P. Jordan

INTRODUCTION

Experience teaches that cities too can die.

Rutilus Namatianus, *De reditu*

"ITIES too can die." How could I have dreamed that one day this verse by a poet of the Late Roman Empire bemoaning the fate of the major cities of the ancient world devastated by the barbarians could be applied to Paris? Certainly it was unthinkable in the 1960s, when in describing the Parisians I thought I had said the last word: Paris was better understood by looking at Parisians than at their city.[1] Still, even then, hadn't things already started changing? This is what I asked myself each year when I began my course at the Collège de France with lectures on the transformations of the city. I needed no more than three or four meetings to be convinced that the subject was neither urgent, important, or interesting. There were some new developments, of course, but they were insignificant from the point of view of history. One of the most important of these was that Parisians had begun to have more children, something, it seems, that had not happened since the end of Louis XIV's reign. Specialists discussed the phenomenon without reaching a consensus. Anyhow, at first glance, it seemed Parisians were now born in Paris rather than in the Auvergne, Brittany, or the heart of Africa.

As for the construction sites of the increasingly numerous and hideous buildings, these were mostly in the more expensive neighborhoods which, for some time (to speak bluntly) had not much to lose. What did Passy, Auteuil, the west end of Paris have, compared to Montmartre or Belleville? At least the easy-going masons, dangling from their scaffolds like sailors from the rigging of a ship, brought some cheerfulness into those deserts of boredom, bantering flirtatiously with women unaccustomed to gallantries that fell from on high. During the apéritif hour, they ended

1. In *Les Parisiens* (Paris, 1967).

1

the working day by amusing themselves in the pretentious cafés of the Sixteenth arrondissement.

Obviously, during this carefree time, there were disquieting official projects of all kinds. There were extravagant projects such as one often sees in the history of cities. Descartes, who had greater confidence in kings than in the city fathers, says somewhere that such proposals are a specialty of the Paris bourgeoisie as soon as they get some power. Even more to be feared than these bourgeois excesses were the extravagances of the technocrats, "brain storms," as they say in America, where they believe in organized frenzies of thought, where a gathering of sociologists is taken seriously only when it starts to resemble a madhouse. Following the American practice, more and more such meetings were taking place in Paris. They generated hallucinatory projects which the newspapers sometimes submitted to public opinion, taking elaborate precautions, as they do in Hollywood when they show a producer who has put up money the model of a costly set envisioned by a director known for his extravagance, his eccentricities, or his taste in drugs. Who could assure me that this or that abomination would not eventually be built?

Nevertheless, I did not become alarmed. The long history of Paris and the inveterate skepticism of its inhabitants encouraged me to be patient. In the past, how many projects for the urban landscape, incomprehensible to most mortals, had been aborted. One plan, I said to myself, had always destroyed its rival. And lack of money, the caprice of politics, the unexpected death of a dangerous individual, or some other intervention of the gods, might always change things for the better, as had happened so many times. As for the works under way, it seemed premature to me to try and foresee their consequences. Why add my two-cents-worth to so many already tottering projects? Reading the then fashionable studies produced by men too anxious to publish the results of their meditations, I thought about buildings hastily constructed over the years, whose faults had often become, in a very short time, their outstanding feature. I thought of those public officials who had the unfortunate idea of ascending to the *terrasse* of a public housing project inaugurated with great pomp—not too many were being built—and then could not descend. The stairway had collapsed, taking with it the elevator and much else. They had to call the fire department.

So, having described Paris once, I did not think it necessary to do so again. The city would not change very quickly and the Parisians even less rapidly for, as the song says, and especially because they believe it, they have "Paris under their skin." Reassured about the future, untroubled by the present, on leave from my city and my contemporaries, I could return to the past: more precisely to the history of the Parisians, to the study of how these curious people had become through the centuries what they had been for so long that we had forgotten how they came to be. For years and years there had been no reason to think the Parisians could ever change, since Paris was essentially unchanging. "To live elsewhere is to exist in the relative sense of the word, *secundum quid:* to live in Paris is to exist in the absolute sense, *simpliciter.*" What the schoolman of Senlis wrote in the fourteenth century seemed to me to express perfectly the relationship between Parisians and their city. As the years passed, I plunged more deeply into history, into the distant past where I imagined things had begun. Those at the Collège de France who attended my lectures, announced as "A Description of the Parisians," found themselves presented with Gregory of Tours and Ausonius. Were they in the wrong room? There was astonishment and some murmuring. No, Paris was in fact the subject. Yet they did not understand. Had the professor lost his mind?

H E had soon to ask himself the same question: Will Paris always be Paris and the Parisians always Parisians? Without doubt. But these towers suddenly thrusting up on the horizon, all at once, in a few months, precisely during these years, like those monsters in Japanese films who rouse themselves from a millennial sleep, get up on their haunches, and destroy cities with their horrible appendages: Tokyo, of course, London (needless to say), New York, which had long had such towers, but even innocent Paris. The towers were there. We had forgotten about them. We thought them abandoned, buried. Yet there they were, everywhere, flaunting their ugly silhouettes, cut off at the top, grotesquely inclined this way and that. Beating their chests, like King Kong, they declared their names in cavernous voices, which the Japanese archaeologists thoughtfully translated for us: "I am Kikuyamata. . . . I am Maine-Montparnasse. . . . I am. . . ." Who listens to them anymore? There will always be time to hear this nightmare catalogue again. We are only at the beginning, just waking up, and I had, as at any awakening, only a confused, obscure memory of a long and extraordinary illusion. The towers were there, the towers and everything connected with them, everything they stand for and declare, like a signal. They were there like Ionesco's rhinoceros: "There is nothing but them. They fill the street." Soon they will devour it, the succulent, appetizing Parisian street, the waiting victim of their dangerous, insatiable hunger. How could I have missed it?

When they first started going up I am not sure I saw them, and if I believe the press releases it is not clear that the most perspicacious observers saw them any better than I. This was not because of some blindness on our part, some inattention, or some conspiracy of the powerful, always capable of deceiving, but rather because habits are slow to change. Perception is itself a matter of habit. Images from the past obscure the eye and mask images of the present. At first we do not see, or we see without registering the image. Then, when it is no longer possible not to see, we arrange things, first instinctively then deliberately, to avoid seeing them as much as possible. We take complicated routes to avoid the monsters or so many other establishments which are equally offensive: all those food specialty shops that kill the appetite, the sex shops that kill love. "I hate the towers of Saint-Sulpice. . . ." Oh, Verlaine! Without going to such an extreme, one can always choose one's subway stop, take another street and even, while in enemy territory, close an eye, open an umbrella. I know a grandmother who regularly takes her grandchildren to the Tuileries. She invented a game, part hide-and-seek and part blindman's buff. By carefully using the trees and statuary—and the statues of country girls erected in the garden of the kings make it easy—one can cross the pathways, going from one to another, in a series of leaps, without seeing La Défense.[2] *Défense de voir la Défense!* Looking at the skyscrapers of La Défense (beyond the Arc de Triomphe) is forbidden. If you glimpse La Défense you are dead. . . . And as this adroit grandmother told me, having read in the newspaper that the towers of La Défense were sinking: "If this continues I will have to find another game, since my grandchildren aren't getting any smaller." The selfishness of grandmothers! I did the same. The more present-day Paris annoyed me, the more I turned to the past, played hide-and-seek. The Gallo-Romans of Ausonius were my trees in the Tuileries, and the Merovingians of Gregory of Tours, or rather the women of the dynasty, were my bronze milkmaids.

I add another consideration which I still find difficult to assay. Georges Pompidou was an old comrade of mine. A comrade is different from a friend, a little less, a little more, but something else. Beyond friendship, which comes in youth, comradeship signifies sincerity, truthfulness,

2. A concentration of modern skyscrapers just outside Paris which can be seen from the Champs-Elysées, looking through the Arc de Triomphe. The new "Grande Arche" has recently been built at La Défense.

equality, or at least the memory of equality which, once it exists, never completely disappears. The statesman continued to associate on equal terms with his comrades. Just as the king is always naked before his old comrades, so at least was this king, whose forbears were peasants from the Auvergne. With a few comrades from the Ecole Normale Supérieure, we had the habit, for fifteen or twenty years, I no longer remember exactly, of lunching together, every second Tuesday of the month. At first these lunches were in a small restaurant on the rue Hautefeuille, just off the boulevard St. Michel, not far from the publishing house of Hachette where one of our number, Maillard, edited a collection of geography books in which he reserved the volume on "Europe" for an aspiring young geographer who had not yet published his *Rivage des Syrtes,* Julien Gracq. The prime minister remained faithful to the habits he had as a teacher and student. He came on foot to the smoky cellar of the restaurant without disturbing the other clients, who knew the ritual. He came without a policeman (or maybe with one cleverly disguised), without a single journalist, and it should be said, in those simpler times, there were no bomb threats. Nevertheless sometimes the get-together, as we called it, was at the Matignon Palace and later at the Elysée, that uncomfortable and somber palace, so misnamed, so unlike the carefree place visited by Aeneas in book six of *The Aeneid.* The Matignon had more charm, more whimsy. Maybe we were just getting older, but the lunches now took place only quarterly, in this heavy, overwrought decor which hardly complemented the things our comrade loved, or at least thought himself obliged to love because of his position. Who would want modern art if the president had spurned it?

And what did we talk about? Everything except questions of art. Our host, seeing with an ironic eye the way we sat uneasily in his uncomfortable chairs and how we glanced at his walls with perplexity, had decided that we would never understand such things. We talked about everything that deserved interest and was worthy of a well-laid table: of our youth, of love, of poetry—but never of philosophy, which we hardly understood—and, of course, never, absolutely never, of politics. And also never of Paris. Yet, God knows how, some days the subject imposed itself, burning to be brought out, hot from the oven, and set on a platter in the middle of the table. This happened the day after a certain declaration about La Défense and its great towers appeared in the daily *Le Monde* (which I will discuss below). As I sat down at the table it was still stuck in my craw. It seemed to me—and perhaps this was an illusion—that Pompidou, knowing what I thought about this subject, which was exactly the opposite of his views, cast a stern and mocking gaze in my direction that said were it up to men like me the Parisians would still be living in the huts in which Julius Caesar had found them. What could I say to break the silence: that the plates served us contained choice delicacies and that the Cantal (by no means my favorite cheese) was a gift of the gods? One cannot love everything, not even the towers of La Défense.

Having decided not to talk about Paris with the man whose opinion was most important to me, how would I later be able to write anything at all about the city, telling the president through an intermediary, so to speak, what I did not want to say to his face, declaiming in a public voice what he knew perfectly well. It was not that he attached the least importance to my opinion, or that I was exposing myself to disgrace or risking the Bastille. It just seemed impossible. Thus I decided to abandon contemporary Paris to its sad fate. I would content myself with assembling the evidence which would permit others, and the later the better, to write the chapters on our own times, including the chapter on Pompidou, in which I would not get involved. I filed everything in boxes and earmarked them for posterity without concerning myself, as a good historian, with what could become of it in the future. The "archives of contemporary Paris," of which Pompidou knew the existence and about which he had vaguely suggested that they might be housed in the Beaubourg Museum, would end up on some riverbank or other: that of the Seine or, if no one was interested in them, in some more welcoming harbor. Having thus made up my mind, I felt relieved. I even asked myself if Pompidou had not been for me the unexpected excuse for not having to describe a city that no longer gave me the joy it once did and which interested me less and less. Even more, this was an excuse for not seeing—or what can be called seeing—what would finally kill sight itself: the fact that in a few years Paris had completely vanished, to be replaced by something else.

M Y feeling intensified, little by little, like a sickness. Fleeting impressions, street scenes, overheard words, empty passageways, sad doorways, the impression of dragging my feet where, only yesterday, there was a bounce in my step, of marking time when previously each second was an adventure: all this eventually spread over the city itself a gray dust, a kind of sadness, lassitude, decrepitude. Paris was getting decrepit. Or was it me? A moment of fatigue, feeling out of sorts—everyone has these feelings, even lovers of Paris in the most charming neighborhoods. "This afternoon," wrote Julien Green in 1935, "I meandered between the place Clichy and the place Pigalle. They were taking down the market stalls in an unrelenting, fine rain. I believe that of all the great cities that I have known, Paris is one of the saddest, despite the reputation for gaiety it inherited from a happier time. . . . Nevertheless . . . I attributed this to feeling out of sorts." Feeling out of sorts is an old theme of Parisian literature, but it is a temporary state, a heartbeat. After having blasphemed, Baudelaire adored. There was none of this in what I felt. I did not think it was age: the old Victor Hugo spoke of Paris like a young man, always ready to be gallant, to caress a round bottom or try even more. It is true, as Léon Daudet observes, and he was himself an amorous sensualist and a great connoisseur of the city, "this lyre has solid strings." Not for a moment does Hugo doubt the seductiveness of this sumptuous creature. Not even when he has some reason to complain about her or to feel uneasy about his subject. "Old Paris is no more and new Paris does not yet exist," he writes in *Les Misérables*. "Of this new Paris," he adds, "the author, long absent, knows nothing." At least he knew that this new Paris would always be Paris, "the city of cities, Rome and Athens together." What astonishing certainty. Despite the works of Haussmann, despite the detested Second Empire, despite exile, despite so many reasons for hate, for doubt, he had not the least uneasiness. For the Paris of the future he had only a blind, total declaration of love.

"Old Paris is no more and new Paris does not yet exist"? Shouldn't I rather write "Paris is no more" while the much vaunted "New Paris" has nothing in common with what Paris has always been. Indeed it is this "New Paris" that opened my eyes. In the 1960s, when I wrote *Les Parisiens,* an unscrupulous advertising campaign was launched naming everything and anything "Paris." The wicked step-mother tried to supplant the real mother, dispensing favors, cajoling the child and, better to accomplish her designs, donning the clothes and jewelry of the original.

Historians will have no difficulty writing the history of this litany of imposture. The documents exist, puffed up with pompous words which, one will see, change over the years. The word "prestige" for example, overused at one time, eventually evoked suspicion—a prestigious apartment, what does that conjure up?—and was replaced by the word "standing," which sounds impressive and has the advantage that no one knows exactly what it means. These impostures are everywhere, highlighted by the grammatical errors which accompany successful promotions (yet another word whose history one could write), applied to the poorest cloth as well as the cashmere jacket or the ocelot coat, the velvet jacket, which will replace the delicately soiled shirt, the faded, expensively threadbare jeans.

In July 1966, for example, the Municipal Council of Paris indignantly declared: "For several weeks now a huge advertising campaign has been covering our walls and filling our newspapers. It announces the birth of a new city to be called Paris II. . . .We must fight back. They have stolen Paris by confiscating her birth certificate." Without understanding very clearly what had happened to him, the sacrilegious developer had to retreat and dream up something less insolent, but no less offensive, to baptize his project. The first syllable of Paris—at least so I imagine—was joined to the last syllable of Marly, which obviously they thought redolent of the age of Louis XIV, of a *fête galante* including the elaborate pumps at Marly that fed the Versailles fountains. If only he hadn't been so hasty. Two or three years later what couldn't he have gotten away with? He could have had his Paris II, his Paris III, his Paris IV. In the great airports of the world one would have heard: "Passengers for Paris III . . . the next flight for Paris II," for these other cities of which the real Paris would eventually have become the dilapidated suburb. The first-class passengers, destined for Paris II, for Paris III, would have dinner with champagne, a film, and soft music. The others, bound for Paris I, the ignoble poor, the immigrants, the students or teachers, would have no room to stretch out their legs, would be served cold cuts, some mineral water, and an after-dinner mint. Yes, what might have been. As it turned out, according to the latest news, those on the organized tours to Parly 2 are encouraged to make a detour by way of Versailles.

If the advertising history of Parly 2, perhaps because of the proximity of the Sun King at Versailles, reads like Molière's *The Bourgeois Gentleman,* others have different absurdities or convolutions. The advertising theme of the Montparnasse Tower, or rather its melodrama, is of unappreciated beauty. How they try to please! "Oh, I feel so beautiful . . . ," this great homely tower sings incessantly. Bejeweled like a reliquary she shines with all her lights in the evening sky, with no one to contemplate her marvels besides a few cruising taxis. With the coming of the energy crisis of 1973, some said we might not have to see her any more. But no. She held out until things got worse and they finally decided to put out this useless candle, to close the jewel box. Thus deprived, she found it hard to defend herself against misunderstanding or slander. Some found her too large, others too small. Some criticized her color. Those who preferred blondes found her too swarthy; those who preferred brunettes disagreed. Pompidou himself, a connoisseur, told *Le Monde* that he would have preferred another color, without specifying which one. People didn't know what they wanted. And then, speaking on the radio, the director of Le Lucenaire (an avant-garde theater situated in the rue Odessa), who knew the Montparnasse Tower intimately (she is its neighbor), baptized it the big eyesore [*la grande vilaine*], which was soon taken up by the neighborhood. But what about convincing all the others? And the big eyesore is distraught. She wrings her hands in the sky. If only an artist, even one without a reputation, would paint her! Despite enormous financial difficulties she would go so far as to pay for his brushes and even buy the finished canvas. If only a novelist would set some touching love story here, or even if some desperate person would commit suicide from her, as is so often done from the top of the Eiffel Tower, also misunderstood at her debut. But it seems suicide is impossible from the Montparnasse Tower. Confronted with the success of the American film *Towering Inferno,* a facetious filmmaker suggested a similar scenario. The project was rejected with horror. Besides, only the Americans burn their towers. In Paris, when we have only one, we keep it.

So it is that from year to year the historian, walking past the billboards, will come upon all the most recent outrages which make it even more obvious where we are, as I write these pages, and where Paris is. Not far from the Montparnasse Tower, for example—her again—is a hotel whose advertisement declares that it was not by chance that Hemingway wrote *A Moveable Feast* in Montparnasse. From this one should infer the necessity of installing oneself in Montparnasse, in the hotel in question. But one says to oneself, contemplating the building, that rather than stay there Hemingway would have preferred to face all the bulls in *Death in the Afternoon* or the great white fish in *The Old Man and the Sea.* In any case never would he have had the notion of writing at the head of the final chapter of *A Moveable Feast* "There will always be Paris." Even more presumptuous, more definitive, another hotel, near the Porte Maillot, put it bluntly: If you visit Paris in order to know Paris you can do it without inconveniencing yourself. Visit the ground floor of the Porte Maillot, where all the major streets of Paris and their shops await you. "It is not you who come to Paris, it is Paris that comes to you." I went to see for myself. To my great satisfaction the shops were without customers. Some even had no merchandise. A jewelry shop had been cleaned out by a gang of international thieves who arrived by airplane the evening before. And a woman had been attacked in an elevator. Without customers, sinister doorways loom here and there and say to the occasional passerby, do not linger here. This is not the rue de la Paix but the menacing exterior boulevards.

Even more than the material changes it is the advertising, it is the words, the moneylenders in the temple with their vulgar cries who have forced me to realize the temple is gone. I was not the only one to see this. I would have been even less isolated if people were not so easily satisfied with words. But deep down they agreed. They even said so, when we knew how to get them to say so. "That's Paris? Are you kidding us?" This was more or less the conclusion of a public opinion poll that the Paris administration took—partly on my sardonic advice—around 1972. We were then in the midst of prosperity. The official hymn was to Paris in the year 2000. They preferred to silence this discordant note and to hide the truth. I even think they asked me, very courteously, not to speak about it. Things have changed today.

"T HAT'S Paris?" Numerous Parisians—several hundred thousand if I believe the poll—wondered about this in their innermost selves. Many had known Paris before World War II and some even before World War I, yet they could not readily respond. The years had already taken their toll on memory. This is an old theme of literature about Paris. Viollet-le-Duc, in 1860, gave the definitive response to this perennial subject, which, literally applies to our day: "It is remarkable with what ease people in Paris forget the old things. This is a blessing but also a great curse if they have neglected to preserve in some reliable form what they heard and what they saw in an earlier time. A Parisian told me that the tower of St. Jacques was surrounded by a *place* since the French Revolution. Another, relating an event that had occurred in 1848, told me: "I am certain of what I now recollect, and the proof is that the event took place on the boulevard Sébastopol, at the corner of the boulevard St. Denis. I feel as if I were there." Everyone knows the anecdotes told by Fouché, minister of police under the Empire. He recounted a conversation he had had with Robespierre, when, because of a particular circumstance, he had believed himself bound to oppose him: " 'Duc d'Otranto!' . . . Robespierre said to me, 'you play for high stakes.' "[3] Viollet-le-Duc adds that people are not longer absolutely sure whether there was a *flèche,* a pointed ornamental tower on the roof of Notre-Dame, above the nave, before the one he himself erected and which our contemporaries consider a masterpiece of the Middle Ages. What does it matter so long as it is beautiful? It still takes one's breath away. "How

3. In the first two anecdotes reference is made to parks and streets that would later be built by Baron Haussmann. Fouché was made Duc d'Otranto by Napoleon years after Robespierre's death.

lovely the *flèche* of Notre-Dame is this morning" wrote an unfortunate man some years ago before jumping from the top of the Eiffel Tower.

If the Parisians who have known the Paris of yesterday, the Paris of an earlier time, forget, how much easier will it be for those who have never known it, the young, who are scandalized to hear me disparage a city that seems to them more beautiful than any of those they have seen. Today's youth are different, for they travel throughout the world and can make comparisons. In listening to them ennumerate, in support of their views, their favorite neighborhoods, all that is vibrantly alive for them is moribund for me. I recite to myself the passage from *Les Misérables:* "The horizon, the trees, the green fields, the sails of ships at sea." In place of the beauties of nature which are vanishing, in my mind's eye I see those of the city which give the same satisfaction, the horizon still intact, the fine articulation of the bell towers, "the ocean of clustered rooftops," as Henry Miller saw them around 1935, in *Black Spring.* "My eyes still see them. Darkness closes my eyes: night."

Vanishing, this is the theme of my book, the certainty that in a few years, easy enough to calculate, no one will have any idea of what Paris was. In barely fifteen years it will be gone except when we conjure up its image—always inadequate—from books. There will no longer be the faintest imprint of a footstep, as it was possible to find in an earlier time, no longer the smallest stone where one sat daydreaming or grafting the city's past onto one's own. Ineluctible intolerable oblivion. How can we not hear mounting from the kingdom of shadows the cry of Dante's *Inferno?* "I also have lived in this city." I was this city. "Have you forgotten me?"

I F vanishing inspires my book, it also fixes its purpose: the description of how a place has disappeared, root and branch. The first signs were barely visible. "The eye saw no changes." Man "is not uneasy. What is there to be uneasy about? But he feels something." What the author felt from day to day over the years and, along with him those whose testimony he collected, this is the subject of an account which values memories—which are in themselves texts and evidence—above actual texts and recorded evidence. And then comes the final word: "night." The night once fallen, who can continue? It doesn't much matter what comes afterwards. Once Paris was gone, who could care much about what remained? Life is short. Why waste it in describing what everyone can see? Why even go to see for oneself? When I told one of my former students, who had become an important man, that I was going to describe the recent evolution of Paris—a prudent way of expressing myself—without ever having set foot in a "new city," he was dismayed and directed one of his colleagues, intimately familiar with such cities, to get me to visit one. I no longer remember which "new city," for I confound them all, despite the care taken to make attractive documentaries about them to fill the empty time between films in the movie houses. We arranged a meeting. The colleague had his offices—needless to say—in the middle of Paris, on the banks of the Seine, not in the new city in question. He put himself completely at my disposal. He had only a single letter to sign before we departed. The car was waiting for us. The driver was passing the time by looking around at nothing in particular. It was one of those winter afternoons wrapped in fog when Paris has an indescribable added charm. From what I observed, my guide was as anxious to revisit his little marvel of a city as he was to throw himself into the river. As I was no more anxious than he, I said, to his great relief, that we might reschedule the visit for the spring. We would invite a few students, which would be splendid. We would picnic on the grass; by the way, was there any grass? And so I shall die without ever having seen a new city. In any case this is not at issue here as long as I don't speak ill of what I have never seen, for the guidance of future generations who might otherwise be able to deceive themselves about the sentiments of the men of our time by reading misleading documents.

THIS account will show when it was all over, when night descended, between 1960 and 1968. Things moved quickly long before May 1968. The transformation was so far along that it is hard not to see in the revolt of May 1968, among other things, the refusal to live in this new urban milieu, in this city that had been "Nanterre-ized," this city whose boredom, hideousness, rawness, whose reinforced concrete condemned students to a kind of captivity and summed up all they detest.[4] Fantastic transformation! The young now spit on Paris, Paris that had for centuries been their paradise, the city to which they flocked, convinced they would find there all they dreamed of—pleasure, love, success, glory, in a word life itself, the "vivre à Paris" of the medieval student: "Paris for us!" The change is significant. For our purposes it shows that by 1968 darkest night had already descended.

But in what year did it begin? If it were only a question of describing the general history of Paris in modern times, nothing would be simpler.

4. Nanterre is the "new" city whose university was the cradle of the student revolt.

It would suffice to begin with some great event, the liberation of Paris from the Nazis, for example. But the sapping of the city's life, when does that begin? Should I attempt to fix the moment when it seems to me—from my own experience or that of others—that Paris began to change? Or should I—through a retrospective survey of circumstances and responsibilities—ask myself when exactly Paris began to change? There is no compelling reason for choosing any particular date after World War II over another.

For a work of this kind, though, which lacks the chronological framework of traditional history, some authorization for the historian to begin, some point of departure, is needed, as with the three blows struck offstage at the theater to announce the raising of the curtain. There are so many difficulties for those who would set out on their own! The novelists, for example, have the same problem when they have a historical bent or write a historical novel. What pains Balzac takes in the opening lines of his novels when he fixes the action not only in space but in historical time—the year, the season, the day in relationship to the great events of the hour. "At the time when this study opens. . . ." The first pages of *Eugénie Grandet* are a chronological outline. This is also so in Victor Hugo, and more dramatically, this obsession to establish a necessary correspondence between his story and the immensity of the moment: "1817 is the year that. . . ." It is the year when *Les Misérables* opens, an insignificant year, "a year now forgotten," the year when this gigantic work begins. A minor circumstance of life, something so insignificant that one is astonished it determined such a choice, makes this year a point of convergence of events and an important date in history.

In what year, and why in this year rather than another, should I begin a narrative for which the traditional documents of history, which history itself will undermine, are less important than personal impressions? In such an account anecdotes would dominate. Anecdotes are not, as Voltaire insisted, "this small field where one gleans what is left from the vast harvest of history," but rather lovely bouquets of history, at least when it concerns Paris, where the anecdote is at a premium. In such an account facts, usually thought to be of major importance—command decisions, celebrations, inaugurations, scenes worthy of the movies—would have a lesser role than the minor events, incidents from daily life—in a word, mundane details. "These details that are erroneously considered of little value," writes Hugo à propos of 1817, "are useful. From the physiognomy of the years is the face of centuries made." These details, as he imagines them, show us "Chateaubriand standing every morning at his window (27 rue St. Dominique) in trousers . . . his eyes fixed on his mirror. . . ." Why am *I* not a novelist, able to describe this or that man in his undershirt? Why can't I invent? As far as I'm concerned, it is ungrateful to speak thus of a novel that gives such pleasure and embodies so much truth. Rather than invent, it is preferable, as Hugo himself had done, and without embarrassing myself any more, to choose some personal historical fact and begin.

I will start in 1955, when I happened to make the acquaintance and to become the friend of the man who was, without doubt, the last prefect of the Seine, in the full sense of the word, the last prefect endowed with the traditional grandeur of the office, Emile Pelletier. He gave me an office not far from his own, in which the windows look out on the *place* of the Hôtel de Ville. I was by title counselor to the prefect. What counsel did I have to give? Fortunately for myself, but especially for him, hardly any. There always was in the city administration, at least in the pre-technocrat era, some inoffensive and perfectly useless person: a poet, a dreamer, a novelist, a hanger-on. The sinecure in these years was held by myself as historian. The purely honorific functions allowed me to add some supplementary bits of information to those accumulated by a Paris stroller. So, among many possible dates, I would choose this one. It is not that I was overcome by some novelist's inspiration and wanted to organize around the year 1955 a collection of bric-a-brac comparable to the venerable characteristics of 1817, in order to make a mountain of events of all shapes and sizes. But "in this year, in the day of the motor scooter, Parisians could contemplate an astonishing motorized parade. The celebrated lovers, Tristan and Isolde, Romeo and Juliet, Héloise and Abelard, circled the Etoile on scooters." This is an actual citation from a newspaper. I would not pretend that this year presents some important historic signs of the decline of Paris I and that these can be seen more clearly in 1955 than in the preceding or subsequent year. It only seems to me that, trying today to describe the decline, it is from this year that I find in my memories and in my papers a way of understanding approximately how these things happened.

PART ONE

CIRCUMSTANCES

The individuals charged with deciding where new streets would be cut, despite their authoritarianism and desire perhaps to give their work a personal imprint, have had to bow to the social needs manifest in the city. . . . Their intervention is evident only in the particular forms, in the details, but neither modifies nor opposes the play of collective forces.

Halbwachs, *Les expropriations et le prix des terrains à Paris,*
1860–1900

L ET us begin with some circumstances. Not those men in responsible positions, the guilty ones, the directors, all of those the public adores, and the Parisians probably more than others, if one is to believe history and especially literature. Left to her own genius history would forget them, for they scarcely play an important role, were it not for those specialists "with the memory of an elephant" of whom Lucien Febvre speaks. The thick novels, on the other hand, full of emotions, punctuated with portraits, solidly built up out of sentences and literary devices, reawaken the passions, recapture feelings and behavior, orchestrate scandals, those character assassinations in which the public takes so much pleasure. One would have to be Madame de Sévigné to remain faithful to Fouquet languishing in the Bastille.[1] The years I am about to describe are those of Zola's Second Empire, with its bankers, its businessmen, its widespread corruption, its appetite for pleasure that inspire so many comparisons in today's newspapers, so many judgments that can even be quantified in opinion polls conducted by men who have never read the twenty volumes of Zola's Rougon-Macquart novels. But this is the Second Empire of the novelist, not of the historian. There is one his-

1. He was Louis XIV's finance minister. Confined to the Bastille after his disgrace and fall, he would become the first martyr to arbitrary imprisonment in that dreadful place. He also built the chateau of Vaux-le-Vicomte (which Louis confiscated) whose gardens are said to be the inspiration for those later built at Versailles.

torian, however, or rather a sociologist turned historian, unique of his kind, Halbwachs, who in studying the building of Paris in the nineteenth century underscored the fact that Baron Haussmann concerned himself only with what was essential in a city that had become unlivable, in short, in material reality.

It is precisely this city, overwhelmed by its population, fatigued, sick, that I was then studying. The book on which I was working, *Classes laborieuses et classes dangereuses à Paris pendant la première moitié du XIXe siècle,* no doubt reinforced, over the years, this same way of seeing the city where I lived. It is because I had written this book that I spent the greater part of my time in the Hôtel de Ville. I did not have a guilty conscience or the impression of uselessly taking up space. To make my case more compelling, I even had two of the prefect's charming secretaries type up reports on prostitution, on crime, and on executions (they were more anxious to devote themselves to my manuscript than to the official prose of the prefect). All this was done with the permission of the principal assistant to the prefect, Roger Sicard, happily someone who loves history. Seeing these horrors come to light and often seeing his secretaries sitting in the Place de Grève in front of the Hôtel de Ville or in some dive, he contented himself by saying: "Type quickly, ladies, and do not be deterred from your goal." Immersed in the nineteenth century, where I rediscovered violence in the spectacle of les Halles, which I never failed to walk through on the way to my office, what I remembered from the Paris around me were those things the city expressed and symbolized: the city of stone described by Halbwachs who, in his dealings with the population, both satisfying and difficult, was able to distill, without much control over the outcome, the best, or more often the worst. My city had failed to adapt to its population, just as it had failed in the middle of the nineteenth century, but in another way and with different consequences. This fact seemed indisputable to me. As to what followed, this I would have to view in another way. It is, then, with this interpretation that I shall begin.

Chapter One

The Mystery of Charity

A decent man who writes *Caractères*, as does La Bruyère, ought always to paint scenes and not portraits, to paint men rather than one man. Even so people will always suspect bad intentions because particular examples are always the first concern of louts.

Montesquieu

I N one of the cafés near the Hôtel de Ville frequented by the staff of the Prefecture of Paris, where one sometimes hears crude stories, one icy February morning in 1954 two functionaries whom I knew slightly were laughing uproariously while reading their newspapers.[1] What was so funny? It was an account of a gala to benefit the good works of the abbé Pierre that had taken place the previous evening at the Théâtre des Champs-Elysées. An edifying film had been shown to the cream of Paris society, a film calculated to open even the most tightly closed wallets, for God knows the Parisian upper crust is notoriously tight. "Until quite late sedans left the theater filled with those who had attended and thus announced to the world that Paris society was not unconcerned with the disadvantaged of the capital, those without food or a roof over their heads." Mentioning a well-known building contractor, almost as renowned as the abbé Pierre (but in a completely different way), the darling of the elite of Paris society whom he never failed to invite to sip champagne when he opened a new building (which happened often), one of my interlocutors suggested that the abbé had in a way created the social elite of builders. The man in question is the very archetype of building contractors. If he didn't exist he would have to be invented. But since he existed, why did the ingrates, his rivals, want him to die so that the pope could canonize him? Rather they should have held

---

1. Emile Pelletier had been appointed prefect of the Seine in October 1955. I had been doing research in the Bibliothèque administrative, on the top floor of the Hôtel de Ville.—Author.

his hospitality in high esteem, since they had no idea what sainthood was. I might add that at a gathering devoted to the construction industry where the talk was mired in material matters and interest rates, I once clearly heard with my own ears a man little suspected of mysticism elevate the discussion by bringing Saint Vincent de Paul into it. He was ignorant of everything concerning the saint's century.

> From the first night society women and recidivists, touched simultaneously by the same grace, went together to seek the homeless in the freezing streets in order to give them a roof over their heads and some bread.
>
> Thierry Maulnier, *Preuves*, April 1954

THIS recollection of Thierry Maulnier sums up what I am attempting to do. First, there is the abbé Pierre and the arrival in Paris of those who were probably not hungry—the rich, when they think about such things, always exaggerate—but had nowhere to live, "to crash" in popular language. Not even a pallet of straw and all that that evokes—some temporary shelter, an attic in Belleville, a garret near les Halles, as well as the warmth of a stable, an ass and an ox, the infant Jesus, even the Magi on the horizon. High society likes to masquerade as the Magi, wearing a silk turban, bringing myrrh, incense, and those useless but inexpensive presents which, as is well known, give the masqueraders such pleasure.

What happens to these new arrivals who don't have any idea where they can stay? Why do they come? Who has put this idea into their heads? Do they still think they are in the Middle Ages when people flocked to follow some mad monk who promised a land of plenty? It is true that the abbé Pierre . . . but leave that be.

In the provinces this migration is probably useful because it gets rid of a "surplus" population, as officialdom puts it, and loads down Paris and the Parisians, those patient beasts of burden, who pay taxes and endure exactions. But Parisian good will has its limits. In October 1955 a municipal councilor declared that, as a result of the preaching of the abbé Pierre, there was a huge immigration of provincials who hoped to find a bed and assistance in Paris: "We will never clean up this mess." The prefect was forced to distribute in the provinces a circular designed to discourage this immigration, which was getting out of hand.

During these years, then, the internal immigration to Paris, which had been interrupted by the war, resumed. It began as a kind of festival, immediately after the Liberation, indeed on the very first evening. The huge bell of Notre Dame had scarcely ceased piercing the night, the beautiful summer night, with its heavy bronze vibration, when the new immigrants were in the capital. They flocked from everywhere. In trucks bearing provisions they sat among the potatoes and rutabagas, on scooters, on foot, by any means, they roamed the city. It was extraordinary. They formed joyous groups within one immense happiness. I can still see miners from the Nord, their faces blackened by coal dust, around the Châtelet. They had no idea where they would sleep. I thought it useless to tell them to "be very careful not to catch anything. A single night celebrating the Liberation of Paris would not be worth it." Then there were the Marseillais, as if fallen from the sky. "It is impossible that you have come from Pigalle. It shouldn't be Pigalle but the old port of Marseilles. Besides it's a bit late to seize the Bastille!"[2] I thought of the Marseillais whose grotesque faces Chateaubriand describes: "Marseillais worthy to sing the *Marseillaise*." Irresistible logic. I then thought, once the *Marseillaise* had been sung and the street lights extinguished, these Marseillais of the Place Châtelet were finished and would return to Notre Dame, unless they really were crazy or really were the Marseillais of Pigalle. On the other hand I asked myself if, once having discovered this Paris refuge, my miners from the Nord had returned to their mines. I know a priest from the Vendée region in the west of France who still has not forgiven himself for having "borrowed" a truck so that his young parishioners could celebrate in Paris itself the liberation of the capital. When he returned, a few were missing.

There was, then, in the years following the war, as after all wars—those of the Revolution and the Empire, those of 1870 and 1914—an enormous movement in hearth-bound France, which at times just wants to take to the road, suddenly mobile, adventurous, disoriented. But this never lasts for long. Between the two world wars immigration was halted with the approach of World War II. When it started again, after the Liberation, its character changed rapidly. To single men, to lone individuals who saw a chance to live their own lives, to escape "the chill of provincial life" Balzac speaks of, were now added young couples, more and more often with children. But above all, in a few years, unnoticed and ignored, the original immigration—celebratory, carefree, welcome, even encouraged—gave way to another influx—needy, burdened by and angry at everyone, loaded with problems and unable to solve them alone, reduced

2. A reference to the arrival of patriots from Marseilles in the French Revolution, who carried with them the song, the *Marseillaise*, that would become the national anthem.

to seeking public charity, with no other hope but Divine Providence, a miracle, the abbé Pierre.

Certainly these new arrivals did not inflict upon the city the over-crowding and the ever-changing street scene that I found in Paris before Baron Haussmann. Nevertheless the diverse facts regularly reported in the press, of suffering and of sights in the streets, presented a picture of Paris in the 1950s that needed only a great novelist or a maker of epic movies to be as agonizing as the Paris of *Les Misérables*. In the winter especially, the harsh long winters of 1954–55 and 1955–56, when the cold and the snow lasted for weeks, the temperature fell to minus 10 degrees and slabs of ice floated in the Seine, as during the great winters of history and legend when wolves roamed the cities. On some mornings the bodies of men frozen to death were found in the streets, hunched up on a bench or on the steps of a metro station, huddled in the barely sheltered corner of a doorway or in some hallway whose door was un-locked. "If this continues I think my entryway will be mistaken for a morgue," a concierge told a municipal ambulance crew. She had twice found what she called "a stiff" while putting her garbage cans out for collection. And the asphyxiations. Chance, a diabolical stage director, weirdly arranges its presentations. One December night in 1955, in Montmartre, on one of those streets that precipitously descends from the top of the hill to the boulevard below, in the rue des Trois-Fréres, a few yards from the Dullin theater, a family accidentally asphyxiated itself trying to get enough heat for their hovel. In a neighboring house a sick woman without a penny committed suicide by turning on the gas, killing her son along with herself. "They found two empty wallets on the two corpses," the newspaper reported. Usually indifferent, the neighborhood was sick of it. A grocer who refused to give credit had to close his store. Ironically it was in the privileged neighborhoods near les Halles, which was overflowing with food, sometimes in the stalls of the market itself, under the groaning board, so to speak, where the most miserable lived.

During the evening scene, in the very heart of the festivities, suddenly among the panhandlers a face from the lower depths, wrinkled, dirty, emerged into the light. A bony hand was thrust forward. Daytime misery, which is no less ragged, has a different face, a different age, other diffi-culties. Paradoxically the nighttime problem is to eat, that of the daytime is to sleep. Part-time laborers by chance or habit, newly arrived in Paris, said one could always find work at les Halles. They were soldiers free of army discipline, opportunistic adventurers scarred by their deeds, a world apart—it was impossible to know where it began and where it ended, who belonged to it. There were *clochards*,[3] occasional clochards, or merely the wretched who while waiting for work would rather keep warm and sleep somewhere other than in a metro entrance or in one of those cheap movie houses where the ushers won't let you snore. Where can one find refuge or lodging? Single men solve the problem by not looking for lodging, by camping out of doors as in the days of François Villon. But what about families? In January 1955 they found homeless children (Oh Gavroche!).[4] Police patrolling in Citroen 2CV's tried to pick them up. There were hotel rooms available, but they were expensive, and hotels that rented by the month, fearing they might not be able to dislodge these homeless people, threw them out into the street before the month was up. Cooking was forbidden in the rooms. Neither dogs nor children were permitted. During the winter months those without a home of those miserably housed, whose jobs were in other parts of the city, forced their way into empty houses, old buildings, closed hotels (often shut by the police for having too indiscriminately accepted lodgers). Under the inspiration of the abbé Pierre temporary encampments were organized at various places. There was one under the Auteuil viaduct. The most spectacular was that on the quai Henri IV, next to the Hôtel de Ville, almost under the windows of the prefect. There, in full sight of everyone, entire families—women, children, dogs—lived in tents, risking finding themselves under water should the Seine overflow its banks. This too was doubtless a part of the overall strategy of the abbé Pierre. "It is better," grumbled a municipal councilor "than if this meddlesome priest had chosen the Place de la Concorde."

These people had to be housed. Everyone agreed. But how? That is another matter.

> The astronauts say the moon is the color of plaster of Paris.
> A newspaper article, July 1969

THE only solution was to build, or rather to start building again. It was essential to have those who had built Paris over the centuries again put to work, and if they were no longer interested to find some other means.

It is because of the bourgeoisie, the owners of buildings, much more than the kings, the emperors, the ministers, the prefects, that Paris became this enormous conglomeration of stone and plaster that Balzac's

---

3. A kind of French hobo; Samuel Beckett's play *Waiting for Godot* is about clochards.
4. The street urchin in *Les Misérables* who eventually is killed fighting on the barricades.

characters love to contemplate from some elevated spot. It is this "plaster casting in the Seine valley," this vast collection of houses, this gray ocean whose beauty exalts the city and makes it incomparable, much more so than the triumphal routes, the grandiose perspectives, the bell towers, the palaces. The history of the building of Paris is part of the history of the Parisian bourgeoisie. More than the work of historians, who are too specialized, too diverse, it is the novelists who tell in successive chapters the adventure of a particular family. In the beginning there is a piece of luck, the purchase of a bit of well-situated land: the speculation of César Birotteau around the Madeleine or of Boussardel on the Monceau plain. Then, after two or three generations of opulence, in the wake of some crisis, some ill-considered deed or just plain dissipation—extravagant parties, gambling, or a dubious descendant without any interest in business, and sometimes even a taste for culture—comes decline, ruin from which others, who also rose from nothing, will profit, on which they will build their own fortune, until the day when they too will suffer the same fate.

This had been the case, more or less, since the Middle Ages. It came to an end with World War I. Real estate had not been profitable for nearly forty years, construction was almost totally suspended. When the first shot of that war was fired, rents were frozen and remained so until 1948. But whether frozen or not, most people didn't pay them during the war. After the war the French bourgeoisie suffered numerous additional difficulties: the unpaid loans to Russia, innumerable crises, the fear of economic collapse. As for the industrial and financial bourgeoisie, for whom the defeat of the empires of Central Europe opened up new opportunities, they were busy accumulating vast fortunes in Europe or the colonies. The Parisian molehill did not attract them. They preferred to invest elsewhere than to embroil themselves in real estate development, which had so interested their predecessors in an age when construction paid and above all when investment in apartment buildings represented the major part of bourgeois wealth. When the postwar bourgeoisie needed a place to live, they didn't build, they rented in the best neighborhoods created in the happiest years of the nineteenth century, the "lovely neighborhoods" of Louis Aragon; these were neighborhoods whose town houses and sumptuous apartments had been abandoned by their former owners who had been ruined in the war. The new tenants, rather than rent a single apartment, rented two, on different floors. A fashionable decorator connected them with an extravagant stairway, like the boarding ramp of a transatlantic luxury liner.

This is why there was no building, or very little (and that mediocre) in the years after World War I. Scattered here and there, the houses built in this period are easily recognized because of their contrast with those built before the war, especially those opulent buildings erected between 1880 and 1910, with their facades of cut stone, their balconies, their caryatids, their sculptures, their nobility or at least their dignity, and their lodges for their concierges (comfortable lodges, compared to the foul rat-holes provided in other buildings, fought for by the better concierges). The postwar buildings are marked by facades simultaneously pretentious and banal, from all indications hastily built, finished off with "arts décoratifs" details. In place of the sinuous, the playful, the undulating contour, the contrast between shadow and sunlight, there is the straight line: a page-boy cut to replace the flowing locks of the prewar years. The materials are of poor quality, brick and reinforced concrete. A mason, recollecting some of the buildings he had once worked on, told me that nothing in the world could get him to put his family in some modern structures: "When I pass through the neighborhood I am astonished they are still standing." Unstable at their creation, old before their time, the gray cement hostile to light, thus do these skins appear, rough and cracked, already withered in their first flower. André Malraux's program to clean the buildings of Paris could not help them. Cleaning has even intensified their disgrace by contrasting them with their opulent predecessors whose cleaning has made them more appealing. In addition, the layers of paint applied to them and instantly fouled by the dust remind one of those aged actresses whose makeup, just applied, cakes, the colors running, so that her face looks like a messy artist's palette.

Then came the Depression. It hit France around 1930–31, a bit later than elsewhere. Brutally it stopped everything, nearly permanently, ruining at a single stroke those who had not seen it coming or who obstinately continued to believe in the solidity of stone as they had been told to believe. I still see the distress of one of my comrades from that time, whose father, infected by the virus for construction, had begun to build, around 1930, near Charenton. His very choice of site was fatal. When the universal disaster hit, he was not able to make his payments. The bank from which he had borrowed seized the unfinished building. This story is not unusual if we are to judge by the numbers of such buildings that were seized on the eve of the Second World War.

From 1914 to the end of World War II, during almost a half century of the history of families, of fortunes, of lives, most bourgeois proprietors had not derived any benefit from their real estate. As a result many were impoverished, some were ruined if they had no other source of income. Rents, when they were paid, which the Depression made a haphazard occurrence, did not even suffice to pay for the upkeep on the buildings. In bourgeois neighborhoods and commercial neighborhoods where rents were higher, especially rents on commercial property, numerous apartments had been transformed into offices. Yet even in these fortunate parts of the city, in commercial Paris, great problems remained; the smallest repairs cost a fortune, especially in these areas. For the landlord there was not the least hope of living mostly off his real estate as his forebears had in the nineteenth century. As for the poorer neighborhoods and the older part of the city, away from most commercial activity, roughly everything east of the rue St. Martin, the rents were so inadequate that everywhere, little by little, the buildings were abandoned to their sad fate. This happened in the Marais, for example, for years deprived of its former splendor but which still, before World War I, contained the artisan community described by Alphonse Daudet and his brother Léon, who were born at 24, rue Pavée, in the Hôtel Lamoignon. In places the Marais looked like an urban ruin.

Not only did the owner not derive any benefit from his property, but in a sense he had been dispossessed. Since 1914 the regulations governing rentals had had the practical result of transferring some property rights to the renter. The stupefying history of repossessions, of irresponsible subleasing, seems to belong to the realm of phantasmagoria, of sleight of hand, of smoke and mirrors. Comparing the landlord from the period between the wars to his ancestor at the time of Balzac, of Gavarni, of Daumier, one can say that the latter—criticized, vilified, detested, caricatured, battered, deceived (sometimes by his wife)—at least had from his property that which consoled him. Even in the midst of the worst misfortunes his property gave him the calmness, heroic or merely bovine, that we admire among his traits. The landlord of the period between the wars had less luck. His ancestors had been accused of despoiling the poor. It was now the landlord who was despoiled. Caricaturists and satirical songwriters now directed their barbs elsewhere. Small consolation.

What did the landlord do? If he was well off he bore his difficulties with patience, even if he had the soul of an old Parisian property owner who would rather die than sell a building long in his family, even if it brought nothing in and cost money to keep. This was especially true if he had one of those town houses built long ago in such large numbers that one still sees them along entire avenues in the most elegant streets in western Paris, their facades untroubled, caressed by foliage. Thus they remain despite a century of demolitions, of pillaging, of robberies, of shady deals, of depreciation, of tasteless remodeling, despite the ruin of so many illustrious houses lost through gambling, playing the horses, pursuing women, and above all through ignorance or disdain of economic matters. In the first heady years after World War I these town houses were much sought after by the nouveaux riche, whatever the source of their money or their social milieu, by rich Americans in quest of a title, by celebrities of the automobile industry, by champagne-makers, by clothes designers, by stars of the theater or the music hall, by gold-diggers (as they were called) and by some of the great demi-mondaines, representatives of an illustrious race who, on the eve of their extinction, enjoyed a final efflorescence. Sometimes these town houses were sold, but rarely, and usually to restore the family chateau in the country that was badly in need of attention. More often they were let at an enormous rent, almost for amusement. These stately mansions had seen similar inhabitants, under the frivolous Regency after the death of Louis XIV and during the carnival that was the Second Empire. Besides, in Paris such fashions do not last long. The vogue was only temporary and it would have been stupid not to profit from it. A thorough cleaning would suffice afterwards. In the meantime, take down some of the tapestries, roll up some carpets, put away some of the knickknacks, lock up the venerated room where one's ancestors had died, guard against the worst by covering up things here and there.

The Depression brought its own difficulties. Let us not even speak of those tenants who disappeared over the horizon like traveling hucksters, long before the curtain came down, before the applause stopped, before they stopped paying, before bankruptcy was declared and the representatives of the law appeared on the scene. Often they left scattered about, as a repulsive reminder of their tenancy, empty wine bottles, perfume flacons, and all the ridiculous paraphernalia of frivolity, along with cream pots and dog droppings. At the same time that repairs cost more and more, the price of these mansions fell. Tastes began to change. People thought less and less about living in a historical monument, compelled to follow complicated rituals imposed by the size of the place and the arrangement of its rooms. The young especially did not see things as their parents had. Rather than ruin themselves repairing a roof while skimping on a car, why not sell the mansion and buy a more modest apartment on the top floor of an ultramodern building—on the avenue Foch, for example—that was not yet sullied by having been lived in, or a villa at Louvenciennes? They reiterated to their old-fashioned parents that it was completely ridiculous to condemn themselves to an impossible life in an uncomfortable ancestral house, or rather one that had the comforts of a bygone time, with enormous rooms in which one could not feel at home, with fireplaces that did not draw, with a kitchen so far away that the food was always cold by the time it reached the table, with an elevator that clanked like the movable stage at the Opéra: "When you ascend to your room, Mama, in that rickety elevator cage suspended from a cable, I always have the feeling that one day you will be trapped at the top of the shaft, like the Queen of the Night in some amateurish production of Mozart's *Magic Flute*." Nevertheless they sold only rarely and then only because they might lose the mansion. They sold when they had no choice, because of death, taxes, or division of property. Otherwise they kept the property, out of devotion to the family's past, as one guards an old treasure.

Of course there was an overwhelming majority of Parisian landlords who had no connection to the Crusades or the Court, who did not risk disturbing the eternal rest of an ancestor, who had no claim to a coat of arms. There were those who belonged to various professions, the backbone of the Parisian bourgeoisie, a bourgeoisie whose diversity reflected its many professions, each clearly defined, rather than the blurred outlines of social groups. The same was true of neighborhoods. In numerous neighborhoods those of the same *métier* owned the buildings and congregated. Thus the important "masters" of the Sorbonne in former times owned property in the Latin Quarter and were detestable landlords (it is said), as one might expect of a profession that had a sense of tradition. In the same way butchers, bakers, wine merchants, lawyers, doctors, pharmacists—virtually every profession and *métier*—eventually bought their buildings, whose prices fell as their incomes, especially in times of economic crisis, continued to rise. The practices of these property owners, these bourgeois of every origin, every occupation, every neighborhood, hardly differed from those of the titled property owners of the elegant neighborhoods. What is more, they did not sell their property, partly because they too did not want to be propertyless. In certain *métiers* in which the old provincial and Parisian habits predominated, many always arranged things so they would get by, at the least cost to themselves, when others failed. The merchants of les Halles did this. Owners of the buildings in which they did business, they also were often owners of neighboring buildings where they stored their goods and merchandise (as did their salesmen and acquaintances), which they piled up carelessly. They had their employees, during slack times, even on Sunday mornings, fix up the floors and ceilings of these buildings, the stairways, the roofs, and restore the facades with bright new coats of paint, apple green or blood red. It hardly cost them anything, maybe an extra joint of meat or a round of drinks at an Auvergnat's bar nearby.

The Auvergnat was himself a property owner.[5] This was the case in and around les Halles (and elsewhere), and generally in the older neighborhoods where one could always find a bargain. It sometimes happened that an obscure but well-located café, well run, after several years of hard work and saving by the proprietor, of many towels worn out polishing the zinc bar, moved to a place only dreamed of, pouring its light out onto some boulevard or the Champs-Elysées. As the owner of a café or of some other business—a scrap-metal yard, for example—the Auvergnat proprietor had the advantage of his provincial origins, which influenced the conduct of this Parisian proprietor who was hardly even a Parisian. I knew such a man who, I would say, with scientific objectivity, represented the Auvergnat proprietor par excellence. He had arrived in Paris some years before World War I as a café waiter. Then, I don't know exactly how, he became the manager of a building, the owner of a building, then two, then three buildings, which in turn led to other buildings. The only ones he could afford were old structures, somewhat decayed, located near the Marais. Once he had fixed them up a bit he turned them into hotels, without being too fastidious about his clientele. When repairs became urgent, when pipes burst, he did not call in a professional, he came himself, with his toolbox. When the roof sprang a leak, he climbed up, assisted by his son and his wife, put on a patch, and covered it with tar. In the beginning this allowed him to hang on, and eventually he became rich. After some twenty years he bought, after World War II, more substantial buildings that other owners, less resourceful or from a less serious region of France, were forced to sell, driven to the wall by the constant devaluation of Paris buildings.

The war had only made the situation worse. Not only did the buildings no longer bring in anything, they ruined those who owned them. There was no other solution but to abandon them to their sad destiny, that is, to stop maintaining them, letting them decay, or, better yet, when there was no other choice, selling them, and of necessity at a low price, for there were no buyers. But if there were no buyers to whom could one sell? To prudent men like my Auvergnat. In truth there were few such

5. The Auvergnats have traditionally dominated the restaurant and café trade in Paris and have acquired a reputation as shrewd property owners.

men! Had there been more, the prices would have risen. Usually such buildings were sold to insurance companies which, during these years, acquired vast real-estate holdings at the lowest cost. In the face of such economic power, when a property was sold by notary at auction, it was difficult for a modest would-be buyer to compete. One had to be an Auvergnat, or better yet my Auvergnat. La Fontaine could have made a fable about this. On the back slopes of the area around the Place de Clichy a block of houses was for sale. Not perhaps the most desirable, but full of potential. Rather than going himself to bid on them, to show himself interested, my Auvergnat had the idea of asking a businessman, himself an Auvergnat. Everyone knew this man represented a large insurance company. My Auvergnat knew him personally, I don't know how. Perhaps they had made their first communion together or met at some Auvergnat celebration. When the representative of the company interested in the property saw this man before him he immediately gave up any thought of bidding, never imagining for a moment that behind this formidable facade was my Auvergnat. Thus did my Auvergnat, who would have been unable to compete, get the houses for a song. When he recalls this deal he still laughs. Or rather he smiles to himself, with a slight batting of his eyelids, with the faintest modulation of his voice, with a quiet and personal satisfaction at his triumph both modest and a bit submissive—a state Balzac has so well described. When you hear an Auvergnat, in a low voice, describe this or that sharp business deal, you always have the impression that he wants it understood that it is far less difficult to extricate oneself from difficulties in Paris, to get the best of a Parisian, than it is to budge a stubborn cow or to make a good cheese. However that may be, and as a fable would say, the moral of the story is that the building is not logically attached to anything.

> God does not so quickly call worthless men to himself.
>
> La Bruyère

THE old builders of Paris, the Paris proprietors, had long since ceased to build. And with them the financial institutions which had also played a part at times, although a less important one, had turned their back on building. Construction no longer being very attractive, there was no building now, or almost none. Certainly there was not enough to house the population, neither those camped along the Seine nor those who were tempted to embark on a Paris adventure after the Liberation, as had their parents after World War I. Is it worth citing the statistics? A speaker, wanting to give the Municipal Council a precise number and finding himself entangled in his figures, said, "ten thousand, or rather twenty thousand apartments are needed." Is it 10,000 or 20,000? The speaker concluded, with embarrassment, "it's a lot." He had no reason to strike "a lot" from the official record of the meeting, although it was lighthearted and brought laughter. This "a lot" said exactly what he wanted to say. Paris did indeed lack "a lot" of apartments. The responses imagined, the means invented, the measures taken, the plans made ready to launch construction were of several kinds. First there was a rent increase. From 1948 to 1954 rents increased sixfold, so much so that the cost of living doubled. Who was not pleased to have a few coins in his purse? For so many years the landlords had had nothing. For them here was the chance to set things right. Not by throwing themselves into new construction—"once burned twice shy"—but by repairing what had never been repaired. More often than not they profited from this unexpected manna to enjoy themselves, again allowing their old buildings to decay. There were not even incentives created, incentives to build, such as tax advantages more favorable for building than for other investments. Prefect Pelletier's predecessor addressed this question on June 30, 1955, telling the Municipal Council: "We must maintain the principle" (these grand principles)—"that those who build affordable housing, whether companies, individuals, or investors, be assured a sound capital investment. If not, the source of necessary capital will dry up as it did between 1918 and 1949. We must, consequently, fix the principle"—again the principle—"that housing ought to be worth its cost to the builder, by granting some relaxation in the laws. . . ."

Who did the building? In answering this question we see that there were few individuals involved, few of those traditional Parisian bourgeoisie who own a building, a piece of real estate, and want to build using their own or borrowed capital. In place of construction financed by the landowners came all those other means, correctly alluded to by the prefect, involved in "the production of housing for profit," which were studied for the first time, in 1947, by Christian Topalov, in a book that marks an epoch. Capital was independent of real estate. But it could not be invested in construction unless the owner of the real estate was willing to sell his property or found himself constrained to do so by the new regulations or by force of circumstance. An unwilling landowner, a difficult character or one totally disinterested, for whatever reason, could block or compromise or even destroy construction plans, or, as they soon were saying, the urban renewal of a neighborhood, which meant (as became apparent) the destruction, pure and simple, of the neighborhood in question. A single landowner who did not want to be "renewed," who did not understand the new jargon of renovation, or who understood it all too well, was sufficient. Obviously men of this stamp were the scourge of builders, were even public enemies, it being assumed that construction is always for the public good. Such men made the great "principles" of the prefect mere talk. These men were even more despised when they were insignificant, unimportant individuals: mere insects who prevented decent men, the benefactors of mankind, from doing their proper duty. If the building in question, the old Parisian structure, with plaster walls and a slate roof, was well located (for the builder this meant it was in his way, for the owner it meant his building was poorly located), it was lost amidst the tall buildings going up. It was tormented by cranes, by cement mixers, enveloped in noise so hellish that it made life impossible. Permanently in motion, some ten or twenty meters overhead were great, menacing blocks of concrete which, should a chain snap, would demolish the poor place. How infuriating it was for the builders to see appear at some cracked window, between two flower pots, a brave man, an intrepid woman, who had the appearance of bearing their plight with patience (could they be deaf?) or to see the neighborhood character at an attic window thumbing her nose at the workers below!

I speak of "builders," using a word that is today obsolete but was current some years ago. "Developers" is now the preferred word. People are beginning to use it without understanding very clearly, as their usage shows, what the word signifies, or better still what it conceals. Many remain ignorant. But if no one understands exactly what a developer is, at least people know, no matter who they are, what the developers have done. What is certain is that they are the most hated group of our era. Compared to them the tax farmers, the grain speculators, the creators of artificial shortages in the eighteenth century were the adored children of the Parisians. Comes the revolution they will be the first to be guillotined, on the mall of the Montparnasse Tower whose cement would not absorb their blood, or on the esplanade of La Défense where, for the first time, there would be something to see resembling the violent upheaval caused by that development. The list is ready and the developers know full well that their names are at the top, as the *sans-culottes* of the French Revolution said. There is no need to name them. The man in the street could instantly provide a name. On the scaffold awaiting them they could show courage. Even better, let them stand on the edge of the pit into which Jean Giraudoux has already cast their precedessors who, compared to the new variety, were as infants making sand pies on the beach. Writing about the revival of *The Madwoman of Chaillot* in *Le Journal du Dimanche* (February 2, 1975), Pierre Marcabru said: "The Madwoman is right. Everything Giraudoux says pertains to our own situation. We have caught up with him. What does he say through this brightly bedecked beggar woman who dominates over those simple folk around her? She says Paris will not survive the brutality of those who covet her. . . . That we have to throw the financiers, the developers, the speculators into an enormous pit, which is done in the last act. Only thus is the plague arrested." The developers at the bottom of a pit—that is clear, simple, definitive, and adequately expresses what they deserve. There is no reason to explain further either the opinions about developers or the developers themselves. The word itself, as it comes from the pen, falls like the blade of the guillotine: developers!

What was the origin of this term? Who invented it (if we can speak of invention), when, how? What significance did it have? "Developers," like "housing developments" and other such creations, await invention, change, circumstances. They can all be dated from the same year, they are cut from the same cloth, they are of the same family, emanate from the same sterile brains which are, however, confident (and justly so) about the enormous power of ignorance and the idiocy surrounding it, and the stupidity of the multitude. We can believe, moreover, that through the centuries the ignorant have made considerable progress. The most unscrupulous businessman of the ancien régime, at the end of the evening, after washing up after his dinner and having just undressed for bed, is careful to find a new word for what he does that would not smack of his boorishness, his nastiness, which would not inspire scorn or, worse yet, laughter. The Balzacian businessman also tampers with the language. The businessman of our own day, without great effort—the how or why doesn't matter—some morning while shaving, or having an aperitif before dinner, or in that moment of intense inspiration that comes between the fruit course and the cheese course, hits upon the new word "developer."

In his *Mémoires d'un architecte,* so useful a source for these years and also quite brilliant, Fernand Pouillon writes: "Certainly I knew well the profession of 'the real estate businessman,' (the term 'developer' was later invented by Larrue, the director of the Comptoir national for housing, created in 1954−55)." In the beginning no one knew precisely what this meant, not even those who had made it up and began to use it to enhance their logos and their office doors. Why didn't they know? Because, more than others, they were convinced that it was unimportant, indeed they were even reassured by not knowing. Just a word like any other, not at all pejorative, and even somewhat flattering. We do a double take in leafing through the *Bulletin municipal officiel* and seeing the Communist councilors (April 1954) flatter themselves for having been "the real developers" of the changes in their neighborhoods. Two or three years later they will avoid the word like the plague.

The earliest uses of the word expressed the needs of its inventors. "These men functioned as middle men," Pouillon notes, "go-betweens, real estate speculators looking to make their fortune. Today we call them 'developers,' those who get things started. It is by this activity that they wanted to define themselves." There was more precision in "development" than "developer." It is no more than a new twist on an old story. As Ernest Labrousse, the master of economic history, writes: "urban civilization is a civilization wrought by conquest." Times have changed, real estate that had not been worth anything began to attract money. Men from the most diverse professions, the most unlikely men, sometimes the most laughable among the ambitious and the hungry who only yesterday were doing something else, set off in pursuit of the Golden Fleece. This fierce desire to try one's luck was fixed on the real estate business, and for those already in it there was the desire to get rich quick, which is the main topic of Balzac's *Comédie humaine*. There are imbeciles in this world, those who forget to get rich, or don't know how to go about it, and there are those who think of nothing else and are unconcerned about the means: "Murders on our highways I consider charitable acts compared to some financial deals," Du Tillet (that is, Balzac) asserts in *César Birotteau*. This is his judgment on speculations that were then thought to be completely honorable. In every period, but especially in these years I am discussing, one finds such appetites everywhere, but more prevalent, keener, more open, in Paris. It is also true that the pie to be divided is much larger in Paris. And what a pie! The recipe is simple and the dough easy to make. One doesn't even need a lot of capital. A little luck and a lot of audacity is enough to leverage big deals, as they say. And in less time than it takes to say it, certain anniversaries, of which an admiring press informs us, are henceforth marked not by the year but by the hundreds of millions of francs involved.

At first there is a small advance of capital. Then comes the purchase, at a good price, of a piece of land not zoned for building. Then, at the wave of a magic wand, some good fairy appears and the land can be built upon. Why detail the rest of the scenario, which is already familiar? At the outset, unlike the builders themselves, we don't see very clearly because we are blinded by the short-term economic advantages, by the shell game of the con men. If there is any point in recalling this it is to underline how long it takes for the most obvious things to be recognized and understood. Even though the deception had gone on for some time, it was only in 1955 that the Communist members of the Municipal Council, otherwise so vigilant and informed, started to denounce and expose a system that led to this: the buildings constructed were "luxury apartments, made possible by allocations granted by the State . . . and since two-thirds of this money comes from indirect taxes the workers are paying to house the rich, since it is they who pay most of the indirect taxes" (session of September 15, 1955). And again, on December 10, 1956: "The actual system of advances and subsidies has become a veritable scandal." There are examples to prove it.

Thus we see a motley group, always available, throwing itself into the real estate market, which becomes consequently a market for "developers." Those involved in buying and selling buildings—which in practice is buying and selling land—that is to say the rental agents and real-estate brokers, are at the heart of the problem. They need only a little money, a handful of collaborators, above all a secretary endowed with all the necessary gifts, a Circe responsible for seducing the sailors, or rather a Penelope (often enough the devoted wife of the owner). In addition they need an established agency, and an architect to draw up plans. To verify these plans or make it seem as if they had been verified, they need a technical department, or at least a department calling itself technical. We should not be surprised if, in technical matters, they stumble from the unexpected to the undesired. In the years under consideration the vaudeville shows and the music halls, often the most useful source for the sociology of housing, and anyhow the most amusing, found some of their best material in these misadventures. I can still see a skit at the Olympia, played by a celebrated pair of comedians, in which the rental agent shows a young couple a little jewel of an apartment. "When we have children . . ." (we were then in the midst of the baby boom) "it will, of course, be a bit small. Exactly, madam. We have made it small for your benefit, thinking of the time when you would have children. It is when you have children that you will see the advantage of its smallness and thank us. You say the toilet is too close to the kitchen? This is deliberate. From the toilet you can keep an eye on your cooking and on the children playing at the same time."

In addition to these people connected to the real-estate business were those who came scurrying from the most unrelated occupations, sometimes the most unbelievable. Those without a profession, or those who made a profession of not having one, never having lifted a finger, those too lazy or too important to work, too disreputable or too distinguished, suddenly found a way to work without exerting themselves, to get rich without tiring themselves. Thus was formed in these blessed years something new to Parisian society or, as Balzac would say, a new social type; this was a world apart, the bizarre herd of those in real estate, the real-estate fauna. Of course this mongrel battalion, this happy soldiery untroubled by doubts, was soon to lose men, as time went on, while simultaneously renewing itself, recruiting from new sources. Perhaps it thus changed, or at least it made every effort to give itself the appearance of change, to make itself wise, to regulate itself, to make itself moral, to conform itself to what the image makers of the developers did not hesitate to invoke: the good, the true, and the beautiful of Plato's *Republic*. Yes, even the beautiful was invoked, would you believe it? The original mercenary without faith or laws, the mercenary out for his own advantage, is to be replaced by the mercenary interested in the good of others and—why not?—even the good of mankind. To read the self-professions made in the 1960s by the developers one might think one was reading something from the age of *La Légende des Siècles,*[6] tales of visionaries, or paladins. The developers rush in where angels fear to tread. They become the protectors of widows and orphans, their concern is selfless, they give from their own purse, sacrifice their health, even their life, they bleed themselves white. They are the leaders, the champions, who overturn the traditional order of the world with its injustices. They are the "developers." Without doubt they will astonish themselves some day when they discover that their pockets are full of money, and that they don't know exactly who put it there, and when they learn, from public rumor, that they own chateaux, hunting grounds, and villas on the Côte d'Azur which they have never heard mentioned. What malevolent wit has taught them such deception? Who can imagine it? Perhaps in another age, but not today. What a transformation! The black sheep in the fold have been slaughtered, some have been eliminated by examination, the profession has been purified, business has been carefully regulated. Habit has taken over. In a word, there is honor; not the old honor renewed but a young honor, completely new: the honor of burgeoning corporatism.

In a few years, it is true, the original management had been replaced by another group, and not so much to change its appearance. This was

---

6. A cycle of poems by Victor Hugo, published in 1859.

the Far West, or something very similar. Thus did they describe themselves when speaking of their beginnings, using this analogy borrowed
from the American Westerns they watched on television at night to make
the point. It was a kind of Far West without law and order, or at best
only nominal law, without a sheriff, or with one just sworn in who takes
some old regulation, some prewar rule, out of his pocket in order to settle
a difficult dispute, much like the judge in the Westerns who takes a tat-
tered Bible and a flask of whiskey out of his coat. In fact I am thinking
of a particular developer, now departed—he died in harness—whose
memory haunts these pages. This is how I envision him. Was he or did
he only call himself developer, builder, or simply architect? I no longer
know. Anyhow, these words were hardly distinguishable at that time, at
least to me. I saw him as a cowboy contemplating his herd, tall in the
saddle, perched on a promontory, happy, amiable, with an infectious
laugh, a dazzling smile, an intense voice, much embraced, with a circle of
warm friends, generous in his hospitality, offering standing invitations to
dinner, irresistibly persuasive. Of course, it goes without saying, he had
long arms, powerful hands, seven-league boots, all-seeing eyes. This cowboy was everywhere at the same time, he knew everything and, for a time,
he had a hand in everything. He would have had it all had he not had the
bad habit of playing Gary Cooper, walking into the saloon to settle things
with his six-gun, if he had not so often treated his partners as renegade
Indians. Breaking into laughter he said what he shouldn't have, for example that his project was not very beautiful but there were worse ones.
Besides, the neighborhood was so wretched that it hardly mattered. To
those who objected that his model of the development had more trees
than his concrete would support, he admitted, chortling, that he agreed:
no one had ever seen trees grow in a housing project. Inappropriate
words, useless cynicism, which disconcerted his colleagues who agreed
with him but did not say so publicly.

A cowboy! He did so much swaggering, he and his friends, that the
authorities had finally to pass a law. By then he was dead and those like
him, risk-takers, jugglers, and smooth talkers, were also gone. Only the
most staid, the most prudent, the most circumspect remained. They ex-
changed, so to speak, greater power and a broader range of action for
staying power. Those who endured were more careful when they spoke
and were on guard against saying what the architect in *César Birotteau*
said: "An architect calculates the cost of a new building to the nearest
penny, since I do not know what it is to deceive the bourgeoisie . . . excuse
me, the word slipped out accidently." The French bourgeois wants to be

deceived but he doesn't want to be told about the deception. Those who survived were those who had had the luck, who had stumbled upon a good deal, who had been in the right place at the right time. They were also those with the greatest assets, the most money. Money? The major different between the phase that now begins and that which preceded it is, since 1960, the participation of the banks. They will now intervene either indirectly by loaning money or directly by undertaking their own real-estate developments.

Without doubt the entry of the banks transforms this new phase into the golden age of the developers. The triumph of the developers! Had the subject not been overly symbolic and had the crisis along with the ill feelings of the public not counseled discretion, what an excellent theme this would have been for the ceiling painting of these new cathedrals: the commercial center of some Parly 2 or that desert, the waiting room of the Montparnasse train station. Now came a stretch of good weather. No more uncertainty, no more tempests to fear. The storm was followed by calm. The scandal of the CNL had obviated any other scandals.[7] The new day's dawn was marked by a propitiatory sacrifice. The temple had been purified. Who would even imagine it could once again be defiled? Why take special precautions for the future? A rigorous, official code of behavior had been established. One had only to apply the rules, the rules of the game with higher and higher stakes, fantastic stakes, a game where one won with every cast of the dice: a game that required little effort. It wasn't even a gamble, it was a money-making machine. The possibilities were unlimited, its capacity enormous. The authorities were supportive, almost complicit in their behavior, for reasons we shall examine. The minister was at the head of the line, in direct contact with the developers, so courteous, so accommodating, so zealous: "But how can I help, dear friend." That is the word, "friend." Why hesitate along such a promising path? Why stop to rest? Fatigue is not a factor since the machine, once set in motion, runs almost unattended. Why tamper with its workings? Why even hide them or dissimulate? Project after project rises up. Remember Hugo's *La Légende des Siècles:* there are always the paladins. It is true that there is limited land and the city is even more limited. It is sufficient to come to an agreement and then divide things among friends. This piece and a bit of that for me, and for you that piece and a bit of this. For me the Opéra and a corner of a wretched suburb. For you the

---

7. A huge real estate and building scandal which involved not only developers and bankers, but also compromised several political figures.

eastern quadrant of Paris. Why scowl? Take for compensation this fertile grain-growing land, these sumptuous forests, with Versailles in your backyard and a view of the chateau: Louis XIV for a neighbor! We could continue like this and revisit these inimitable times. It is difficult to do otherwise. What we are examining is not administrative law, nor the science of finance, nor sociology. It is not even urbanism. It is comedy.

In much of the writing and in memory itself we already confuse the preceding years, so inspired, with those that followed. The comedy had already begun, but we were only in the first act, in which the characters are presented, or rather at the moment when we discover them with surprise. We discover. . . . But why not use the first person and put myself into the play?

I discover a humanity that I had thought only existed in my beloved classics. There they were in flesh and blood. Yet they were different, and the differences riveted my attention. Forget the extravagant accoutrements, the big, flashy cars—the carriages of their forebears were no less lavish—the memorable ribbon-cuttings, the extraordinary feasts. Forget the pink blouses, the velvet jackets, the lace collars, but let me note in passing that in the days of Balzac and Zola the most flamboyant businessmen thought it prudent to dress in the most staid manner: Saccard wore a black frock coat and the most beautiful peacocks kept their tail feathers un-fanned. Yet I find their modern counterparts more rapacious, less scrupulous, more cynical, and more vulgar. Of those he calls "the mafia of apartment builders," F. Pouillon writes: "The best one can say of them is that they are not idealists."

I have often heard this said of this or that developer. My cowboy, whom I have introduced, had not the slightest concern for ethics, he even bragged about it, going so far as to dismiss the idealism of others as a manifestation of what Kant would call pure idealism, a complete abstraction. Once I heard these lords of construction, these men without ethics, complaining among themselves that in the Paris of their day only the most insignificant undertakings were permitted: "We're talking about peanuts," said one. The other retorted: "Everyone knows you prefer caviar." Hearing talk like this in the highest circles, an old Parisian could only feel ill at ease, unable to smile, even to participate in so distinguished a conversation. He would rather pretend not to have heard, as if he had stumbled on some sordid deal, some division of spoils.

"Men without ethics." We could add "blind to nature," that is to beauty, which they do not hesitate to trample under foot; blind to sentiment, which they unscrupulously shove aside; but above all blind to gen-

erosity, to compassion for those immaterial flowers that materialism
sometimes causes to bloom, for those unexpected consequences of the
most cold-blooded deals, for those hands that open after grabbing money.
The history of capitalism in Paris reveals such instances of generosity. Yet
this was the least unselfish form of capitalism, the cruelest, the most sordid, if one is to believe Karl Marx, who knew it well and who wrote the
most terrifying chapters of *The Communist Manifesto* in Paris. None of
that in these later years. Whatever profit was made in real estate was
reinvested in real estate or some insane venture. Profit is profit. There is
no act of generosity—which happens only in the movies—not even a
donation to cancer research, which these men of finer substance are unconcerned about. As for the old story of the generations who consume
what their fathers have amassed, which is a kind of revenge of society
against family egoism, there is not in these succeeding generations even
the embryo of a poet or a musician, not any young boy with a gift for
amusing others, a lover of literature, a budding Latinist, a collector of
Merovingian coins, to break the pattern. They don't even have a man of
letters, one of those rascals that the tax collectors in Montesquieu's *Per-
sian Letters* so liked to have at the foot of the table for their dinners.
Nothing. Nothing. Nothing. Some say that such miracles only occur at
the end, at the moment of a final reckoning, before the last breath is
drawn, or in the second or third generations. The crisis has come too
soon, even before we can speak of the first generation. We shall never
know what their successors might have done.

As for diversions, it is only a question of making as much money as
possible without letting anything interfere. Projects are piled on projects,
operations on operations, the public sector is soon abandoned for the
private sector, which is more lucrative. Above all, the better neighborhoods are targeted, those where one earns the greatest profits, enormous
sums, by skirting the rules, cramming too much into the available space
by erecting what will soon be called deluxe housing projects, or more
accurately false luxury, tangles of Lilliputian apartments in place of spa-
cious residences that had a certain stateliness to them. These old townhouses, pushed thickly together in certain streets where more of the
nobility and the wealthy lived than in others, began to disappear, sacrificed by their owners and massacred by the developers. During the Second Empire Saccard saw them in the distance, lit by a thousand candles,
without a care in the world, unaware that many of them were doomed to
die. It became a slaughter. If we believe Jean Bastié, meticulous observer

of Parisian buildings between 1945 and 1956, the greatest construction activity was in the sixteenth arrondissement, the richest and best endowed with housing. In December 1956 a municipal councilor noted that there were more requests for construction permits for the sixteenth arrondissement in a week than there were for a six-month period in the eleventh arrondissement. Need we say that it was not a municipal councilor of the sixteenth arrondissement who called attention to this fact?

The communications presented at the opening of each session of the Municipal Council by the Communist members who specialized in housing questions constitute the most accurate and implacable record of the evolution of building in the course of these years, and show the correspondence between the geography of construction, financial speculation, and rich neighborhoods. A little later it was the turn of the fifteenth arrondissement. In April 1958 the Investment Company of the fifteenth arrondissement requested a contract—a small, inexpensive venture—to make a study of the neighborhood. "This study is ominous," a municipal councilor observed. And then letting the cat out of the bag he continued: "The company doubtless doesn't want to undertake this study merely to get a ten million franc fee, but because they hope to get, without competition, the advantage of carrying out the project. There is thus reason to think that important interests would be involved. . . ." The fate of an arrondissement with 260,000 inhabitants: a straw in the wind!

And then, very quickly and at the same time as these projects that had the excuse or pretext of improving housing were multiplying, projects that would transform entire neighborhoods yet not touch the essence, not strike the city in its vital organs, there appeared even more formidable projects that seized Paris by the throat. The plans existed, already worked out, detailed, deadly. But the developers still did not dare to show their fangs. A curious, even comic sight soon became an alarming one. It was usually at the end of a meeting, when everyone was relaxing, that someone was emboldened to propose—apologetic, mumbling, ill at ease— some astonishing project. I once saw an architect, if one can use this divine word for someone who so little resembled Eupalinos,[8] propose something important in the manner of a big, unkempt baby who doesn't know how to tell his father or mother that he has soiled his diaper. Two years later the same body will be stronger, will have changed his tone,

8. *Eupalinos ou l'architecte*, a work by the poet Paul Valéry, cast as a dialogue between Socrates and Phaedrus, published in 1921.

the mess in his diaper will have become monumental, an excremental masterpiece that will be displayed to all eyes and before which each will have to declare his admiration.

We are still only at the stage of infancy, timid, virginal, a time without audacity. Or rather if there is audacity it is through a surrogate; the astonishing is presented by means of a straw man, or better yet by someone a bit bizarre, eccentric, who can be disowned if need be, or sent to the country if the scheme is rejected, who can be dismissed with disbelief by those who still have the power to decide: "Build towers there! Do you know this guy? He's a dreamer! Ever since he won the Prix de Rome...." Or "because he never won the Prix de Rome he thinks he's Michelangelo building the dome of St. Peter's. Don't worry. This is not a real scheme. Even he doesn't take it seriously. I know him, he's a good old boy, a kidder. What he's proposing is the kind of practical joke they play at the Beaux-Arts school, an apprentice's fantasy like those described by Hugo, Murger, Carco. Haven't you read *De Montmartre auq quartier Latin?* Picasso said, to shock, people, 'when you paint a landscape it should, above all, look like a plate.' This is the same thing. You don't know your classics." "Do something outrageous" is an exaggerated way of saying "Make yourself noticed." Those around you will laugh, pleased to have in their midst someone so entertaining. Jules Romains, who always was catnapping or seemed to be, thought himself back in the time of *Les Copains* (His novel of broad farce). In truth it was rather *Donogoo* they played with him, or that they got ready to play.[9] To play *Donogoo*, to deceive everyone openly and with the consent of those who are deceived, to enjoy completely the collective illusion, other conditions have to be met. Yet many of the conditions already existed. Soon public opinion would gallop. For the moment it walked.

> Clients are always attracted by appearances.
> La Fontaine, *Les devineresses*

OPINION? What I mean is public adherence to the schemes of the developers, to the myth of construction at any cost, to the promise that each could become the owner of his own apartment. I mean the support of almost everyone, even of those who had no interest in such things. Perhaps the only exceptions were the clochards who preferred the old squares or the metro entrances. They were the last lovers of Paris, in

9. One of Romain's tales (its title was *Donogoo-Tonka*), which he dramatized. It turns on a political imposture.

the full sense of the word love: they loved unselfishly and with peculiar preferences, private tastes, a wholly secret sense of discovery, without repugnance for the hidden corners of the city, face against face, body against body, lying on the bare ground. The important fact is this general conversion to construction, to its rituals and its works, this almost unanimous acquiescence to undertakings whose consequences most did not foresee. Most were incapable of imagining what the impact would be, what they themselves would think when the time came (and it came quickly) when they went looking, in vain, at the open construction sites or the new buildings, for a bit of the city of their youth, the city of yesterday. Moreover it is this consenting, hypnotized public opinion, this blind, hysterical crowd, that drove the builders to ask for more than they otherwise would have dared, to abandon all prudence, all precaution, whether of form or substance, to cast aside all moral scruples. This is what pushed the authorities, for a period of several years, to grant the unimaginable, to concede what they had refused the night before, to consider what they had before shouted down: sacrilege, destruction, rape of the landscape, and, of course, plain robbery. Not only did they accept all this, but they ran ahead of what they believed the will of the people to be. They proposed, even before they were asked, what those who had the most to gain and who were the least restrained by scruples would probably never have dared suggest.

As I listened to some of these official speeches, with an unfamiliar new tone, noticing especially the murmurs and voices on all sides, in offices, waiting rooms, stairways, and even on the sidewalks of the Hôtel de Ville, which echoed the official view, making it reverberate, amplifying it, it seemed to me that all the employees of the city, with the exception of some anarchists, huddled at the back of the stage (in the recesses of the temple), clothed in the white tunics of one of Racine's choruses, chanting at the command of the high priest, who would perform the sacrifice: "Behold a new Jerusalem, born in the depth of the desert, dazzling with light, a Jerusalem made more brilliant, more beautiful." Behold Paris, more brilliant and more beautiful and, to speak in images as does the Bible, behold Paris reborn! But to the voices of the temple servants, were added numerous other voices which we will shortly identify, voices sustaining the chorus of initiates, dominating it, supporting it, leading it. In the end it was a universal chorus.

It is this assent that matters, this massive expression of opinion. The acolytes of the temple would never chant what some outsider told them to. "Bred in the seraglio, I know its mysteries," and I know as well as anyone that if they today sing one motet tomorrow they will sing another. If Joad got them to sing to the God of the Jews, Mathan, who sees this, is certain that he can get them to sing the hymn to Baal tomorrow. They can't help themselves, they should not be reproached. The powers that be can themselves do nothing about it. Believing themselves leaders were they not themselves led by forces which, at the time, I could hardly discern?

Finally the most vivid of my recollections of that time—and for the moment I want to remain on a superficial level without additional analysis. I remember the sound of the crowd, this public voice of general consent, nay, pressing, exigent, supporting what was not for the benefit of all, rather supporting different interests. For some—the majority—it was simply a question of finding housing. For others it was an opportunity to make a fortune, to seize the moment so long awaited, to corner Dame Fortune. These two motives had nothing in common. Nevertheless they applauded as one: those who were predators and those who were the prey. "After more than a millennium of open war, the wolves made peace with the lambs. It was apparently good for both." We know the rest of the story: "The lambs were all devoured, only one escaped." Even the pasture itself disappeared. The fable ends in carnage and so does our story. But at the time, at the outset, in the euphoria of reading the first verses of the fable, in the enthusiasm that accompanies beginnings, everyone was in agreement. He who wasn't was thought perverse. I remember, around this time, I was actually insulted for having dared to say that the plans to demolish the neighborhood around the Place Maubert made me a bit uneasy. And what did I propose to do about the wretched people forced to live under bridges, those poor yet good-humored unfortunates on whom, one Christmas eve, the archbishop of Paris thought it Christian to go and bestow his blessing. Even the Church was against me, from the top to the bottom of the hierarchy, from the abbé Pierre to the archbishop. All that was left for me was to say my *mea culpa*.

The wolves and the lambs? Surely there were some species in between. Besides, who is really a wolf, who a lamb? I would have to concern myself here with natural history and I prefer to bequeath the task to our children and our children's children. They will have the necessary leisure to untangle these complex yet simple matters, so close to us that they only elicit a yawn. The mechanics of real estate, coproprietorship, the problem of knowing precisely who was the seller and who the buyer, what were their social and occupational profiles, broken down by neighborhood, perhaps even by age or for different stages in their careers, that is to say their lives. Such are these simple yet complex matters. If I am to believe a Parisian *notaire*, depending on the profession, those who had recently taken a step up the ladder of success were the ones who bought real estate. Buying an apartment was, in fact, a kind of promotion which might perhaps make the word promoter (ridiculous in itself) acceptable. An entire natural history to study, a zoology, a sociology.

Nevertheless I prefer La Fontaine to Buffon, the fabulist to the naturalist. The sheep were in harmony with the wolves. They howled with them as if they had become not wolves but fierce sheep, as sometimes happens in fables. But doesn't the fable exaggerate? The two in harmony? Is not the fable a bit simplified? Doesn't it lack something additional to provide verisimilitude or, as they say in the *contes*, a final device? The word means many things, but in particular a machine. A machine? Exactly. Those who were not convinced we needed housing were won over by a less costly but more common machine, the horseless carriage, or to speak in ordinary language, "wheels," a car.

Chapter Two

The *Bagnole* and the Tree

There are no people in the world who use their coaches more than the French. . . . The ponderous carts of Aisa would give them heart failure.

Montesquieu

THE *bagnole?* An old country word as well as a slang word for an automobile, whose original meaning, which explains certain ambiguities in current usage, is today forgotten. The Littré dictionary tells us that *bagnole* comes from the Gaullish *banne,* a kind of cart, and that in spoken Parisian French of the sixteenth and seventeenth centuries the *banne* was a basket—for example the *panier,* used by the baker—as well as a charcoal-burner's cart. Sometimes it meant "the *bannel* used to take a condemned man (ignominiously) to the scaffold." Perhaps it was already thought good usage, by some ignoramuses, to speak of one's *banne.* Pure hypothesis on my part, unsupported by anything in La Bruyère or elsewhere.

In the middle of the nineteenth century, *bagnole* was used in several provinces to designate a cart or wagon, usually one in a sorry state. In the Ardennes, but especially in Normandy, in Picardy, in the area around Paris, and doubtless in Paris, the vehicle appeared because of internal immigration. The word smacks of provincial popular speech. It also—a hypothesis as unsubstantiated as my suggestion above—eluded the notice of a bourgeoisie guarding its language, and flourished among the decaying nobility that wanted to be close to the people, or rather mingled with the vulgar. There is not a shred of evidence in Balzac or Eugène Sue. It is none the less true that the word *bagnole,* such as we find it today, solidly entrenched in our own speech, posturing with the unconcerned air of a disheveled *parvenu,* benefits from this etymological history. Even if the etymology is reconstituted from pieces and fragments, from suppositions rather than proofs, this is faithful to the most authentic linguistic tradition (although very far from the high-powered acrobatics of structuralism or semiology).

Both vulgar and refined, pejorative or favorable—a useless fragment of iron or an elegant tool—changing meaning depending on place, user, image, manner of pronunciation, whether uttered in a resonant or a throaty voice (or a combination of the two), with the mouth open or closed, it seems that this protean word, this indefinable word that eludes the grasp yet is understood by everyone, sums up excellently all the aspects of this invasion by the automobile which much more than the need to build, overwhelmed Paris.

The *bagnole,* in 1954, was in Françoise Sagan's *A Certain Smile* just as in 1961 it was in *Petits enfants du siècle.* It is her *bagnole,* baptized Jaguar, or better yet "Jag," that, whatever its make, was "always a fast convertible that handled well," driven by her with bare feet and filled—the *bagnole* that is—with whiskey. And there is also the *bagnole* of Christiane Rochefort, supported by the pooled resources of friends: "They calculated for an entire evening on this matter of the *bagnole* . . ." There is the *bagnole* of the rich neighborhoods: "I will wait for you *en bagnole* in front of chez Francis . . . you know the bistro in the Place de l'Alma." Bistro, *bagnole,* words of the same kind, taken from the same sack, surely not from yours, Oh Madwoman of Chaillot. And then there is the popular *bagnole,* a worker, one could almost say a working-class leader in that it occupies a place in the sociological production, in all its patterns reflecting the conditions of workers and their changes. One could extract from this plethora of inquiries a statistical study of the use of the word *bagnole,* or rather of the word *voiture.* Sociology directed toward the working class is prim and has a holy horror for François Sagan's affectations of vulgarity. Is there still a working class, a proletariat, or is it dead (from natural causes), before our very eyes? Questioning what he calls "the new working class," Pierre Belleville wrote in 1963: "The most optimistic already say, looking at the statistics on departures for ski vacations or the growth in the number of automobiles, that the working class no longer exists."

Bagnole or car, the writings of this period let us better understand its impact by highlighting certain nuances which then appeared obscure. Certainly there was general agreement: "Ah! pretty woman, I have a car," had been a commonplace for some time. The worker, by rejecting the metro, committed himself to paying the expenses of a car which he could have done without. And when they discussed questions of traffic flow at the Municipal Council, those representing rich neighborhoods as well as those representing poor neighborhoods were equally concerned for their constituents' cars. Why try to support this observation with statistics, why trouble oneself with the number of cars and their distribution by class, to try to fix the responsibility on one group or the other? Why even call this sociology? Each person had or wanted to have his car and was determined to use it, accusing everyone else's car of preventing him from doing so, and accusing Paris itself of being ill adapted for cars, of putting a spoke in his wheel. On the surface this appears an adequate, simple explanation. Why dig deeper?

In the texts, enquiries, chronicles, novels, there seems more to it. First is the fact that not only were all the automobile owners in agreement, but they shared the same spirit, had the same perspective. This is not a question of class, a problem for sociology, but a fact of psychology and of Parisian psychology. In a word, a French phenomenon. Observing how people's tastes differ from country to country in the matter of cars—a banal observation—one can ask oneself (and the inhabitants of a given country), without descending to a meaningless game of words, if there is a psychology of the car. Is there, for example, a German psychology in which German brutality is clearly seen and which transforms every car into a veritable armored vehicle? Solidity, robustness, force, maybe even the gray color, or no color at all, these are the bone-chilling qualities described by Tacitus. Of course I am exaggerating these questions to the point of absurdity in order to rouse the car owner from his placidity and elicit some response.

Isn't there an American psychology? What a pity André Siegfried didn't think of it.[1] It is true that the American literature on the car is abundant. So too is its treatment in the movies. The subject has been well explored. And what about a British psychology, or Italian, or Spanish, and others as well, whose main interest for us is to highlight a French psychology that might go unnoticed without such comparisons.

Let me cautiously propose two traits which may be the most striking. First, the instinct for property, the old peasant instinct by means of which I would like to explain the Parisian politics of the car. The Parisian owner of a car should be able to use it, and thus use the tiny bit of Parisian land—road, sidewalk, or public place—that he is fully persuaded he has

---

1. Siegfried, who makes several appearances in this book, was a celebrated professor of "human geography" at the Collège de France, who regularly contributed to *Le Figaro*. He was the author of numerous books on the United States, the most famous being *Les Etats-Unis d'aujourd'hui* (1954).

bought along with his car. Thus does the instinct for property come into play. It is sacrilege to bar access to a piece of land. Such a blow to the ego is deeply resented. Read Balzac, read Tocqueville. And why not Descartes as well? Can we not see his mechanistic view of the world in the engineer designing a complicated machine, not so much to go from here to there as to demonstrate the superiority of its inventor. The same is true of the Parisian, under the hood of his car, assembling, disassembling things for the pleasure of tinkering? Tinkering, in the period we are discussing, is a dominant theme in the sociology of the car.

More dangerous for the city is another trait of Parisian psychology whose analysis needs no learned sources: newspaper accounts suffice. Over the years, one of their favorite themes is the pleasure of strolling in the city, the pleasure of the pedestrian, which is also the pleasure of the driver who has, according to all indications—unfortunately for Paris— the soul of a stroller. One has only to leaf through the papers of the day, or, building on memory, to imagine them.

A story in *Le Figaro* brought to my mind the rendezvous by car in front of the bistro of the Madwoman of Chaillot, which in turn took me back to a street near the Place de l'Alma. I have mislaid the newspaper item, even forgotten the author, but it seemed so charming, so pertinent to me, compared to the boring contemporary sociology of the car, that I think I have remembered what is essential. It happened on the avenue George V, at the time of the automobile show. A sports car stopped on a dime at a red light. A young man with a Marlon Brando haircut was driving. A horn sounded behind him. No, it was not Françoise Sagan attracted by one of those shaved necks she describes in *A Certain Smile* and finds so irresistible. Rather, it was some blonde girlfriend, a Brigitte Bardot type, herself in a car. The horn blast said: "It would be fun to smoke a cigarette under these lovely trees." But the light changed to green, which signaled their dilemma. Still, what luck to have been able to honk at her friend. So charming, so seductive, as long as she didn't mean "You jerk," which doesn't matter for my story anyhow. What a body (I'm talking about the car)! What luck, in a word, to have been able to behave like a pedestrian, to taste a moment of forbidden pleasure, and especially on one of the marvelous avenues that lead to the Etoile. The avenue George V is one of the loveliest; it is the avenue de l'Alma of the Belle Epoque, the avenue of the height of elegance. Everything was present to make this minor episode into a kind of apotheosis. The decor, the broad, shaded walks, the people strolling, as in the time of those handsome gentlemen who served as Toulouse Lautrec's models. The handsome, sedate facades of buildings whose ground floors still shelter, like a collection of jewel boxes, tiny and luxurious shops, were indifferent to this scene. So too were the passersby, whom one would not encounter elsewhere. Familiar faces, ideal people who, suddenly embodied, looked exactly as they did on stage or on the screen, as if they were still playing a role. I saw Gérard Philipe here, radiant in his youthful glory, flying by in a convertible, like some Prince Charming in the ballet of the Marquis de Cuevas then at the Théâtre des Champs-Elysées, a few steps away. Smiling and polite, well-mannered and pleasant, Rodrigo acknowledging, with a wave of the hand, the innumerable hellos of Chimènes.[2]

In the Paris of these years there were those who drove and those who walked, those who used public transportation and, if I accept the results of a poll conducted by the IFOP (in November–December 1954), constituted 66 percent of Paris adults.[3] Here I have inserted a statistic since it fits my purpose. But the point is, those who drove behaved more like pedestrians, believing themselves still pedestrians, despite appearances, despite their armor, this enclosure, this body, these extra wheels. Like pedestrians—that is, the Parisians whose greatest pleasure was to explore, without getting bored, a city that was still a city of pedestrians, as Jules Romains depicts it at the time of his *Men of Good Will*.[4] The only difference is that in greater numbers than before these pedestrians are now in cars, causing enormous complications, horrendous traffic jams and great anxiety for the city. In an earlier time weren't those who went by coach even more annoying? Although less numerous, didn't they cause greater difficulties and weren't they more disagreeable? Disorder for disorder, isn't the avenue George V or the Champs-Elysées of the 1950s still charming and preferable to those congested scenes so dear to Parisian literature in so many texts? The most disgusting is surely Boileau's poem, so often quoted in official speeches, which is nothing more than a bad and pretentious translation of Juvenal. The cacophony of metal striking wood, the clatter of wheels, the crack of whips, the sound of horseshoes—without mentioning the smell of manure, compared to which the

2. Rodrigo was El Cid, the hero of Spanish history, and Corneille's hero in his *Le Cid*, considered Gérard Philipe's greatest role. Rodrigo loved Chimènes as young Parisian women loved Philipe.

3. The IFOP, or Institute français d'opinion publique, of which Chevalier was co-founder, was one of the first French opinion polls.

4. The collective title of twenty-seven related novels which together depict French life and thought between 1908 and 1933.

odor of gasoline fumes is the perfume of Arabia. Reread Mercier for the
eighteenth century or Zola for the nineteenth, who adored describing this
tumult, disentangling this confusion. Thus in *Nana* does the latter describe the chaos of coaches on their way to the Bois de Boulogne one
glorious racing day: "dog-carts, victorias, landaus, light tandems, as delicate as pieces of jewelry, threading their way amidst the clang of bells . . .
four-in-hands"—I don't know what these are and probably Zola didn't
either. How much easier it is simply to say *bagnole!* There is not much
difference between this scene before the Franco-Prussian War of 1870
and that after World War I, the scene that Raymond Radiguet describes
in *Le Bal du comte d'Orgel.* A long procession of automobiles on their
way to some country spot in the environs of Paris, with a crowd massed
at the Porte d'Orléans like a guard of honor: "After dancing at Robinson,
those who liked to stroll along the outer boulevards and the young people
[*braves gens*] of Montrouge came to this *porte* to admire the upper crust.
The curious who made up this impudent line pressed their noses against
the windows of the cars, the better to see their owners." Always the spectacle and the spectacle of the spectacle! My spectacle on the avenue
George V is not so different.

The setting, the cars, the people, a similar kind of pleasure: even in a
car to feel oneself still a pedestrian. The difference is that this kind of
pedestrian occupies more space. The pleasure he takes in wandering
through the city will eventually destroy it. The pleasure of driving in the
city will become, as the city is gradually effaced, the pure and simple
pleasure of driving, the automatism of the automobile. "It is clear that
the frequent passage of coaches is enlarging the streets," writes Hugo, in
book IV of *Les Misérables.* Great good sense, words of a titan, an ava-
lanche that sums up the issue. The passage of automobiles is enlarging
the streets. In so doing it sacrifices the trees, which for the most part date
from the time when Hugo wielded his gigantic pen.

To sacrifice the trees is to sacrifice the city. Even more than one might
think.

> There used to be so many trees in the city.
>
> Hemingway

S ACRIFICE the trees? The city had always done it. Obviously the
city had been able to be born and to grow only at their expense,
the expense of the forests, the fields, the groves, the gardens. Without
going back to the very beginnings of Paris, St.-Germain-des-Prés and

St.-Martin-des-Champs carry the names of what they replaced. There was no opposition until the sixteenth century, which furnishes a celebrated example. The students protested against the extension of the faubourg St. Germain at the expense of the Pré-aux-Clercs: "These students demolished and wrecked a large field belonging to the abbey, tearing up the vines, attacking the houses of the *seigneurs* and bourgeoisie located in the above-mentioned woods." This made many Parisians, for whom Corrozet's account bestowed the prestige of a kind of epic—Charlemagne himself was in the background—take notice of what was exceptional and what was useless in the affair.[5]

Through the ages the spread of houses and men has been accomplished only to the detriment of gardens and trees. Should one be astonished at this, it is important to note that, despite the centuries of men laying down stone, there have endured, here and there, in the most neglected corners, the most hostile places, the most unbelievable gardens, miracle gardens, those "fugitive gardens" of Colette, where a wall has been knocked down, at the rear of a courtyard which itself is within another courtyard.

It is also worth noting that the developed land, which is the old Gallic land, remains alive, not ossified, and is still able to nourish these tenacious roots, to support vegetation whenever there is an opportunity, whenever stone and concrete reveal some crack, an overlooked fissure. How surprised Hugo was to see a tiny flower growing behind a stone wall, among the calcified ruins of the Vaudeville theater, burned in 1834! "This wild flower, growing tranquilly and following the gentle laws of nature, in the earth, in the center of Paris, between two streets, a few steps from the Palais Royal, only a bit farther from the Carousel arch in the Tuileries, in the midst of passersby, boutiques, carriages, buses and the wagons of the king, this flower of the adjoining fields of paving, opened in my soul a chasm of reverie." How much more profound was the chasm opened for the Parisians of our day by the enormous hole in the ground where les Halles had been, now so smoothed out, so devoid of buildings, that there is no longer the slightest chance that anything will grow there, whatever it is, unless it is imported or transplanted, but not sprung from the bowels of Paris.

In contrast to this significant, pitiless fact is another, seemingly different yet identical, which Colbert mentions, with superb simplicity, in a

5. Gilles Corrozet (1510–1568) was a writer whose most notable works were *Hecatomgraphie* (1540), and *Richart Sans Prour*.

manuscript note: "Plants everywhere to continue. Arch of triumph for earthly conquest. Observatory for the heavens. Pyramids." And plants did continue so that in the seventeenth century the public parks and gardens of Paris were considered, without any exaggeration, as the most beautiful in the world. The French Revolution held its festivals in these gardens and ruined them. The Empire only had time to clean them up, to restore them, to impose the symbols of its victories, to make its triumphal arches the gateways to the gardens of the kings. With the Restoration and the July Monarchy, while the romantics were celebrating nature, stately trees, and tiny birds, the city showed itself more hostile and destructive. "Plants everywhere to continue." The plantings of the Second Empire were born from this imperative. The woods, the parks, the squares, were "the Paris of little creatures," as the *Contes de lundi* would have it, sheltering themselves from the carriages. Along the new boulevards and avenues, there were those enormous trees which have survived to our own day, or almost. The Second Empire created the foliage amidst which we have lived ever since.

The Third Republic actually added very little except the poplars and plane trees of the quays. On the other hand how many menacing projects, how many dossiers were prepared, some successful at once, others having to await their time. In 1894 came "the project of the Tuileries gardens"—it being understood that henceforth what they baptized as the "project of the garden" in fact called for the destruction of the garden, or as much of it as was required. It was a question of linking the Solferino bridge to the rue de Castiglione by a road cut through the Tuileries gardens. In 1938 it was the project of the Palais Royal garden, although the gardens and the palace had been declared a national historical monument in 1920. The Municipal Council then turned to the idea of a subterranean road linking the Bourse to the avenue de l'Opéra, which would extend as far as one of the pavilions of the Palais Royal. Since the proposal submitted to the assembly seemed to suppose, for economic reasons, that the road would be built above ground, through the gardens, the Commission du Vieux Paris, on the recommendation of Victor Perrot, opposed the scheme (March 26, 1938), which has since slumbered in its file. I suppose it is still awaiting another opportunity. There are a number of these dormant, sacrilegious projects that so much recent experience has shown usually end up by being realized. This was true of the Marché St. Honoré, an old project that was realized in 1959, without a struggle.

Immediately after World War I, when the mood was patriotic, they proposed erecting a monument to the glory of the French army on the site of the Marché. Around the monument would be considerable masonry. But it was necessary to pay the merchants huge indemnities to acquire their long-term leases. Things did not go smoothly and at the time it seemed not worth the effort. The scheme was set aside for another time, but it was a close shave. The world economic crisis saved the Marché this time, as the war itself had saved the Tuileries Gardens. Thirty years later, to do the deed, it was no longer necessary to invoke the fatherland: the sacred love of the automobile sufficed.

Meanwhile, before attacking the city in its very heart and essential arteries, the automobile had already done considerable damage. Not much noticed, sometimes even insignificant. The accumulation of these small but dangerous blows prepared the way for greater crimes while preparing people for these crimes. It seems to me that around 1953–54, maybe a bit earlier, people began to speak more and more frequently, more and more strongly, more and more forthrightly, in a voice carrying real authority, as they say, of how difficult it was to drive in Paris. Such talk may not actually have begun then; the theme is an ancient one, if we remember Boileau. One turned, in fact, more and more often, on every occasion, to cite Boileau. Stories and news items in the press, both more numerous and more dramatic, wrenching radio reports, described the weekend exodus—which had replaced the "country outings" of the *Comte de'Orgel*—as transformed into a dangerous time, a wild migration before which the old accounts of the barbarian migrations pale. These are recorded in the most somber poems of the *La Légende des Siècles,* for example the one that begins: "When with his infants dressed in animal skins."

At the Municipal Council, discussion of the subject became more and more frequent, more and more prolonged. Statements came from those of every political persuasion and received unanimous support, except from some stubborn character always ready to sniff out some suspicious motive in this drama, and even to lament the first decisions made to ease the flow of traffic. The chronology of these decisions should show us, year by year, these first wounds inflicted by the automobile, isolated, limited, sometimes sincerely regretted and irrigated by tears. In fact these decisions paved the way for the great ravages, the real massacres which would come some years later, to be greeted with enthusiasm and tears of joy. The enumeration of these massacres would be interminable. They touch all neighborhoods, all avenues, all boulevards, ultimately even all trees, wherever or whatever kind they may be. Each place suffers from the damage done to others, and the good fortune of some spared avenue is only temporary, and no consolation for the misfortune of another where the ax has fallen.

1955 was a bad year for the lovely Paris avenues. During the spring, the work of enlarging the avenue de l'Opéra began at the expense of its broad sidewalks lined with trees which led to the sculpture of Orpheus playing his lyre, on the façade of the Opera itself. The avenue had been so beautiful to contemplate during intermissions, like an unrolled carpet. In October of the same year they attacked the sidewalks of the Champs-Elysées. In October 1957 six government ministers along with the cream of Paris society (as was correct) rode the metro to inaugurate the Franklin Roosevelt station which, according to an official speech, "was one of the most luxurious in the world, with its windows depicting famous paintings with cut-glass replicas." Less enthusiastically, some malcontents commented that the uglier things got above ground the more refined they became below. As the Champs-Elysées, with its shrunken sidewalks, began to resemble a used-car lot, the metro, in contrast, was made beautiful. They even considered having music in the station. It would have been installed if those responsible had been able to choose between classical music and pop, a serious problem that remains unresolved as I write these lines. Also in September 1957 came the turn of the avenue d'Italie, and in September 1959 that of the boulevard Malesherbes. As many massacres as there were Septembers. Black Septembers.

All this was accompanied by numerous explanations and justifications: work on the gas mains, on the electrical system, or the water and sewer pipes. But above all the bad condition of the trees, old and diseased, threatened the safety of pedestrians. Official texts did not, obviously, pass over in silence the question of traffic flow, which they insisted was "imperative." The age of the trees was not mentioned. Nothing is better known to Parisians, at least the ages of certain celebrated trees, certain heroes of yesteryear. Stories abound, illustrated with photos. The estimates of age vary. Some are as unbelievable as those of Russian demographers who study longevity in the Caucasus. There the people eat yogurt. What is the secret of the trees? The acacia of St.-Julien-le-Pauvre, for example, the uncontested grandfather of them all, dates from the beginning of the seventeenth century. Is it not this tree that Huysmans saw "through the white windows," this "tree that sways and adds the moving tracery of its branches to the lead tracery of the windows"? It was by that time probably too stiff with age to move, and burdened with how many other afflictions that mark the history of so many other trees, almost as celebrated—the paulownias of the Contrescarpe,[6] for example, whose mysterious name, some know, came from that Anna Paulowna, the daughter of Tsar Paul. The crowds knew only that the trees bore enormous purple flowers in the spring, splotches of unusual color in this already multicolored place, this haven for beggars and clochards. Hemingway, who lived not far from here, at the top of the montagne Ste.-Geneviève, saw them in another season: "the cold wind would strip the leaves from the trees in the Place Contrescarpe. The leaves lay sodden in the rain and the wind drove the rain against the big green autobus at the terminal and the Café des Amateurs was crowded and the windows misted over from the heat and the smoke inside." In fact they had stopped flowering before 1939. The automobiles having disappeared during the Second World War they flowered once again, only to cease—and this time definitively—in the years after the war, until they were cut down.

If many Parisians know the destiny of a few celebrated trees that mark the broad contours of history, they know even better about those trees that make up what government functionaries call the Parisian forest, the widespread collection of trees that until very recently contributed so much to the beauty of Paris. Above all the chestnut trees, "the huge, sleek chestnut trees with red flowers" of Colette. "Who knows," she asks, "as well as the Ile de France how to plant chestnut trees as a roof against the rain, an umbrella against the sun?" "The chestnut trees of the Champs-Elysées that Napoleon's son dreamed of when a prisoner," writes Charles de Gaulle in his *Mémoires de Guerre*. We could reconstruct the history of Provence by recounting the stories of its plane trees and mulberry trees. For the history of Paris—the Ile de France—we could collect an anthology from those who have celebrated its chestnuts. The writings of women especially would be helpful. It was in the shadow of a chestnut, at the abbey of Livry, that Mme de Sévigné wrote some of her letters. I read in the *Courrier des Arts* of August 1963 that Lady Blanford, the first wife of Aristotle Onassis, wanted to purchase a pied-à-terre in Paris and could not decide between an eighteenth-century town house in the faubourg St. Germain and the fifth floor of a new apartment building on the avenue Gabriel, where *Caroline chérie,* that is, Martine Carol, had lived. "The apartment faced the chestnuts of the Champs-Elysées. She finally chose

6. A small *place* at the top of the rue Mouffetard dear to Parisians as a piece of old Paris. M. Chevalier lives nearby on the same street where Hemingway once lived.

this apartment because of the chestnut trees." *Chéri,* the creation of Colette, ends with the image of the book's heroine walking, carefree, under
the flowering chestnuts. In the opening lines of *La Fin de Chéri* the chestnuts are ever-present. They were there only yesterday. A parking lot has
killed nearly all of them. If they are not completely dead those that remain are moribund.

Such are the final consequences of automobile traffic, the last chapter
of a story which has been accelerated and whose episodes have become
as familiar to Parisians as a song whose chorus is endlessly repeated.
Gasoline asphyxiates trees.

Not only are trees old, but they are sick, dangerous. They must be
chopped down. This will be good for the tranquility of people and even
for the beauty of the city. This is the official theme, incessantly played
and recapitulated, for example, in this declaration of an official (*Le
Figaro,* January 16, 1959): "Along the Champs-Elysées there were
75 chestnut trees, 59 of them more than a hundred years old and with a
circumference between 1.80 and 3.30 meters. Only 16 trees are relatively
young and vigorous. We were hopeful, we were patient, until an old
chestnut tree was uprooted by the wind (February 4, 1955). I want to
remind you that we are devoted to beautiful trees. We also have the responsibility for human lives."

Indeed never did we see so many accidents of this sort than in 1955
and the years following. In 1955, 1956, and 1957, the wind uprooted
ten trees a year in Paris; seventeen in 1958. A woman walking in the Bois
de Vincennes was killed, not by a murderer, but by a worm-eaten oak.
Evidently no one questioned these facts, the bad luck as well as the enormous concern of the functionaries, as passionate about the trees as anyone, nay more so. One could not help but notice that the bad luck was
relentless and timely. These accidents happened repeatedly, always in the
same way and always coinciding with some expansion of the street system: by unexpected chance, by a kind of happy circumstance, and with
hardly any questioning, in these years, of the need to improve the flow of
automobile traffic. These were trees that died providentially, that fell
from old age or disease (one did them a service in cutting them down),
not to mention those poor pedestrians whose lives were saved! And all
this care was taken to assure Parisians, by every means, that all would be
done in such a way that they would not even notice, that nothing would
be changed except for the better. It was too perfect!

Along these lovely avenues, slowly destroyed—and always during the
summer months when no one was in Paris—who would not think of the

Paris administration as one thinks of the weasel in the fable "Is This a ruse"? From the simple enlarging of the streets there soon came other operations whose linkage eventually became so well known that it surprised no one. From the first blow of the pickax everyone knew the outcome. First parking lots on the surface, at the expense of sidewalks already narrowed, or of those quiet, unassuming promenades which ornament the center of some lovely place, indifferent to surrounding traffic, set aside for the pleasure of another century. From Barbès to the grounds of the Parc Monceau, and above all from Pigalle to Clichy, with their fairs and the undulating decors of *Jésus la Caille*.[7] Now came the turn of a boulevard that had escaped the Germans, who had wanted to make it a military thoroughfare. It was also the turn of the avenue Henri Martin, the former avenue de l'Empereur, the counterpart of the avenue de la Impératrice (whose name was changed to the avenue Foch). In 1959 the rough field that had been used as a parking lot for a long time, amidst the mud and the noble droppings of horses, gave way to a modern parking lot, that is, a paved lot which caused everyone to ask themselves if this was not the harbinger of an underground parking garage.

This is the final phase, prepared by a few prototypes and some more or less successful experiments. It would be full-blown only after 1965. A number of circumstances, besides complete uselessness, explain this delay. Stupidity itself, some say, for the scheme, which far from solving the problems of traffic, could only aggravate them: disastrous for the many, profitable for the few—the builders and, by a fitting paradox, the muggers. But this new chapter in the lower depths of Paris will be discovered only later. Entering the underground parking garage of the Hôtel de Ville for the first time and thinking of the criminals of the first half of the nineteenth century who, Balzac reports, did their dirty work around here, I could not help murmuring to myself: "Ah, if Lacenaire had known this cutthroat!"[8]

Among the circumstances that stall so many impatient projects is Parisian archaeology. A construction site is an archaeological site. One never knows precisely what will be discovered. The contractors do the

7. The most celebrated novel of François Carco, set on the boulevard de Clichy in a bar on the Butte Montmartre. Chevalier says he was inspired by this novel when, as a young man, he often walked in this quarter, which would subsequently be the subject of his *Montmartre de plaisir et du crime*.

8. Lacenaire is one of the most celebrated assassins (who also wrote poetry) of the first half of the nineteenth century. He was executed in 1836, at the age of 33.

digging and the Commission du Vieux Paris oversees the work. At least the construction of underground parking garages has enriched the history of ancient and medieval Paris. In 1970–71, for example, the excavations on the rue Soufflot helped Paul-Marie Duval to sharpen the description of Gallo-Roman Paris that he had presented in his *Paris antique,* itself resting on the discoveries made at the end of the nineteenth century when the street was originally created. "The archaeologists," he recounts, "working underground for several months on a delicate job, amidst the bulldozers, exposed the outlines of a small, rough stone wall with rectangular niches, with traces of the marks of the original builders scratched or painted on the exterior." The diggings under the *parvis* in front of Notre Dame began in 1965, following two years of probings. Closely supervised by Michel Fleury—you could not pass in front of the cathedral without seeing him—they had to use the utmost care to preserve the Gallo-Roman wall and the remains of St. Etienne, which they discovered. An extraordinary museum was created, with difficulty, by rescuing a part of the *parvis* garage from the cars. Here was a huge, subterranean cathedral of which Fleury was the *maître d'oeuvre,* a modern-day Maurice de Sully, the medieval builder of Notre Dame. Soon, on the ancient site thus transformed, a new and unexpected chapter in the great, picturesque history of Paris was opened. This is, it seems to me, a kind of consecration of this new scene, this extraordinary "theater" of the young. Assembling in crowds from the four corners of the earth they come to Notre Dame on Sunday mornings to dance, to sing, to celebrate some strange rite known only to them. Through the open portals of the cathedral they see the mass being celebrated and hear the organ reverberating under the vaults. Sometimes they squat, contemplating the enormous facade with the sunlight playing upon it, like some great phenomenon of nature rather than of art: or perhaps the emotion conveyed by art becomes, in these confused souls, these simple souls—the souls of an exhausted civilization—something identical to the emotion derived from nature. Seeing them thus sprawled I thought of the monster gatherings in California's Big Sur, where, from the cliffs, the bearded crowds watched the play of light, the clouds, the storms unleashed over the immense Pacific Ocean. Sometimes a sea monster, a whale, swam by, indifferent to humankind and their corruption. Everyone stood up as if to watch the creation of the world. Squinting in front of Notre Dame they similarly gave the impression of asking themselves what would emerge from this sea of stone.

But if this particular underground garage created a kind of Miracle of Notre Dame under the parvis, what can we say of the others? What about that of the church of St. Sulpice, whose four sculpted bishops, atop their fountain, seated on their thrones, give the horrified impression of having become parking-lot attendants and feeling all this noisy traffic passing under their soutanes? And what about the garage I said should be consecrated to those great criminals, Lacenaire or Vautrin, the garage under the Hôtel de Ville which, by magic, miraculously exits in the department store, the Bazar de l'Hôtel de Ville. More especially what can one say of those garages that have annihilated so many marvelous gardens filled with trees, under the pretext of saving them? Sometimes they even prided themselves on improving these gardens, ennobling them, promoting them to the dignity of "French Gardens" which, as everyone knows, have no trees. Even better, without inventing the "French Garden," they made them into paved gardens that pretend to have trees but have none, or have such ridiculous trees that it is best not to speak of them. With the coming of parking garages the old taste for a tree with a decoratively trimmed branch again makes sense, as one sees by the skeletal plantings in so many squares. The square of Anvers, for example, that place they have the effrontery to call the square of Anvers. Formerly so protected by verdure, so hidden from sight, that in the night of Montmartre some years ago members of the Resistance would meet there, a few steps from German soldiers strolling down the boulevard Rochechouart trying to pick up French girls. Jean Moulin held an important rendezvous there.[9] Lack of soil, insufficient drainage, concrete that prevented proper watering, these are the reasons given to explain what happened to the trees in the square of Anvers, as elsewhere. There are only stunted trees now, trees that seem to belong to another species, caricatures of trees, dwarf trees, aborted trees, stillborn trees, shaving-brush trees, broomstick trees—whisk brooms or feather dusters like those used by the local concierges—miniature trees to put in one's button hole, potted trees such as those seen on Parisian balconies.

What has become of these "rustling organisms" that Hippolyte Taine's tree called to mind; "this lovely thing glistening with rain, flooded in light by the changing aspects of a beautiful April day" that Maurice Barrès went to honor? And what of the smell after a cloudburst, this breath of

9. Jean Moulin, himself a polytechnicien, was a Resistance hero and de Gaulle's personal envoy to the Resistance in France. Captured by the Germans, he was hideously tortured and killed by Klaus Barbie.

the forest, this exhalation of incense! Too much pollution has accumulated, too many exhaust fumes from trucks, to make grow what doesn't
want to grow, trees that would prefer not to grow—like the malformed
and dismembered who hide themselves. Such trees reek of rottenness. As
a clochard, the most wretched living in the gardens next to the tower of
St. Jacques, exclaimed: "Now they will say we smell bad!"

> It is not the woods that you cut down. . . .
> Ronsard

THE sacrifice of the trees signifies even more. It is the first act of the
sacrifice of the city itself, which it prefigures and announces, accomplished amid a general incomprehension and indifference. Because the
trees of Paris are not like trees elsewhere.

The fact is Parisians do not love trees. The observation is not mine but
that of an official responsible for the trees who, at a gathering in the rue
St. Guillaume[10] in the 1960s, responded to the question of an indignant
Parisian: "How do you explain the differences between this and other
cities . . . London, for example?" The official replied: "The explanation
is that Parisians do not love trees." The public bridled at this insult, yet
it came from a technocrat. As for myself, I see in the remark confirmation
of what I already thought. Having heard, at the first meeting of the Economic and Social Council of Paris, an official declare, to underline the
interest he had in the deliberations of the gathering, that he kept thoughts
about "green areas" in Paris to himself, I thought that he was mocking
us. What more could one say about this abused subject, so sterile, and
stigmatized as "green areas"? No one knows precisely what they are,
beyond some vague green indication on an official plan.

About the attitudes of Parisians, and indeed the French generally, there
is much more to be said, and it is said in a quotation from *Les Misérables:* "As one goes about one's business in one's natal province . . . one
imagines these trees are the first to grow. When one is no longer among
them one realizes that one cherishes the streets, misses the roofs, the windows, the doors, the walls, and the trees are beloved." Beloved? But not
more than the other things in the list, relegated to the last, even the end
of the list, the place of least significance.

Compared to the place occupied by trees in the literature of other

---

10. The location of l'Institut d'études politiques, known familiarly as Sciences-Po, where
Siegfried and Chevalier gave courses and where gatherings such as that here described were
sometimes held.

countries, other capitals—London or Berlin—how modest, indeed how insignificant is the place of trees in Parisian literature and French literature, where the sound of ax against trunk resounds continually. In addition it seems in these texts that the Parisian, believing himself to love trees, loves them as he would objects, as things that belong less to the world of living things than to the mineral world, stones among the stones, just as devoid of life, or having another kind of life, that of manmade monuments.

The tree is, in fact, history's monument. One can say of Parisians planting trees what Bossuet says of peoples: "They had made monuments of things that had happened to them" (*Histoire,* II, 3). The attachment of Parisians to such living monuments is strange. Should the trees die, they are replaced with others, in the same place, rooted in the same soil. These monuments, moreover, are worth more than others. One can admire a tree, as did Taine, but less often a statue, at least in Paris. Where in Paris are the fountains that grace Rome? I do not know what storyteller invented the history, the nightmare, of the statues of Paris, putting them in motion, parading them through the streets. Horrible carnival, pitiful procession. The fat figure of the Place de la République passes by . . . then. . . . But to remain in our own epoch, let us add to the parade of statues that of General Leclerc which stands at the end of the avenue d'Orléans. When someone expressed astonishment to Pompidou on the choice of this statue, he answered that clearly they had chosen the ugliest. He understood his times. It is true that had he himself chosen we would perhaps have seen erected there something or other by Calder, more costly and more deplorable than this inoffensive soldier cast in lead.

To the monuments of public history I add those of private history, of which literature preserves some trace. Each Parisian has his own tree, his "beloved." He knows them thoroughly and venerates them, not as trees but as monuments of his own past. Such a monument is the oak tree in the Bois de Vincennes under which Rousseau, on his way to visit the imprisoned Diderot, wrote in pencil to the spirit of Fabricius. Or the monument behind Père Lachaise cemetery, the walnut tree where Rousseau walked in reverie and which Michelet loved to visit, transforming it into a monument of his own life (*Journal,* Pentecôte, 1834). To Rousseau's tree to Michelet's to Taine's, to so many famous trees and others like them, I would add Daniel Halévy's tree. "The reason for my letter," the author of *Pays Parisiens* wrote to me (July 26, 1959), "is the lovely tree which is growing before my window, first in the row of trees along the quai de l'Horloge. This tree has a deep wound which has been neglected for several years and which certainly ought to be looked after. They tell me that there is an office in the Hôtel de Ville, occupied by a functionary of the Department of Waters and Forests. It seems to me that this is the door where I should knock in order to have my tree attended to. Could you tell me his name? I believe that in such a case a recommendation could be useful, and the magnificent tree that I am speaking of is one of the beauties of Paris." The tree of Daniel Halévy has continued, for many years since this letter, to bow its crown, heavy with years, over the barges gliding along the Seine.

Although it concerns one of the "beauties of Paris," this intensely vibrant text is an exception, as is Taine's celebration of his tree, which it resembles. It is a companion piece in a literature which persistently treats the tree not even as a monument but as a thing, a stone like any other in this universe of stones that is in the city. Parisians refuse to admit it, but the fact is so evident in all the known texts one could write a book on the subject. This is a book I shall never write. Besides, it is already half-written in the literature of Paris. The proof of this assertion is important for my views. Therefore these pages will sometimes touch lightly upon this book to be written, as well as on other books in limbo. *Poèmes à faire.* The title is Baudelaire's. Why not "books to write," of which this is one?

Books to Write

LEST my proposal seem paradoxical, as if it were one of those dissertations of the old school where the subject, when it is finally announced, still appears enigmatic, I am going to make my plan clear, in good pedagogical fashion, at the outset. Moving from the most obvious to the most surprising, from the least convincing to the most probing, we will successively see the insignificant place of the tree in the most curious, the most meticulous, or the most sober descriptions of Paris. In addition, we will see how the tree is represented when, by chance, it is discussed. Finally and most importantly we will see at what point it is overlooked where one most expected trees, as would be the case in describing a forest where nothing is lacking but the trees—the Bois de Boulogne, for example, that figures in so many descriptions of crowds going to Longchamps racetrack. Coaches, seductive cleavages, men of the world and easy women, horses (of course): everything is included, the necessary and the superfluous, except the trees, which are missing.

Trees scarcely appear when one reads descriptions of Paris, whether these are informed by observation of sensibility—qualities that are as distinct as two streams those waters never mingle and that inform the best work in this genre. Consider the sketches of Paris, an inexhaustible literature which can be traced back to the Middle Ages. "Love of the countryside and agriculture, which is universal," writes Mercier (in 1785), the greatest master of the genre, "still manifests itself in the great stone pile Parisians inhabit. Here a tiny garden, no more than a yard long, there a pot of flowers which occasionally falls on the head of some pedestrian." These lines encapsulate the various guises, some of them rare, assumed by trees or tree surrogates growing amid a pile of stones. This is an image one finds in Balzac, or in the "pot of flowers," which is the title of one of Mercier's chapters. Villon comes to mind: "The rue Galande—where there is neither forest nor land." Even more striking are the chapters in Mercier in which the Parisians walk just outside the city gates or in the neighboring countryside, and always in a place strangely devoid of trees. Trees are almost never present, except for those planted along the major roads around the capital and which say more for the Parisian administration and policy than for a general concern for trees. These are the "handsome routes, unknown in England," that Chateaubriand admired when he returned to Paris in 1800. "Approaching the capital, between Ecouen and Paris," he observes that "the young elms had not been cut down" although all along the route the chateaux had been destroyed and so had the tall trees. It is true, even in *Les Misérables*, that if a tree does appear along the country promenade of the four lovers, at the Carré du roi it is a special tree. "A plant recently brought from India . . . that drew all of Paris to St. Cloud . . . a curious and charming little tree with a tall trunk": in a word, a monument.

No less striking is the absence of trees in Baudelaire. *Paysages sans arbes* could be the title of an unwritten poem about all of Baudelaire's Paris scenes. Indeed the subtitle of this *Poème à faire* would be "Parisian things." There are similarly no trees in *les Fleurs du Mal*, that quintessential expression of the poetry of Paris. There are trees only in the cemetery where the kind-hearted maid sleeps: "And when October breathes, the scourge of old trees / Its melancholy wind around their stone roots." Trees and pavement, there is the whole of my theme. And the same is true of his vision of autumn: "When the burning log hisses and sings" and "I already hear fall with deadly shocks / the trees resonating on the paved courtyards." A sound already familiar to Parisians. Describing an agitated evening in the Marais in 1830, in *Choses vues*, Hugo notes: "The soldiers arranged their bivouac. We heard the sound trees being felled on the pavement, fuel for the night fires."

Not only do trees hardly appear in these descriptive or imaginative works, but when they are evoked, or rather mentioned in passing, it is to highlight a world without trees. The tree in a city is not really a tree. Giraudoux, in his *Pleins pouvoirs,* writes about a gardener whom he admired; "he opposed the authorization given to an employee of the Ambassadeurs Theater to cut down twenty young elm trees on the Champs-Elysées in order to add two meters to the establishment." The gardener had no love for the country. "'I'm a city man,' he said. 'I love the sense of freedom here and I love the gardens'." For Collete, "The lassitude of May overwhelms the planted areas. Will I soon be the only provincial woman seated in the Tuileries garden on her chair of yellow iron?"

Our administrators, so solicitous in finding titles of nobility for themselves, would have difficulty seeing in these "planted areas" the "green expanse" of their forebears. The gardens of these Parisian administrators—"city men" with no love for the country—like the "planted areas" of Colette, who prefers the country to the city, signify that it is basically a question of the city: trees are only a part of the background, in the most material and precise sense of the word. They are the stage scenery of the city. They are like theaters which often, before presenting their shows, present themselves and thus become a part of the great theater of the city. "The row of gas lanterns ablaze on the cornice of the theater," Zola writes of Nana's appearance on the stage, "cast a blanket of light on the sidewalk. Two small bright green trees were clearly visible in the bright light." It was perhaps a descendant of one of those trees, now a century old, that only yesterday was defended by Marie Bell on the sidewalk in front of her theater, using all her art as an actress. And I think, in 1935, I saw Artaud under the trees in the Place Dancourt, illuminated by the lights of the Atelier theater, telling his young disciples how much he admired Jean-Louis Barrault's first play, which he had just seen. But maybe I only read about it.

The whole city is a kind of theater, or at least it was, with its special scenes, its drama, its promenades, and its gardens. This was as true only yesterday as when La Bruyère wrote that "one comports oneself in Paris as at a public rendezvous, to be looked at, as they do every evening in the Tuileries Gardens." The faces of people are more important than the scenery. "Whether foul or fair, it is my custom to take a walk, at 5 P.M., in the gardens of the Palais Royal." Diderot says not a word about the trees in the Palais Royal, nor does Rousseau about those in the Luxembourg gardens.

Trees are not only the background decor for the theater of daily life, they serve the same function for the great events of history. Without comment here is what Chateaubriand says: "I went to the Champs-Elysées . . . the prostitutes straddled the canons . . . the king's carriages followed: they rolled by in the dappled darkness of a forest of pike-staves." Pikes rather than trees. Sometimes the trees give the impression of being more contrived than the scene itself. In 1841 Victor Hugo (in *Choses vues*) witnessed the return of Napoleon's remains. "The wagon bearing the Emperor's ashes appeared. The sun, until then hidden, burst forth from the clouds. The effect was extraordinary. In the distance, in sunlight and shadow, one saw, against the gray background of the trees of the Champs-Elysées, as through a group of large white statues resembling phantoms, the slow progression of a kind of golden mountain." With this "gray background," these "phantoms," this mountain, this vehicle, we are in the world of the unreal, the fantastic. All the more fantastic since Hugo certifies, "here is an absolutely true detail: when the Emperor's wagon appeared, the sun, until then hidden, burst forth from the clouds . . . the effect was extraordinary." The *effect*.

If trees hardly appear, or appear deformed or denatured in these privileged parts of the city, in great historical scenes, all the more reason for their absence from lesser neighborhoods, popular neighborhoods, shabby or sinister, where poverty and degradation, as well as a fragile charm, express the desolation and the hidden treasures of such places. Thus, in *Les Misérables* does Hugo describe the area around the Porte d'Italie, in the Gobelins neighborhood. "A huge elm tree, three-quarters dead. . . . The sinister traditions of the place . . . along the old carrés that looked like ditches, glimpsed between the trees. The day was foul, the evening lugubrious, the night sinister . . . the wretched elm trees, decapitated by the gate of St. Jacques and mercifully hiding the scaffold," made the trees a part of the environment of the scaffold, the setting for the place of capital punishment as well as a bit of camouflage which, once the "deed was done," remained as a kind of mockery. "Nevertheless, at nightfall, at the moment when the light vanished, especially in winter, at dusk, when the cold wind strips the last russet leaves from the elm trees. . . ." Here already is the tone of realism. These trees are those of Bruant, illustrated by Steinlin. The tree, the gas street-lamp, and the urinal, the Holy Trinity of the outer boulevards, the three props for tragic drama, as indispensable as the oversize bed, the dressing table, and, hidden by a Chinese screen, the immodest bidet are to that other genre, the "comédie de boulevard."

Like the gas jet and the urinal, the tree has a metallic quality. This is

Zola's scenery. The scenery of the novelist Carco: the rue des Poisson-
niers, "the rue par excellence" (his novels were printed at number 17,
chez Busson), "so close to the workshops of the railroad serving the
Nord," with their blind walls, their chimneys belching dense black
clouds, their street lamps, where one can still read these words from another time: "Bosquet Gardens." It is the setting in particular, in 1914, for
Jésus la Caille. The night of the neighborhood of the Place Pigalle and
the rue Blanche, with its feeble, flickering light and its sharp, penetrating
winter wind "that whips the pavement with long stripes and reverses the
flow of water in the gutters. A few leaves, the last stripped from the plane
trees, fall to the ground like wounded birds."

This is the scenery of Paris, the scenery of the people, more regal than
that of the royal gardens. The evident beauty of the latter obeys rules.
The mysterious beauty of the former violates all of them, in every way.
This kind of scenery is celebrated throughout the world, and the for-
eigner can perhaps best read about it in literatures other than ours, especially that of the Americans, who are not inhibited and who speak
frankly. Perlès says that the room where his friend Henry Miller lived in
1927 "looked out on the tiny triangle of the Square du Maine, formed
by seven barkless trees and a few wooden benches where the beggars and
the sandwich men of the neighborhood came to eat their bread and
cheese, washed down with cheap wine drunk from the bottle. On the
other side of the square he could see the cheap prostitutes now and then
hook a client from the regulars of the Edgar Quinet market."

Here on the same stage are glory and misery, born of the same history,
of the same happiness or the same bad luck, of the same inspiration or
the same chance, sometimes, it seems, made from the same matter:
marble, stone, plaster, zinc or corrugated iron, rarely wood. Hemingway's Luxembourg gardens are mineral rather than vegetable. "The bare
trees look more like statues, and the wind whistled over the surface of
the ponds and the fountains." Sometimes it is stone imitating trees, following a Parisian habit criticized in the eighteenth century by Mercier:
"these columns recall the branches of trees, these stone brackets the
wooden supports for beamed ceilings, these ornaments, vases filled with
plants; they are ingenious but I have seen it a thousand times. . . . I accuse
architecture of overwhelming monotony." Clearly this monotony is more
significant. It expresses this indifference to trees, to what they actually
are, to how they are viewed elsewhere.

This absorption of trees into the decor appears even more astonishing
in the descriptions otherwise so detailed, so meticulous, in which the

trees that we know were there, suddenly disappear without the slightest trace, without the slightest mention. Everything happens as if in another galaxy, millions of light years away, or as if it were part of a reality in which the naming of things came from a foreign language, a vocabulary whose secret would have been lost. On the first pages of *Bouvard et Pécuchet*, along the banks of the St. Martin Canal, heavily shaded by trees, which is where the novel opens, Flaubert's eye—this unsentimental eye that, alas, nothing escapes—sees only a stone Paris, baked and rebaked under a hard sun, completely petrified. The verbal details make this precise and weighty, as if it were the announcement of a public works project. The facades, the stone roofs, the granite quays, "their eyes wandered over the piles of building stone": this is a desolate universe.

In conclusion: the tree is the city. The sacrifice of a tree, even the most deformed, the most misshapen, the puniest, one that looks as if made of metal and is only held up by stakes and wire, even this is to sacrifice the city. It announces, it authorizes, it excuses, it even glorifies the sacrifice.

HOUSING, cars, trees, Paris itself pulled out by its roots, like a tree, dead leaves blown about by the wind, these are the images conjured by my memories of these first ten or fifteen years that encompass almost the whole of my account. But there are also other memories, if one relies on documents from the time, on written memory. Taken together they make a tapestry of a developer embracing the abbé Pierre, as St. Christopher embraced the infant Jesus. Or maybe it's the contrary! Nevertheless, what has happened subsequently, and what could not have been foreseen, necessitates attempting to peer more deeply into this great mystery of charity.

Chapter Three
"La Grande Bouffe"

It seems to me that I have only been in the parterre or at best in
the orchestra, playing and amusing myself with the violins. I want
to ascend to the theater proper where you see scenes not worthy
of you but at least a bit less unworthy of your attention.

Cardinal de Retz

WHAT came into being—no mystery about it—was what
would soon be called "the consumer society." A phenomenon
originally confined to the educated and wealthier classes, the
phenomenon spread within a few years throughout society. In my course
on recent history at Sciences-Po I used the expression for the first time
around 1964–65, I believe. Books dealing with "the consumer society,"
mostly translations or rehashes of American works, were causing a big
stir at the time. My students expected the subject to appear on exams
prepared by young economists: I had to speak the same language as the
faddish. I still remember the annoyance I felt.

In good French, *consommation* never had the meaning given it in
America. How could French society be led to this kind of organized
feeding so foreign to Rabelais's joyous cry, "tout pour la tripe"? It reminded me of those suction pumps one sees in the streets when they clean
out the sewers. "Let's get blotto," "Let's jump in the septic tank and do
it gaily," generations of students have sung, without attaching any significance to the song. "Let's get blotto," (omitting the out-of-fashion
"gaily") now symbolized for me the mechanistic image of consumption
being forced upon our society by a crew of sewer-pumping navvies,
namely, the sociologists.

Ten years later the image no longer seems to me as compelling, as
worthy of consideration, and even less appropriate. The consumer society
has become the subject of a host of books which, for the most part, are
not so much descriptions of this society as products of it. Some bookstore
displays look more like supermarket shelves than serious presentations.

And the most trivial poster on the subject says as much as most books. The passageways of the metro are as informative as the lecture hall. Radio and television have miniaturized the lecture hall, putting it in one's home, one's pocket, one's ear. The consumer society manifests itself didactically—sermonizing, in an unbroken discourse, or rather a discourse in which the international situation and laundry soap, political crisis and shaving cream, alternate. A significant amount of time is given to the news: some political crisis, a threat of war, a famine, all demand attention. But not without apologizing to the listeners. An abrupt raising of the voice, a tone of conviction, of pathos, of exultation, all signify that the great moment is that dedicated to some cosmetic or some new miracle detergent. And the music mixed with the message is not avant-garde stuff that puts everyone to sleep, or anything deafening, or the senseless music of aesthetes, but Vivaldi, Mozart, Beethoven. As I write these lines[1] France-Musique[2] is not much interested in classical music. And if listeners complain, if they want to hear Beethoven's Ninth Symphony, they can always turn to another station and put up with the commercials, or better yet, go to the movies, where, at the blessed intermission, they can join the crowd on the screen going in procession to one of the department stores along the Seine:

> Joy, thou source of light immortal,
>   Daughter of Elysium,
> Touched with fire to the portal
>   of thy radiant shrine we come.

No one now can be unaware of this so-called consumer society, not infants in the cradle, who prefer vitamin-fortified preparations to their mothers' milk, or the most retarded, the village idiot with his transistor, watching his cows. If one expresses personal views or teaches people something they do not already know, one must be "gifted" or miraculously inspired. A few manage this. Amid all the twaddle Jean Baudrillard's book *La société de consommation* (1970) is an exception.

Familiarity with this subject is especially impressive in Paris. One reason is the never-ceasing talk that continues day and night. But primarily it is because many Parisians can compare what is told them and shown them with what they remember from an earlier time, what remains in the

---

1. At the end of 1976.
2. The music station of the state radio network.

mind's eye, what they recall from great books or know by heart. Who will ever see in today's shopping centers, in the subbasements of the Montparnasse railway station for example, that termite nest of shops where a cow, even a Breton cow, could never find her calves; who will ever see there "those mysterious and undulating beaches" that Louis Aragon discovered in the shops along the boulevards and in the mysterious *passage* near the Opéra that he described in 1924: "Metaphysics of place, it is you who gently rock infants, it is you who people our dreams"?

Thanks to the so-called computers in certain shopping arcades along the Champs-Elysées there is no longer any such thing as the unknown or the mysterious. What unfair competition for some poor fortune-teller who, from her stall near the Porte St. Denis, divines the future. This naive creature more often predicts consuming passions than business successes. Zola's *Le bonheur des dames,* however revolutionary at the time and hurtful to the small shops even then being supplanted by department stores, was in its novelty faithful to what the simple word *bonheur* means in Paris: precisely that happiness specific to women which concurrently brings happiness to man. In his notebook Zola writes about Mlle Dulit, the saleswoman who inspired the portrait of his heroine: "She gave the impression of never withholding herself from a man who pleased her, yet appeared well-balanced, steering her ship with confidence and intelligence." Love and intelligence, happy stories of men and women, are found in all the departments of the store whose name is the title of the novel, in every chapter of this golden legend of Parisian commerce.

The *drugstore*[3] is a universe, not of men and women, but of objects— a subtle but essential theme for Jean Baudrillard. It is objects that exist, that are alive, that obtrude themselves, that give commands. It is objects that matter, not people, at least so long as people do not become objects (which they frequently do): wretched objects that are moved about, that have built-in responses for controlling actions—heartbeat, salivation; human objects that are manipulated and lumped together precisely as the social critics of 1968 described. It is objects that see and observe, not human beings, who, unless they were objects themselves, would be incapable of seeing them or distinguishing them one from the other. In contrast, note this observation by Marx, cited by Baudrillard: "In the busiest streets of London the shops are crowded one against the other, and in

---

3. A unique Parisian phenomenon composed of pharmacy, restaurant, book shop, perfume boutique, and novelty shop.

their windows, glass eyes without sight, are ostentatiously displayed all the riches of the universe, Indian shawls, American revolvers, Chinese porcelains, Parisian corsets, Russian furs, tropical spices. All these articles, coming from so many countries, carry the same white labels on which are written arabic numerals followed by the letters *L.s.d.* [pounds, shillings, pence]." What breadth of cultural knowledge it takes to see this! All of geography, of history, of Marxism. Looking into a store window of the consumer society, one is in no need of being a geographer, a historian, or a Marxist, because the origin and nature of the things on display are of no importance whatsoever. It is the objects themselves, with their shrewd eyes, that make choices. It is a given that these things live, so they must end by dying, and usually very quickly, which makes them different from their predecessors. Their death is not the saddest or most puzzling aspect of the whole affair. Before the funeral dirge for things became a favorite topic (not forgetting the calls of the Paris junk collectors, who know firsthand about the death of objects)—the poisoned pastry of a particular literary genre and a popular interpretation of modern art, which we rediscover when we ask ourselves about Pompidou and Paris—the glorification of debris had made its appearance in German art following World World I. As René Huyghe has pointed out, the word *Merz,* which seems to come from *Kommerz,* is an astonishing anticipation of our consumer society. How can we be surprised if, despite its seeming newness, it smells so strongly of corruption?

We are a long way from the *Bonheur des dames* and from Zola, who, though accused by his detractors of being obsessed with filth, would never have had the thought of emptying what were not yet called *poubelles* (the word for garbage cans, named for the Paris prefect who first distributed them throughout the city). Also, in this world of products, of the relations between products, the good sought is not happiness but fascination, enchantment—although these words are too noble, too evocative for the subject. Mindless enthusiasm is a better description, collective irrationality beginning with the client, who is the hopeless enthusiast, tied up hand and foot, swept away. Listening to the advertisements of our supermarkets, we find ourselves mumbling the lines of Baudelaire: "Here one finds only order and beauty, profusion, both peaceful and voluptuous." "Our former life" has become our daily life. All one has to do is cross the threshold of one's house. "It is there that I have lived in peaceful voluptuousness, amidst the blue, the waves, the splendors, and the naked, perfumed slaves." If we continue along this path we might ourselves see one day such naked slaves, or at least nubile girls, in scanty costumes, like those who already are waiting tables in the restaurants of some American shopping malls.

Nothing brings the consumer society home more forcibly to Parisians (perhaps more than to other city dwellers) than the newness of things, the absence of the familiar. And nothing can be clearer than its responsibility for the disfigurement and—eventually—the destruction of their city. I gave a few examples of this in the last chapter, as well as in the opening pages of this book, but these are so singular, so overpowering, so obvious—the Montparnasse Tower and the others—that they pose unique problems. These are the great beasts, the man-eating ogres, and they have already taken their first big bite. All things considered, even if they continue, here and there, to ravage and sometimes devour neighborhoods, the evil they are capable of has largely been accomplished. All that can be done now is to curse them, to refuse them forgiveness, and also to try to contain them.

It is different for their numerous progeny, small ogres, birds of prey, who have a hearty appetite and who feed everywhere, almost to satiety. Small predators can often do more damage than large ones. More damage certainly to the feelings of someone who stumbles upon one of these lion-cub feedings. In place of a restaurant, for example, or a café, or even a movie house which isn't doing a very good business or is tempted to sell, there suddenly springs up a new supermarket ready to gobble up all the shops in a neighborhood—the grocery store, the bakery, the butcher shop, the whole array. Which is to say, it destroys the joy, the life, the sense of the expected and the unexpected, the particular structure of the place, the variegated colors of the streets which henceforth become sterile, oppressively boring, commercially ruined, ripe for some developer to pluck. Already it can be foreseen that the neighborhood itself will soon be obliterated, replaced by a new neighborhood, if such uniformity can be called a neighborhood, which is by definition diverse. This uniformity we all know too well, this ideal neighborhood in an ideal city, the consumer city: buildings cheaply thrown up around a supermarket in the middle of a parking lot, a desert of poured concrete with a few stunted trees and abandoned supermarket carts. The supermarket is the raison d'être and the moving force of the place—the brain, the heart, the stomach, everything. It tries to say, with the student song, "Let's get blotto . . . gaily." But it is lugubrious, despite the deafening music and the red balloons given to the children as a way of enticing their mothers, despite the artificial good cheer and the smiles of the first few weeks. You cannot make a silk purse out of a sow's ear.

The disadvantages will appear soon enough, three or four months later, when there is no longer any competition to be feared and everything in the area is dead. "I can't bear to think," the prefect Pelletier said to me in 1965 or 1966—on his way to see me at the Collège de France, he had passed one of these great devourers of a neighborhood—"that as prefect of the Seine I had the duty of reassuring the residents of that neighborhood and promising them a commercial center, which they passionately wanted." I myself hate to go over my own memories of those years, the judgments I made, the stories of crooked builders, the accounts of renegade champions of the automobile that have filled the preceding pages. What has come to be called the consumer society had then not begun to appear, to reveal its nature, to show its true face: the face of the supermarket.

There are other faces as well, few in number, to be sure, and there is no point in naming them all. Each tells the same story with more or less the same grimaces. The face that shows the least yet says the most is probably that of the banks. It is the fundamental face, the first, the original, the model, the mold, the ideal face from which all others derive, of which all others are only imitations. The proliferation of branch banks in Paris, beginning in 1966 and accelerating since then, would have something sinister about it were it not for an admixture of the grotesque. Let's begin with the grotesque: opening branches where they can attract only the housebreakers who live in the neighborhood or offer checking accounts for a clientele without money. Or to be in the area around Barbès, or better yet Pigalle, where the location of a bank urging people to open savings accounts and invest their money next door to an infamous bistro was a source of great amusement to observers of a quirky turn of mind. Around Strasbourg–St. Denis we see the same thing, and here a daytime holdup might add piquancy to the attractions of that intersection.

Still, taking everything into consideration, the sinister outweighs the grotesque. The sinister includes the wounds inflicted on the city, the destruction, the ravages, equal to those of the supermarkets. And the cafés driven out of business, the restaurants, even movie houses, all kinds of little shops replaced by hideous, identical facades, despite the proprietors' best efforts to satisfy and get free of their creditors—these too could be added to the list. The same sinister aspect marks the destruction that results when such changes spread onto avenues where there is no commercial advantage to be gained. Here there are no customers in sight—

they have already been taken care of. There are no delinquents to be tempted—the safes are virtually empty or not worth the cost of the acetylene gas needed to crack them. Some neighborhoods, inoffensive, well-constructed, stable, apparently happy, built to survive for a century, are already targeted by the banks, like some mad surgeon marking in red the incision he plans to make in a perfectly healthy body. But the surgeon I am talking about is not in the least mad, and the operation proposed is on a grand scale; not a bit of snipping here and there, but the amputation of a noble, even vital, part of the city. This is the beautiful Paris of the second half of the nineteenth century, the Paris that stretched from the boulevards and the Opéra to the foot of Montmartre. The man with the golden scalpel never gave up the hope of making it a financial and commercial neighborhood, a neighborhood of business, which is to say, a neighborhood of banks, the kingdom of the golden calf—a dead neighborhood. If the crisis had not come when it did, paralyzing and overwhelming—first of all by ridicule of the would-be perpetrators' megalomania—the deed would have been done: it would have been in the bag, and that would be that.

As a pessimistic historian who thinks the solution chosen is usually the worst, I am persuaded, as I write these lines, that the worst will yet come to pass, that some day or other the entire area will be destroyed. A morose view, but one that will be supported by what I shall say in the rest of this book—unless things move so quickly that the evil will have been done even before these pages announcing it appear in print.

> It is beginnings that matter.
> Deparcieux, *Essai sur les probabilités de la vie humaine,* 1762

RATHER than prophesying about future misdeeds of the consumer society, or lingering over those of yesterday or today, which everyone can see, it is more to my purpose—which is explication—to return to how and why it came into being and was so named.

The so-called scholarly literature—a sizeable collection of books on the consumer society—hardly helps to explain it, any more than it has helped to describe it—excepting always the work of Baudrillard. It is obvious at the outset that the economy played a leading role—the "conjuncture," as they say. I recall that thirty years ago, when André Siegfried asked me why I indulged my taste for the outlandish by talking constantly of "conjuncture" and not simply of "circumstances," I pointed out that *conjoncture* is an old French word. Corneille was partial to it, since it has a kind of stateliness and many rhymes: "I know their various

elders and of what nature / Are the duties of a prince in this circumstance," we read in *Cinna*. La Fontaine uses it in *L'horoscope*, evoking
those who say they can read the stars: "I don't believe it was nature's
design / To tie its own hands or to tie ours / To the point of fixing our
destiny precisely in the heavens: / [Rather] it depends on a concatenation
/ Of time, of persons, and of place. / Not on the conjunctions of all these
charlatans."

Siegfried could have objected that the old meaning of *conjoncture* implies uncertainty, chance, and applies to nature, while *conjoncture* as
used by economists today implies certitude, but a certitude so often belied
by the facts that one would be tempted to speak of their use of the
word—echoing La Fontaine's wordplay—not as *conjoncture* but of *conjunction* (as of planets), a conjunction, dare I say it, of charlatans. This
recollection and this dispute over words sums up what I think, not about
conjoncture, which I would not know how to talk about, but about what
I have read and what I have been told about the consumer society by
those who know something about it.

Following World War II France enjoyed, contrary to all predictions, an
economic boom that sustained itself almost continuously, with only minor slowdowns, and never stagnating, until 1974. This is obvious to us
today. At the time it did not appear so. We are now faced with the essential job of understanding the causes of the boom. But can we hope to
succeed in this? The explanations economists gave us for the economic
collapse of 1929–30 make us skeptical about their interpretations of the
last thirty years of economic growth, for the theorizers are often the same
people, who have only aged a bit and have lost none of their confidence
in their economic theories or any of their youthful enthusiasm. But how
can we concern ourselves with the consumer society unless we try hard
to understand its economic causes, first of all by asking the experts?

Yielding to a natural penchant I would be quite satisfied to say that
boom follows bust and bust follows boom, without knowing precisely
why or how, just as peace follows war and war, peace, day follows night,
famine follows abundance, scrawny cattle follow fat cattle—and vice
versa. To disguise the simplicity of this, which is much too biblical in
tone, I could speak of biological and physical, perhaps even metaphysical
necessities, of stars, of sunspots, even of those rains of blood described in
Virgil and Lucretius. After war and destruction, peace, a joy in living,
and then a rage for life, as in the age of James Dean. I could speak of
circumstances, I could say that this is how things work, I could cite the

conjunctura rerum of Tactitus, for whom the glow of the stars on certain momentous nights of history was much more than an artistic device or poetic license. But how could I simplify all this? Did I have the right to do so? When I began to think about this book, the economic crisis did not have the gravity that it has as I write these lines. Things had not gone so far. When things do go bad, even the most skeptical feel religious fears stirring within them. Those who one day will write the history of these past few months will note the point at which the most serious economic texts had recourse to hypotheses and to language that reflects the fears and impotence of human beings—language that might have been borrowed from some bleak chapter of the *Annals* of Tacitus. When things go bad it is Tacitus's turf. When they're going well it is the economists'. And when I took up this work things were not yet very bad.

So I consulted those who knew. May they forgive me these lines should they ever read them. I would have done better to consult Mme Soleil [an astrologer], a woman of great common sense. Or I should have remembered Pompidou's response when one day I imprudently asked him—I don't recall the circumstances—why he did not take the advice of a certain very distinguished economist endowed with a kind of pontifical infallibility, why indeed he did not invite him into the councils of government. Pompidou shot me a derisive glance and returned to the financial pages of his newspaper.

Listening to the experts explain the causes of the burgeoning prosperity of the postwar years, thoroughly confusing me in the process, I was reminded of John Maynard Keynes saying, completely artlessly, in *The Economic Consequences of the Peace:* "What an extraordinary episode in man's economic progress ended in August 1914." That is all I ask for as a description of our era. Rather than these intellectual acrobatics, just the simple song of Alceste: "Et je prise bien moins tout ce que l'on admire / Qu'un simple chanson que je m'en vais vous dire."

> During the 1960s the condemnation of productivity under the expression "consumer society" was the preferred exercise of the *lumpenintelligentia*. Ideological production has not been at an intellectually worthy level. . . . An imbecile ideology can find only imbecilic or trivial refutations.
>
> Jean Baechler, *Qu'est-ce que l'idéologie* (1976)

ECONOMIC analyses taught me virtually nothing about the causes and origins of the so-called consumer society. Besides, the concept had already appeared in Keynes's work in 1920: "The new rich of the nineteenth century preferred the power that gave them access to the pleasures of immediate consumption." In Keynes also one finds "a larger slice of the pie," and "delayed gratification." Sociological studies, even those whose theme, often reflected in their titles, was the consumer society, were no more helpful to me. They were only minimally useful in describing what every Parisian can see around him, fleshing out the words with innumerable stories. Even less did these works help me uncover and date what was most essential to my work, the origins of the consumer society. For the most part these were translations of American books that began to appear after 1965 and concerned the United States rather than France. They became fashionable after 1968, appearing in waves. Setting down a string of qualifying terms in 1969, Edgar Morin spoke of the "society of consumption" as being technological, bourgeois, capitalist, individualistic, industrial, and bureaucratic. From that time forward the expression "consumer society" was generally thought of as including these attributes, and everyone understood what the expression meant.

Not only did most of these books arrive late, too late to answer my questions, but while describing almost mechanically, over and over, the inevitability and durability of the consumer society in all its glory, they appeared in the bookstores at the very time when the consuming society was dying on the vine. Seeing them in the shop windows, mocking us, brought to mind a picture of well-meaning people paying a visit to someone they haven't seen in a long time, arriving with smiles on their faces, loaded down with gifts, only to find the family in mourning and a wake in progress. They have brought champagne, but a funeral wreath would have been more appropriate. It is in this spirit that we read in the 1973 book *Innovation* (published in France the following year) that "innovation is the principal activity of a modern society. Three thousand new products appeared in the United States in 1970 alone. Fifty percent of the products now in existence did not exist ten years ago. Eighty percent of the products that will exist in 1985 do not exist today. Citing additional statistics would provide only a glimpse of the importance of innovation in today's industrial societies." But what products are involved and where does this glorious innovation lead? "Pharmaceuticals and cosmetics, packaging, toys, etc." For a reader in 1974 the list smacks of the absurd. Yet at the end of 1973 it seemed normal to publish such nonsense, for the consumer society appeared to be a golden age of humankind, and the mere mention of the consumer society was thought natural, satisfying, reassuring. In his *Critique du capitalisme quotidien* Michel Bosquet reports the reception given to Ralph Nader in October 1971 by several French journalists. "The introduction of cosmetics," said Nader, "gave us halitosis, then the smell of armpits, then female body odor, and now smelly feet. Television commercials show us a husband with his feet on the table. His wife walks by and passes out from the smell. In a few months they have thus created a $50,000,000 market." An ad man responded to the charge: "I have studied the matter. Market research proves that the foot odor of men really does offend women." Marvelous anecdote!

Les Images

SINCE there are few books that deal with the subject and even these reach us too late, obviously those who want to trace the first appearance of the phenomenon and the earliest attempts to find a descriptive word for it should turn to memory—to recollections used with the greatest care. First impressions, because they are first impressions, are often still fresh. It is a good idea, however, to try to verify and sharpen the recollections by using written material; by this means we can often enrich conscious memories by calling to mind what we thought we had forgotten. As a historian I have observed that literature, whether simple or sophisticated, often unknowingly registers social change long before the best observers have noticed it. *Les Misérables* is a case in point. The word *misérables* has greater meaning, because of what was happening at the time, than Victor Hugo thought he was giving it. I believe more strongly in involuntary and spontaneous literary testimony than I do in the divinely inspired science of books by specialists.

Along with literature, of course, I include the cinema. Conferences on the theme of the cinema and society abounded during the period we are speaking of. I myself organized one in Monaco. The prince had been my pupil. When prefect Pelletier became a minister of state in the principality of Monaco he wanted to do me a favor. The stars being favorable, a center had been created which, after having focused on the human sciences (anthropology, psychology, sociology) declared itself an institute of "cinema and civilization." But there were problems from the outset. The prince had a falling out with his minister—I don't know why—and the French government was pretending to be angry. Most important, Prince Pierre of Monaco, the father of Prince Rainier, died. He had been as much interested in science as in art and supported my undertaking. During his reign the principality enjoyed one of the most brilliant periods of its history and, indirectly, of French artistic and literary history generally of the period between the wars—as will be seen from his correspondence if it is ever published. Anyway, my conference ceased as abruptly as a fireworks display, and I never knew exactly why. Yet my memory of those debates about the cinema and society remain vivid. Pierre Billard defended reason and Jean-Louis Bory defended emotion. The debates were about society proper, not the consumer society, whose effluvia had not yet reached the refined nostrils of the principality of Monaco.

Let us begin by noting the slowness and almost complete indifference, the uninterested, even scornful way French literature and movies recorded the first symptoms of the phenomenon, compared to its description in other countries. The contrast with America is the most glaring. "We're back in God's country," says Charley Anderson, Dos Passos' returning soldier. "I can't wait to have a real American breakfast!" Dos Passos devotes an entire page to its description: "Grapefruit . . . cream . . . ham!" And a beautiful girl: "A beautiful girl and an American breakfast, there's heaven!" It's not this way in Paris, where steak and fried potatoes alone are enough, or perhaps a woman (without the steak), which is also not bad. "And after a huge steak, beautiful women," as Louis Aragon says, but not both on the same menu. Of course a steak is not breakfast in France, but that is unimportant.

Then he has a whole chapter on food advertising and on ways to eat without getting fat, the latter doubtless more important than the former in some segments of society. In the years after World War I, American men, we observe, began to be concerned about their weight after having long admired corporal bulkiness. To hungry immigrants the paradise of the New World offered the chance to fill their stomachs. Portly magnates—copper kings or railroad barons—at the end of the nineteenth century saw corpulence as symbolizing success. American women had already become concerned about their waistlines, although the fashion among Parisian women at that time was still "to remain obese," if we are to believe the French clinician, Heckel, writing in 1911 (*Les grandes et les petites obésités*). "In order to have desirable shoulders and cleavage a woman ought to have some fat around the neck, fleshy shoulders, and ample breasts. Slimness is a real sacrifice for a woman, for it means renouncing everything that society most admires in her."[4]

If we consider Dos Passos' words in the abstract, it is the consumer society that he is describing, and at an advanced phase of its evolution,

---

4. I owe my erudition about obesity to Hilde Bruch's *Les yeux et le ventre*. She is a professor of medicine at Baylor University.—Author.

marked by a preoccupation of people with their bodies and all that is related to them, including the somewhat tepid sexuality of the overfed: "Good wine puts me to sleep." We see it also in the ambiance. The publishers of a 1946 French translation of Dos Passos' book thought it useful to explain the word drugstore in a note: "Typical of New York. A store that sells everything from pharmaceuticals to ice cream sodas." What a way to disgust French readers! But a way that disgusted some Americans too. Five or six years later Henry Miller, evoking his bohemian years of undernourishment when, like François Villon, he had often dined on the smoke from the rotisseries of St. Séverin, wrote his friend Lawrence Durrell to discourage him from coming to live in the United States. Miller told him he could not imagine the horror of it, the nausea one felt in possessing and seeing a well-stocked refrigerator. No, you cannot imagine it! And it is not as if food is confined to the refrigerator and the kitchen. It is everywhere, in the churches, in the museums, in the concert halls, in the movie houses; and not only in the simple form of ice cream bars—there are also hot dogs. The Chicago novelist, James T. Farrell, writes somewhere that the smell and the crackle of grilling hot dogs once ruined a film about Polynesia for him: the residual odor lingered on the nightstand and in the chewing gum of the pretty and the not so pretty when they made love.

Such remarks are banal these days. Parisians have only to look around them to see that from now on they are not special, that they are feeding from the same trough, stuck to the same chewing gum. Indeed it is true that the story of chewing gum helps to date the arrival in France of the consumer society. As much as many products and better than most, because of how it is chewed, gum perfectly sums up everything mechanical that is evoked by the French word *consommation*. The American word *consumption* includes the notion of commerce, trading, the dollar, even a sense of adventure, a feverishness, life itself. In Spanish, *consumacion* carries the suggestion of a fire that devours and annihilates: here is not life, but death. In German "the word for consumer society," Robert Minder, the great Germanist writes me, "is *konsumgesellschaft. Konsumieren,* the verb, has the same connotations as in French. Before 1914, *konsumgeschaft* meant a gourmet food shop, and some of this has survived in the word *konsumgesellschaft,* although not consciously." In the French *consommation,* dullest of all, there is this mechanical aspect that evokes the pump of the old song, this movement of the jaws that is identical to masticating gum. Remember that the word jaw is also used of machinery.

The funny stories about chewing gum, in the true French comic vein, best expressed by the burlesque farce of dubious politeness, are those about trousers getting stuck to movie-house seats. Some elderly usherettes, the three Fates of those dark places they illuminate with their flashlights, say that pants stuck with chewing gum began causing trouble ten or twelve years ago, both for them and for Parisian husbands who came away with a ticket stub stuck to the seat of their pants and had to confess to their wives that they had not spent the afternoon at the office. Here is true drama. Drama is to be seen, too, in an incident of 1965 (the daily press is the authority for this important date in the history of the consumer society) concerning the misadventures of a young man from the Strasbourg-St. Denis neighborhood who put a poor girl in the hospital because she had the misfortune to be chewing gum while they were making love. But for me such coarse stories fade before the memory of an elderly woman, supremely elegant and wonderfully preserved—a role for an Edwige Feuillère—whom I overheard giving a lecture on beauty culture one Sunday some ten years ago to two young girls who were vigorously chewing gum. This was in the metro and the lecture was quite unsolicited: "You are very pretty, young ladies, but take care, you are working the muscles of your jaw to no good purpose. When you are my age, you will regret it: you have to think of these things when you are young. Don't get a double chin! Here, look at me." And she pulled back her fur coat to reveal a neck as unwrinkled as a swan.

The ubiquity of the consumer society in American literature and movies is so obvious, so striking, so long-standing that citing texts and images from the period between the wars, and before 1914, is interesting only to point up, by contrast, our own backwardness. Doing so puts us in another world, on another planet, in another epoch outside the chronological limits of an essay committed to clarifying and dating what happened in France. It is more useful to compare ourselves with our neighbors— with England for example, and with the precocity and intensity, indeed the selfishness, of English images. "I wanted an Aston-Martin," the hero of John Braine's *Room at the Top* says in 1956. The book appeared in French in 1958. "I wanted a three guinea linen shirt. I wanted a woman tanned on the beaches of the Riviera. I was entitled, I knew it intuitively. . . . It was as clear and irresistible as the sense of vocation that calls doctors and missionaries. But evidently in my case my vocation called me to do good works for myself and not for others."

It seems there is more in English literature of the first years after World

War II than in our own lighthearted celebration of the *bagnole*. In this need to enjoy and not just purchase an Aston Martin there is, more or less consciously, an anger at life, a defiance of death, a grandiose and sometimes desperate feeling about being itself that needs the invocation of great names. In a novel of those years—*Saturday Night and Sunday Morning*—and in a movie based on it, both of which can be interpreted the same way, an unskilled worker from Nottingham recites Shakespeare to his girlfriend. This is unimaginable in the working-class suburb of Saint-Ouen. The depiction, in Stanley Kubrick's *Clockwork Orange* (1972), of a consumer society reaching a state of frenzy in the last stages of its development is Shakespearian: the angry cries of the actors, the baroque scenery, the deafening sound track—Beethoven, Rossini, Purcell. Some of the scenes recall the bloody and subtle buffoonery in Elizabethan plays that often precedes catastrophes or accompanies monstrous crimes.

As for Italy, its cinema makes us think of Dante: film after film depicts stages of the consumer society, from its dimly seen beginnings to its end, but here the decline is not marked by anything resembling convulsions of British plays and films. Paradoxically, at the culmination of this evolution appeared a film made by an Italian director, Marco Ferreri, using French actors and a Parisian setting: *La grand bouffe*. A capital document this, which gives me the title for this chapter of my book. It is also a document in the history of Paris, at least of the savage corner of the city where the action takes place, and which no longer exists. During the summer of 1975, the profound quiet of August when Parisians, as always, are away on vacation, a huge segment of the boulevard Exelmans is demolished, its shrubs uprooted, its rows of lime trees cut down, and in their place— in the place of these survivors of a society nearing its end—is built the North Vietnamese Embassy. How Italian this image is, though set in the middle of Paris. One thinks of those gluttons of Dante, in a freezing rain, wallowing in the contents of their stomachs as they had been in their pleasures. "But who are you," I ask, "you who are suffering a punishment greater and more repugnant than any other?" He answers: "Your city, which is filled to overflowing with gluttonous desire, was my home during a tranquil life. You, my fellow citizens, called me Ciacco the glutton."

The Parisians of *La grande bouffe* resemble the gluttons of Florence, themselves descended from Trimalchio of the *Satyricon*. They are peaceable forty-year-olds who confine themselves to the opulence of western

Paris, but whom one would more likely see in some wealthy Italian suburb, stuffing themselves, enjoying a little philandering between the fruit
and the cheese, for sexuality is a supplementary refinement, a touch of
spice. Hovering over everything, mixed with the smells of the cooking
and the stench of vomit, is the odor of death, which, we know, fills the
third circle of the *Inferno.*

Compared to this, how puerile, feeble, and, truth to tell, common,
almost banal, is French imagery, whether literary or cinematographic.
Only one book, though an important one, deserves mention: Christiane
Rochefort, *Les petits enfants du siècle* (1961). It deals with the consumer
society of working-class Sarcelles, but even more with the consumer society itself, in its essence, its soul, its laughable and abominable preten-
sion of bringing happiness. "At dusk, instead of coyotes, announcers
howl at us telling us how to have gleaming teeth and shining hair, how
everyone can be beautiful, clean, healthy, and happy. The happiness is
killing me." Thus speaks the terrifying young girl in Christiane Rochefort's novel. And again: "There were only lucky families, fortunate families, happy families at Sarcelles." How many happy creatures we find
here! "Oh brave new world!" In a condensed universe of this kind, in
Sarcelles as in Brasilia, everything is the same: "If you know one city you
know them all, for they are perfectly identical, as much as the natural
characteristics of the site permit." Thus wrote Thomas More in 1516, in
Utopia. In these utopian universes the rule is to make people happy in
spite of themselves and without asking their advice. Get up, shower, have
breakfast, watch television until bed time. Go to bed, make love, wash
up, sleep. Have pleasant dreams. This is hell. Long live the little girl of
Christiane Rochefort's novel who says "Merde." It is only one book, but
what a book!

As for all the others, descriptive articles and literary critique, which
appeared in significant numbers only much later and are of little help in
writing the history of these years, such work being, in general, no more
than a derivative of sociology, a residual reworking of familiar themes,
ersatz. After May 1968 they became political pamphlets. The same was
true of the cinema. We see the congenital impotence of French film, a
kind of insensitivity to visual images, compared to the Italian nervous
energy, such as that of Fellini, which is akin to that of Virgil or of Dante:
"these images that turn constantly in this eternally dark place, like the
sand when blown by gusts of wind" (*Inferno,* 3:28). Is mine an ico-
noclastic hypothesis—or absurd? It is easy to see in this bankruptcy

the effect of a mediocrity that developed a few years after the war and reached its apogee between 1965 and 1970. But one can also see here the expression of reality. Perhaps it is a late development in consumer society, less accentuated here than elsewhere, perhaps a repugnance against it, or at least a lack of enthusiasm and, so to speak, of appetite; or perhaps both together, caused by the slowness of life and the indifference of people.

Whatever the reason, there are some exceptions, and significant ones, which perhaps confirm the hypothesis. An example is the work of Jacques Tati, from *Jour de fête* (1949) and *Les vacances de M. Hulot* (1953) (where, of course, one does not see any foreshadowing of what is not yet even in the air, as it were) up to *Mon Oncle*. In this film (1958), the contrast between the modern neighborhood—absurd, hostile, deadly, impossible, shot on location amid the huge buildings in the suburb of Créteil—and the old neighborhood—alive, charming, joyous, friendly, filmed at St. Maur—corresponds to the first pages of my own book, which evoke this very year (and those immediately before and after), attributing these developments to new construction and the *Bagnole*, under the inspiration of abbé Pierre. Things are already ugly, hateful, but we have not yet arrived at the consumer society. These are only its first steps, its first works, its first compositions, its first style, all done in ugly poured concrete which, at least, doesn't pretend to be marble.

With *Playtime* (1967) the consumer society has arrived and it kills the cinema. The very title of the film is a manifesto. "I deliberately chose this title as a challenge," Tati says. "English words have invaded our vocabulary. People live in a "building," they put their car in a "parking," they eat a "snack," or a "self" [service], they shop in a "drugstore" and "supermarket." Hence *play*, meaning game, and *time*, meaning time. I hope that playtime will one day be a part of our vocabulary." We know that this did not come to pass and also that the film did not enjoy great success. Perhaps this is for the reasons given by the film critics, but maybe it is also because, in 1967, the consumer society had so penetrated our habits and appeared in such glowing colors that the stupefied public could not laugh at it, assuming they were still capable of laughing. We know the story. A group of foreign tourists arrives to visit Paris. At Orly they find themselves in an airport more or less similar to the one they departed from. They take a similar airport bus, along a similar highway, lined with similar street lamps and similar buildings, and with similarly idiotic ads for similarly insipid products. They arrive at similar hotels, have similar cells with similar wet bars, similar beds, and with bilingual scriptures (*la Sainte-Bible/The Holy Bible*) on their night tables. Fortunately, there are M. Hulot and M. Marcel, and a few courageous men who still exist, who have seen clearly.

Maybe they are fewer than Jacques Tati thinks. Chatting about *Playtime*, some years later, and more especially about Tati's satire of a uniform, international style, with some friends who do a lot of traveling on movie business, I was horrified to hear one of them (who specialized in foreign films) maintain—perhaps to tweak my nose—that this similarity was all quite nice, reassuring. It made one feel safe to find the same hotel room, the same bed, the same breakfast, the same shops, the same surroundings (or at least they were presented in the same way, wrapped in the same cellophane) separated from the traveler by the same safety glass, everywhere tinted the same color, so that the Atlantic Ocean, the Mediterranean Sea, the China Sea, the Pacific Ocean, the Dead Sea, or the Red Sea all look like the same green watery expanse, the healthy color of chlorophyll, or have the same rosy hue, the color of optimism.

What has become of the wildness, the intrusions of an unhealthy nature that is without pity? Where are the powerful odors, the smells by which one recognizes so many cities—the stench of blood from the old Chicago stockyards, of rancid oil from Arab quarters, the salt smell, like decomposition, of Tunis, the smell of pepper and fish in Hamburg, of jasmine in Cordoba, the horse-droppings mixed with gas in old Paris, here the sweat of labor, there that of pleasures, the smell of thighs, the odor of armpits or the stench of what made Henri IV (who was noted for the smell of his feet) just another man, that is, another king.[5] We don't have to fear any of this. The consumer society is a closed universe, disinfected, deodorized, devoid of the unexpected, without surprises, with nothing shocking, a well-protected universe providing one does not leave one's room and understands that one can always be attacked in the elevator. But if one can leave one's room without mishap to go, without difficulty, to a tiny bit of international rented paradise, one is saved and even happy. At least this is so for those who thus describe to me the state of their souls, or at least what they believe it to be: "You cannot know how pleasant it is, upon arriving in Paris, to believe oneself still in the Waldorf Astoria." I must add that their wives don't seem to me to be

---

5. To those who love the sweep of history I offer the hypothesis that Henri IV was as great a king as he was only because his mistresses never bathed.—Author.

in full agreement. Some even confess they feel themselves becoming en-
raged at this static happiness. Instead of a personal paradise it is the "air-
conditioned nightmare" of Henry Miller they are describing. Always and
everywhere . . . and always . . . and always. "Veal, always veal," as they
sing in the music hall. This could drive one mad. Let's be honest about
it: no one has dared add "always the same husband."

These are but a few remarks, some comments about Jacques Tati's
film. The excuse is that this is a document, and virtually the only one of
its kind. We will have almost completely exhausted the meager list of
such French films if we add two by Pierre Etaix. In 1966 *Tant qu'on a
la santé,* a picture about the "tent cities" which appeared around this
time, the first of them at the Paris Fair in 1964. Then in 1970 *Le Pays
cocagne,* whose title, though more esoteric, carries the same connotations
as *La Grande Bouffe* and lets us fix an evolutionary moment with precision. Finally, in January 1968, Jean-Luc Godard's *Weekend,* a black
comedy about weekend amusements which turn into cannibalism amid a
jumble of smashed cars. *La Grand Bouffe* in the form of *le grand bar-
beque* was already foreshadowed. If I remember rightly, beyond some
interesting remarks by a few inspired critics—Jean-Louis Bory in *France-
Observateur* (January 1968)—not many saw that beyond this confused
tangle of twisted metal, this striking, chaotic, outdoor barbecue, there
was already the image of the consumer society, an unfamiliar society
whose name was scarcely used, but which we recognized from the first
scene of some hippies knife-fighting around a bonfire. By the time of *La
Grand Bouffe* (1973) the consumer society was full-blown. This was no
longer the world of *Weekend* in 1968, a few months before the great
revelation and endless talk of May.

Contrary to the picture presented by so many descriptions, which remove it from the historical milieu, contrary as well to what we have come
to believe because of advertising, which similarly presents an ahistorical
phenomenon, as old as the world itself and as eternal (the forbidden fruit
of knowledge in the Garden of Eden presented as a supermarket) the
consumer society, if we judge from literature and movies and take into
account the slowness of the French cinema to incorporate changes in
society, was hardly visible in France between 1960 and 1965. In addition
the emergence of the consumer society scarcely evoked such dramatic nor
frenzied spectacles as those we observed in other countries. It is not
Shakespeare or Dante that we think of. More appropriate, and this is
more than the consumer society deserves, it is the comedy of Molière.

Statistics

Y OU have looked only at literature and film, the social scientist objects, which leads me to seek more precise information, more exact
data, more of an orderly evolution in the vast materials, the numerous
official inquiries and other sources that can be quantified by year, by
social class, gender, age, place, changes in standards of living, in life-style,
in desires. From the outset a single conclusion emerges. Whatever the
nature of these investigations, whatever might be the criticisms and interpretations made at the time and those that can be made today, whatever
the discussions that might begin tomorrow and agitate the meetings of
professional historians and economists and social scientists for centuries,
it is evident that a consumer society, defined as a general improvement in
the standard of living and the democratization of comfort and the expectations of comfort, hardly appears as an incontestable fact before 1960.

The investigations of consumption before 1960 do not demonstrate an
improvement among the different socioprofessional categories, but only
among the "workers." In addition, in 1958 and 1959, an economic and
financial crisis caused a loss in the purchasing power of workers. It was
clearly manifest in a drop in orders for refrigerators and washing ma-
chines, and fewer purchases of clothing. Yet during these two difficult
years purchases of cars continued to increase, bought by these very workers who, with the exception of expenditures on food, apparently preferred to economize on everything else (including housing). In most of
these studies there is a correspondence between the purchase of cars and
deteriorating housing. More useful than these general statistics are the
investigations of the IFOP, especially on the psychological aspects of the
cost of living, which is how the cost of necessities of life are seen. Drawn
up by Jean Stoetzel in 1952 and constantly referred to ever since, these
statistics reveal the change, over time, in the amount of income thought
necessary by each person. This study also reveals the change in the desire
of some to share in the national prosperity. These figures express what
Renan, describing the society of the Second Empire, called "the material
interest." An essential theme for our study.

From 1956 on, fairly regularly, there are studies of the condition, the
attitudes, and the aspirations of the working class. Questions are asked
about housing and life-style. For example: "In the following list which
items do you now have and which do you plan to acquire in the near
future? A radio, a hot-water heater, a washing machine, a car." It is surprising to note, since we tend to forget, that in 1958 none of the conve-

niences in this list, except a radio and running water, existed in more than 20 percent of working-class families. In 1958 workers hoped to acquire a hot-water heater and a washing machine in a few years. They wanted a house of their own, a car, and a separate bathroom, but thought these beyond their means. They almost never wanted carpeting in their house or a fur coat for their wives. As for the desired but unobtainable car, 69 percent hoped to have one and 21 percent only thought they might have one some day. In addition, with regard to a car, a unique case, the desire was strongest among those who were mostly poorly housed. The prestige of having a car was enormous, and what workers knew about cars was astonishing. A survey taken in fall 1955, after Citroen, which had not introduced a new model in years, unveiled its DS19 at the auto show in October, made this clear. We are back to the whole question of the *bagnole*, but supported by statistics, incontestable and distinct from my recollections and seemingly vague descriptions. Apparently equally useless, but quite interesting, was a survey taken around the same time about New Year's gifts. Among the things men most often wanted were an electric razor (8 percent), an automobile (8 percent), a book (6.5 percent), money (6 percent), a telephone (6 percent); a record player or a tape recorder were desired by only 2 percent of those asked. Among women a fur coat (9.5 percent), a washing machine (9 percent). . . . The wise and foolish virgins of the Bible story.

Statistics and Images

F ROM survey to survey, statistic to statistic, those who prefer quantification to film images and literary depictions can follow, year by year, in great detail, the evolution of the consumer society to its mature development. Usefully combining quantification and impressions, while offering the advantage of continuity of text and ideas, a document of another kind, *Les Temps Modernes*, seems to me to sum up these early surveys very well, linking them with the impressions from films and literature. Two numbers of this revue, edited by Jean-Paul Sartre, do this marvelously. Without embarrassing myself in the world of philosophy I would liken these two thick productions to two issues of a popular magazine listing all public entertainment, which is not to slight those brave texts but rather to give them an additional glory, that of the theater and the cinema.

The first issue, of July 1952, reminds me of one of those popular songs that lament life's difficulties. Raymond Aron called it to my attention. On the front page of *Figaro Littéraire,* of September 27, 1952, in an article entitled "Jean-Paul Sartre and the Proletariat, or the Fear of Incorrect Political Thinking," Aron wrote ironically about "the erratic sensibility of the philosopher" so concerned about "the sufferings of the female worker. She was born in the Kremlin–Bicêtre neighborhood . . . her father was a stable hand . . . then apprenticed as a lathe operator . . . preoccupied with getting by . . . at Saint-Ouen. . . ." This sounds like one of Aristide Bruant's songs.[6] Before others discovered him Sartre was already playing "Hearts and Flowers" on the violin with the support of banal arguments and using statistics as his vibrato. He also attacked a heartless *Figaro* (which would soon pay him back in kind), as a newspaper for aging society women who know the people only as those who gossip in the pantry. "These old society women love servants," writes Sartre. "The workers don't particularly love them." Here you have society ladies as depicted on the popular stage, women clearly debauched, reading *Le Figaro* and throwing themselves at the butler in some elegant boudoir, thus creating another beneficiary of the will of some noble family. Here was Sartre's idea of the society woman who bore a great name. In contrast was "the woman of the people," the unfortunate working woman, whom the villain Raymond Aron mocks, as one would expect from someone who writes for *Le Figaro.*

There you have the farce played out by two former comrades from the Ecole Normale Superiéure, to which I add, with all due respect to my elders, my own kind of joke! It is clear that this issue of *Les Temps Modernes*—and I use the word issue in all its connotations—presented a situation in 1952 which did not in any way presage the consumer society. This situation will last for several more years, with now and then the appearance of some indistinct symptoms that were more or less correctly interpreted. There are some examples in *Les Temps Modernes,* but above all there is the debate that emerges from one of the principal themes proclaimed by Maurice Thorez in his report to the Fourteenth Congress of the Communist party, published in *Les Cahiers du communisme* (July–August 1956): increasing pauperization. "The quickening pace . . . that leads the worker to sickness and extermination. . . . Given this undermining of health, the situation of the proletarian is degraded even if his salary is augmented." In hindsight, this document—the text itself, the

6. Bruant (1851–1925) was a celebrated composer of songs that depicted the realities of life.

examples chosen, the images, the very words—seems to me to express perfectly this intermediate period. It expresses my recollection of the discussions it provoked, at least in the circles I traveled in. In the INED [Institut National d'Etudes Démographiques] of Sauvy, I can still see some demographers with opposite points of view thinking Thorez was right, but most, including one communist, thinking he exaggerated. Rereading this text closely, comparing it to others at the time and especially to *Les Temps Modernes,* relating all this to recollections of those years, considering both texts and recollections together in the light of what has happened subsequently, one can say that Thorez never would have spoken of the fear of pauperization, despite all the grounds he had for speaking out, if the nature of those years (the 1950s) and the unmistakable impressions of people who read the period correctly—contrary to what the demographers and economists said—had not given him reason to do so. Moreover, my rereading of these texts, which is more focused on what lies behind the words than on their literal meaning, reveals in certain sentences a meaning that they perhaps did not have at the time or, rather, that was not then recognized. The first indication of what lay ahead I find quite apparent in the concessive clause "even if his salary is augmented," which concedes a fact that no one could possible deny. I see a more strident manner in these apparently common words: the imperative for the masses to struggle against the trusts, against big business, "against the disdain and aversion they show toward French intelligence."

French intelligence? One may see—and people probably did—in this defense of French intelligence the prolongation of an old historical protest. At the time of the Popular Front, workers marched in delegations to the congress of writers. "One of them, once, I recall," says Jean Guéhenno, "read a paper. He and his comrades complained to us that they had always been excluded from culture." And again, in 1968, the children of the bourgeoisie took to the streets in the working-class suburbs not so much to bring books to the masses as to instruct themselves, to render homage in these frightful places to unknown gods. "Justice, Truth, Progress moved me," writes Daniel Halévy, "like those primitive, gigantic figures, the Goddesses or the Mothers of Revolution." The Revolution without a revolution, for those who embraced these values. A half-century earlier it was Agricol Perdiguier, and those whom the great historian of the high-water mark of working-class culture, Georges Duveau, studied. How distant those times seem and what a contrast be-

tween those years, not really so long ago, when Georges Duveau, enthusiastic and confident in the future, published his great book—*La Vie
ouvrière sous le second Empire*—and the steady impoverishment and
mediocrity which soon took over. It was signaled for the first time, probably by René Kals, in a study done in 1958–61 and published in the
latter year in *Economie et Humanisme,* and another simultaneously
published (in May 1961 in *La Revue de l'action populaire*) by Jacques
Charpentreau, entitled "Revendications culturelles du monde ouvrier."
In November–December 1964 Michèle Perrot came to the same conclusion in the *Annales:* while leisure-time activities were developing in the
working class, the workers were undergoing intellectual impoverishment.
This is what I had read earlier in the "aversion" for "French intelligence"
that Maurice Thorez denounced in 1956. These were the first symptoms
not only of a decline of intelligence but of a cretinization, a brutalization
which will only intensify in the consumer society, as Paris will soon prove
by ruining so many neighborhoods, erecting so many monuments to stupidity, which have already been glimpsed, now and again, in these pages.
Remember that Rabelais preferred the Lyonnaise to the Parisians, of
whose imbecility he spoke.

The imbecility, from now on, asserts itself, loud and importunate,
gargantuan, like the wicked prince of Rabelais, Picrochole, ambitious
and restless: an accumulation, a flood, not of such Rabelaisian matter
that was pumped in the song earlier referred to, but a disgusting diar-
rhea, deodorized and without substance. This song is the theme of the
September–October 1962 issue of *Les Temps Modernes* which, in contrast to that of 1952, highlights and thus lets us rediscover, without ambiguity, in the texts the significant dates of a forgotten evolution, in
which everything is finally confounded. Here we no longer have the
popular song, some familiar complaint about the condition of the
workers, made into a chant by priestesses dressed in black robes, but
a comic sketch, "Les Jouets" of Georges Michel. Toys that for the
moment one still buys for pleasure and not merely to do as everyone
else does, not merely to obey what the radio commands. Toys? In
a few years people will no longer even dream of giving them this charming name, full of fantasy, childhood, amusement. And a bit later still,
the mere sight of these toys will enrage some grown-up children, who
will smash them for the sole pleasure of destruction. But in 1962
the refrigerator, the vacuum cleaner, the three-speed mixer, the stock-
ings that never run, all these "new gadgets" that corrupt the young

marrieds written about in *Les Temps Modernes,* these toys are still innocent, even useful: the refrigerator, the vacuum cleaner; and those about to be invented.

> Wolves eat gluttonously.
>
> La Fontaine, *Le Loup et la Cigogne*

FROM document after document, display after display—literature, film, surveys, statistics, all in the same package, with Jean-Paul Sartre on top—there emerges a chronology, approximate but adequate, of the beginnings of the consumer society. What is more striking, compared to what happened elsewhere, is its lateness, its slow development, and the lack of enthusiasm, even the coldness, of its reception. This leads us to say, with the husband in *Les Temps Modernes* who is astonished to find these "toys" in his house, which were not there in the morning, "They didn't walk here by themselves!" A sensible observation that takes us to the heart of the question of responsibility.

To confine ourselves, for the moment, to the first point, the triumph of the consumer society, the creation of a consumer mentality was not realized at a single stroke, without preparation. The ant in La Fontaine's fable did not become a grasshopper overnight, not even the Parisian ant who is almost in the same family as the grasshopper. Even more so is this true of the characters in so many fables, which are so many lessons about intelligence, common sense, prudence, defiance, stories of survival where the large always devour the small, stories of deception, of deceitful appearances, of lies, of theft, and also of preservation. If we judge the French by La Fontaine (or by Balzac, who himself says he is a disciple of La Fontaine) it is clear that they—if we didn't already know it from the documents discussed above—could not throw themselves into the jaws of "a wolf in sheep's clothing," the developer posing as a benefactor of mankind. They did not learn, from one day to the next, to buy for the sake of buying. Indeed in matters of consumption they are gourmets, from the most exquisite to the most gross, those who don't wash their hands to those so delicate they eat off silver plates with their pinkies raised. The most refined lesson in culinary art I ever heard was that given on a bench in a Paris square where the clochards compared the merits of various New Year's Eve menus: the turkeys of Bicêtre and those of Nanterre, the former with grilled chestnuts, the latter with boiled. Gluttony is not a part of our nature, or rather is not to our taste, as we see in La Bruyère's Gnafron, and much earlier in the Celts of Gregory of Tours who looked with distaste upon the French, that is, the descendants of Germanic tribes, who were gorging themselves.

There is a pattern in literature, an underlying historical reality that lets us interpret many contemporary documents correctly, documents that reveal if not the distaste for an orgy of eating at least a lack of enthusiasm, a reluctance to join in the gorging. This is the view, for example, of a study by André Piatier on the changes in French purchasing during the last twenty years. "Indulging a passion for cars, forced to pay a great deal for housing, the average Frenchman limits his other expenditures, yet he remains a *bon vivant*. His table is often well garnished, and he ranks in the forefront of Europe in [the purchase of] most food categories." This is a cliché, banal. As for other products—household appliances, conveniences, clothes, as well as fancy food products, which proliferate in multicolored wrappings—"he ranks between sixth and ninth place." Piatier concludes: "France ranks high overall, but low in the purchase of consumer goods. Given our relatively high income of 1970 we still cling to a model of consumption dating from 1930" (*Le Figaro*, January 20–21, 1971). How much more telling would be these conclusions for the ten or fifteen preceding years.

We can get an even more precise idea by examining, among other evidence, those studies of how people respond to advertising on radio and television. This advertising is the principal cause of the triumph of the psychology of consumerism, a triumph that would have made La Fontaine scream, if he was still among us. But he is still among us, he continues to speak to us, and if we happen to pay attention when we find some comment on the subject at hand that is perhaps a bit raw we should not be surprised that it comes from La Fontaine. The psychology of consumerism is stupid. It is the product of the stupidity that advertising teaches, or rather "exhorts," by the arguments that it uses to ensnare fools, as with a net: "I regret that this word might be too old today. It has always seemed to me to have considerable energy" (this from La Fontaine's *The Frog and the Rat*). Thus the husband in *Les Temps Modernes,* who returns from work and doesn't recognize his wife. "What has happened? Are you ill?" She replies: "What a bonehead you are, it is my makeup, which is completely new." And this irresistible line has been declaimed on television: "The Trifecta will not be very lucrative tonight, but what is important is to win it!" Stupidity of a picturesque sort, if one can put it this way. Advertising on television, television itself in a way, is fundamentally, essentially, at least for those who have heard it from the mouth of the master, Alain, and who have kept the faith by refusing to have this instrument of decadence in their house—a matter of an image; and the image itself, whatever it may be, is only appearance, deception, and, if one is taken in by it, idiocy.

The press of these years show traces of the old, popular skepticism. This is especially apparent when the old Chartieriste critical spirit appears, to speak in the manner of the faithful followers of Alain, who called himself *Chartier*.[7] This is the case in the pages of the *Canard Enchaîné* from which the pupils of the lycée Henri IV, preparing for the entrance exam for the Ecole Normale Supérieure, one day in 1932, wrote on the blackboard, along with the sentences from Balzac or the verses from Homer, an unidentified quotation. Taking up the challenge, although he had identified at sight the citation meant to embarrass him— like Socrates crossing the market at Athens suddenly realizing where vegetables came from—Alain announced: "You have given me a wonderful unpublished bit of Descartes." He then set about analyzing this authentic Cartesian text, as was his habit. For him such student challenges had the twofold advantage of always being well-chosen, sometimes even exceptionally so, and of allowing him to forgo preparing for his class.

If I remember correctly, Alain's course met on Mondays. The historian, André Alba, met his class on Wednesdays, and used those handbooks from which everyone in France learned their national history. Sometimes Alba told us: "Wednesday is an auspicious day for me. It is the day I meet you and the day the *Canard Enchaîné* appears." How could one be surprised if the *Canard*, expressing the views of its audience, now never misses a chance to pillory radio and television, which fire advertising from both barrels. For the historian of the consumer society the articles in the *Canard* are the bread crumbs that guide Hansel and Gretel out of the forest. On May 29, 1963, for example, this ultimatum to the government: "Outlaw advertising or shout it down. Advertising is coming out of our ears . . . the coffee break that refreshes, the vacuum cleaner break, the yogurt break, the apple-juice break." And "business yeah-yeah" as the pop singer without a voice but blessed with rebelliousness, this eternal student who starts a ready-to-wear company, says: "The company is a year old, it does about a billion [old] francs of business. Yeah, yeah" (April 29, 1964).

My old repugnance for everything the consumer society represents,

7. Emile Chartier, called Alain (1868–1951), was a philosopher and celebrated teacher at the Lycée Henri IV. Venerated by his students (including M. Chevalier), he was the subject of a veritable cult. His most famous work is *Les Propos*. The "esprit chartieriste" was a self-description of Alain's angle of vision.

stimulated through the years, finds its final, its most flagrant expression—
a kind of manifesto—in one of Pompidou's speeches, in April 1968, announcing the beginning of advertising on television. It is regrettable, he
said, but we cannot do otherwise. Our approaching entry into the European Common Market demands it, "the necessity for our economy to be
able to meet the challenge, in every way and in every area. Advertising is
one of the weapons of a modern economy." Let me pass over the arguments. One phrase sticks in my mind that sums up what I have been
saying and it provides a date: "It is true that France is perhaps more
resistant than other societies to advertising." Oh, La Fontaine!

After this speech our table talk, whether in the dining room of the
Matignon Palace or our little bistro in the rue Hautefeuille, I no longer
remember which, was about La Fontaine and those of like views. "France
more resistant to advertising"? In the Chamber of Deputies there was
not a single pertinent or impertinent question about the speech, not the
slightest reaction to this sentence, to this professorial assertion, such as
Pompidou might have made in his classroom: "The French are like this
and not otherwise." The teacher had spoken. The prime minister meant
what he said. The pupils knew it, so did the deputies. His comrades had
less reason to back off, especially on such subjects where every candidate
for the Ecole Normale Supérieure worth his salt has an opinion. If there
is equality, this is it.

It is worth remarking that when de Gaulle spoke of France he always
seemed to be talking about himself. When Pompidou spoke of France, at
least in this example, he often seemed to be speaking of the Auvergne.
France more resistant? In the Saint-Flour market, maybe.[8] But the peasants from my native Vendée, so fierce when it comes to their neighbors,
are in the hip pocket of the first developer who comes along to take their
sand dunes, their beaches, their vineyards, their pine trees! It is true,
some may say, that the promoter in question carried a magical name, the
enchanter's name, Chateaubriand. Vendean fierceness was taken by surprise. A magical name, to be sure, but belonging to the legends of Brittany. And Breton credulity is so easily manipulated! Here comes a native
Breton who, hardly detrained in the Gare Montparnasse, falls in love at
first sight and that very evening finds herself the owner of some land near
Barbès (which is like buying the Brooklyn Bridge). Pure Breton legend,
the worst kind of Parisian folklore. We know what it is worth. And what

8. Saint-Flour was the old capital of the Haute Auvergne and was used as a metaphor
for a primitive place, at the ends of the earth.

about that terrible Breton we meet in the opening pages of Victor Hugo's novel *1793*, gazing suspiciously at the horizon. It is true he was the last of his species, an aristocrat, and things turned out badly for him. Still, however naive they may be it is important to note the Bretons have better preserved their coasts than have the Vendeans, or even the Normans, whose reputation for shrewdness and a tough business sense, as well as for being litigious (which is so often confirmed by Balzac) is evidently exaggerated, or maybe they acquired these qualities so valued by the Parisians. What a good topic for a dissertation for future students, assuming the great-grandchildren of Edgar (in the sense in which Christiane Rochefort speaks of the *Petits enfants du Bon Dieu*) still write dissertations.[9] Don't forget, we are talking here of 1969, and the fires are still not under control. One day, with patience and prudence, can this blaze be extinguished? This is what Pompidou asked himself, without believing it possible. Whatever happens, provincial resistance, which varied by region, to the developers' disfigurement of the coastline and other places of natural beauty is a splendid subject. Have certain regions, among the most attractive, proved to be the most difficult to convince? As they say of women and horses, are there easy provinces and restive provinces?

9. The Edgar in question is Edgar Faure, the author of the university reforms in France that were enacted in response to the events of 1968.

PART TWO

MEN

A monstrous beast of a thousand feet attacking the stone giant
with lowered head. . . . Sack it, cried the speculators! So did the
king of Thunes. So did Clopin the Fearful. We will pillage the
church!

Victor Hugo

IN the years immediately after World War II we find that circumstances, especially political and even moral circumstances rather than
economic ones, enabled new men to rise to the top in the business
world and to occupy those positions most important for the fate of Paris.
There quickly formed, around these new men, an equally new administrative milieu, which did not differ socially from those that had dominated before the war. The important families did not let themselves be so
easily supplanted. From their point of view the destiny of Paris depended
more on the great families of France than on purely Parisian initiatives.
To understand the evolution of Paris we must examine France and not
just what happened on the banks of the Seine. A new power was constituted, a strange power, not strictly constitutional, next to which political
power (it is important that we begin to distinguish the two) and even
more so administrative power will play only a secondary role in my account, my attempt to understand what happened to Paris.

Finding myself one day in the office of a minister, one of those ephemeral ministers of the Fourth Republic, I remember overhearing a lord of
real estate (among other things) speaking on the phone to this minister—he spoke so loudly I could not help hearing—in a way no aristocrat
of an earlier age would have treated his stable boy. I then realized that I
should shelve my handbooks on constitutional and administrative law,
for there was an enormous difference between constituted power—that
of a minister (not to mention that of a prefect)—and this new power that
commanded the older power, not without enjoying the additional luxury
of appearing to amuse itself at the latter's expense. It is essential to pin-

point the Parisian aspect of this new power, to identify it as something more than a voice over the telephone.

I really don't have a way of doing this. There are no books to consult. There is nothing comparable, for example, to what Anthony Sampson called *The Anatomy of England* in 1962. He offered not the whole body but "the arms, the legs, and the circulation of the blood." "This book," he adds, "deals essentially with the managers attached to industry, government, the sciences, and transportation." Notice that he puts industry before government and the sciences before transportation.

At the time when André Siegfried wrote his books on the United States and England there was nothing comparable to Sampson's work for either country, which was the reason Siegfried gave, in all sincerity, for his own books on these countries when they were praised, or when a geographer, somewhat irritated, expressed amazement at Siegfried's literary fecundity. Another book on the United States! And on England! He had hardly returned, he had hardly had time to breathe the air of Manchester or Lake Michigan and here he was already giving a diagnosis. As if Phileas Fogg were a professor at the Collège de France inviting the ambassadors of the great English-speaking powers to come and explain their countries to his class. And Siegfried observed how insignificant were the available works.

There were books and newspapers in America dealing with these subjects instead of concentrating only on politics, as do French newspapers. And there always were interested parties—industrialists, bankers, even professors—who were better informed about such things (at least this was true of Siegfried's friends) than were their French counterparts, who were a bit ignorant. Anthony Sampson thus explained: "My method has been fresh and direct: I have written to about 200 persons asking them to grant me an interview and I have questioned them about their role. With only a few exceptions all have revealed an astonishing willingness to cooperate. The more one deals with men in responsible positions the easier it is, it seems, to meet with them."

It is completely different in France. Listen to a journalist tell of his repeated visits to the Rhône-Poulenc facility: "A short tour is as inadequate for understanding a large factory as it is for knowing a region or a country. Rhône-Poulenc keeps its secrets. But regular visits, listening to those whose task it is to clean up the sediment from the past and take risks in the future, provides access to revealing phrases, unexpected impressions" (*Le Figaro,* February 20, 1971). Doesn't this sound like the sleuth Arsène Lupin, as depicted by Maurice Leblanc? I remember that the president of Rhône-Poulenc, when he was a teacher at Sciences-Po [Institut d'Etudes Politiques], talked long and publicly about these matters before a huge and attentive audience. In England Anthony Sampson was welcomed by the most distinguished men, with the exception of two vulgarians and a rude aristocrat (whose names he gives), something I would never be able to do. Here when one calls at their offices every telephone line is busy. Having telephoned a friend, an important figure in real-estate finance, to tell him that I would love to ask him some questions about issues related to his line of business, I found myself invited to his country house for the weekend. "My wife will be delighted," he said, "and we will have a chance to talk." These are evidently contrary expectations. I don't think Anthony Sampson had ever been invited to spend a weekend. At an English weekend one does something quite different from sociological inquiry, if I am to judge from Agatha Christie, to whom I owe all that I know of an English weekend. As for books . . .

But why get upset about the lack of books? I can already hear the reader asking. What a peculiar mania for things printed on paper, for texts at all costs, when one already knows a good deal about the subject from other sources. Teaching for so long at Sciences-Po, I encountered every week in the faculty lounge—a kind of universal matrix—many of these people we are here considering, of all sorts, competent and incompetent, with every variety of character (and some without any character), from every age group, including the ageless. In addition, having had more than one of these men in my classes, I am in some way involved in their responsibilities and irresponsibilities. Perhaps I even indirectly destroyed Paris through one of them! To be able to question them, to pretend to know nothing or to know inadequately, surely this is self-mockery. This is how I imagine a former student thinking and responding: he suspects me of wanting to demand of him, even after ten or twenty years, some additional assignment for the sadistic pleasure of once again giving him a grade. "You're joking." "No I'm not joking. I have to refresh my memory, verify my recollections."

In addition it must be admitted, there exists a superstition, a cult of the written document, which is what Michelet, the son of a printer, understood: "Before writing my books I composed them materially. I gathered letters before gathering ideas." The feel, the smell of paper, of ink. I have even done my collecting in the street. Seeing some incident, perhaps a demonstration, or overhearing someone make an intelligent remark, an unexpected remark or even a banal remark, I have asked him to be kind enough to write it down and send me this record, which is merely the simple witness of what I have already seen as clearly as he. The religion of the written document.

But when it comes to written documents on French society there is nothing comparable to Sampson's *Anatomy*. There are brilliant (too brilliant) essays, pamphlets, or apologies, which have the same shortcomings as books about the consumer society: this is not accidental. Around 1965 or 1966, but more in the latter year, they began to appear, washed ashore by the same tide that carried books about society and spoke, with those books, of technocrats. They were much too late to tell us whatever it was that the authors saw, and especially unable to tell us what was most interesting about these technocrats. To begin with, they said nothing about the diversity or unity of the group designated by the term technocrat, which (whether it was flattering or pejorative) arrived as mysteriously and as badly wrapped as did consumer society. Above all they came too late to reveal everything about the question of how it all began, how it all ties together; in a word, they failed to fix a date.

These books are not very important. It is hardly worth going through them. One could even avoid opening them—it would be sufficient to note the author's name, the title, and the date of publication—if in some special libraries (that of Sciences-Po, for example) generations of students had not written in the margins of these books pertinent and often irate notes that are much more important for history than the texts themselves. Graffiti didn't make their first appearance in May 1968. Having had to produce dissertations or essays, that is, sometimes having had to risk their careers on this subject, these students could usually find little substance in the maxims of a writer who thought himself witty, who pronounced impertinences in the manner of the seventeenth-century moralists and threw in some imitations of the great writers.

What is a technocrat? It isn't very helpful to say with Tocqueville, that "it sometimes happens that one sets oneself to direct the fortunes of the state only when one feels incapable of managing one's own affairs," or with Alain that "a bad cause can be well administered," or even more bluntly, with Sauvy, "we call a technician we don't like a technocrat." This is especially so when one has to present a paper on technocracy that has a good chance of being corrected by a young technocrat who is lurking around the corner and expects to be deferred to, one should not be entirely stupid or basely servile; or when oneself is an aspiring technocrat, waiting for a *dignus intrare*, one would like to know more about it, especially when one rejects the charms of style, does not have a shapely leg, or does not know how to dance. Reading the books of this or that author, the pupil at Sciences-Po knows no more than he originally did. In the blank space of the pages he expresses his anger in harmless verbal attacks which interest me more than the text. This is what the *Revue des Sciences politiques* should publish!

More than books, then, the images of Sciences-Po will inform my description, my dissertation. In the absence of books it is still, necessarily, the sketch of a book, a preparatory study, that I am attempting. It is arranged like a dissertation which presents the faces, the men, the circumstances that, in years to come, it seems to me, will be at issue. If the picture doesn't look flattering—and since it is a question of Paris how could it be flattering?—I will make sure that at no time I speak of those who might have had me for a teacher, or rather those I might have had the possibility of having as students. I do not know either why or how, by what chance, what cause, the serious students, the grinds, the maladroit, those who know how to copy, I should even add the chaste, seek other stables, while the race horses, those with imagination, the dilettantes, the lazy, those who despise authority, the habitués of cafés and the girl-chasers, those who never take notes in class and are better off for it, find themselves in my class.

Chapter Four

The Technocrats

Exaggerated sentiments, in ripening, produce the fruit of error,
and the harvest that gathers it has only tears.

Aeschylus, *The Persians*

HE technocrats: clumsily, I have already mentioned them. How
could it be avoided? They signify an epoch. In some future handbook, in some dissertation yet to be written, they will doubtless
speak of the century of the technocrats as one speaks of the century of
the philosophes, but without adding that it too was an enlightened age
and probably without saying it lasted a hundred years. There are other
obvious differences not worth mentioning. Let me say only that the philosophes who most deserve this impressive title, those who thought themselves superior and had good reason to do so, never took themselves so
seriously, except for Rousseau, whose tedious and sententious *Emile* resembles a study on pedagogy by a perfect little technocrat. To love nature
but use it to build sand castles, to be a goody two-shoes, to love one's
little friends, to desire the good of humanity, to guard against superstition, to eschew fables, especially those of La Fontaine, to neglect history
and read as little as possible, except for *Robinson Crusoe,* this is Rousseau's prescription.

The technocrats begin to be spoken of between the years of 1955 and
1960, a bit before the publication of the books that they themselves wrote
and the books written about them which let us date their apogee. They
wrote a great deal yet without in the least resembling the world of Diderot and the philosophes. They inspired each other to take up the pen.
They wrote prefaces and afterwords for each other. They collaborated,
as had the encyclopedists, contributing to collective works which, from
the first line to the last, seemed to come from the same thought processes,
seemed to emerge from the same automatic writing, to flow from the
same bottle of ink. "These technicians whom the deputies keep busy,"
wrote François Mauriac (*Le Figaro Littéraire,* September 21, 1963), al-

ways ready to join the winning side, seeing in it, like the Emperor Constantine, the Christian God. "They can be called technocrats. Television is the medium, carrying them (and it will continue to carry them) God knows where." This sentence fixes a historical moment for the word and its meaning, dates it, is almost an act of baptism—thank God, I say, imitating the saintly familiarity of Mauriac. But it is a delayed baptism, one which does not call forth only blessings, celebrations, and gifts. "Can be called": here is an accusing finger pointing to the sacrilegious, the skeptics, the unbelievers. They were already present at this moment of public joy! How much more so five or six years later—without even looking as far ahead as June 1975 (which is when I am writing these lines)—when my newspaper tells me that, addressing the National Assembly, the minister of economics and finance said, without any change in expression, that he had some claim to be called a "partial technocrat."

Death to the technocrats. Let them mount the scaffold which the aristocrats mounted long ago, without Mauriac to accompany them to execution or to hide the horrible machine from their sight by holding up the cross. They used to be the men who could do everything, who knew everything, who were never deceived. Now they are those who are mistaken all the time. But more than any other group the French technocrats are singled out by the international press, especially the American press, for their feats, or rather their defeats. "A brilliant technical solution. It remains to be seen if it is workable. In the United States the discussion is both more profound and more democratic than here. . . ."

"Incompetent directors and audacious technocrats, who leap easily from a simple insight to massive general applications," wrote *Le Monde* (March 10, 1976). In a few years the word has completely changed its meaning. "A technocrat has a brilliant mind that completely disregards reality." This is the automatic understanding of the word. It is like the quip: "There are three ways of ruining oneself: women, gambling, and engineers who have inventions." Substitute "technocrats" for "engineers."

The awakening is bitter for those who, having known another time, are stubborn and carry on as they did formerly. This was the case of the master technocrat, the pope of technocrats, as they say (doubtless because of the Holy Spirit), about whom the historian Philippe Ariès, as interested as I am in the little details of history as well as the grand sweep of things, recounted a recent misadventure. The incident is insignificant but it seems to me to date an epoch that I myself discuss. Having to reiterate, one day in 1975, what he had always said, to chant his litany in a supposedly welcoming school, he was roughly treated, cast out, without understanding what had happened. He was the doyen whose least word was gospel. Now he was the aristocratic emigré returning prematurely to his estates from voluntary exile, stumbling upon a gathering of sans-culottes.

More inspired than him and more like those aristocrats who, sensing the Revolution, would don a peasant shirt or a gray jacket, are these famous technocrats, these believers in an indefinite economic progress, these unscrupulous builders and destroyers who, overnight, take an interest in the environment, the artisanate, the old stones and the old architectural ornamentation, just as the promoters switch from building high rises to rustic cottages. A technocratic stance which used to concern itself only with poured concrete and steel, mirrored glass, clusters of dead towers, now indicates (on glossy paper) woods,·prairies, clusters of villages. These are the visionaries of the year 2000 who do not hesitate to reduce things to numbers, to cartographic representation, and now lead us back to the Middle Ages or the age of the caves. They throw into relief not the shortcomings and decadence of technocracy but its infinite resources, an adaptive capacity we expected them to have, but not so highly developed and pushed to such an extent, to such frivolousness and cynicism. To describe it we have to borrow from La Bruyère or Balzac their darkest sentences, or say simply, as they do in Belleville: "What balls!"

If the word "technocrat" applies here to an entire period, whatever the moment under consideration, the diversity of the groups, their appearance, this is because behind these differences and changes of opinion, whether they celebrate or condemn, we find a similar way of doing things, of seeing, a similar state of mind, the same way of thinking. I would be hard-pressed to describe this way of thinking if I had available only the works of the technocrats themselves, their self-conscious meditations, their strategic works written as they maneuvered for position, or what they wrote when they were victorious, not to mention what they now write. In the beginning they wrote Caesar's *Gallic Wars;* now they write Las Cases' *Memorial of St. Helena:* a chronicle of triumph followed by retrospective myth-making. Not only do I save myself from the boredom of reading them, I also spare myself the fear that I might be taken in by their prose and the image they present, and consequently judge them incorrectly or fail to understand them. They are better than they appear or admit to be. What is their value? We cannot ask the technocrats themselves.

The technocratic spirit is only another way of referring to what Alain called "the Polytechnique style" [l'esprit polytechnicien], a style he did not much like. But instead of crushing it with his heavy Norman paw, or ridiculing it (as I would tend to do) he preferred to take it seriously. What constituted seriousness for him was Descartes: "Perhaps we should read Descartes carefully in order to understand these pathetic geometricians. They are basically revolutionaries, completely rigid and despotic in their thought, yet in deed they are conservatives, often Catholics, but without a theology." On the one hand their thought is "like a cloistered monastery isolated on a mountaintop," which has been subjugated to the discipline of mathematics and does not know that "to simplify, to flay, to despoil the universe and to create theorems about it is to reject the universe," which always has its revenge. "We have to know that the world exists. But the elite *polytechniciens* showed us during the war, when any man of common sense could judge them, that they knew nothing of the world. These men with ideas . . . were convinced that an undertaking where everything was anticipated would succeed. What actually happened has stunned them but taught them nothing." On the other hand, as Descartes himself saw, what resulted from this kind of thinking was complete submission to established order. "To follow the religion in which God gave me the grace to be raised since infancy" is one of Descartes' provisional rules for clear thinking, while he subjects all his ideas to universal doubt: "This is in the nature of administration. Maybe all these geometricians did not take the trouble to realize it," Alain concluded.

If we want to see the technocrats clearly, whether or not they are polytechniciens who get entangled in their figures, we must start from this kind of analysis, if for no other reason than that it allows us to distinguish clearly between what is and what is not true anymore. But was this obviously the case in Alain's time? The philosopher's generosity perhaps led him to give too much credit to his adversary, as did Descartes himself. In addition his analysis of mathematical thought was perhaps a bit too restricted by the Ecole Normale Superiéure and the memory of mathematician friends, of whom a few were illustrious. Such things should not influence our judgment.

Mathematicians and Mathematicians

I was led to understand the distinction between mathematicians from the Ecole Normale and the Ecole Polytechnique) when I asked a mathematician trained at the rue d'Ulm if there was a difference. "Do you believe there are mathematicians from the Ecole Polytechnique? They are men who want to build a good career, nothing more." Still, he grudgingly granted there were two or three genuine mathematicians. Forced to answer my own question, I found myself hard put to do so, able to judge mathematicians only from the outside, by their words, which usually surprise me—uttered, it should be said, on matters foreign to mathematics. But mathematics seems to me, probably because I am ignorant, to explain the eccentric, even the bizarre. So I return to the texts and to my recollections. To Daniel Halévy, for example, interrogating him about the mathematical genius of Leibniz, trying, as I do so, to understand Leibniz himself. Then turning to Jean Baruzi's *Leibniz et l'organisation religieuse de la terre,* a kind of struggle with the angel, for thus does he ultimately present Leibniz's discovery of infinitesimal calculus, in the town house on the rue de Tournon, where the envoy from Mayence lived and where the philosopher stayed. Rather, to be more precise, in the commons that overlook the rue Garancière, where today the Republican Guard is quartered. This is an important detail for the author of *Pays parisiens:* "The rue Garancière is the place where this stunning triumph of the human spirit took place." Let me cite Alain: "The discoverers, such as Archimedes, Galileo, Descartes, Leibniz, reasoned as a species of struggle, without guidance. The polytechnicien now follows the paths they blazed" (*Propos,* September 3, 1919).

This is even truer today! Applied to economics, to demography, to poor sociology, with even more reason to the problems of our unhappy Paris, it is much less a question of mathematics than of mere statistics, ready to hand for anyone, even if he has never learned to manipulate them, which is my case. Rather than think about this in terms of mathematics, it is better to speak about an imperialism of statistics, a mania for quantification which, for most practitioners no doubt, has only feeble and indirect connections with a kind of thinking Alain could not himself bear but which he respected. I will be unable to do more than he. To clarify my own views there is no need for me to reread Descartes and Plato. That would give too much distinction to those I am here considering.

My recollections of INED at precisely the time I am discussing make clear to me this cast of mind (or maybe they get in the way). I am speaking of the Institut national d'études démographiques, which was created in the early 1950s by Albert Sauvy and his collaborators, including Jean Stoetzel, who introduced opinion polls into France. Sauvy has appeared here and there in this book as one of those who figured in the history of this time and in my personal history as well. A polytechnicien, but one who would also have been able, and even more appropriately, to have another title, wear another hat, or maybe no hat at all (he never looked good in the squashed hat of a polytechnicien). Perhaps we can call him an imaginary polytechnicien to distinguish him from the others, whom he appeared to imitate, surprising them precisely because he seemed to be doing what everyone else was doing. He quantified, but in quest of wisdom. He was curious about what quantification can do and what its limits are rather than about the numbers themselves. He used quantification, making it useful, dividing it, employing it, sometimes throwing petty calculations away instead of saving them, adoring them, hoarding them like those fierce misers who cannot let themselves lose the least bit of what they have collected, even making it grow by earning interest. He was a man who quantified in the manner of the quantifiers of the eighteenth century whom he revered as he set out upon his adventure—for it was an adventure; those who, having other interests, saw things differently, saw and sought other horizons. Some of their names are scattered throughout this book because they too, with Sauvy, figured in the history of their times and in my own life.

Then there are the polytechniciens, who are not among this company. One or two had some intellectual distinction and would have attracted Alain's interest. One of them, Ledermann, they tell me, had genius. The others quantified everything that fell into their hands, even love itself. How could they do otherwise? From seeing them at work I have presented them as they were and shown the possibilities of a quantitative cast of mind, which I don't at all understand and for which Alain had only prepared me to see the summits: a bit like Hegel who would point to the mountain and say: "Thus it is."

From the mountains to the clumps of earth and the rabbit warrens there are numerous intermediate gradations. There are the feudal barons of mathematical economics whom I judge by what Sauvy says about them. Les Propos of Alain and the remarks of Sauvy, on a great many points, are similar. The latter's comments give me a chance to control the former's. Even better, to update them. "Numbers," Sauvy observes, "are the refuge of the economists"; Alain uses the image of a monastery— "They are tranquil living in these abstractions." A place of timeless beauty. Nothing disturbs pure thought. For ten years during this period there is not a single book on unemployment. Life is seen through rose-colored glasses. So too the future, for numbers crystallize concepts which, when they become quantitative become definitive. Without his numbers the quantifier is lost. The "defrocked priest of numbers" goes mad, everything is disordered, everything is thrown together, everything is shattered. He ends up by not knowing how to make a calculation, or so it seems from a few examples. But to play Hamlet one has to be the prince of Denmark and be manipulated by Shakespeare. Our mathematical economist is a petty aristocrat, not a prince.

Since the 1950s economics research and teaching has turned on mathematics. A generation of mathematical economists were trained then, and ten or twelve years later we find them everywhere. Ever since it has been impossible to study the subject without mathematical equations. Afraid to be accused of being concerned only with literature, the university has taken up quantifying its theories. Since the great masters of mathematical economics are *polytechniciens,* certain economists at the university, lacking this skill, are secretly tutored in calculus for two or three years (the less able for even longer) in order to be able to impress their students with their new science, wielding the chalk at the blackboard like a magic wand.

> Your heart swells up and feels the all-powerful cause.
>
> Valéry

THERE is much more to this kind of technocratic thinking, than this polytechnique mentality, this mathematical thinking described by Alain. A great deal more, or rather much that is different and even the opposite of mathematical thinking: "When in the world" (that is to say not in the monastery) writes Alain, "they are all prudence and politeness, not out of esteem for the world but rather from contempt." Respectful of power, they would never think to lay hands upon it or to assert a rival power.

Here we are at the heart of the matter. Different times, different behavior, but not a different basic psychology. To discover the relationship between mathematical thought and political ambition, between the polytechnique mentality and the technocratic mentality, we have to turn to Leibniz, not Descartes or Alain. It is a question of Leibniz's dream, as Daniel Halévy interprets it. "The king of France was young, only a few years older than Leibniz. One was twenty-six, the other twenty-one; how youth unites men! Leibniz saw in Louis XIV a genius of taste, of courage, of heart. Intellectual power is another kind of virtue. Two thousand years earlier the ancient world had seen the appearance of Alexander. And next to Alexander had been Aristotle, his teacher, who had imbued him with the idea of a magnificent empire. . . . Leibniz dreamed of playing Aristotle to this new Alexander." Or consider Caesar meditating on power: "Caesar, calm Caesar, his hand on everything." Why should we be surprised if Valéry is the poet of our technocrats, and almost the only one? In *Le Pouvoir de l'esprit* it is the spirit of power one reads about, well understanding that they embody this spirit, that they know no other.

Alain never suspected this any more than he foresaw the use to which Valéry (whom he adored) would one day be put. "Have you done your work, Orpheus?" he asked Valéry when he met him. But there is a lesson to be learned from the poet (both the best and the worst), I insist, one which our technocrats clearly recognized. Above all there is a scorn for history which we have not seen the end of in Paris. "The ruins bore me," Valéry wrote in Rome. "And when they interest me it is not because they are ruins but forms or shapes . . . interesting, although ruined . . . let those old columns crumble in peace" (*Notes personnelles*, 1937).

I did not recognize this will to power, this overwhelming desire, when its first manifestations were developing before my eyes. These first urges revealed themselves publicly in the years to which I have returned in order to understand what has happened since. It was at the Ecole Normale, at the Center for Social Studies, established by our director, M. Bouglé, that I saw, without understanding, the opening scenes of a strange spectacle. Rather than Alain inviting the future minister Monzie (who had come to visit his class) to have a seat on the last bench in the room, reserved for dunces, or in this case reserved for the only dunce among those brilliant *normaliens,* the opposite occurred. This was not Socrates taking Alcibiades into his bed, it was rather a man who wanted to be minister offering himself to Alcibiades' caresses. I am speaking, obviously, of *normaliens,* who are the only students I know. As for what happened on the other side of the mountain, I have no idea except what I learned, on extremely rare occasions, from a few polytechniciens, when the normaliens paid them the honor of inviting them into their holy of holies.

They sometimes came to talk about what they knew and what they were told to stick to—financial matters, prices, plans, all of it profoundly boring. We listened to them out of courtesy and asked what all this had to do with politics. Politics was a matter of the word, not of techniques, and the word was the business of normaliens, of Jaurès, of Herriot, of Léon Blum, not of polytechniciens. Eloquence was the water that baptized, cleansed, transfigured politics. Of the different modes of genius these precincts nurtured, the word was all, and in no way inferior to the others. Pericles and Demosthenes were of this race, and Jaurès was one of the greatest historians of the French Revolution.

A career in the professoriat or a political career? In these years between the two world wars, in which everything began to churn, some could waver, but they were unusual. Far from admiring those who chose politics, most of their schoolmates were uncomfortable around them as one is uncomfortable around someone coming down with a bad cold, or else they made fun of them, seeing no value outside teaching. I can still see, on the night of February 6, one of these ambitious young men cry out, as soon as he reached the Place de la Concorde: "I would love to be dictator for the pleasure of being unjust."[1] A declaration worthy of Nero. Some wanted to be on horseback, as Napoleon, or pilot a plane, as Mussolini. These were political careers which could not be realized except at the summit. Some years later a few of them had reached those heights, some even responsible for their own misfortune or that of others. When I arrived, in 1933, at the Reims lycée, anxious to be able to follow Georges Bidault, my classmates told me how Déat was tormented by ambition.[2] Déat, the purest of the pure, the darling of sociology, the favorite child of Bouglé. When we spoke to the wife of this philosophy professor, we already addressed her as "Madame la Présidente." Nevertheless, who imagined at that time that one day this little man, in leather jodhpurs, with a wide belt, a sword . . .

Having seen things, and continuing to see them in this way, from the heights of the rue d'Ulm, where a few young men who seem to have stepped out of the pages of a Jules Romains novel saw in the Paris sky some phantom of glory, I knew nothing about the quest for power of others, those who had a different view of politics and saw power differently. All I knew was what I learned from experience, from rumor, from books—Philippe Bauchard's *Les Technocrates de le pouvoir* or Sauvy's *De Paul Reynaud à de Gaulle*. All I knew was what I sometimes learned from the technocrats themselves, much later, when they were already en-

1. The anti-parliamentary riots in Paris, February 6–7, 1934, further discredited the Third Republic, already shaken by the sensational revelations of the Stavisky Affair. Serge Stavisky, an Eastern European Jew with excellent political connections, had been caught selling fraudulent bonds. Public outrage at official corruption brought down the Radical Socialist government of Camille Chautemps. Royalists, seeking to exploit this opening to bring down the Republic itself, staged riots in Paris but were put down with brutal force by the new government of Edouard Daladier.

2. Bidault, born in Moulins in 1899, was several times minister of foreign affairs for France. Marcel Déat (1894–1953) entered the Ecole Normale in 1914 a self-proclaimed socialist and the protégé of the director. He converted to Nazism before the occupation of France and founded a "Légion" of French volunteers against Bolshevism to fight alongside the Nazi troops. He wore a uniform that looked like the SS uniform and used a salute similar to that of the Nazis. Along with Doriot he is considered one of the two most notorious traitors of the Vichy era.

sconced in power, in positions that were not those I imagined, positions one would look for in vain in Jules Romains' serial novel *Les Hommes de bonne volonté*, or better yet, when they had left those positions. As Voyer d'Argenson wrote in 1785, in his *Essais dans le goût de Montaigne:* "Men such as these are very dangerous when they are involved in politics. But when they have retired they are usually charming to listen to."

First, in 1930, came the creation of the group "X-Crise." This was a group founded by polytechniciens, made up of polytechniciens, and devoted to finding some way of overcoming the crisis by using polytechnicien solutions. It was a group outside the political parties but close to them and necessarily having, some day or other, to enter into a relationship with them, to act in concert with them, to use them, to replace them. This is a minor detail in Parisian history. The idea was hatched in a café near Maubert-Mutualité. But which one? None of the polytechniciens I questioned, even those who should have had the clearest memory, were able to tell me. They looked at me with astonishment. What does it matter? Alain had already shown me the curious way they had of seeing things (and not seeing them). Then came the Popular Front, Vichy, the Resistance, and finally de Gaulle.

With the advent of de Gaulle, Leibniz found his Alexander, Valéry his Caesar, the polytechniciens their enlightened despot, who would open all the doors of power for them, who would sit them in his lap, embrace them, have them on his throne. Twice, despite the difficulties some of them had made for him, de Gaulle gave them a place in the government after the Liberation. God only knew what they would do after his fall. It is de Gaulle who took them in when he returned to power, refusing to recognize that only yesterday they had maneuvered against him. Only yesterday they were marching in the Place de la République protesting de Gaulle, and then they were sheltered by the gilded ceilings of the Elysée Palace, which they never afterwards left. The Jean Moulin Club, created on June 18, 1958, in a heroic atmosphere, in response to a fascist attack, provided the Fifth Republic with technocrats, or rather polytechniciens.[3] In addition, and in far greater numbers, it provided functionaries of all kinds whose grasp of technical matters was only feebly related to that of the polytechniciens. After all, as the General would have said: "the Jean Moulin Club remains the best means yet found to get functionaries to work overtime." An ironic and condescending quip, or perhaps a regal aside which will help historians understand why de Gaulle, on two occasions, put men into power who were of a species unknown to him, whom he did not try to know better. These men were completely incapable of understanding him; they were ignorant of the past and did not hesitate, when they had a chance, to spit in his soup.

A personal experience supports these words. Around 1959 I had been appointed to the first Committee of Twelve, whose charge was to set priorities for scientific research. I represented the social sciences on the committee. It had been Pompidou's idea, knowing that, with him, I did not believe in the social sciences, a name he could never pronounce without laughing. "At least," he had said, "with Chevalier there is no risk of going too far." After a year de Gaulle summoned us to the Elysée Palace in order to learn what we had proposed. This enormous man entered the tiny, dusty office exactly at the stroke of noon, sounded by a clock on the mantle that dated from the First Empire. Each of us spoke in turn. He listened to the mathematician politely. He listened to the doctor, Jean Bernard, with respect. With passion and unexpectedly he asked questions of those who had not yet spoken about what possibilities they saw for France: empty-handed, starting from scratch, could France, by force of genius, catch and then surpass the great nations in the areas they dominated—atomic energy and space exploration? When it was my turn he had less to listen to, for I had nothing to say that seemed to me worthy of him. I had nothing to say about demography, sociology, economics, those preserves of the technocrats. I did not mean those princes of technique, or one of their disciples, who probe the secrets of nature, but of mere technocrats, those who, not being able to confront the elements, focus on men and who, without laboratories for testing the truth, erect mountains of theories about the future. I stopped speaking, convinced the General wasn't listening, and then mumbled in a rather confused way something about the technocrats, the very ones who play so central a role in this book. My example is thus ill-chosen, but at least it lets me understand why the reign of de Gaulle was also that of the technocrats, of whatever level of ability, of those who possessed a skill and those who had only a calling card, those who helped and those who helped themselves, exploiting the glory of others and everything that the good name of science promised. Analyzing the problems of Greek democracy (in a book by the same name), Jacqueline de Romilly writes: "The words Plato uses should not mislead us. His expertise, his science, his 'technē,' are part of a moral and philosophical universe. Those Greeks who insist on some understanding called 'technical,' in political matters, do not have in mind anything similar to what our technocrats today mean. . . . Another difference [is that] . . . the science of the technocrats is *a priori,* which is even more foreign to the people than what Plato calls for, since it can be taught. The royal art Plato is talking about, on the contrary, is part of an ideal whose realization is almost miraculous." A miracle of wisdom. We are a long way from statistics.

To the diversity of methodologies we should add that of men. Paradoxically, this diversity is much more difficult to describe because it pertains to so few cases. There are already dictionaries and biographies of technocrats, even bibliographies, since a great many of them write and publish. It should probably not be entitled *The Dictionary of Technocrats* because the term might become unfashionable and the publisher would risk being sued by those not flattered to find themselves thus designated. It should rather be titled, at the outset, something like "those who count," or "the values of France," or "the aspirants" (as they say of bicycle racers). I even recall having seen my own name, though I cannot remember under what rubric, in such a list drawn up by the magazine *Réalités*, which proves that the list-makers are all too impatient, they are ill-informed, or they believe, since the title of technocrat has so far suffered no devaluation, that they flatter men by thus baptizing them. A hostess, without fear of mockery, presented a guest as "a friend who is a brilliant technocrat." We can say that a good hostess, without the slightest mental effort, could name twenty such. With twenty hostesses worthy of the name, knowing each other and telephoning each other, the list would be almost complete.

Not to treat such grave matters lightly, I would say that to the diversity of professions should be added the variety of men, whatever might be the homogenizing effect of their professions. In addition, men change with age and events. From 1930 to the Liberation at the end of World War II, to take only the most dramatic period to help us understand what would happen later in the period I am here describing, God knows how events put everything to the test. Before writing the history of the technocrats as a group, it would be necessary to know the background of each one of those who would one day be thus designated.

Reviewing Vercors' *La Bataille du silence* and the history of the Editions de Minuit (in *Le Monde*), Pierre Massé, then the president of the national electrical power company (EDF) wrote: "It is important to tell the world that France, amidst misfortune and violence, knew how to remain faithful to her most noble character: clear thinking . . . I remember having said to myself: all that remains is thought. And thought was then above all the secret silence of man seeking the beginning of revenge in his own being. It seems to me that the summer of 1940 separates two parts of my life and continues to influence much of what I have been able to do since." This pertains as well to the history of technocracy.

Whatever were the experiences of this or that individual, a general conclusion characterizes these years. There are a small number of men, maybe four or five hundred, of whom maybe a hundred are important. These are the men who have an affinity of character, despite the evolution that caused a divergence between those who belonged to "X-Crisis" (made up of engineers, especially polytechniciens) and those who were the important members of the Jean Moulin Club. There are men, moreover, who knew each other and who held power, certainly after 1958 but already before that date, a kind of shadow power that would operate in place of direct power if it proved necessary. One might, incorrectly, smell a plot, suspect a series of machinations, a net of intricate intrigues, resembling those of the *The History of the Thirteen*. "There was in Paris under the First Empire, thirteen men, all with similar feelings, all endowed with the greatest fidelity to the same ideas, so devoted that they would not betray each other, even when their interests differed, so deeply political that they would dissimulate the sacred bonds uniting them, strong enough to put themselves above all laws, brave enough to attempt anything, and fortunate enough to have almost always been successful," writes Balzac. "One day, one of them . . . decided that the society should be composed entirely of distinguished men who would join to their natural intelligence their education, their personal fortunes, a fanaticism ardent enough to weld these elements into a single unit. Then, formidable in action and in devotion, possessed of their secret power against which the social order would be defenseless, they would surmount all obstacles, annihilate opposition, and give to each member the diabolical power possessed by the whole."

Despite the profound Balzacian genius, despite the absolute belief one has in his penetration, despite the temptation to think of the technocrats as these "distinguished men," this "secret power," this group "formidable in action and in devotion," possessing "diabolical power," it would be too fortuitous if things had happened in this way.

Certainly plots or would-be plots were hatched now and then, even some pacts in the style of Balzac's Thirteen—"the pact to run the Empire as a committee"—on the eve of the Second World War. There were also personal histories that even Balzac couldn't have made tragic. Such was the burglary, around 1961, of the Jean Moulin Club. The prime minister's police were accused of knowing about this nocturnal break-in, and the theft of a card file whose names all the hostesses of Paris knew intimately. Benefiting from protection in high places, and more imaginative than the others, one of these hostesses had perhaps simply used this clever means to avoid having thirteen guests for dinner. Or maybe the prime minister himself, wanting to add to one or another of the ministerial office staffs, had sought, in this file, a member of the Jean Moulin Club who did not already have such an appointment.

There was a kind of plot that originated, I think, in the friendships born in a shared past, especially during the Resistance. These comrade-ships were intensified, I believe, by the unexpected events that followed, events in the evolution of France, even before 1958: the replacement of the old political milieux of those who deliberate and vote by those whose function it is to decide because they are experts, who possess some avant-garde technique, without whom the most prestigious and indispensable undertakings would come to naught. In the great projects of our national destiny politicians who should resolve issues, who should feel themselves, or want to feel themselves, "the necessary cause" play a minor role. The technocrats decide things, and they cannot be bypassed because they guard the secrets of the central mysteries. Also decided in this way and at the same time, in the shadow of old-fashioned politicians and political power (and without their knowledge), were matters that had always re-solved themselves and whose only mystery was that now there seemed to be some mystery attached to them. The technocrat made himself a medi-cine man who, possessed of a heavenly gift, makes the rain fall. This sorcerer with a diploma waters the plants and makes them grow.

This is an enormous power. One technocrat authorizes others, empow-ers others, intertwines with others. They are everywhere, or at least wher-ever it is worth being. They decide everything. The enlightened press spreads their ideas and their images. It even publishes dossiers on them, with their photos, and, next to their height, weight, and the color of their hair, all the bits of information the public wants, including their favorite pastimes, their hobbies. Alain insisted that polytechniciens—at least those he observed on the boulevard St. Michel—always carried a violin with them as well as their sword. He would play brilliant variations on the subject of polytechniciens and their violins.

L'Express, whose first issue appeared on May 16, 1953, played an important role in presenting the technocrats to the public. It chose Sauvy as its subject. It succeeded in the undertaking. The public knew the tech-nocrats although they sometimes confused one with another, which only proves that they knew several of them well. Those in power listened to the technocrats. Why, by what kind of lèse-majesté, by what kind of ridiculous avoidance, by what unreasonable act should those who were subservient to those in power not also heed the technocrats? This was especially true in Paris, at the dawn of this dazzling light. Here we discovered the technocrats engaged in rethinking the city, when it would have been enough merely to think about Paris. They instructed, they transmitted, their message. They selected and trained those who would put it into practice. The word was made flesh. The *énarque* is the incarnation of the word.

Chapter Five

The Enarques

> The state is the actuality of the ethical Idea. It is ethical mind *qua*
> the substantial will manifest and revealed to itself, knowing and
> thinking itself, accomplishing what it knows and in so far as it
> knows it. The state exists immediately in custom, mediately in in-
> dividual self-consciousness, knowledge, and activity, while self-
> consciousness in virtue of its sentiment towards the state finds in
> the state, as its essence and the end and product of its activity, its
> substantive freedom.
>
> Hegel, *Philosophy of Right*

ECHNOCRATS, *énarques?* If we judge by the use of these words
for the past fifteen years they have become synonymous. The
technocrat of these heroic years, "one of those men the rest of the
world envies," the technocrat of the social hostesses, of the high-society
woman who reads *Le Figaro* as well as the enlightened woman who reads
L'Express, both of them readers of François Mauriac, who spoke to the
latter, with special intimacy, of the charms of a private mass celebrated
in some country church at the first light of dawn. There was no need for
him to introduce the famous technocrat at that point. But there was "the
perpetually young and brilliant énarque" who could not help but become
a technocrat in time. Future technocrat, a "technocrat in seed," the famous technocrat who would become the narrow technocrat whose ignorance one mocks, an ignoramus.

The history of the énarques is part of the history of the decline of Paris.
The reasons, if we can find them, are in the milieux of the énarques themselves, not in the usual Paris sources. It is the technocrats who inspire, or
rather it is technocracy, as in the Enlightenment it was philosophy. The
énarques carry ideas through, make them work. They are the secular
arm: Like the intendants, those royal agents of the ancien régime who
had been nourished by the Enlightenment. But this is a strained comparison, for the énarques can only put into practice the technocracy of which

118

they are part, which speaks through their mouths and guides their hands. The reader should not be surprised if, describing Paris, I do not linger over the official files which they have signed. They did not sign them, they countersigned them.

I have no intention of recounting their history, only my memories of it. "Souvenir, souvenir . . . d'automne. . . ." Age encourages rapidity and also allows me to present problems and developments through anecdotes—for the pleasure of it, whether or not they are significant—and to treat grave matters in a lighthearted way.

It was for state service that the Ecole Nationale d'Administration was created and the énarques were trained. They began as civil servants. Often they ended as civil servants, dying in harness. There is an epic quality in my account, as there is in this history itself, at least at its beginnings when we can still hear the clash of arms. Held responsible for France's defeat, the graduates of Sciences-Po had difficulty exonerating themselves. They were able to do so only because of their directors, Seydoux and Chapsal, and because of the credit of André Siegfried and the simple truth. But one still has to know how to speak this truth. In the Boutmy Amphitheater, filled almost to the rafters with students and former students, a great many of whom had just climbed out of General Leclerc's tanks, I can still see Siegfried reciting, by himself, La Fontaine: "You murmur, old man! See the young die—see them work, see them run. . . ." In the place of Sciences-Po graduates or over them, if they could not be swept away, substituting for them in their essential task, a phalanx of competent and devoted administrators for the state needed to be trained, with recruitment not only from the upper bourgeoisie of Paris—the social milieu of Sciences-Po—but from the population at large. "I want the village postman to be able to become a state councilor," said the first director of the ENA at a gathering I attended, in the company of Siegfried, who appeared interested.

Fortunately or unfortunately, one will judge by the consequences, Sciences-Po had a near monopoly on preparation for the exams for state appointments, and during the first years this was a Sciences-Po faithful to traditions they had valued for more than a half-century. It was their greatest glory and earned them their detestable reputation. For me, this well-deserved reputation was one of the surest proofs of how solidly grounded was their glory (a kind of supplementary guarantee). In truth, despite some recent rearrangements that fooled no one and (thank God) do not amount to much, Sciences-Po continues to resemble, as one drop of water resembles another, the Free School of Political Science [l'Ecole libre des Sciences politiques]. Both institutions were devoted to politics (calling their subject "political science" is misleading), and the politics in question was indifferent to what passes for politics in restaurants or garrets or beyond the city walls, or in Plato's *Republic*. It is the politics of the citizen, not that of slaves and valets. As for liberty, even if it has disappeared from their discourse, or rather been erased, it remains the same. Siegfried, who incarnated this liberty, was the living image of what, only yesterday, Elie Halévy was and what Taine had been before him: the embodiment of a worldly personal culture without prejudices, freed of this burden, this baggage, these heavy academic restraints, and able to travel quickly and far. Why encumber oneself with what life itself will soon enough teach? No more than the pupils of the Ecole libre, those of Sciences-Po in these first years did not break under learning, were not abysses of culture.

When I began teaching at the rue St. Guillaume, in 1943–44, my friend, Jacques de Bourbon-Busset, to whom I owed my appointment as *maître de conférence,* had alerted me that the students didn't know much. It was an understatement. Coming from the rue d'Ulm I would say they knew nothing. But after all, to fill important posts in government, even more importantly to succeed the incumbents, was a lot of learning, acquired early in life, so necessary? This is the question that I then posed to myself until I was forced to admit that in a number of places, or at least in Paris, culture and learning, or what passes for them, are more a hindrance than a help. There is always time to learn and besides, in common parlance, the less one knows the better. The intelligence of the young is a marvelous thing, and it should be focused on marvelous things, games and exercises that eventually will be as useful as they now seem useless. Isn't this what Cardinal Richelieu explains in his *Testament politique* (the book I was then using in class), the definitive book by which pupils aspiring to public careers ought to be judged? "To have a bishop equal to our expectations, we need a learned man, full of piety, zeal, and of good birth, for as a rule the authority required by this position is found only in men of quality," the cardinal writes. But it being difficult to find all these united in a single man, "I would insist," he continues, "that excellent manners . . . being assumed, the quality and authority which ordinarily accompany them should be preferred to the greatest learning, since I have often seen erudite men make very bad bishops." Here is the heart of the matter. To be a good bishop one does not have to be a great theologian. Even more is this true for a good state functionary, a prudent businessman. The students of Sciences-Po were hardly great theologians; even the most brilliant of them did not much care about such matters.

With the ENA and above all with preparing for the exams, everything changed. Not at the beginning. The great bishops were still around, as were the cardinals, who were in no way theologians. On the question of theology Siegfried expressed the essence: "England is an island. Having said that, gentlemen, I think I have said all that is necessary." Or, "granite is conservative, limestone Republican," an article of faith and of experience which earned me, however—when I borrowed it to sidestep a question on a geology exam (I almost wrote "theology" exam)—a rebuke in the Sorbonne from the great Martonne , who was completely hostile to such witticisms. But at the beginnings of the ENA wit was still acceptable. Siegfried was there. And so too were some bishops from the good old days, as well as some future canons, on their way to becoming bishops or who already had considerable responsibility, who were as accomplished as Siegfried at constructing a universe in a lecture. Pierre Laroque could do it for the social universe, in a few lessons of disarming clarity. Jean-Jacques Chevallier, could do it for the political universe, white and red bodies whose paths in the sky he traced. Raymond Aron was already an adept. Ten years, fifteen years later they would be replaced by others, by those savants Richelieu was so suspicious of. Statistics, national bookkeeping, quantitative sociology, economic prediction: why should I fatigue myself making a list which no one asked for? Let me say simply that it is the apparatus of technocracy, the machinery of the petty technocrat. And these good little men, thus armed, are so courageous!

From now on it was no longer enough to be erudite. In addition to ability one needed courage, even physical courage, perhaps physical courage above all, and energy, willpower. One had to show he had it, advertise it, flaunt it, shout it, get others to shout it. How many ways they found! What a hodgepodge of genres. Gestures incomprehensible for those who continued in Alain's army, mute about his campaigns and who, with him, scarcely appreciated the tiny, courageous thrusts of Barrès' chin, a gesture he habitually made.[1] "He has stolen the tool," said Alain when to tweak him his pupils wrote on the blackboard a violent phrase from Barrès' *Déracinés*. The tool in question, of course, was the pen, not some warlike instrument. What did this kind of courage have to

---

1. Maurice Barrès (1862–1923), novelist, essayist, and politician, made a long personal journey from extreme egotism to mystical nationalism, which is reflected in his books and the causes—he was anti-Dreyfusard for example—he embraced.

do with the statesman Richelieu, half-dead, borne upstream along the Rhone River in a litter, forcing France's mightiest subjects to bow their heads to his master's royal will? This we shall never understand.

Anyhow, willpower was in style, and not only at the ENA. Around this time geography itself became willful. If I listen to Maurice Le Lannou, it has remained so. Everything sauced with will! At the final exams of ENA a parachute jump was part of the test, it helped rank a man. So too did judgments about employment which provided occasions, especially during these years, to judge a man's character. One of my old chums, then an important personage in the Tunisian government, told me that the director of ENA or the director of placement—I no longer remember which—came to find positions for his charges. He wanted the most inconspicuous positions for them: Tataonine, some godforsaken place of the Foreign Legion. Why not the stockade? It was necessary to explain to him that the graduates of the rue des Sts. Pères ran the greatest risks there, had the most dangerous adventures, and even suffered the most horrible outrages. So what! They would overcome. Everything is a question of willpower. In place of *Men of Good Will* men of willpower.

From the day after the competition for appointments, while waiting to do combat with others, they fought among themselves, for the obvious reason that the final tests were near (we should know better than to call it the moment of truth). Because of a half-point advantage one could become, from one day to the next, an aristocrat in the civil service with a personal functionary to announce visitors, or an indigent. "It was a dogfight," some, who remember with a shudder the months immediately before the ranking, have told me. Perhaps they exaggerate. Certainly there was nothing like the amiable atmosphere of the university exams, at least in my time, when the games were played strenuously, in public, to the unanimous applause of rivals, of which Pindar sings in his odes. But it is rather of Aristophanes we are reminded by so many sordid stories of how the future great personages are distinguished by delivering some low blow against their comrades. These men have forgotten nothing. When they speak among themselves, they think it prudent to keep silent on these matters. It would be even more prudent on my part to be still and not to generalize about the character of this new generation of functionaries. A few of my pupils, men of character, and not only bad character, have not been able to remain silent, and have resigned. Most of my pupils, men of character, and at times of monstrous character, have persevered.

The result of all this is an administrative caste, created to serve the state, which soon took over the state, subjecting it to its views, forming France in its image, or attempting to do so. It is not calumnies or hypotheses that I use in my indictment, but only citations from texts published at different times which say the same things, even with the same words that I use because these are the appropriate words. Seen from a distance and from the outside, this unanimity I here record is worth all the experiments I would be tempted to cite. If a few come to mind they serve to illustrate these texts, not replace them.

It all began early on, in a pleasant enough way, with some congeniality. There were no *apologia* or pamphlets, as would later be the case, but sketches of manners, chronicles, a novel. I hope the énarques will forgive me—they already have a great deal to forgive me—but it is *Le Grand dadais* of Bertrand Poirot-Delpech (1958) that seems to me to inaugurate this multiplication of texts and documents. "It was enough," the hero of the novel thought, "to enroll in the school for important administrators and to graduate near the top of the class. Everything else would take care of itself." Women, women, women. "Dozens of girls would be willing to scratch each other's eyes out to go to the movies with me. Of the one who went they would say, 'she is the date of one of the twenty top students.'" As a responsible textual critic, I chose this text about getting oneself invited to the movies as a kind of rare deviation, for it does not seem to conform to the facts. But everything else, the hero's delicious maladroitness, his innocence, his lack of information, seem perfect to me. "The school for important administrators." But of what school, young man, do you wish to speak? How far we are from the verities that should follow. My students at Sciences-Po, those from some fifteen years ago, helped me describe, in my book *Les Parisiens,* marriage in the faubourg St. Germain.[2] The marriage of their elders, not their own. Now they describe to me the changes wrought in nuptial strategies by ENA, which is no longer "the school for important administrators," without even taking into consideration several other novelties for which those interested are solely responsible.

At the balls given by families in the best neighborhoods, the mothers always sit together in one corner. But now instead of asking each other if a guest has money they ask if he or she has a "situation." The answer is that he or she is preparing the ENA or else that he or she has completed

2. Historically the residence of the aristocracy and now still a wealthy neighborhood with many of the old sumptuous aristocratic houses serving as government offices and departments.

the ENA. She as well as he, please note. This career is now the crown of a woman's life, the image formally used by those to sum up everything. A young *maître de conférence* at Sciences-Po who had just finished the ENA recently reproached a charming young woman, who had different ideas (and also some money), with "Mademoiselle, you have no ambition." She reported these words to me with astonishment.

From 1963–64 the texts are abundant. The speech of General de Gaulle to the Association of Alumnae, then the departure of the first director of the program, were occasions for the press to write about this "nursery of important state administrators." *L'Echo de la mode* itself. In a book published in 1963, *La Mystique du Plan,* Philippe Bauchard writes that "the ENA takes power." This is an important phrase that dates the fact. It tells us that the ENA did not have power yesterday or in the three or four preceding years. It also says that this power came suddenly, or at least that one had the impression of it happening suddenly, which seems to me precisely the case. One could count the old énarques on the fingers of one hand; and then, all at once, with numerous promotions, they were everywhere. Two or three years later the ENA's modest origins had been forgotten. They were firmly entrenched in power as if they had always been there. They were not so much in power, they *were* power, they were the "énarchie," a word to add to Montesquieu's list of political entities, an intermediary political force between the monarchy and the aristocracy, an aristocracy who aspired to monarchy although they incessantly proclaimed themselves a democracy, which some reproached them for not being. I only interpret the increasingly numerous texts which make the point. Two are especially important.

In November 1965, an issue of Pierre Mendès France's journal, *Le Courrier de la République,* carried an article entitled "*The Reign* of the Young Gentlemen" [La Règne des jeunes Messieurs]. I emphasize *The Reign.* The argument of this classic article is—and guided by Montesquieu's example I reproduce substantial extracts from it—that the connections between the administration and the state differ from what they were under the Fourth Republic. The administration has monopolized the state, that is to say the social milieu from which the administration is recruited has monopolized the state. The most important administrators now see themselves treated as indispensable collaborators, close to the decision-making power, sometimes even summoned directly to government councils. And this administration represents a social class, as is shown by the increased proportion in its ranks of the sons of directors of the administration, of members of the liberal professions, and more gen-

erally of the upper bourgeoisie of Paris. In place of an administration, in
the traditional sense of the word, we have created through new privileges
an administrative corps, an aristocracy of a few thousand young men
convinced that they are destined to maintain among themselves and for
themselves, the direction of the state and especially of its most prestigious
bureaucracies, as well as of other things that will be discussed later. The
second work in question is the pamphlet of Jacques Mandrin, *l'Enarchie,
ou les mandarins de la société bourgeoise* (1967), which posed the question of what kind of scoundrel hid behind the name of an honest man.[3]
Let us remember these mandarins, whom we shall often encounter. China
represents for us what Persia did in the eighteenth century, and our picture is as false as was theirs. In fact the mandarins resembled another
administrative corps: "the French administration is more or less," as
Michel Debré imagined, "like the empire of Philip II of Spain, on which
the sun never set." The new directors of the empire would be henceforth
chosen, almost without exception, from the énarques. The former pupils
of the ENA held (in 1967) seven of the eleven directorships in the Ministry of Finance. Of the twenty-nine ministerial offices, sixteen were con-
trolled by them. The only exceptions are the technical ministries, the
prefectorial corps, and perhaps also the foreign service. Still, the first
steps in the career of the énarques were not so impressive. To succeed in
a diplomatic post, at least at this time, one still needed imperfections
which one couldn't learn in the rue des Sts. Pères. The énarque who believed he had a vocation for diplomacy but lacked the gift for it or only
did it to please his wife, saw himself posted to Tirana. But wasn't Sten-
dhal the consul at Civitavecchia?

When these arguments were being made the énarques were everywhere. They had overcome all resistance. They had vanquished. The
ENA has become the school of schools. I see the proof of this in the fact
that more and more pupils at the rue d'Ulm passed the ENA exams,
presenting themselves along with candidates from the ENA. Whether the
polytechniciens choose to enter the ENA is their own concern. But that
the normaliens thought of this as a promotion, mooned over the ENA,
that the rue d'Ulm should be absorbed by the rue des Sts. Pères, that is
what surpassed understanding, especially for those of my generation who
saw the ENA rather as a demotion, a loss of status. To be able to open
Homer or Thucydides and read it off the page, and to end up in the ENA!

3. The author is punning on Mandrin, who was a celebrated bandit. The Mandrin here
is probably a pseudonym.

Of course I found some striking exceptions in the interwar period, some who even took a detour from the royal road that led from the school to literature by way of the Quai d'Orsay, "the school of the Quai," which was the case for Giraudoux and Mistler. I find these exceptions in the most austere administrative careers, in the most prickly men, which is not the norm at the Quai d'Orsay. It is very difficult to describe them. The beginnings of adult life is a theme for a novel. Let us imagine, a bit updated, a supplementary chapter in *Men of Good Will.* Once upon a time, in 1927, three of the most brilliant normaliens, and the jewels of the rue d'Ulm, decide to begin a career in the *Cour des comptes.*[4] They are completely uninterested in an administrative career in itself, they are the most unbureaucratic bureaucrats imaginable. They could readily produce a work of literature or philosophy, but they imagine nothing better than civil service. Richelieu would have loved them.

The court welcomes them with enthusiasm, or at least this is true of one of the most influential judges, delighted to see normaliens enter the rue Cambon. "To pass the exam you have only to read Allix's 1,200 page handbook, which for gentlemen like you is nothing." Actually some of the other judges are less enthusiastic. "If the normaliens prepare themselves to join our ranks what will become of our brothers-in-law?" It is thus that young men who had left a brilliant memory in *khâgne,* which is recorded in the annals of the qualifying exams, entered the rue Cambon.[5] Their schoolmates still tell about the exams in philosophy conducted by an extraordinary panel of examiners—Jean Baruzi, the expert on Leibniz and St. John of the Cross, Guéroult, the Descartes scholar—as though before Pascal and Descartes. One of these young men, responding to the question "What is the nature of thought?" suddenly stopped and exclaimed: "But this is the beginning of morality." This was a thunderbolt. I forgot what I was saying. At this time and a few years later, when I came to the rue d'Ulm, I occasionally saw a person of this kind seek a civil service career, but for noble motives, without losing any respect in the world, without being judged badly by his comrades, who expressed only a little surprise. It was the Cour des Comptes or a provincial high school: one could hesitate over the choice. The choice only troubled us when we learned, some years later, that our comrade Pompidou had taken a diploma at Sciences-Po without our knowing and without cele-

4. A French court with no American equivalent, specializing in financial matters.
5. The lycée class that prepares students for the Ecole Normale. *Khâgneux* are those enrolled in the class.

brating it, no doubt because he saw nothing to be proud of. We were a bit surprised. Sciences-Po! What a curious idea! I confess that even today I still find it hard to understand. That the polytechnicians went to ENA was not unusual. It was to be expected. It only proves the beginning of ENA omnipotence. But that normaliens should rush to the ENA en masse, shamelessly, without even feeling the least twinge of remorse, as did normaliens of my day when forced to write their exams for certification or to be licensed while sitting next to ordinary Sorbonne students, on the same benches, their privileged behinds rubbing against the common posteriors of others, thoroughbreds yoked to drays, this is what surpassed all understanding. Here is irrefutable proof of the growing importance of the ENA.

What is more serious still is not only that they are omnipresent, in major and minor positions, not only that they all know each other and are often on the friendliest terms, but that they resemble each other, as if cast from the same mold. Of course they have individual characteristics. It would be unreasonable to insist otherwise. Some are blonds, some brunettes; some fat, some thin; some chaste, some voluptuaries. But I do not have the impression that these natural differences have the same importance they had in the days when Alain explained the careers of his former pupils to the *Khâgneux* of the lycée Henri IV, as Socrates had explained the destiny of his young disciples, by the submission of the passions to the soul, the body to the spirit: "Mark my words," he seemed to warn them. They had much in common. A woman who sometimes fed them and knew them somewhat said: "When, talking among themselves, they say 'so-and-so is so unbelievably Quai d'Orsay, or so unbelievably Conseil d'Etat' I swear I cannot follow their allusions." I myself, going to say hello to a friend, at some council or court, am always surprised to run into, in the corridor or the library, some former pupil, completely ensconced, whom I thought worked elsewhere.

The énarques resemble each other, but how? We already get a glimpse of the answer. But it is better to return to the documents. Some of them appear impartial, scientific, and have been published as such in scientific journals, even enhanced sometimes, with statistics. The *Revue des Sciences politiques* itself, usually better inspired, devoted a bizarre issue (April 1964) to "the managerial class." Among other pearls of wisdom we find that compared to the "Sciences-Po" style the ENA style has "a more democratic and virile, but also less intellectual manner" and that "a neutral stance is cultivated, inspired by reading *Le Monde*. But the two are equally brilliant." This "equally" is worth its weight in confetti.

No less striking is the example of the brilliant *D'Etat et le citoyen,* published in 1962 by the Jean Moulin Club, a *De l'Esprit des Lois* about which no one will say that it is de l'esprit *sur* les lois. Here is another absurdity: "This is not an antiquated, inept administration devoted to red tape, but a muscular and dynamic one." Always these parachute jumps in the desert *"au peril de la mer."*

There is much more to be extracted from the critical texts already cited, whether pamphlets or accusations, while noting that political bias gets in the way of judgment and that the "young gentlemen" of today will soon become well-established gentlemen if political chance is favorable, the latter giving way to the former, who resemble them in everything essential. La Bruyère said, with a wicked tongue it is true, one is in a position of authority or one is not, and this fact makes all the difference between them. This doesn't prevent these harsh documents from telling the truth, even if the nature of politics skews the judgment, and I'm not so sure it does. If they exaggerate some details, among them the material interests we are considering, still these texts clarify the essential, above all what the word "technocrat" means, *énarchie* becoming the equivalent of technocracy.

Let me enumerate. First there is the control of the techniques or pretended techniques, which have nothing to do with Plato's *Technē* and are indeed its opposite. Then there is the power that comes with these techniques, thanks to the superstition perpetuated by the mystique of words and also thanks to the conviction of the self-interested: "Doubt troubles them less and less. The assurances of their elders and their own confidence convince them that it is sufficient to advance resolutely under the protection of their expertise" (*Cahiers de la République*). In *Le Point* (1975) Olivier Chevrillon, describing "the ENA, this Great Wall of China"—again this recurring comparison to China and its mandarin class—writes: "How often have I seen mayors, heads of unions, or CEOs mute with rage by the reception they received from an énarque? They expected, naively, an exchange of ideas: they got theology instead, shameless logic-chopping lessons on industry, unionism, or municipal administration."

There you have the essence: a system of belief masquerading as reason. Let us take a page from their book and talk about culture. Their culture, or what they call culture—never has there been so much talk about culture, writing about culture—is certitude. Rather than "all I know is that I know nothing," all they know is that they know something. They know what they have been taught, which has allowed them to succeed in what

they believe to be the most difficult of all competitive exams, the memory
of which makes them break out in a cold sweat, and they will cherish
their success until they die. They know what their masters taught them,
or rather those whose courses they took, distinguished economists, high-
flying technocrats, who were themselves convinced they knew something,
these popes of technocracy, as they are called, whose infallibility puts that
of the pope to shame. The infallibility of the popes of technocracy is
a certitude. They will never abandon their faith, whatever doubts arise.
Constant organization and development will continue. There is a cor-
relation between this development and what they call the quality of life.
At last comes Paris of the year 2000 which *Le Canard enchaîné* judged,
from a first glance, "Yet another stupid gamble."[6] How truly they spoke.
In sum this is a culture fixed once for all, certified with a diploma, tied
up like a dossier, sealed like a tomb. In that tomb is Paris.

6. A pun on *pari*, a gamble, which is pronounced the same as Paris, the city.

Chapter Six

Business

M. de B., I say to myself, is a man involved in big business and has important connections.

Abbé Prévost, *Manon Lescaut*

T HIS tomb recalls to mind another characteristic without which one cannot understand the disastrous history of Paris. This characteristic, or rather poisoned arrow, I found in the *Cahiers de la République*. "The young men become part of a network, the heirs apparent of their superiors in important public and private business." The énarques lending themselves to business? We have to seek further. The businesses in which they came to interest themselves were but, as they themselves were, the fruit of technocracy, grown on the same tree as they but a few years earlier. It was a fruit that might call to mind the tree of the knowledge of good and evil, although such terms are excessive, especially the former.

The Important Families

I N the years after World War II a new class replaced the old class of wealthy business executives. The new class, based on what, in the marvelous language of our times, is called "gray matter," was understood to be incompatible with the old business executives. Without even turning to Zola, who had a taste for the "decline of a family," the "degenerate heirs," we know from the most mundane experience that one is always surprised, meeting a descendant of an old family, when he is not a complete idiot. The theme of the inevitable decline of dynasties—from the genius creator followed, in order, by the debauché, the poet, and finally the cretin—is a novelistic conceit that opinion has ratified, and is always happy to discover (or rediscover) in the great books but especially in films and comic strips.

The war, defeat, occupation, collaboration, whose history Robert

Aron has written, destroyed the old ruling class. A number of business families were ruined or weakened. To this should be added the postwar crises, decolonization, the loss of fortunes dependent upon the empire—plantations, mines, ports, navigation companies. A bourgeois bound to the old business practices found himself ill-prepared for the new and vast possibilities opened up by the postwar economy, one into which a new generation of businessmen leaped, men who had learned in the United States how to take advantage of these opportunities. Few men succeeded, temporarily or permanently, during these years without having made this pilgrimage. One has only to read their biographical sketches, among other documents. In a recent trial that caused a stir, one of the principal defendants explained: "When I was twenty I went to America to study. There I learned the methods of commerce, I was introduced to the study of marketing and to all those concerns we today call *management*." The journalist adds: "M. certainly has the lingo." And for those who might not understand, he adds: "Marketing, in real estate as in everything else, consists, above all, in finding the catchy advertising that gets the public one wants to reach where it lives. The defendant was an expert in such matters." A trip to America was necessary for anyone who wanted to learn American techniques. The preceding example seems to indicate that—at least in a great many cases—these techniques were quite simple and that there was no need to travel so far to learn how to fool the public. Of course, I oversimplify. Usually this pilgrimage had other goals and aspects. Between 1950 and 1960 when one of my excellent pupils at Sciences-Po failed to enter the ENA, which was often the case with the most brilliant, I would help him get a scholarship for an American university that had a business school: "I do not know what you will learn there that is not already in La Fontaine, but at least you will be able to work in American business before starting a business of your own." A few have had enormous success, some surpassing those who outdid them at the ENA and even eventually employing them. Business, difficult at the outset, became easier and gave them the edge.

Business is the consumer society that we have treated above as a general economic phenomenon. Now let us return to the subject, examining it in the faces and the histories of the actors, those who have climbed to the top, or rather insinuated themselves, and who could people Balzac's *Comédie humaine*. One finds among them, at the outset, especially at the outset (things would go on by themselves later) some of those inventors of genius whom Balzac loved. Born into misery, or near-misery, virtually unknown in 1950 except in the rue Belleville or Montmartre where they went to school, they found themselves ten years later at the head of king-doms, sometimes empires—builders of businesses, that is, builders of the consumer society, which itself began at the same time. Alongside them, often more powerful than they were (although born a bit later) imitating them, following their example, using their recipe, were those from other kingdoms, other empires, who were anonymous. And behind them were the banks. For both types the goal was identical: conquering the market-place. In addition, the same salaried personnel worked for both. These up-and-coming directors, these managers as they were called, held the secret of making business take off, and knew that they could not be pro-moted unless their business succeeded, that they could advance only by improving business. The only chance for quick success was in the com-mercial sector, catering to needs, or better yet creating them, replacing one product with another, scarcely different (sometimes identical) but wrapped differently, in a timely fashion when sales slumped. Among these managers a great many, including those who were most successful, were self-made. This was especially true at the beginning. They were like those who employed them and employed them for this reason. They were products, like their employers, of the thousand and one perils of Paris, Balzacian characters, retaining an illusion of adventure, chance, freedom, in the enormous machine in which they were a cog. They were still street-wise, but most felt more strongly the influence of school, the great tech-nical school, the factory that made them, with diploma, or rather working papers, in their pocket. Then came the énarques, those who after having spent some years in state service went into business, which in the language of the Ecole Polytechnique is called "pantoufler."

The Revolving Door

I admit to being embarrassed in treating a practice that explains, in large part, the misfortunes of Paris. It is not that I fear that those involved would be able to recognize themselves in the most faithful por-traits, suffering as they do from a psychological trait that La Bruyère observed long ago in those he scarcely treated with indulgence: deafness, blindness, indifference, aloofness, arrogance, or as the popular writers say "uncommunicativeness," that comes from their social status. In a word, social snobbery. Rather my embarrassment is because there is little chance that I can today correctly describe, even by reading the writers who deal with the phenomenon, something I have never understood very clearly. Writing the word "pantouflage" I recall the astonishment, better yet the disgust that I felt when I heard, immediately after the war, a young polytechnician tell me, with admiration, of one of his older friends who, he said, had "pantouflé." I had never heard this word in the rue d'Ulm. What was he trying to say? I pictured Anatole France in old age in his dressing gown, like a potato in its jacket, with carpet slippers [pantoufles], near the fireplace, rheumatic, with his cane and his herbal teas. This is the pampered life, the cocooned life. "A people seeking a fat belly, carpet slippers, of course. Their back to the fireplace, their belly against the table, the ideal of Béranger and M. Prudhomme," as Larbaud says. "At 9 o'clock," writes Mme de Sévigné, "November 2, 1673, the abbé de Grignan . . . entered my room to chat intimately [*raisonnée pantoufle*]." The image seems to me hardly elevated. A strange kind of ambition at age twenty! Surely the dictionary would clarify this: "*pantouflage,* slang of the *Grandes Ecoles:* to leave public service to enter the private sector, paying an indemnity, if necessary, for interrupting one's service, is called "pantoufle.'" The dictionary even cites Daninos (*Un certain M. Blot*): "Many of them were *Polytechniciens* who, having quit public service, *pantouflent* in insurance." It remains to explain what images—and this is the most important—what sentiments, what part of one's self one attributes to the word at different historical times. When Balzac used it, he always associated it with the sense of ruse. In *Le Député d'Arcis,* for example: "Philéas . . . earned . . . each year, a sum equivalent to that of his expenses, beyond the interest from his capital, in turning his métier into a kind of retirement [*pantoufle*], to use a proverbial expression." Is this what is generally done today and especially by énarques?

Recent texts provide little help. Perhaps they even add to my embarrassment by the annoyance I believe I can see in them. Maybe it's a simple illusion, a spontaneous reaction completely normalienne. Yet it seems to me that, with the énarques, I don't find this sense of the word—ease, satisfaction, complete innocence, a clear conscience—which is clearly there in the polytechnicien's use of it and in the polytechnicien's description of the practice. One could say that the shift from public service to the private sector is not necessarily natural as it now manifests itself among the énarques (but no longer the polytechniciens). It has the appearance of posing some subtle problems which are familiar to the scientific normaliens who, already in my day (in small numbers, it is true), worshiped the Golden Calf. I still remember, just after the war, one of my masters at the rue d'Ulm confessing to me, with a red face, that his son, my school chum, had gone into business. He had the appearance of the noble father in a melodrama who saw the comfort of his old age, the hope of his house, mount the scaffold. The hurt is even more obvious when the text that tries to explain such events is as inept and maladroit as the wretched article I read recently in the *Revue des Sciences politiques:* "They are certainly less resistant to the pressures of private gain than their elders." Or when an appeal is made to noble sentiments, to the well-known selflessness of some: "I don't know anyone who would hire themselves for a quarter of the salary they could earn in the private sector." The fact is evident, but this "I don't know anyone" is still extraordinary. Obviously the subject is delicate.

Trying to understand the differences between the practices of yesteryear and today and convinced, because of the difficulty, that they are important, I turn to a great public servant of long experience, who like those of his time knew the classics and his own language. Listening to him I can hear a more indulgent La Bruyère, a less corrosive Balzac. How were things done formerly? There was always, needless to say, the great man with a passion for public service, proud to embody the grandeur and authority of the state, which was at times the expression of his own will to power. Such is the public servant Richelieu describes. "The great personality," "the superior being," to speak like Balzac, who reserves these words for important occasions. We are speaking of a man who "prefers," as Cicero says, "to command those who have money rather than to have it himself" (I take the quotation from Pierre Escoube, *Les Grands Corps de l'Etat* [1974]). To echo *Les Caractères* there was or there is, for example, the director of the treasury who tells himself that one or another of his comrades will seek him out to arrange a loan, to get financial assistance, and that he will make him cool his heels in the waiting room. Then there were those who passed quickly from state service to private service. It doesn't matter which lists of the important *corps* we use to get an idea (that of the inspector of finances, for example), of how this was accomplished through promotion. As for the reasons given, it is easy to imagine them. It suffices to compare the words used by men today with those of their ancestors. Whether they speak or write—and they write a good deal—the latter always have state service on their lips; even if they go from state service to private service, it is to serve the state better. One thinks of Valentine Tessier explaining to Pierre Renoir (in Marcel Achard's comedy) that if she has deceived him it was only to give him additional proof of love. Men of an earlier generation explain things by simple, very natural reasons, or by drollery: "You forget, my wife's fur coat." Witticism for witticism, I prefer the fur coat to state service.

If you use historical example we leave our own times.
                                                          Balzac, *La Maison Nucingen*

I T would seem that this practice did not have the importance in the first years after World War II—without going back to the Third Republic—that it would later have. It did not play an essential rule. One could examine and treat in depth an important economic problem, for example, consider the politics of provisioning or the organization of Paris, without alluding to these matters, or hardly at all and from a different angle. They counted much less than other practices which attracted attention, which burdened descriptions, which unleashed passions, and in these days no longer interest even the satirists.

This is the impression one gets from rereading, after more than fifteen years, the book on *Les Groupes de pression* [*Pressure Groups*], which Jean Meynaud, then a professor at rue St. Guillaume and an economist specializing in financial questions, was working on in the mid-fifties. At that time we sometimes spoke together about Paris problems and especially about les Halles. Rediscovering this book, published in 1958, I rediscovered my memories and compared the ideas I then had (as well as those of others), with the way these questions were treated some years later.

Enumerating the various kinds of pressure or influence, an American expression that first appeared in France and whose meaning needed clarification, Meynaud referred to the practice I am discussing here, but he attached less importance to it than to other facts. Of principal importance for him was the identity of the social origins of the great functionaries, the directors of private enterprise, and the heads of certain unions. The same milieu made the functionaries of the state more receptive to the requests of their representatives. Worldly relationships play a role, as Alain taught: chaste philosophers and radical thinkers ought to beware of beautiful women, perfumed and corrupting. Otherwise it was a question of political milieux rather than administration. The deputies, the ministers, directly or indirectly influenced by their entourages, by their chief advisers, by directors of *bureaux* drawn from the corps of engineers, that is, those who attended the same schools as the captains of industry; or by members of their staffs that they had not selected with enough care, as several scandals of the Third and Fourth Republics make clear.

Scandal? In the final analysis it is in this light that the influence of private interests on politics was analyzed. There are scandals like a thunderclap and those that begin meanly, nastily, and crawl along ignominiously. "Qui vole un oeuf. . . ." [1] Things often begin like this. An invitation to lunch, the Pied de Cochon gambit, which was occasionally discussed by the Municipal Council, but as something to laugh about. Councilors or department heads let themselves be wined and dined by those anxious to obtain some favor, or sometimes with no other idea than to eat well in good company, to have a good time. When they reached for their wallet, there was the envelope left on the table or slipped into a hand at the end of a visit or a copious meal. This happened not at a meal in les Halles, in the joyous les Halles, debonair and nonchalant (unfortunately for les Halles), but in one of those restaurants in the fancy neighborhoods that cater to business, veritable institutions with well-established reputations. Here one can encounter a political adversary, and much more. One would have to be a fool or a shrewd reader of Machiavelli—irreconcilable hypotheses—to go to such places. A city councilor, a director of the prefecture, even the prefect of the Seine could be seen at a table in les Halles in the company of the most crooked merchant without being accused of compromising himself. It is not the same for certain restaurants, closed or inaccessible to mere mortals, with rooms hung in plush and with deep-cushioned chairs, which automatically classify their clients.

When the INED was not far from the Champs-Elysées, which made the study of demography more attractive, there was such a restaurant in the neighborhood. Drinking my cup of coffee not far from the place, I one day overheard an inexperienced waiter telling of being sacked for having asked a table of important diners if they wanted anything else at precisely the moment when they should not have been disturbed for any reason. I thought, hearing the poor fellow lament, of the story Tardieu told about the terrible Mandel asking a deputy: "And what did you say to him when he gave you this check?" And the deputy sputtered, "I . . . thanked him." Some accept the check, others refuse it (not without a sharp physical recoil), if they are young functionaries being offered their first bribe. Abellio, a polytechnicien, tells such a story. Anyhow, the theme of the check should not be overlooked. Believing he had covered everything about the national markets in a presentation at the rue St. Guillaume, a pupil was asked by his teacher (who told me the story) if he hadn't forgotten something.

1. "A man who will steal an egg will steal a cow," is the French saying.

This is, nevertheless, insignificant, and thus is it considered. "Most deputies and political parties have difficulties at the end of the month," Jacques Fauvet writes in *La France déchirée* (1957). The same year Meynaud noticed the same thing, and it is not just coincidence. Well, it's not worth making a fuss about, as the saying goes. Or put another way, there isn't enough for a scandal; or rather, what we today call a scandal was formerly an "affaire." "It is terrible what a scandal the 'affaire' of the poisons has caused," writes Mme de Sévigné. She thus helps us clarify a distinction that still exists. It is the "affaire" of the poisons that creates scandal, the "affaire" of Marie Antoinette's necklace. "And don't you see," Pascal pleads in *Les Provinciales,* "what a scandal it would be to surprise a priest in such a state, in such a disreputable place, clothed in his religious habit?" An example one doesn't want to be a part of. What about the Panama "affaire," "a scandal carried out with panache," as Léon Daudet says, in his *Vie orageuse de Clemenceau.* What about the Stavisky "affaire." In our own time we speak of scandal rather than "affaire," and this change has significance.

When the trial of the CNL [Comptoir national du Logement] began, in the spring of 1963, *Le Canard enchaîné* asked, as did many others, what was this tale from another time, this scandal (or seeming scandal), which they performed every day, as if it was the most natural thing in the world, operations which, if they were not what we would call scandals, were certainly scandalous. "We see a promoter purchase, for 100 million old francs, a piece of land not zoned for construction. Soon this promoter, thanks to his connections and some bribes, gets the desired permits for construction and the land is sold, for 400 million old francs, to a real-estate group whose founder is our promoter. Such practices remaining perfectly legal two years after the scandal of the CNL, one asks what was the use of the trial. . . ." To express myself in the language of psychoanalysis or religious psychology, I would say that it is a question of what the ancients called a rite of passage, a kind of propitiatory sacrifice, or simply a sacrificial lamb. A sacrificial lamb that I rediscover in La Fontaine in the guise of an ass: "The ass comes in his turn and says: I remember, while passing a field belonging to the monks, my hunger, the temptation, the tender grass, and I thought (what devil tempted me): I cropped this field. I had no right to do so, since I must speak frankly. At these words they indignantly denounced the ass. . . . Eat someone else's grass, what an abominable crime!"

Henceforth these things will be legally done, in the way *Le Canard enchaîné* explains, whether or not there are enormous bribes, with their old importance. The word has aged. "It is a faithless man who grabs with both hands—and doesn't sign without at least a bribe [pot-de-vin]." This is Regnard, but it could just as well be Balzac or Zola. It is an old expression we already miss, partly because of the importance of wine itself, as it should be, and also because of the services for which a pot-de-vin paid. Their enumeration, when one rediscovers them in the newspapers of the postwar years, in the pamphlets or in the books that speak of this time, gives joy even to the teetotaler. These were innocent practices which could not possibly have any consequences, cause any great harm. Paris hardly suffered from them. In a 1953 book, *Crise du pouvoir et crise du civisme,* Paul Delouvrier describes the pursuit of information, "the constant efforts of various groups to be informed at once, not only about projects, but of the intentions of decision-makers." Clearly if one buys land it is important to know whether Paris will expand toward Puteaux or Boissy-St. Léger. "The need for fast information," Delouvrier continues, "has raised indiscretion to the level of an industry or even a national institution." If we believe La Fontaine, indiscretion is essentially feminine. "Never confide in a woman. . . ." More important, never confide the direction in which Paris is going to expand. Not even to your secretary. Whatever her age, some promoter will eventually send some hired Don Juan to speak to her about love. If need be, he'll go himself, this adolescent of real-estate promotion, not being without the ability, at least in these heroic times. Such anecdotes surface periodically in the newspapers. They are not unique to this or that period.

Finally, the Parisian who attentively reads his newspaper believes in the composite story of the faithful collaborator suddenly swept away by middle-aged desires or devoured by the flames of an autumnal passion. But there is no reason why the weaker sex should enjoy this privilege. If I believe Balzac, who was much interested in such cases—and the documents of his time provide testimony—the contrary is more frequent and more to be feared: the demons of the flesh, if one can speak thus, causing the greatest ravages to some important personage rather than some secretary who has reached the onset of middle age and become a little crazy. This is not just the stuff of novels. Why do special-interest groups go to so much trouble to get information, sifting through wastepaper baskets, seducing middle-aged women? Why should they make an effort to win over the public authorities, using those pressure tactics that were described in the mid-fifties, since at around the same time one finds essentially the same men in and out of government, this being the most natural thing in the world and for the greatest good of the state. As the author of the article in the *Revue des Sciences politiques* dealing with an important administrator said, in all simplicity: "Among the directors of important projects in the private sector, public directors find reflected their own interests in expansion and modernization. Generally hostile to traditional family businesses, even the largest, they naturally prefer firms where the decision-making power is in the hands of the managers. More concerned with increasing production than in its distribution, they consider capitalist profit legitimate because it drives expansion." This is exactly the accusation of Pierre Mendès-France: the énarque serving private enterprise considers himself and is considered as serving the public good. More to the point, Pompidou, in *le Noeud gordien,* gave them his blessing. If they left public service for the private sector, the fault lay with the state. Otherwise they went back and forth from one sector to the other, without one knowing precisely, at any given moment, where they were and where they were not; without knowing if the moment when they seemed to be *here* was not the precise moment when they were *there*. An elusive game of musical chairs but not difficult to see through.

How does all this relate to Paris, which I have never lost sight of, and how can we talk about Parisian authorities and the choices they have made? "The Fifth Republic," Mendès-France writes, "is increasingly and proportionally dangerous to the degree that she convinces the most influential part of the public sector and the private sector to join forces for the systematic exploitation, like a recirculating fountain, of French politics." And Parisian politics most particularly. Already during the Fourth Republic, and again especially in Paris, things began to be like this, things and men. As to the particular moment, however, I do not have direct knowledge. Nor of the men who thought they were calling the tune. At least that is how it seems to me as I try, today, to recapture those years.

PART THREE

POWER AND CHOICES

With no more ado each of them got a piece of the pie. What I
think I make out here is the image of a town.
La Fontaine, *Le chien qui porte a son cou le diner de son maître.*

"THEY want to demolish St. Germain-l'Auxerrois to align a street
or a *place;* one day they will destroy Notre-Dame in order to
enlarge the parvis; some day they will raze Paris to broaden the
plaine des Sablons" (Victor Hugo, *Choses vues*). This was in 1831. From
nothingness to nothingness, by way of nonexistence, as quickly as possible. For the greater good of the plaine des Sablons, the land bordering
the Bois de Boulogne. For Hugo this meant complete obliteration, a desert, a black hole, La Defense or Parly 2, or whatever new city (the name
doesn't matter, so much do they resemble each other in their existence or
nonexistence). From nothing to nothing and nothing in between. Zero
total. Zero plus zero is always zero.

This is perhaps to oversimplify and to move too quickly. "Some day,"
says Hugo. That is, the day when circumstances might be favorable or,
better yet, when authority, whoever or whatever it may be, judges that
circumstances are favorable, that the hour has come for the plaine des
Sablons. When that day comes everything is ready and waiting. The great
beneficiaries will be the architects whom Hugo held in absolute contempt, comparable only to the contempt we have for the promoters and
developers. There are those who have nothing to gain from the matter
but who are attracted by the Sablons. All is ready and waiting, as for the
sacrifice of Iphigenia: "The army and the winds of Neptune." The winds
and Neptune: everything is ready.

Neptune above all, if we can thus baptize the powers that be, bedeck-
ing them with a beard made of wind, hair of algae and clouds, and carrying a trident. Neptune rather than the favorable or unfavorable winds,
whose caprice is not important and does not much affect the decisions of
the gods. To return to earth, it seems that the gods, in the years here

141

under consideration, were not agreed among themselves. Their power was feeble, illusory, contested, always ephemeral, and they also had too many irons in the fire at once so that Paris was the least of their concerns. They were minor gods. Paris was not so badly treated by them.

Such is my memory of the final years of the Fourth Republic, so old in my mind but also so young, as young as the Trojan War sung by Homer or by Racine, or even by Giraudoux. It is true that Giraudoux's republic was the Third, ours is the Fourth, but as far as the relationship between Paris and the state, there is little difference. The state was as "powerless" in his time as in ours: Giraudoux need not have troubled himself. This was the way I looked at things at the time. I don't look at them much differently today, despite all the political science—constitutional, administrative, institutional—and all the Dalloze's of the world who would insist otherwise. I make the easy judgments of the traveler without baggage.

In truth, as I evoke those years, administrative exactitude does not torment me more than at the time when I settled in the Hôtel de Ville and began accumulating these experiences, these anecdotes from which come my words, these impressions from which, bit by bit, there emerges an interpretation so simple that many, more learned, will find it simplistic. How much science, how much political and administrative experience might have been needed and how much would one need to identify and judge correctly, to know and recognize with discernment who was responsible and what were the responsibilities of the authorities, as people say. The authorities? At the sound of this all-powerful word official pomp is manifest. The red carpet is rolled out in front of the steps of the Hôtel de Ville under a canopy, the kind that is proper for a bourgeois wedding and that does not match the stature of some of the great of this world. Green plants are unloaded from trucks, along with those uncomfortable chairs of gilded wood, which are, alas, unbreakable. Then there is the crowd, held back behind barriers which were formerly made of wood and are now iron, gazing at the backsides of the horses of the Republican Guard, trying to attach a name to the faces before them, or if not a name at least a title, a function, even though this title would say nothing and mean nothing. They were often wrong, mistaking the neighborhood police chief for the prefect of the Seine, the prefect of the Seine for the prefect of police, a university dignitary in robes of I don't know what color, for the papal nuncio. By minimizing the uniform and concentrating on the face, television, which is always pernicious, has begun to eliminate these confusions which gave our fathers pleasure. They have undermined the old Parisian theme which caricature, until recently, made its bread and butter. Thank God, some of it survives. Seen from the crowd, an official procession always gives the spectator great pleasure. Even when they get lucky and win over media techniques, they make a lot of mistakes, unless television itself is the cause of these mistakes. The crowd still deceives itself a good deal. But this has little importance. The public is the first to be aware of it; it recognizes, without rhyme or reason; it puts the wrong hats on the wrong people knowing full well that it is mistaken 75 percent of the time. But it persists, for it enjoys the spectacle, takes pleasure in recognizing, rubbing against, being near something powerful, no matter what that power, no matter how minor it is and no matter what is closest to hand that represents it, a hat or a pant-cuff, or simply the pleasure of shouting as if it were the night of July 14: "Oh la belle rouge! Oh la belle verte!" [responding to the fireworks].

I have been and continue to be a part of this innocent admiration inherited from the ancien régime or the Middle Ages, an onlooker who fools himself and is not overly troubled by this, who rather takes some pleasure in it, as the mark of good Parisian health. Long live Jehan Dumoulin, the touching scoundrel of *Notre-Dame de Paris,* the brother of the bad priest! Curled up on one of the window ledges of the Palais de Justice, among some of his disreputable kind, what pleasure he takes in identifying, without reason or justice, the high and mighty personages as they appear, losing himself willingly in their titles, tossing them like a salad but never losing sight of the essential: the face, the character, the gestures, the badinage—about these things he is not wrong, never deceives himself.

I will therefore set aside the administrative analysis that anyhow I would be incapable of providing and hold myself to the essential, to what then seemed to me, and still seems to me today, at least for those first years and before the mechanisms that I am about to decry were set in motion, which I did not discover—nor did others—until much later. Whatever the details, political matters were done in such a way that without distinguishing the greatest good from its own good, which usually worked, Paris avoided the greatest evils. A certain beneficial impotence appears, in hindsight. We ought to have regretted much more than we did in those years when we often made ourselves miserable over something that in retrospect was worthy of celebration. What we had was a Third Republic, prolonged into the Fourth Republic, which found the means to return in another form, with another constitution, under another guise, with different men, or with men who seemed different but who, at bottom, were the same. In any case in these matters, at least in Paris, whatever the regime may be, a man in power is always a man in power. This observation would be banal if it were not Alain who inspires my judgment today as he did in an earlier time. Ignoring institutions and even usage or habit, making serious mistakes—which included parking my car on the sacrosanct spot reserved for the prefect's car, and consequently being reviled and cast out into the hell of the parking space in front of the Hôtel de Ville—I then quite naturally applied to things Parisian (and continue to do so), concepts from the past. I reflect on the inherited power of my masters and of their masters who transmitted the lesson. It is saying too much to say I "applied" concepts. I saw things in this way and could not do otherwise.

Chapter Seven

Those in Power

In memoriam

T HE man who had power over Parisian affairs at this time was the prefect of the Seine. That is what Parisians thought. The prefect of the Seine is like any other minister except, perhaps, the minister of the interior, a bogeyman who inspires some fear even in the most virtuous men. To confirm this it is enough to reread the great Parisian novelists, especially Balzac, who best understood these things, or to take an imaginary poll, or, more simply, to question people, those who know their city well, taxi drivers for example, or to use one's own recollections. The minister is an abstract being who is spoken about (we know him vaguely from the newspapers); he lives in a distant palace, across the river, a palace whose location we know little about, and we confuse him with his ministerial neighbors, those of agriculture and education, in the rue Bellechasse and the rue Varenne, respectively: go and look for them! The offices of the Council (of Paris) are easily confused with a ministry or an embassy! Sometimes the taxi drivers themselves get lost, as did formerly the coach drivers of *Père Goriot*. Only the most cultivated know where this or that hotel is: "To the hôtel Beauséant. 'Which one?' says the coachman. A sublime word that confounds Eugene." How many Parisians know that the Ministry of Justice is in the Place Vendôme, and would even imagine it in so lovely a location? People know where the Elysée Palace is, but they don't know very precisely where the other branches of government are, and sometimes they mistake the Place Beauvau (that is to say, the Ministry of the Interior) for an annex to the Elysée Palace. This is a serious error.

The prefect of the Seine exists in a way the prefect of police does not exist (with the exception of a few celebrated prefects of police whom the Parisians still remember). This is explained, no doubt, by a material fact, by the real grandeur of the Hôtel de Ville, which is visible to all who see

145

it, which perpetuates the significance of the institution and the man who represents it at the moment. Everyone knows the Hôtel de Ville is the prefect's home, where he has his office, where one is sure of finding him. Everyone knows which windows, sometimes lit up long into the night, are his, while no one knows very clearly where the prefect of police has his office. We know where police headquarters is, but not where the prefect is. For Parisians the prefect of the Seine holds the power in Paris. More to the point, he incarnates this power. He is the power.

He is also for me, as for all Parisians, the one who articulates this power. I have an advantage here for I have known the man who was probably the last prefect of the Seine, Emile Pelletier. All the intelligence and charm of his successor, Benedetti, and the friendly atmosphere surrounding him could not mask the decline of the institution that set in with the Fifth Republic. As for Benedetti's successor, he was nothing but a man who carried out orders or rather who saw projects through and who acted only as an administrator. It was at this time that I left the Hôtel de Ville, or decamped, or disappeared, or was driven out, I no longer know. The nature of my views of Parisian affairs after my departure have been bookish, or picturesque, seen from the angle of an outsider, which is perhaps not myopic, but no longer from the Hôtel de Ville, where I never again set foot.

We are talking here about the final years of the Fourth Republic and of the power the prefect then had, and thanks to him, through him, of the power of the prefect of the Seine itself, which existed throughout its long history.[1] The prefects were independent of regimes, whoever might be at their head, and whatever their character, their work, their luck (or their bad luck), whatever memory they might leave behind (the most forgotten sometimes having been the best, the most useful).

Theirs was a unique power, difficult to understand even for those who knew the documents and could cross-examine them. To see this clearly, those just passing through have it explained to them, at the prefect's table, for example, during a coffee break, which is a good time for meetings. Or another way is that of a certain American senator more interested in the facts, however, few, than in documents: "No, no, don't interpret for me. The alleged lucidity of the French language creates the greatest obscurity. Tell me about it." This is what I myself would say. At the outset I remind the reader that the prefect represents the executive

1. A history whose beginnings Jean Tulard recounts in his great (and handsome) book, *Paris et son administration (1800–1830).*—Author.

power and that his authority is only an emanation of that of the state. Still, to this power conferred by the state and which, from one day to the next may be taken back, another is joined, which comes from different sources, mysterious yet beyond dispute, which makes the prefect the representative of the city less by the force of law than by circumstance, sometimes in opposition to the former power itself, but formidable, jealous, suspicious, and intolerant.

It is with this power that we must begin, this power visible on the horizon from those palaces in the rich neighborhoods that the prefect can almost see by leaning out his window and looking up the Seine. One must begin with the Lion. Thus he was dubbed by Alain making a commentary on La Fontaine. The old lion? The sick lion? This is unimportant: it is still the lion, the redoubtable king of beasts, with his fearsome claws, who considers everything his domain, who wants to dominate everything. And he has his lioness, sometimes more than one. And his lion cubs as well. His ministers are lions in their own right who have their own lionesses and cubs. There is an entire leonine society, roaring and difficult to manage, which says it speaks and commands in the name of the Lion. When the night is silent, les Halles not having yet begun their tumult, what distant and menacing roars does the wind blowing from the west sometimes carry to the ears of the sleeping prefect. From the heights of the Latin Quarter one hears the groans of the stuffed lions of the Jardin des Plantes. From the prefecture one hears the host of ministers and a crowd who cry out, who are disquieting to the prefect, who knows them well. Did he not come from among them, is he not still one of them? Alas, he will perhaps rejoin them one day, sooner than he might wish, in some bureaucratic cage, if in the meantime someone has not taken his place.

The ministers have only too many occasions to get involved in the affairs of Paris. Some of them, as they say in administrative parlance, because of their "attributions," some because they insist on it or simply intrude, thrusting a paw into their neighbor's territory, into that of the Parisians. And not without having their eye on the choicest morsel. This is how the lion behaves, not so much on his own initiative—he has other things to do—as on the prompting of his lioness, goaded by some Parisian incident, by some common disagreement, by who knows what, which she considers intolerable. This at least is what wicked tongues say, for example, attributing the idea of a Right Bank expressway—but here I am confusing regimes by anticipation—to one such woman outraged at having missed her train from the gare de Lyon and complaining about it to her husband, in the manner of the first act of *La Reine morte:* "My lord, I have a complaint. . . ." Is this true or false? Even the falsity is probably not far from the truth. Let us therefore say it is true. Otherwise, as is apparent, all this is fable, imitating La Fontaine or Alain.

As a good radical Alain did not despise the lion, not the real lions—Caesar, Alexander, Napoleon—the lions who founded the Third Republic or won the First World War, like Clémenceau, with his rugged tenacity. Nor did he despise the lioness. Alain believed in the wisdom of women, in their taste, and the history of Paris gave him good reason. Not only because it belongs to another epoch is my example of a Right Bank expressway ill chosen. The beauty of Paris owes a good deal to the feminine temperament whose discernment was not perhaps exemplary but who, in questions of taste, were unquestionably lionesses. More dangerous are ministerial offices and the pretentious functionaries who infest them. The prefect often has to defend them before an exasperated Municipal Council. If Alain was apprehensive about the polytechnicians, he did not even take seriously Sciences-Po, where he saw only jugglers, in the true sense of the word; men whose principal talent, along with those essential to success, was knowing how to juggle, how to dance like a prize-fighter. For a normalien, knowing how to dance was unthinkable, as one saw at the school ball, even though it only involved the *sévriennes,* who also couldn't dance.[2] But, if we are to believe the records of the municipal debates, the énarques—having replaced Sciences-Po and beginning to invade these offices and soon afterwards be attached to the prefecture of the Seine—are not even dancers on this order. They have, and it is very unfortunate, other ideas. These ideas affect Paris, and we must look at them. We have seen some of this in what has already been said. Now we come to the offices of the ministers, that is, to the department heads, often important personages, and the functionaries serving under their order, all those who, having been there longer than the ministers, know more than they and, because of this fact, in some cases have more power. It sometimes happens that the prefect of the Seine, representing the executive branch of government, might be charged by this or that minister to bring some project to conclusion for which he has no enthusiasm, or even of which he disapproves. It might be a project that he knows will, moreover, provoke identical reactions among his own col-

2. Formerly the ENS was separated by gender: the rue d'Ulm was for boys, the Ecole de Sèvres for girls, called sévriennes.

laborators, his own staff, in the city administration itself, and finally among the Parisians.

Even before 1958, the majority of the projects most destructive to the Parisian urban fabric were of this kind, outside projects, set in motion in this way, imposed. The minister wanted it, the prefect wanted it. The prefectorial administration itself had to want it, was obliged to do the work, in cooperation with the ministerial staffs (I don't very clearly understand how) on projects the opposite of those they themselves were interested in, to do the contrary of what they had always done and what they thought appropriate, for technical and other reasons and often compelled to destroy what they had always wanted to protect. If I am to judge these things by the people I have known, whatever might be their original training (even polytechniciens), their career, their rank, their competence and qualities of mind, the personnel of the city brought to the study of Parisian problems not only rare abilities that stand in contrast with so many fantastic proposals, technically unworkable, that came out of some ministerial desk drawer, but also experience, taste, an active vigilance, I would even say a love which has always seemed to me incomprehensible to outsiders. But I suppose that in this Paris is like other great world capitals. I have heard competent administrators in New York, as devoted to the skyscrapers as a hen to her chicks, complain bitterly about projects forced upon the city. It is possible that in Paris this civic attachment could be even more intense, the caretakers more meticulous—"How much trouble has this dear head cost me!"—the fear of doing damage and doing the wrong thing even greater. There are a number of reasons. One is location. The Hôtel de Ville is in the heart of the city, penetrated by the city. One enters the Hôtel de Ville through open, unlocked doors, as one does a department store. It is not like this in the rue Barbet de Jouy where the district administration will have its offices. In this aristocratic neighborhood (the Seventh arrondissment), elegant in its melancholy, not far from the bishop's palace, next to foreign embassies and the Ministry of Agriculture, everything will be different. But in the years I am thinking about the offices of the city were still in the Hôtel de Ville, not in the avenue Morland building. Everything and everyone was mixed together, the general population, the administration, the councilors, those who could not be easily classified, down to the sparrows of Paris who hopped about on the sparse lawn. This created an extraordinary concentration of information, and even more precious, a sensitivity to the city which eventually won over even the most resistant, a sharpness of perception that affected even the most myopic. The exchange of ideas was complete and free. When the newspapers began to speak of a Right Bank expressway, I one evening saw an important administrator pinned to the wall of a corridor by a hefty woman who looked to me like a cleaning woman, her work finished, about to leave for the day, adding this little footnote: "You have no shame. . . ."

In this sensitivity to Paris even the poetry of Paris plays a role. It is sometimes in the very heart of the Hôtel de Ville. It even sometimes happens, and this is the most extraordinary thing, that the city supports, with its own money, a functionary who has almost nothing to do except praise the city, if he is moved to do so, although the city is not obliged to have or employ such a person. Should it happen that there are several such they could form a kind of troubadours' "court of love." I have never heard of American writers employed full-time by the city of New York. It is true that the movies, which feed American writers well, fill their leisure time, while the poets of skyscrapers, anxious for the apocalypse, seem to belong to a damned species. But Paris has had Verlaine . . . Jehan Rictus . . . Charles-Louis Philippe . . . and less disquieting, Albert Samain, among many others. So many charming writers who, beyond the fact of having spent some time in the offices of the city, all resemble each other in manner: they love the streets, the art of sketching, having the ability to do other things, and write a poetry that is both light and serious, like Villon's. These verses of their colleague Verlaine sum them up perfectly: "Bibi Purée / Astonishing type / And so droll," and especially "I idolize François Villon / But how can I be him?" And what does one do in the meantime? One follows one's calling honestly. Need I add that these amiable writers are not in any way Stakhanovites. But does that term fit better those who are not writers? And perhaps without being as useful to Paris as these useless children of Verlaine and Villon. I have known a few of them, functionaries at the Hôtel de Ville during the years I am writing about obliged to undertake (sometimes because of me), incredible statistical labors, veritable punishment, which they carried out with complete cheerfulness. Incredible tasks? I am mistaken. There are no statistics concerning the city that don't have their charm. The figures for the consumption of flour have the perfume of warm bread and a flaky morning croissant. National statistics are often indigestible: not those of Paris.

It is no less true during these years that the way power was wielded, in general and in the various ministries, was not what it would eventually become. Certainly power is always power. There is no minister who is not tempted to use it. If he was reluctant his entourage would push him to do so. Power corrupts, said Alain. Still, before 1958, even the minister had many fewer means of corruption. Perhaps his own power was limited; perhaps another minister had another idea and countervailed what he had decided, which in turn let those who were not in agreement to play off the minister who said white against the minister who said black. Perhaps there wasn't enough time to decide, or it was equally possible to play off the minister in power against his successor, who might see things differently.

It is impossible to talk about Paris without evoking the history of the Fourth Republic, that vast disorder, that great confusion of men among which a number of them were remarkable, often more remarkable—I speak here of certain big talents—because formed in a hard school, than those we would later see. The prefect of the Seine, although an agent of political power himself, disposed of a power that was more formidable in proportion to the weakness of the power he represented. In addition, he was certain to last longer than the head of government who had appointed him. Obviously, this was not without some risk. Some sudden, unexpected shift of authority, an inexplicable change, a violent change, a political tempest, a disgrace whose victim would be the last to discover the cause—the prefect would be asking himself how it happened until the day he died. I have always thought that a prefectorial career was the worst calling and I have always counseled my most brilliant pupils against it, providing them with proofs. How many times have I unfolded for them this discouraging spectacle of injustices, hazards, settling of accounts, this uncertain battle, this sacrifice of brave men, this administrative Iliad where the Greeks, treacherous, mediocre, and pusillanimous, almost always end up triumphing over the brave and loyal Trojans, my students.

The prefect of the Seine in his domain thus still wields a power comparable to that he has always exercised and little different from that which public opinion attributes to him, although it is less royal. He is the boss. By brilliantly playing off one minister against another, by taking his time, by insisting on the proper forms, by using to the fullest those qualities without which he would not have become prefect of the Seine, he can put unwanted or bizarre projects on the back burner; so it was with an unbelievable exhibition mounted under the Eiffel Tower which began as a technical exhibit and gradually became a fair devoted to ham—Auvergne smoked ham. More commonly he can let himself run things for the benefit of his city by staying well-informed, making a decision, and then getting a favorable vote from the various assemblies.

He is the prefect, which no analysis of institutions could express as well as the enormous corner office where the marble bust of Haussmann is enthroned.

To understand the power of the prefect of the Seine one has to be here, amidst this heavy decor compared to which the offices of the Elysée Palace are nothing but elegant salons to make the prefect uncomfortable, while visiting the president of the Republic and seeing General de Gaulle's impressive size in so modest a tabernacle. It is to the prefect's office one must go, under these heavy ceilings caressed by the reflection of the Seine, with the city so close one hears it rumble. One must penetrate into the holy of holies or linger nearby to see the men who arrive, who wait to enter the enormous doorway. The comportment of these visitors is more instructive than a long speech. First are the familiars, the assistants, the staff the prefect has generally brought with him from the provinces. Everyone at the Hôtel de Ville knows that one judges a prefect by his colleagues, by their seriousness and above all their kindness. Arrogant or unorganized colleagues indicate an incompetent and odious prefect. If the office has an easy and friendly air the prefect is a good boss! Those who work at the Hôtel de Ville are not mistaken by judging in this way. Years later they still talked about a prefect they thought hateful. His chief of staff told his chauffeur to wear white gloves when opening the door of the chief's limousine. As one might guess, the gloves came off when the chief of staff and his boss were discussed in the city garage and the neighborhood bistros, where I picked up these precious details.

More important for someone who wants to understand how the prefect is kept informed and how he decides, are the visits of directors, department heads of the important services for the department of the Seine, themselves accompanied by their assistants. These are high and mighty personages, most of whom have held their posts for a long time. Their careers depend on the prefect, on the relationship they have with him. In fact, should there be a vacancy in a directorship caused by retirement, it is rare for the prefect to impose a man wholly of his own choice, at least in this age of old republicanism. These men know their business. They often enjoy a great reputation, as had some of their predecessors who left an illustrious name in the history of Paris. The prefect arrives. He is not up-to-date on the situation. Their job is to inform him, competently and loyally. Their job is also to point out to him the technical, administrative, and also political aspects, helping him to understand the relevant files, pointing out problems, and informing him that behind this project and that neighborhood lies this or that personage. Finally, as experienced Parisians, they never fail to underline for the prefect the Parisian angle of pending decisions, with all their subtleties and complexities. I reiterate what I earlier said: they are part of a place frequented by poets. How could they be insensitive to the beauty of Paris when they employ a genuine Parisian writer?

Nevertheless, the most complete and conscientiously kept files cannot relieve the prefect from the responsibility of informing himself, either in person or at least by some other means than his department heads. There are files on Paris, and because there is Paris, Paris the monster, Paris gives one vertigo, as Alfred de Vigny, alas, says: "Vertigo makes me stagger and weighs on my eyes. / Do I see a fiery disk or rather a furnace? / They call it Paris." There is mysterious Paris, dangerous Paris, Paris unknown even to the prefect, who declared himself "an old Parisian" in his first public speeches, almost alone in that distinction: there is hardly a Parisian who was not born in the provinces, with the exception of the prefect of the Seine, who is always Parisian. How can he know Paris when Paris hardly knows itself? I could even say it is preferable not to know Paris at all, or not to know it well in order to accept the prefecture. If he truly knew Paris, the chosen prefect would withdraw in terror.

Be that as it may, if he wants to be better informed there is no other means than going to see for himself. Not in an official car, but alone, on foot, like the prefect Pelletier, whom I met one morning on the boulevard Sébastopol, on his way to see les Halles. At least he had an idea about what went on there. He had seen it, smelled it, heard it, understood it. He would never say to me, pretentiously, as did the newly arrived assistant of one of his successors—the man of the white gloves, as you have correctly guessed—"The problem of les Halles? Surely you mean by that the problem of the central market of Paris?" No, I mean the problem of les Halles, over there, a few hundred yards from your office, just outside your windows. The prefect goes to see it and his wife goes, and his children and his assistants tell him about les Halles. His assistants are as new as he to the job, but if they are like Pelletier, they are just as curious, and in addition they are younger.

He also reads the newspapers. If need be he uses them to destroy or temporarily stall an annoying ministerial project: for example, the exposition under the Eiffel Tower, thanks to an article by Pierre Brisson, and the exhibits of the Ministry of Agriculture—the "affaire" of the rue Barbet de Jouy, where the ministry is located—thanks to an article by André Billy. The columns of *Figaro*, the articles of *Le Monde* work in different ways, but both are equally influential and sometimes feared. In the *Aurore* it is Jules Romains who speaks about Paris. But I have always had the impression, chatting with those who read *L'Aurore,* that even the greatest admirers of Jules Romains are more interested in the newspaper than in the beautifully crafted prose of the father of Jerphanion, carefully thought out and tested on the tongue.[3] It is easy to believe that Jerphanion himself, if he had read *L'Aurore,* would have attentively read the various details about Paris, the articles on crime, the steamy stories of sex, rather than the prose of Jules Romains. I don't think that radio and television have ever had, and I hope they never will have, a comparable role in questions concerning Paris that the press had in those years on this or that important matter. As they say, what is broadcast by the media goes in one ear and out the other; and that's usually what it deserves.

The prefect also gets information from another source, Parisians who come to speak to him about Paris. Why are we surprised to find among them the cream of society? The marks of consideration with which they surround him are surprising, rather like those shown the marquis making his entrance in *Les Précieuses ridicules.* I reiterate that the prefect of the Seine is usually a provincial, even though he won't admit it. I would add that if he had not been a provincial he would never have arrived at the summit of the administrative hierarchy. "It is in the provinces and under the watchful eye of those who, as they say, put in an honest day's work that one learns self-consciousness . . . to say only half of what one wants to say. The Parisians know only how to roll over on the carpet, like a small, pampered dog. This results in them sometimes getting kicked, and only rarely do they learn how to live" (Alain, 1908). The prefect of the Seine has found the secret of success in the provinces. History shows that the greatest number of successes come from the Auvergne, and Balzac explains why. Whether from the Auvergne or elsewhere my prefect is a provincial. Hardly has he arrived in Paris than he is declared a member of the Parisian elite. This impresses him enormously, but less so if he is from St. Flour in the Auvergne than if he is from Plougastel in Brittany. Whether an important functionary or a chestnut peddler, the Auvergnat in Paris is always more or less convinced that whatever Parisian he is doing business with, even if he is a member of the upper crust, is a perfect imbecile. But all the prefects do not come from St. Flour or Guéret. France is a big country, the Parisian upper crust is a select group. It is they who are at the prefect's door and who show him their Paris.

3. Jules Romain is the creator of Jean Jerphanion, a character in *Les Hommes de bonne volonté.*

1. The first Paris skyscraper: The Montparnasse Tower with the Montparnasse Cemetery in the foreground. (Roger-Viollet)

2. The café culture along the boulevard Montparnasse: The Dôme café (which still exists) as it looked a few decades ago. (© Harlingue-Viollet)

3. Old boulevard life: The boulevard St. Denis and the Porte St. Denis (the triumphal arch built by Louis XIV). (© ND-Viollet)

4. The nineteenth-century center of Paris: Charles Garnier's opera house and the Place de l'Opéra. (© LL-Viollet)

5. The nineteeth-century palace: The New Louvre with the Carrousel arch in the foreground (the section to the left of the arch was built in the nineteenth century by Emperor Napoleon III). (© ND-Viollet)

6. The twentieth-century palace: The pyramid of I. M. Pei (with the equestrian statue of Louis XIV, by Bernini) in the courtyard of the Louvre. The Renaissance core of the great palace is behind the pyramid. (© Roger-Viollet)

7. The last major public monument: The Basilica of Sacré Coeur, at the top of Montmartre, was consecrated in 1919 and was the last substantial addition to Old Paris before the construction of the buildings discussed by Chevalier. (© Collection Viollet)

8. The old courtyard: The Cour d'honneur of the Palais Royal, relatively unchanged since the eighteenth century. (Roger-Viollet)

9. The courtyard transformed: The Cour d'honneur of the Palais Royal with the columns designed by Buren. (© Roger-Viollet)

10. The heart of Paris: Two views of the old iron and glass sheds at les Halles, interior and exterior. On the left is the flower market. (© LL-Viollet)

11. Paris's artificial heart: The Forum des Halles is in the foreground, the church of St Eustache (contemporaneous with Notre Dame) in the background. (© Harlingue-Viollet)

12. Paris's artificial heart: Crowds on the esplanade of the Georges Pompidou Center at Beaubourg. (Roger-Viollet)

13. Infinite perspective: Looking west on the Champs-Elysée through the Arc de Triomphe before the skyscrapers at La Défense were built. (Roger-Viollet)

14. Before: The Place de la Bastille with the July Column, looking east.
(© Harlingue-Viollet)

15. After: The Place de la Bastille and the July Column with Carlos Ott's new opera house. (N. D. Roger-Viollet)

There are other visitors as well who are also not what one would hope for! Obviously, those who try to get in to see the prefect are, in general, those who, under the pretext of having information for him, want something from him. Among these importuning informants let us concentrate on those whose visit is most concerned with Parisian matters. What old defender of Paris seeing certain of these pests show their faces in the antechamber and respectfully give their cards to the majestic usher, would not eavesdrop and cry "Fire!" For example, when they see certain architects arrive, seeking a commission, their arms filled with models as were those of the Magi with gifts (and let us not forget the incense!). Those who do not come to see the prefect are those who have no requests, whose business is doing well, whose glory is established. They do not come and offer advice because they wait to be invited, and they are not invited because usually, in official corridors, their very existence is unknown. Celebrated throughout the world, unknown in Paris. It is the careers of Parisian builders I'm talking about here, with their enormous fortunes, and their disastrous buildings, that give them away. One morning the Magi arrive, or a rug merchant appears. . . . At first they are received with caution. Then they are frequent visitors, and soon they are at home.

This is even more true when the visitors are from the Academy, I mean the Academy of Beaux-Arts. Just as the provincial prefect takes Parisian high society at face value so he takes the Academy seriously. What a pity he has not read Hugo's *Notre-Dame de Paris:* "All these masons pretending to be architects are paid by the prefecture or by his underlings"—by the Elysée Palace we would say these days—"and wear the green outfits. All the injury bad taste can do to good taste, they do. As I write, what a deplorable sight! One of them is in charge of the Tuileries, and scars the face of Philibert Delorme's chateau. It is certainly not one of the lesser scandals of our day to see with what effrontery the heavy-handed architecture of this fellow everywhere destroys one of the most delicate façades of the Renaissance." These lines were written on October 20, 1832. They apply equally well to the time I am describing. They would apply even more to subsequent years. It is true that after 1958 the Academy of Beaux-Arts would be less important, with so many flooding the profession, the masons, to speak Hugo's language, although he was wrong to misuse, to disparage this noble word. These architects will make us miss "the bad taste," the taste of those who "wear green outfits." Yet it is to these architects that we owe some of the most deplorable buildings of the final years of the Fourth Republic. At the time there was consternation, but this was nothing to match what soon would emerge from the earth. The place was badly chosen. It was one of the most beautiful in Paris, along the Seine, behind Notre-Dame. Two sacrileges, both endorsed by a member of the Academy of Beaux-Arts, which certainly would not have been permitted except by the act of an academician. Around 1955 the land was purchased on which was going to be built, for the administrative services (alongside the old building housing the archives of the department of the Seine), the Morland building with its pergola shaped like a Chinese hat. Chronologically, this was the first historic horror and it was built for the city services. Then, a few years later, came this Maison des Arts building which, when the first model was maliciously published on page one of the *Figaro*, caused an outcry. A Maison des Arts in Paris, where there were so many wonderful locations, and perfectly comfortable ones, from bistros to the garrets, perfectly suitable, and without costing anyone anything, not even the artists. All the painters of popular sentimental scenes, and doubtless all the hangers-on of the earth and the protégés of foreign governments would find bed and board there. As for those with genius, if we believe the history of Paris, they have a tendency to flee these official barracks. But it is a waste of time trying to convince people of this and one is criticized for speaking thus. I could cite Henry Miller: "the best way to kill an artist is certainly to give him everything he needs" (*To Paint Is to Love Again* [1960]). From model to model, which went from bad to worse, the building was finally born, fortunately squat, but gimpy, wearing thick glasses and standing cockeyed. And it had an underground garage—much maligned at the time—which was doubtless for the artists' cars. I can still see, in my mind's eye, a meeting about Paris at the Institut d'Etudes Politiques, when an old woman leaned over to the person sitting next to her (whom she did not know): "And this Maison des Arts, can you imagine anything so horrible?" Her confidante, who didn't know how to respond, was the academician responsible for the horror.

Thus, from visit to visit, from consultation to consultation, by bits and pieces, the time passes and the prefect acquires an idea of his responsibilities and of his power; of what he should do and what he can do, of what is essential and what is not, of what perhaps can be done and what is best avoided. In general, the necessary sweeps all else aside. The necessary means the projects underway or planned that the various departments of the city know better than anyone, that they have minutely overseen for a long time, for which they have fought and which it is up to the prefect to see through to completion. There is continuity, but not to the exclusion of novelty, that personal yet anonymous contribution that every prefect of the Seine wants to add to the work of his predecessors, which will mark his tenure. I do not think history has taken adequate notice—with the exception of the career of Baron Haussmann—of what the urban fabric owes to the personal initiatives of the prefects who have succeeded him, to their personalities, their ways of seeing the city, their tastes, and also their entourages, their families, often their wives and friends. This neglect of history contributes to the glory of the prefects, certain of whom, their Paris work finished, disappear from the Parisian scene and from the public eye, without compensation or special advantages, without even their former colleagues, collaborators, and pretended friends retaining the least memory of their tenure, the least recognition of what they owe them, not even in those who ought at least to remember how their bellies were then full. The degree of oblivion adds to the grandeur of the work. The contrast between their power and this kind of professional penury, between the celebration (by an enthusiastic entourage) and this silence, between the attention of courtiers and this abandonment, has always struck me. I suppose this is the case for all great careers and not only administrative ones. But in the case of the prefect of the Seine, and history (and it is not only contemporary history that supports the observation—the Third Republic was especially forgetful) it has always seemed to me astonishing, shocking, disgraceful, precisely because of the power attached to the job and also the reputation for power that extends beyond the real power itself.

Whatever the reality, it is true that the prefect's power is not limited to having control over Parisian projects that the city departments send to him, but extends to the solution of numerous problems, material problems which are what I am here interested in, questions of housing and transportation, for example. These are the areas in which the prefect can take the initiative, be creative, depending on the conception he has of the city and that he shares with those who have, quite naturally, become his friends. Perhaps I have painted too darkly circumstances and especially the men, their talent, their competence, their objectivity, their loyalty.

I see the hand of prefect Pelletier in the urban fabric. I see it in numerous places in the city, some of which have been subsequently destroyed, but above all I see it in a place which, as I write, is still intact: Montmartre, the old Montmartre, the village. What a marvelous location, however, for the builders! To have an apartment on the heights, with Paris at your feet. This development will be called—take your choice—"cancan," "Moulin-Rouge," "Utrillo." "And why not Toulouse-

Lautrec?" an inspired promoter asked me one day. "Don't you think that this name would simultaneously express elegance and low-life?" I answered that all things considered I would prefer "La Goulue."[4] That made him laugh. At me, no doubt. As with many Paris projects, what saved Montmartre was an old project. Prefect Pelletier decided to see it to completion, with the assistance of Claude Charpentier, out of love for the quarter.

I have carefully described the reception rooms of the prefect, filled with suppliants, architects waiting to be received, squirming on the benches upholstered in worn velour, trying to be unobtrusive, squeezing behind a door, behind a curtain, in the shadows; if the usher had not been there they would have gotten down on all fours under a chair in order not to be caught red-handed peddling their wares by their colleagues. Sometimes one would see Claude Charpentier arrive, immediately and warmly received. It was another story with him. He bore a celebrated name and the promise of what the opera *Louise* evoked: music, generosity, unselfishness, love of love and love of friendship, in a world the old Montmartre, its streets, its residents, its soul and that special view of Paris that one can have only from an elevated spot.

If the prefect can thus take the initiative and if his undertakings are often good, how many contrary examples are there in the history of Paris of projects that would have been disastrous if carried to completion. When one comes across such proposals in the archives one thanks God (with a retrospective tremor) that some unexpected twist of fortune came in the nick of time, or, more often, that prudence taught restraint— prudence, that marvelous talisman of prefectorial careers. My final advice to those who would pursue such a career: appear bold, practice prudence. What prefect of the Seine hasn't said to himself that it is better not to tamper with Paris than to risk the worst opprobrium. If he himself has not said it, others have said it to him. Anyway, he ought to hear it said to him, as I have myself said it, and as I suppose others have. He who would go far looks ahead. You never know what you're going to step into, so in Paris the better part of wisdom is to do as little as possible or, even better, nothing at all. To cut into a neighborhood, tear down a house, modify a street or a sidewalk, change a one-way street, move a bus stop or a taxi stand, sometimes raises an opposition whose power is greater than the prefect's. The grocer defends the place where he displays

---

4. La Goulue, literally "big mouth," was a dancer at the Moulin-Rouge whose portrait Toulouse-Lautrec painted.

his vegetables, the café is jealous of its terrace, the garage owner is concerned about his gas pump; lord knows what these men have up their sleeves, what unexpected resources they can tap, how fortune may protect them. Chance itself often looks out for those the authorities don't look out for.

This is especially true of those whose intentions they do consider, those whom the prefect's entourage always greet diplomatically, from the usher who feels the first shock, to the smooth office manager exercising all his charm. Often it is some important woman, indignant at I don't know which municipal employee, perhaps some minor official connected with streets and sanitation, one of these street sweepers who have yet to make their mark on history, who has done or is in the process of doing something to her. To the unsophisticated glance of the young men who work in the office I prefer that of the usher who was not born yesterday, who has seen other women like this, and who is not one of those created overnight by power, as Richelieu says. What one must guard against is not stunning, self-assured beauty, an irresistible smile, a dress from Lanvin. "Wouldn't a gallant man and a Parisian sensitive to beauty regret not being able to do what is asked of him with so much charm and moreover, so justly?" Getting out of such an obligation is easy, made even more so since the terms are so often sincere. But things usually don't work out like this. Stunning beauty is not the real issue: it is rare that one has to deal with it. The same can be said of beauty that pleads, as with the charms of Racine's Junie: "I have seen it happen in these places—Sad, raising to heaven her tear-wet eyes . . . / Beautiful without any adornment." Beauty is not what is essential. It is even superfluous, distracting. When it exists it is sometimes hidden, camouflaged with banality, dressed in sackcloth and ashes, surrounded with the mystery of ordinariness that one is never sure, if one is Parisian, whether it is hiding something extraordinary, if some force is not masked by such mediocrity.

Only as a messenger did I ever play such a role. My anecdote is insignificant, a trivial story in this great swarming history. But for me it sums it all up. It made me remember a grande dame on whose behalf I intervened, without shame, with an understanding prefect. An intervention crowned with success. I had known her for some time. She had been what they called, in the language of the rue d'Ulm, my "tapiresse" [a private tutorial student]. A "tapir" is usually a charming child from a good neighborhood whose Latin composition is none too correct, whose French prose in uninspired, and who, with the aid of an impecunious normalien, turns in to her teacher minor masterpieces but who eventually fails the baccalaureate exam. But there are "tapirs" of a completely different type, of another time. During the Popular Front one of my comrades drew up the social platform for a businessman interested in politics and for whom, clearly, social questions, even on a national level, held no interest. As for myself I had the good fortune of being asked to give history lessons to the owner of one of the most famous racehorse stables of the time. On Sunday mornings her name was on everyone's lips in all the cafés of Paris.

The woman I'm speaking of had come to the rue d'Ulm and had asked the director of the school for a normalien who was not too boring. I gave her history lessons and we ended up becoming great friends. She died at an advanced age. She was an extraordinary woman. She had to find some way of getting history tutoring between visits to her stables or the races of Auteuil. At Auteuil she had the reputation of being quite a character which, along with her celebrated horses, made her well liked. Instead of haughtily frequenting the stands with her peers and their wives she took pleasure (a somewhat malicious pleasure) in sitting on the grass, in the middle of a crowd, on a little stool that she carried, dressed like everyone else and taking in from afar the top hats, the monocles, and all the elaborate trappings of her associates . . . And she was equally extraordinary for other reasons. I would love to write a book about her some day because her personal history sums up for me large parts of the history of Paris. But let me skip a number of years.

Knowing that I was involved with Parisian affairs and assuming that I knew the prefect, she telephoned me one day. Her chauffeur had told her that it was impossible to drive through the Bois de Boulogne to go to the races at Longchamps without seeing debauched men on the prowl and pimps everywhere. It was a deplorable sight! I wasn't sure what she had in mind. Wasn't it obvious? she said. The only way to deny these undesirables a pretext for their loitering was to build in the Bois de Boulogne, not far from the racecourse, what she called a *châlet de nécessité*.[5] She asked me to convey this proposal to the prefect. Pindar, when he wrote an ode for the Pythian Games, was no more embarrassed than I was as I wrote to the prefect. I wrote a splendid letter that doubtless will one day be found in the archives of the city and which will surely surprise its reader.

The point is that in Paris everything is complicated, sown with land mines, booby-trapped, unpredictable. This is only the beginning of the

5. A public toilet, although it could also be translated as a bawdy house.

prefect's problems. The most difficult remains: to persuade the elected assemblies that govern Paris.

> I know that you love portraits and I have been irritated, for this reason, not to have been able to show you until now any which were not in profile and which have been, consequently, highly imperfect. It seemed to me that I hadn't enough light in this vestibule.
>
> Cardinal de Retz

I F the prefect is kept informed of Parisian affairs in a number of ways, principally by the department heads, he is also informed by his almost daily contacts with the presidents of the two Assemblies and their staffs, and by the officials one could see among his visitors who consulted him on matters they were responsible for.[6] Here was exceptionally solid information, not contained in general and abstract files but coming from specific cases and numerous (often contradictory) statements, from which evidence and need could be extracted. The prefect used them to his advantage. They also helped him understand the city. A councilor decorated with the ribbon of the Legion of Honor revealing his experiences and an urban sociologist both have the feeling of telling the story of "The Ass's Skin."[7]

But ultimately it is the Assemblies that decide. They vote the budget and have the last word. This is the overarching power to which the prefect accommodates his own power. Over the years the Assemblies have been satisfied to resolve those problems, for better (or at least not for worse), without ruining the city, now and then casting regrettable votes, but refusing to do something disastrous. This judgment is quick and imprecise: history will have the necessary leisure to verify and see all the nuances of their work. She will study the projects one at a time, year by year, analyze the records of legislative sessions, which reveal practically everything, even what is not expressly said. History will dissect the votes, count the voters, penetrate to motives both conscious and unconscious. Perhaps I will be accused of being mistaken about this or that, of having haphazardly distributed praise and blame. And as happened to a well-

---

6. There are two deliberative bodies governing Paris: (1) the elected council of the department of the Seine (in which Paris is the most important entity), the *Conseil général,* and (2) the elected *Conseil municipal,* composed of representatives of the twenty arrondissements of Paris.

7. *Peau d'âne,* one of the tales of Charles Perrault. To avoid a criminal marriage a princess flees disguised in an ass's skin. A prince falls in love with her and her true identity is revealed by a ring which will fit only her finger.

known citizen of Florence who found in the lowest circles of Purgatory those whom he thought were in Paradise, my imagined future Parisian, led by the hand of history, will perhaps be surprised to find those he had considered innocent burning for eternity or suffocating in gasoline fumes which are, as everyone knows, the punishment of those who have sacrificed the city to the automobile. "Don't you recognize me?" I paraphrase Dante, "I also lived on the banks of the Seine. I have even sung the praises of the Seine and its bridges!"

While awaiting such an unlikely *Divine Comedy*, I shall offer the judgment that my recollections of these years suggest as clearly as would a reading of the *Bulletin municipal*. These Assemblies—"This Paris parliament presided over by the prefect of the Seine," as prefect Pelletier says in his *Mémoires*—are the Municipal Council and the General Council. I have principally in mind the Municipal Council. Its composition during these years, its diversity and its unity, explain why the city, momentarily, escaped from the worst, from what circumstances and various forces bring in their train, those blind social forces and their clear-sighted exploiters. The contrast between these years and what happened immediately afterwards, after 1958, is so striking, so wrenching, that it is unnecessary to linger over the nuances.

The diversity of the Municipal Council came above all from its political diversity. It was impossible for any one party to make law by itself or if it was the party in power, to impose its wishes upon Paris. There was not a municipal debate which did not pit the parties against each other, which did not raise political opposition, even if the subject had nothing to do with politics, and even less to do with Paris. Great international events provided the pretext for these confrontations. The invasion of Hungary by Russian tanks, or American intervention in some corner of the world, caused one councilor to be called a CIA agent and another "a spy who came in from the cold." There were less dramatic occasions which should not be glossed over when the curé of Batignolles had the unfortunate idea, in that period of clerical arrogance, of organizing a procession outside his church: he was seen as Father Combes risen from the ashes.[8] There was an oratorical joust over a charming project to name a pathway in the Bois de Boulogne—proposed, indeed by the Right—"Countesse de Ségur"[9] an unnamed pathway still, that today one

---

8. An ironical name given to the violently anticlerical politician Combes.

9. French writer, born Sophie Rostopchine in St. Petersburg (1799–1874), who wrote children's books, *Les Malheurs et Sophie* and *Le Général Dourakine*.

would name "Madame de Genlis."[10] M. de Vécourt says "Mme de Ségur was born Rostopchine, doesn't that name intrigue you, M. Boisseau?" M. Boisseau, does it need saying, is a spy who came in from the cold. In this verbal battle children's literature immediately had its revenge, and Robespierre, a few hours afterwards, made him pay for the affront made to one of Mme de Ségur's books. The historian, Pierre Giraud, my friend from the Sorbonne, having proposed to name a Paris street after Robespierre, on the occasion of the bicentennial of his birth (1958), there was a great hue and cry. Since the whites [the Bourbon colors] remain Bourbons and the reds [sans-culottes] the *conventionnels,* as irreconcilable as in 1793, wanting to separate themselves from the counterrevolution, they (the latter) could think of nothing better than to suggest the *place* of the Hôtel de Ville for Robespierre. "The *place* of the Hôtel de Ville will be appropriate, it will be historic." (In the fullest sense of the word "history.") Pierre Giraud adds: "It seems to me important today to see if, in a city that has honored men as controversial as Danton with a street and a statue, they will refuse to name a street after the Incorruptible!"

The Incorruptible? The allusion is obvious. Why not take the opportunity to speak henceforth of Topaze? There was a Topaze before Marcel Pagnol created him and one doesn't have to go back to the nineteenth century, let alone the ancien régime.[11] In 1928, at the Variété theater, Lafaur starred in the Pagnol play. In 1932, Jouvet created the character on the screen, with Edwige Feuillière and Pauley. Contempt for parliamentary government was in full swing. "Down with the crooks!" The national deputies were readily upbraided, even more than the municipal councilors (at least those who were not also deputies). I myself shouted "Down with the crooks!" in front of the Palais-Bourbon, along with my comrades, among whom were future deputies and ministers. Clearly, we didn't believe exactly what we were saying, or at least it didn't upset us. Were they actually crooks, these pathetic creatures we often saw on the terrace of the Assembly, looking bored behind a stone balustrade, whom we wanted to throw into the Seine? This was of least concern. Rather we wanted to cause a stir, to create one of those great popular uprisings we had so well described in our dissertations, to live history instead of writ-

10. Tutor of the duc d'Orléan's children (1746–1830), who also wrote books on education and was thought his mistress.
11. "The young Mirza had two favorites who served as his secretaries, grooms, maîtres d'hôtel, and valets. One was named Topaze: He was handsome, had a good physique, was as fair as a Circassian girl, as docile and ready to be helpful as an Armenian . . ." Voltaire, *Le Blanc et le noir,* 1764.—Author.

ing about it. Returning to the rue d'Ulm in the evening I was Cardinal de Retz describing his latest action in the City.

In the spring of 1928, that is before *Topaze*, the *Mercure de France* had published two articles on the Hôtel de Ville by Léon Riotor, councilor of the Fourth arrondissement since 1919 and vice-president of the National Assembly. He told the story of the quarrel between two councilors who, "if one can put it this way, had each stolen the other's wife." One of them was Topaze before the character was invented, a man whom Jouvet would have found it hard to incarnate. He had "a thunderous voice and an obscene vocabulary which made the Assembly tremble." He had launched the celebrated aphorism: "The municipal councilor who doesn't earn 60,000 francs a year from his office is a jerk"; around him, Riotor writes, there grew up a legend of venality and corruption. "I spent ten years," he adds, "on the Municipal Council and I never saw anything to support this accusation." As for the man himself "he ended up with a comfortable sinecure, the management of a railroad company." Here is a character worthy of Pagnol. Léon Riotor had to resign from the vice presidency of the Assembly. In the meantime Topaze had seen the light, the Topaze of Pagnol who gave a name to the character type and became a part of public opinion.

Under the signature of a certain "Albert Manteau, Paris taxpayer"—I don't know who was concealed under this mantle—there appeared a violent pamphlet in 1931, *Les Comptes de Topaze et de l'Administration*. The accounts of Topaze recalled those of Haussmann.[12] It is more interesting to rediscover the opinion itself, at work in the stories they still tell today about the Hôtel de Ville. Such is the story of councilor Fiancette hailing a taxi. Fiancette, who was himself a taxi driver as a young man, tells the story. "'Take me to the Hôtel de Ville.' 'To the Bazar de l'Hôtel de Ville [a department store]?' said the driver. 'No, across the street.' 'Chez Topaze!'" he answered. As for the allusions to Topaze, especially made by the councilors themselves in the records of their meetings, before 1958 but especially afterwards and in a much less pleasant manner, they diminished until the personage disappeared almost completely from the debates, or so it seems to me—the historians will verify this—for the reasons explained in the preceding chapter. I admit to missing him, like those old Parisians who, during carefree moments and when things were

---

12. A bitter pamphlet, *Les Comptes fantastiques d'Haussmann*, by Jules Ferry, was instrumental in Baron Haussmann's fall from power in 1870.

going well were close to finding the character of Topaze attractive. "After all," one would hear, "he hasn't done anyone any harm." A recollection about les Halles explains these immoral moods, this guilty indulgence of which one could find many examples in the history of Paris. When I was studying les Halles during these years, assigning my students subjects for papers—you do vegetables, you do flowers, you do meat, you do fish, you do prostitution, you do religion, you do politics. One of them who wanted to look into corruption heard incredible stories from people. It would have taken a dolt, an innocent, to see a subject for study there in terms of morality, where everyone else saw only a way of doing business, one's own as well as everyone else's. It was earning a living and letting others earn one, closing one's eyes to what was going on and what did no harm. What meat wholesaler didn't know that his salesmen, and the salesmen of his salesmen, did not merely eat huge steaks that didn't cost them anything, but also furnished their families, their friends, their acquaintances, even the bistros where they bet on the horses, with meat? Even more: one of my students who worked nights at les Halles—what wouldn't students do in those days to please their teacher?—had even brought their teacher and his comrades much more than the teacher asked: a box of steaks. "Here," his boss told him, "give the sociologist some steaks." And he had added: "Young man, to find steaks like this you have to go at least to Batignolles." "Why to Batignolles?" my student asked. "Ask Julot," the boss said. And Julot, without batting an eyelash, said "Because I live in Batignolles."

In so diverse an Assembly, the Assembly as it then was, other qualities mattered more. Above all how well they saw, how well they knew, how well they understood, in a word how much they loved Paris.

This assumes, obviously, some small degree of judgment to begin with. There was some in this Assembly as in others. "Common sense is the most widespread quality in the world." Yet the words reported in the minutes belie Descartes' optimism, especially in the debates on traffic circulation that seemed to undermine common sense. "Doesn't the Opéra," insisted a councilor, "owe its oppressive heaviness to the fact that it is stuck like a bottle cork at the end of the Avenue that bears its name, and literally prevents breathing?" (BMO 22 July 1955, p. 469). The naysayers insisted automobile circulation was asphyxiating the trees. A car fanatic countered that, on the contrary, the trees were dying precisely where there were no highways: highways simultaneously made cars and the air flow rapidly (BMO 10 April 1957). One could fill pages like this.

Historians of the future, get your note cards ready. We should not confuse insensitivity with cynicism (which often resemble each other), the latter the basis of a thought, the former a baseless thought. No less astonishing, for example, although in another register, is this assertion that a deluxe high rise built overlooking the Bois de Boulogne, despite all the restrictions, all the regulations against such a building, all the rules protecting parks, will be a means of easing the housing shortage in Paris. "I know full well that the floors set aside for apartments are very expensive, but the people who will come to live here will vacate other apartments." Doubtless apartments in the poor Belleville or Glacière neighborhoods.

To declarations such as these that, consciously or unconsciously, fly in the face of common sense, we can add others, a much greater number of them, which only express personal ideas, a bit ridiculous perhaps, such as we all have. One of the charms of Parisian literature is that it is full of such ideas. Parisian novelists, from the greatest to the most minor, are often curious, even bizarre writers. It is sufficient to pay attention to the things Victor Hugo recounts in *Choses vues*. The fantasies, the manias, sometimes the single-mindedness or even the obsessions whose power suddenly manifests itself and is amplified by the right that every councilor has to harangue and badger his colleagues, if he pleases, for they are obliged to listen. Sometimes this springs from wisdom, competence, and authority in other fields. When I was a student, Raoul Brandon, councilor of the Sorbonne, saw exploited children everywhere, tiny urchins out of the pages of Dickens, which led him to receive, posted at the corner of the rue d'Ulm, the most pitiful supplications of these unfortunates who convinced him that if they were prevented from begging along the boulevard St. Michel it was the same as if they were forbidden to take a taxi to Auteuil. The note was signed "The children caught with their hands in the cookie jar," which apparently left Raoul Brandon perplexed. What could this mean? Riotor says, in the *Mercure,* that Brard, an old sewer worker who exuded alcohol and the sewer, spent hours in the sewers; what was worse, he took his friends and their wives there. Then there are those who study the clochards and, more redoubtable, those entranced by the spectacle of prostitution. These latter will complement those who want to uproot les Halles, the enemies of les Halles. When the final debates take place their brief, or rather their sermon, will cause astonishment. The decision to move the markets that was unaffected by traffic jams, by rising prices, by spoiled vegetables, will be brought about by the streetwalkers and will then turn les Halles into a center of pornography.

Given the diversity of the Assembly, there are other differences which play an even more important role in Paris. Certainly the councilors are distinguished one from another by the parties to which they belong and the arrondissements they represent, by their original professions, their education, their careers, their intelligence and their talents, their culture and the work they do and also by the degree of seriousness they bring to a study of the issues before them. In the administrative library (in the Hôtel de Ville) I have often seen councilors from the poorer neighborhoods, who no doubt have a great deal to learn, and almost never those from the better neighborhoods, who have acquired their advantages by birth. They also differ in the liveliness of their personalities, by a mixture of the unexpected, the foreseen and the unforeseen, by a disarming eccentricity or an even more disarming banality, by a disorganized palette of traits, by a hodgepodge of the surprising or the extraordinary; in a word, by a life that is never only the life one sees, or that one observes in so many other places in Paris, and with what interest, what pleasure. Reading the *Bulletin municipal* for these years I thought about the wonderful painting that adorned the lounge of the Assembly, a place off-limits to ordinary mortals, and it is clear why. I gained entry only under the protection of a librarian of the Hôtel de Ville, Roussier, a great lover of history. I slid in for a peek, which is the impressionistic basis of my description. In the painting, I saw, amidst the greenery, the councilors spread out haphazardly on the grass, on benches, and even on the tree branches. In the window of a country café one of them was depicted putting on his suspenders, and Clemenceau was doing I don't know what. This was perfect for the countryside and an outdoor café. It was still somehow representative of Paris. However, for the Paris of yesterday and for the Assembly of that epoch I would rather have chosen the boulevards or some neighborhood of the time, even les Halles (then in its glory), for some of the meetings of the Municipal Council duplicate the spectacle of les Halles, the movement, the noise, the splendid variety, order and disorder, life itself.

In sum (recalling the spectacle of the city itself), what is most important and creates the sharpest differences between the members of the Assembly—more than their material interests, their arrondissement—is how they see Paris, how they love Paris. This counts more than their political allegiance. Let me rather say "perhaps more," or "in most cases." Old Parisian acquaintance and friendship may distract me and make me exaggerate, for there are many acquaintances and friendships involved. And conversely I harbor hostilities, there are those I cannot forgive. History will have all the necessary leisure (and my permission) to nuance these judgments. I am, however, compelled to say that in all the decisive votes on essential questions, it is always the same men who are against (I mean against Paris) and the same men who are for Paris. Of those who are for Paris it is always the same few who speak of beauty and history, who say what needs saying, who utter the necessary words, in all the major votes, all the major decisions. But they also speak out on the multitude of incidents that make up the daily life of the city, against those threats against a street, a facade, a garden, a tree, artists' studios in danger of destruction. Thus it was in 1955, with the *impasse* Dantzig (in the Fifteenth arrondissment), a haven for artists, that a building company threatened and which Picasso and Cocteau defended in *Les Lettres fran-çaises:* they proposed to provide housing for the artists at Drancy, a name that inspires horrible memories.[13] The same happened to other studios, in Montparnasse and Montmartre, also in 1955. Above party, beyond the barricades, history reconciles those who in every other way were ene-mies, and lets me unite them in my gratitude. There are those hermeti-cally sealed against history, who do not understand that history is an essential part of the present city. And then there are those who need no explanations. They could better explain things than the historians of Paris: this councilor representing the faubourg St. Germain, . . . this councilor from the Champs-Elysées who then so admirably represented his area. Or the councilor from the Eighteenth arrondissement whom I sometimes met by chance at the bus stop in front of the Tour St. Jacques. We rode together, and it was rare when we did not find ourselves in agreement. Naturally his approach was not that of the councilor from the faubourg St. Germain or the elegant representative of the Champs-Elysées. He came to the reality of Paris by way of injustice and poverty, the others by way of beauty. But the result was the same; their enemy was the same, as were the choices they made: they voted identically.

Of the several discussions that best reveal these two casts of mind one of the first (and most instructive) takes place in July 1954 and concerns the southern toll road. The plan originated in the Ministry of Public Works and proposed that the highway penetrate Paris by the avenue of the Parc de Montsouris after entering the city at Denfert-Rochereau. The two psychologies—for and against Paris—were immediately manifest. For one, Paris didn't even enter into the equation. The planning for the

13. It was at Drancy that prisoners to be deported to the camps in Nazi Germany were held by the Vichy government.

toll road is and could only be technical, with all the ruthlessness that implies, but it was also blind and, in the final analysis absurd, with arguments and language against which one could do nothing since they belonged to another universe.

Then there was the other Parisian psychology which focused on all that would be done to the city, not merely the avenue of the Parc Montsouris, but the rest of the city. It would be necessary to destroy the sidewalks of the boulevard St. Michel, uproot the trees, ruin the boutiques, and this would spread to the avenues that intersect the boulevard St. Michel, and eventually all of Paris would be cut in two by an urban highway, like some vulgar Chicago. At first rejected, the project was again brought up for discussion two years later, and it suffices to read the minutes of the session of December 3, 1956, to see that the adversaries of the highway are from all parts of the spectrum. The communist Albert Boisseau said: "What will happen if you approve this proposal? They will invoke the decision of the Municipal Council tomorrow to get approval of turnpikes that go to the Place de la Concorde, the Place de la Bastille, the Place du Châtelet." Paul Faber added: ". . . or maybe the Place de l'Opéra!" Boisseau continued: "Why wouldn't Paris one day, M. Faber, be completely traversed from north to south, east to west?" Ribéra said: "Yes, that's exactly what must be done." Livéqui seconded this: "Yes, that's exactly what must be done." Boisseau: "And so we'll have a city cut to pieces, divided into portions like a tart, under the pretext that it's essential to drive cars quickly into the center of Paris." "Permit me to agree with M. Boisseau," said Frédéric-Dupont. And when the project of the toll road was reintroduced on April 1, 1957, Frédéric-Dupont continued: "And then . . . bear in mind that if you approve the southern toll road you will be obliged to let the northern toll road cross Paris." André Fosset: "Personally I favor that." Frédéric-Dupont: "And thus you will have transformed Paris into a bad Chicago. The engineers of the Department of Roads and Bridges, the polytechniciens who specialize in these matters—and the Ecole polytechnique is also against me—the polytechniciens who specialize in cement, are enamored with Chicago. . . ."

During the years I am talking about the very diversity of the assembly explains why certain disastrous projects, like the southern toll road, had been shelved or set aside for later discussion without ever being considered rejected, and hence returned each year for consideration. Political distribution was chiefly responsible: there was no majority party to vote *en bloc* for a government project. But it was also a question of different tastes, different languages, and above all of the presence in the assembly of men, above party, who were temporarily aligned by their attitude toward Paris. This group was then numerous, although they would not be later on. Over the years the arguments of the "old Parisians" weakened. "Let me assure you," Frédéric-Dupont declared on July 1, 1954, "that if you want to turn Paris into a new Chicago, with highways and elevated trains, if you want to build buildings like the College of Medicine in every neighborhood, there will no longer be a Paris and we will have helped destroy one of the most beautiful cities in the world." In 1954 the College of Medicine was still thought of as an eyesore, a horror, a terrible mistake. It still functions as a reference point, and serves to illustrate an epoch and the Parisian sensibility of those years.

There was also in the 1950s, along with the diversity of the assembly, a unity which, on several occasions, saved the city: it was hostile to intrusions, aggression, to the heavy hand of clout. In the case of the Southern toll road the clout came from the Ministry of Public Works. Not from some transient minister but from the stable administration that took advantage of the minister currently in power to bring to fruition old projects, such as the toll road. "The representative of the Department of Roads and Bridges assured us," said Frédéric-Dupont, "that the project for cutting a toll road through the Parc de Montsouris had been abandoned. I'm not so sure. . . . There are dead horses that have to be beaten because the Department of Roads and Bridges is tenacious. From the moment it put this project into its files—assuming a fire doesn't destroy their offices—the danger persists."

When the proposal to cut through the park failed, they fell back on building along the avenue of the Parc de Montsouris, in July 1954 and December 1956. With more and more insistence a kind of chorus (crudely exploited by the spokesman for Roads and Bridges) emerged, reiterating my theme of collective opinion and the *bagnole*. "Should the Southern toll road be completed, in 1958, all the Paris motorists will want to use it. . . . We will then be on the eve of elections and the Municipal Council will be pressured to yield. . . . This is only natural and when this happens we will be able to envision the entire project, but what will be our position with the ministry? We will go and say to them: "Minister, what we did not think ourselves able to do yesterday, we are ready to do today! . . ." And the Minister will respond: "Gentlemen, you have made your choice, live with it: ask the Parisians for the millions now needed to connect the city to the new highway." Here's a fine Parisian comic scene, like so many others. And I mean this as a compliment, not criticism: As Molière says: "You asked for it, George Dandin." [14] And in the same vein, when the project was reconsidered, in 1957, an important councilor who made an about-face was thought (with good reason) to be a friend to history. "I think one must choose the lesser of two evils, and I side with those who want to bring the Southern toll road into Paris." But he insisted on protecting the boulevard St. Michel by widening the rue St. Jacques, up to where it intersects the rue Soufflot. This solution appeared as frightening as the original proposal, but in a different way. The administration, that is, those with clout, was again stopped.

In this mobilization of the Assembly against ministerial power, there were other matters at the same time that point up the contrast between the former and the present sensitivity to Paris. In July 1954, for example, the government brought to the Municipal Council's attention, with a model of their proposal, the decision to build the headquarters of UNESCO at the Place de Fontenoy, on land belonging to the state. "Under the circumstances," a council member argued, "if we do not give our answer now we run the risk of seeing the government ignoring our advice and building the project. It will be difficult to protest later. " In fact if the land offered to UNESCO was indeed the Place de Fontenoy, the international group of architects in charge of drawing up the project had made it known that this site did not fit the kind of building they were considering: "They want to erect a building which will be, it appears, a symbol of contemporary art and building techniques. They think that the very nature of the Place de Fontenoy—and it is a function of the site itself—is not appropriate, from the point of view of perspective and the buildings that surround the *Place,* for such an edifice." The government had, consequently, offered another site, on the edge of the Bois de Boulogne, at the Porte Maillot. But it appeared that the proposed structure would be so tall "that it might look like a hat set atop the Arc de Triomphe," according to a statement of the prefect that should be underlined in red, blood red. In 1954 they were concerned about the Arc de Triomphe! They went back to the Place de Fontenoy. The commission on sites only insisted that rather than a massive structure 60 meters high, the building could not be more than 28.50 meters in height "so that the perspective of the Champ-de-Mars would not be disturbed." The council did not render an unfavorable judgment on the construction of UNESCO head-

---

14. The hero of a play by the same name in which Dandin, a rich and vain peasant, marries the daughter of a country gentleman who treats him with contempt (as does her haughty family). A satire on social climbing and social pretentiousness.

quarters until its session of July 1, 1954. The question would be considered again in December of that year.

It is, however, the matter of the wine market [la halle aux vins] that puts this unified action of the Municipal Council against the initiative of the executive branch in high relief. It shows their resistance to this kind of incessant aggression, this threat of rape which now seems so innocent, compared to what would come later. A few years afterward the Assembly would ask nothing more than to be raped over and over, without shame, without even saying, as they did in the music hall: "I want you to violate me. I only insist that you ask my permission." The story of the wine market could be written as a mock-epic poem. To tell the story one would need to enter into the spirit of Villon. Everything about the market is unique and mysterious. First there is the place itself. "A dull part [of Paris]" writes Hemingway, "where there was a bleak, windy stretch of river bank with the Halle aux Vins on your right. This was not like any other Paris market but was a sort of bonded warehouse where wine was stored against the payment of taxes and was as cheerless from the outside as a military depot or a prison camp." And by chance (although it was not by chance) this prison camp calls up violent and criminal images, a setting for crime stories. Wine, blood, night, the bargemen, the slant toward the river of Maubert, the handsome men and beautiful women in search of adventure (that sometimes goes sour), the illicit meeting-places, and the ambushes behind piles of boxes or wine casks. Through the nineteenth century the literature set on the banks of the Seine is considerable and it all has the same characteristics—from police reports to the *Annales d'hygiène*—the same interest in mortality, beginning with Jean Valjean fleeing Javert: "He left the rue de la Clef behind him, then the St. Victor fountain, ran along the Jardin des Plantes, following the wretched streets to reach the quay. He looked around. The quay was deserted. The streets were deserted. There was no one behind him. He took a deep breath. He reached the Pont d'Austerlitz." A lovely place, in a word, and it was a question of tearing out the bad to create good, to consecrate the place to science. The Science Faculty is built here.

Evil, that's what all these images invoke. These images were used identically for the wine market and les Halles, where virtue would also cause a stir, some years later. The only difference between the two is that at the wine market one doesn't have to go in search of crime and prostitution, as at les Halles. One could have found crime without much difficulty in news items of the time: a naive boy just arrived from the provinces, a traveler wasting an hour between trains, a bourgeois walking his dog, might be killed on the quay or behind the railway station. As for prostitution, one would have had a bit more difficulty finding it, except in some old, drunk, depraved woman living on the streets. But why search? A word sums it up: wine wholesalers. Pompidou used to tell the story that he had one day seen, from his windows, a tower being built on the quay at Béthune which he had never heard about. Someone asked him how they had been permitted to erect, along the Seine, what an American novelist had called "Sing Sing in Paris." "The wine wholesalers," he answered. He meant to say that there was no answer to this argument, "the wine wholesalers," the enemies of French thought. We are intellectuals, we drink only water and milk. "Death to wine wholesalers!"

It was, in fact, this theme that dominated much of the discussion, and well before this time, well before the July 5, 1958, meeting when they finally voted "the resolution concerning the definitive transfer to the University of all the land covered by the St. Bernard warehouses." The words "wine wholesalers" or better yet "dregs of humanity" were, above all, insults that they flung in each other's faces: one was for the coarse red table wine guzzled by the poor, the other the Taittinger champagne reserved for the orgies in the posh Sixteenth arrondissement. But more decisive in the decision was the fact that the Municipal Council had learned in the press, in January 1956, "of the decision to expand the University of Paris by taking over the wine market." This was unacceptable behavior, or rather an unacceptable procedure. Frédéric-Dupont's speech puts the two themes together. "When you move the most learned men in the world to the new science building, you are moving them into a building constructed on piles above the wine cellars and storage tanks." This would lead, as was soon proven, to the elimination of the cellars and storage facilities. More convincing was his second argument: "It is impossible for us to continue to be treated this way by the government. The very dignity of the elected representatives of Paris is in question. If we had a Municipal Council and a mayor of Paris which were like any other mayor and council in France, something like this would never happen. This came about because the administration of Paris is little more than an extension of the national government. The city administration is, at base, the national administration."

Thus, for reasons related to the diversity of the Assembly and also to its united resistance to "the power," certain projects languished indefinitely, from session to session, so that even an authoritarian minister could not send in the bulldozers! This provoked such protests that the projects, even those about to begin, had to be more moderate, one had to aim lower, sometimes to take another tack, and the architects gave up trying to adorn Paris with modern masterpieces. The council did not hesitate to get involved with questions of architecture and to give its advice freely.

This phase came to an end after May 1958, affecting the wine market along with everything else. "For two years," a councilor declared, speaking to the Science Faculty on July 5, 1958, "nothing was done because during this time certain departments didn't know exactly what they wanted. But since then . . . there have been changes which now permit the established authority to act quickly and, I hope, well." Quickly and well. Quickly, goes without question. But well?—that is another matter.

Chapter Eight

Choices

How lovely, bailiff! You have a fine bit of our Paris in your teeth.
Victor Hugo, *Notre-Dame de Paris*

"I T is impossible to accomplish what must be done in Paris." One heard these strident words around 1955 in those Parisian circles closest to the ministries, the legislature, and the Hôtel de Ville, where the movers and shakers—men of action or men excited by action, bold innovators and profound thinkers (or those who fancied themselves such)—talked gravely among themselves about the bitter realities of politics. During these nocturnal hours, Paris being quiescent and the women left to their own devices, the men could finally, in a moment of euphoria, explore the most elevated themes, face reality head on, pick at the constitution, unmask government institutions, expose men, confuse Flaubert's *Dictionnaire des idées reçues* with a chapter from Montesquieu's *L'Esprit des lois*. "It is impossible to accomplish what must be done in Paris. With all the good will in the world. . . . It is not good will that is lacking, but authority."

Authority crept in, riding the wings of political philosophy, or by some other route I know nothing about. The Municipal Council learned with astonishment and anger, one day in June 1955, of "the creation of a commission for construction and urbanism for the Paris region, charged with coordinating the several departments, powers, and authorities— those of the city, the department, and the state—in order to create units of power that are simultaneously ministerial and prefectorial." I had to risk boring the reader by citing the text itself. What it means is that another political appointee whose responsibilities are not clear—and the council has traditionally been a stickler for precise administrative responsibility—has been created. What is clear is that the appointee is a state, not a city, functionary and that this is a state intrusion into city government. The prefect, representing the executive authority and responsible for presenting both the new level of bureaucracy and its first director to the Municipal Council, carefully mobilized all his abilities and hid his claws under the soft pads of his paws. The assembly was defiant: "this whitewash doesn't hide anything." The Council did not want to understand, or rather they understood all too well, and in the June 30, 1955, session said so.

The Council spoke through the mouth of one of its most influential elder statesmen, as he christened himself, Victor Bucaille, councilor for St. Sulpice for three decades. Possessed of great talent, simultaneously passionate and stubborn, he alone was able to enunciate what everyone thought, and with universal support. Even the Communists applauded. Read the record of the session, and add to the words a face worthy of Roman portraiture with his wrinkles incised in marble, a withering stare accented by thick eyebrows and white hair. Standing under the crest of the city, he spoke in a penetrating voice which would have been heard above any tumult if there had not been absolute silence at his first words. As he talked with a mixture of majesty and simplicity, courtesy and plain-speaking, and in a graceful way that gave even to his most elaborate phrases, his most intricate (and irresistible) reasoning, an air of improvisation and simple common sense, his most telling blows appeared as good-natured advice, an easy lesson. He could have worn a Roman toga. He was Cato, and the councilors, riveted to their seats, suddenly like statues although ordinarily so animated, were the ancient conscript fathers who admired the entire assembly incarnated in one of their number, and who spoke through him.

Who is this curious functionary, Bucaille asked, who is under the prefect's authority and obeys him, but is charged, at the same time to head a delegation appointed by the minister [of the Interior] who also appoints the prefect? He is able to give the prefect orders, in the name of the minister. And what is this coordination all about? Why create a functionary to find usable land, to discover polluted parts of the city—as if we didn't know where they were!—to build upon. Who do the department heads of the prefecture serve? And what about the prefect himself? "You say, Monsieur le Préfect, that we need coordination? No, no, no. I have the unmistakable impression that the nomination of this secretary general constitutes, on the government's part, not only an act of defiance against the city, but manifests their desire to interfere in the normal functioning of our administration and replace it with something that will, perhaps function less well. Remember, the state earned no glory in its previous interventions in questions of construction in Paris. They are responsible for those two 'admirable' monuments, the Ministry of Communication and the Ministry of Merchant Marine." Bucaille then told a personal anecdote about how, when he was a young councilor, he went, with a few of his colleagues, to defend the threatened perspective of the Ecole Militaire, before minister Loucheur, a long drink of water, as he put it. Loucheur had said: "That means nothing to me." Bucaille, with his common "that means nothing to me," invoked an earlier precedent. "There's a decree dating from the Directory which authorizes me to build where I want in Paris. If I want to build a fifteen-story structure tomorrow on the avenue de l'Opéra, I will do it!" He didn't, however, build it. And what about the places affected by NATO! And what about this edifice for the United Nations we anticipate, "which will resemble whatever one could hope for, except a Parisian building!" But let us not make recriminations. There is a commissioner whose job it is to build. Let us therefore welcome the commissioner—"I very much want such a commissioner"—and let him build, if he can. His ministerial backing will facilitate things. It will open the doors of the Ministry of the Interior, and those of the Ministry of Finance as well, but maybe not the right doors. If you could chat with the minister himself, things would get done without a hitch. If you could chat with some director-general, it would be a bit more difficult, but there would still probably be a chance of being heard. But when you find yourself before some junior financial bureaucrat or functionary who has scarcely begun his career, you should begin by saying: "Everything the Municipal Council does is ineptly done, they are nothing but a bunch of Topazes." "I hope, Monsieur Commissioner, that at the right moment, knowing our assembly better, you can set them straight." Anyhow, we'll see. Lest the commissioner forget, in his innocence, his greenness, he will learn that the Municipal Council also exists, that it has considerable power and that it has been around for a long time. Here it is useful to cite Bucaille's text itself, the most Roman part of the speech about a Parisian Rome where the cooking smoke drifts up to the Capitol to fill the nostrils of the senators: "We still carry some weight with the ministers, and with the deputies, and in public opinion. You treat us with scorn and contempt, as if we didn't exist. I have received, as have some of you, a letter telling us that our salaries will be increased by 150 francs a month. Clearly, all this is hardly fit or elegant. What do you want? We have to take things as they are. But as for myself, I am not inclined to do so. Though I seem to accept this state of things, I don't. I consider a municipal councilor of Paris to be important not because of who he is but because of the city and its residents that he represents. He is in a way the expression of the most profound views of the populace, because he has been mandated by them. It is sufficient, to justify this assertion, to cite the period since 1871. With regularity over a long period of time we have seen that Parisian elector remain faithful to his municipal councilor, while at the same time we have seen prefects of the Seine and of the police come and go. Permanence, length of service, power, are all on the side of the councilors. The texts, the decrees, do not change this fact."

It is thus, or rather under these auspices (to retain the language of Rome) that the commissioner for construction and urbanism of the Paris region—the former prefect of the Loir-et-Cher department, Pierre Su-dreau—would begin his work. I was at the Hôtel de Ville, since the fall of 1955, as a kind of resident historian, and quite naturally I became the historian of the group to which Sudreau turned for help, at the beginning, in the task of (to use a then current term) "rethinking" Paris. For a historian of Paris to "rethink" Paris boded ill. Yet "twenty years later," to echo Dumas, I am astonished at not having more strongly resented the implications. Friendship doubtless played a part, inasmuch as Sudreau was then like d'Artagnan, without myself being the wise Athos or the devious Aramis. I was without suspicion, as were most of those who participated at the same time or were aware of what was going on and applauded the work. I did not see that this consideration of the city would prepare its replacement by something quite different, which the most ardent partisans of change and modernity would one day demand, revealing what they had hatched. "Where on earth does this bastard off-spring come from?" one might have said. Others, more qualified, and with better documentation will recount this episode differently. As a historian, and for that reason perhaps not qualified to write the history of my own times, it is this blindness of the most clear-sighted, the most perspicacious, and even of those Parisians who were most fierce to preserve Paris, that surprises me. At least this is what I remember from those years, or rather the way that I retrospectively see them.

Brain Fever

THE first task, then, was to "rethink" the city, as if it had been previously thought and if this had taken care of its past, its present, and its future. As for the rest, the new commissioner was not asked to think or "rethink," but to build, if he could. I can still see the terrible Bucaille crossing the antechamber of the "think tank," mistakenly opening the wrong door and quickly shutting it, muttering sarcastically: "They're thinking."

These thinkers and rethinkers, in the beginning, to court the favor of the muses or to fend off evil spirits, cited at length those who supposedly thought the city before them, and often would have been better off not to have done so. I have never heard the name of Claudel so often invoked, which would have made Jean-Louis Barrault jealous. Unbelievable texts flowed from them as if from a baptismal font. As introduction, as conclusion, in the body of the discourse, the Claudelian oracle substituted for argument. "To reside, to circulate, to work," this expert (whom I cite verbatim) tells us, "are the three functions which must be facilitated by the urban organization. To best meet this obligation, the city ought to have a separate place for each." This is clear, perhaps too clear, even disquieting because it is clear. Let us turn to Paul Claudel. Hadn't he written, "Throughout my life I have thought about cities"? And the flood of his thought sweeps everything in its path: "In a city the streets serve two purposes. Firstly, they are the arteries which provide general movement, which serve for comings and goings and move men and goods. Secondly, they are a canal which, by a series of lateral "locks" provides access to houses. Emanating from these bustling streets is a dense mass of tentacles reaching into the courtyards and gardens where people live. . . . There are currents of life and the secret places where things human are." The tentacled city! O Maine-Montparnasse, O marvelous coelenterate! And the coral reef of the waterfront in the Fifteenth arrondissement!

But Claudel can surprise. If you read him carefully, instead of being seduced by vague words, drugged by the opium of images, dozing with your head in your arms, there is a chance he will say the contrary of what one wants him to say. Besides, did he himself know exactly what he said? Giraudoux, doubtless more lucid, is more useful. He is courageous, which so pleased his contemporaries. He made one of Richelieu's mottos his own: "I am determined to do the impossible." What was impossible for Giraudoux becomes, if we explicate Valéry's poem, the *Cimetière marin*, what is possible for Pindar: "O my soul, aspire not to eternal life, but exhaust the possible." What a motto, what an article of faith, what a credo for the innovators! It is the Cartesian credo, in fact, which is the credo of Giraudoux, of Valéry, and also, although they are unaware of the fact—Giraudoux being better known to them than Descartes—the way of thinking of those who want to "rethink" the city.

These are the common assumptions it now seems to me—and it then seemed to me, however vaguely—that animated those I watched making these pronouncements (in all innocence) during this *cogito urbain*. Differences of career, profession, expertise, didn't matter. I would except those who were less preoccupied with thinking than with trapping their prey, these great beasts of the coelenterate city whose huge maws I can still see opening and closing over the coral reef of the waterfront of the Fifteenth arrondissement. Logical and lucid, the French are nevertheless willing to live in enigmatic cities that most resemble a pile of pick-up-sticks." These are Giraudoux's words, but this is very like what Descartes says in the *Discourse on Method,* which is the heart of the matter and, it seems to me, should be remembered. On one side—and I was among them—are those unworthy of Descartes yet still Cartesians, but of another sort, from another page of the *Discourse:* "It is observable," Descartes writes, "that the buildings which a single architect has planned and executed are generally more elegant and commodious than those which several have attempted to improve by employing the original walls which had been built for other purposes. Thus also, those ancient cities which from being at first only villages have become, in the course of time, large towns, are usually but badly laid out compared with the regularly constructed towns which a professional architect has freely planned on an open plain." There you have a pile of pick-up-sticks of Giraudoux. Paris needs "rethinking," turning on this enigmatic and disorderly city a kind of thinking—which in Giraudoux's method, in his judgment, also means courage. It is Cartesian, because, in France at least, he sees no other mode of thinking. When I reread the minutes of meetings where we thought and rethought Paris, it is this almost unconscious Cartesianism that I see in so many, with the exception of those hopeless coelenterates sitting at the table.

What order was to be followed in discussing problems? The order of importance. To reside, to circulate, to work. But where should we begin? By that activity the others depend upon. What about pleasure, asked a wag, or rather a sage. I have the impression, he said, that in all these categories pleasure is not considered. Yet in Paris this activity, in no way to be condemned, enjoys a major role, perhaps even the most important and central role. By beginning with the question of pleasure, all the rest will follow. Let's be serious, interjected a Cartesian. And, true enough, it must be said pleasure hardly has a place in Descartes. Let's begin with the most serious then, let's begin with work. To manage the city is to categorize its activities which history has scattered at random. Put industry where it ought to be located, but where is that? The service sector, which no one has successfully defined, should be in one place. Those catering to the luxury trade should be together. Each person, according to his fantasy or rather his way of thinking, goes into the minutest detail, using the most bizarre phenomenon as evidence. The newspapers will all be concentrated in one neighborhood, although we hope, one dreamer says, that the journalists, who should not be restricted to one quarter, would sometimes be able to go elsewhere: if they couldn't, what deadly prose they would write! For reasons I have never understood, the fabric merchants would all be put together; but they already are, at Sentier.[1] No less odd is the insistence that all of the crystal-ware makers be together, although they already are, on a street with an extraordinary name, the rue de Paradis. Too bad for Sentier and Paradis. Fabric and crystal will have to pull up stakes. Where will they go? Elsewhere, a sublime word. It reminds me of a discussion in the Municipal Council about the flower and bird market, one of those non-Cartesian corners of Paris, a niche next to the Tribunal du Commerce, under Paulownias as lovely as those that formerly graced the Contrescarpe, and which also had—though I never understood why—ferocious enemies who were willing to do anything, even cutting off the water supply, to force the market to move. But where would it go? A cruel female councilor answered simply: elsewhere. *Imperatoria brevitas*. For more details see the *Bulletin municipal*.

There you have Descartes, a simplifier who categorizes things and people intellectually. To work, to reside, and also to circulate. Perhaps for some Cartesians to circulate is most important. "The problems of circulation," one fellow observed, "influence everything else, because the separation of modes of activity depends on the vocation that will be attributed to this or that existing, modified, or new thoroughfare"—it's a strange vocation that is "attributed"! Vocations change remarkably, which this formula recognizes and as will be subsequently demonstrated. To facilitate circulation why not pave over everything that can be paved: the railroad tracks, the railroad stations, the St. Martin Canal, which have till now escaped this fate. And while at it, why not the Seine, at least for part of its course. After all, the bridges with their arches accomplish in miniature what could be done on a grand scale: in place of merely crossing the river, traffic could flow along above it. The suggestion seems a bit exaggerated. Will it always seem too much? Then limit it. Why not use the embankments? Put this way attention is shifted and the storm abates. We leave the realm of pure speculation, the free play of imagination, and enter that of projects. There are already files on using the Seine embankment. The Municipal Council requisitioned them, and one day, sooner

1. The Paris garment district, near the Porte St. Denis.

than one imagines, they will consult these plans. I don't have much reason to be skeptical.

During one of those apparently free-wheeling meetings, with Cartesianism as the unspoken agenda, I heard these words pronounced: "What
a terrible idea to have buried the unknown soldier under the Arc de
Triomphe!" I was inclined to agree, but not for the reasons the speaker
had in mind. This passage from Jean Guéhenno's *Journal* came to mind:
"The dead rested in their great, silent cemeteries, wise, so wise, laid one
next to the other, set in a final order, as if for an eternal parade,
smiling. . . . Then came a stroke of genius. The idea came from some
minister—who might it have been?—to move one of these poor dead
soldiers and entomb him in the middle of Paris." This is certainly how it
happened. "Ah, if only we had not been so supine. We would not have
put up with such scorn." It was truly a question of a great outcry! Such
scorn? No, rather we should speak of a deplorable action. "Soon, traffic
on the Champs-Elysées will be impossible. Why not think of something
else?" In the general stupefaction, there was a silence in which I believed
one could sniff the vague fear of sacrilege. "Yes, why not another place
After all Paris does not lack sacred places or those fit to be sacred." To
exacerbate the problem, "Montmartre has already been taken over.
Mont-Valérien remains free. One could build a monument, a temple,
worthy of the city. The glorious cadaver could be transported there with
all imaginable honors. And then, on the Champs-Elysées. . . ." In our
mind's eye we already saw the two corteges, the official, passionate pomp,
winding toward the top of the sacred hillock, and then waves of vehicles
passing under the Napoleonic arch finally freed of its burdensome quest.
Would they similarly pass through the Porte St. Denis or St. Martin to
defile the remains of Louis XIV? Waiting for that to happen I return to
the scene then being imagined by well-known fantasists, little different
from those described here. It was also a question of circulation and
bottlenecks, and the projects suggested were hardly less astonishing than
those proposed around our official table. "They say the Latin Quarter is
cut in two by the boulevard St. Germain. Why did they build the Odéon
theater where they did, and what purpose does it serve?"[2] Aping the prefect who was attacking the Right Bank: "There is no other solution. The
Odéon has to go. I'll take the Odéon and move it to Clermont-Ferrand.
The Auvergnats will figure out what to do with it. They'll make it into a
covered market."

2. The Odéon was built long before the boulevard St. Germain.

It was Cartesianism gone mad, but Cartesianism still, which had started to malfunction, like a machine out of adjustment, a computer gone crazy. Delirious Cartesianism because directed toward subjects for which the rigidities of Cartesianism do not work. As Descartes himself advised, a few lines later in the second part of the *Discourse on Method:* "It is true that we do not want to tear down all the houses of a city for the sole reason of wanting to rebuild them and thus make the streets more harmonious; but it is obvious that some should be torn down and rebuilt and that even at times they must be torn down for reasons of safety lest they collapse of their own accord because their foundations are weak"; or for some other reason, whether real or invented, when the only need (or pretext) is that of building anew or, as they say today, the need for innovation. In cities as in institutions, in questions of politics or religion. "I in no way approve of those ardent and restless characters who, called to public affairs neither by birth nor fortune, always want to reform things."

Seeing my technocrats giving themselves up, without knowing it, to their Cartesian natures—but without any of the restraints Descartes himself imposes: experience, wisdom, prudence, respect, religion, and doubtless even superstition—I applied to them the analysis that follows, no less Cartesian than the other, without which the most rigid Cartesianism would run amok, as I have seen it do.

From such a Cartesian interpretation we learn, even more for the subject at hand than for other questions, that it was not a question of black and white: on the one hand a kind of innovative and absolute thought alone worthy of expressing itself, and on the other some retrograde and superstitious attachment to obscure values which are best left unarticulated and of which one scarcely speaks except through politeness to those who represent them, giving a kind of honorific bow to these ideas which encumber, are perfectly useless, even ridiculous, and absolutely inflexible. For the most part the technocrats accommodate themselves, as long as the customs are followed: always on the hostess's right hand, which is where one puts a member of the Institute at a dinner party. Better yet, they fail to understand what they mask with so many reassuring words: the historic quarters of the city which, clearly, would never be touched, those quarters which become more rarefied and circumscribed from year to year, so much so that they were referred to in official texts (after 1960), as "the sacred triangle," like the fig leaves put on statues of nudes, or mini-bikinis that hide nothing, like Tartuffe's handkerchief.

It seems to me what Descartes taught was that there was not one language of technique that was the language of reason, and that opposed to it was history, poetry, old songs, popular ditties, old wives' tales, banal refrains. Beauty was not sharply separated from utility. I never heard beauty spoken of at these meetings, even though Descartes insisted that the destroyer of a street have the intention of "making lovelier streets." But doesn't Valéry write somewhere—I owe the reference to Yvan Christ— that beauty is a kind of death? What is beauty? There is some agreement on what makes a beautiful man or woman. But what about things, monuments? Maybe the beauty of monuments should reproduce that of people. "It is true," Michelangelo wrote in 1560, "that the elements of architectural construction are related to those of man. He who has not been or who is not an accurate depicter of the human form, and especially who does not know anatomy, cannot understand this in the least." There were no anatomists among those I met with. What is this certitude Michelangelo speaks of that is so hard to prove and which I myself would have had difficulty proving?

Behind every aesthetic judgment I sniff some settling of scores. "The Sorbonne," Alain wrote, "is one of the ugliest places I have seen. I am amazed that those men of taste—and there must be a few—who teach there, put up with the constant outrage to their sensibilities caused by this nasty architect." Evidently "this nasty architect"—an epithet worth remembering—is less the object of Alain's wit than Alain's colleague, a functionary at the Bon Marché department store, "a cordial philosopher, always opening the glass doors like a zealous chief buyer." And Alain added: "But I name no names." I shall try to imitate him.

How can one not also be reminded of Descartes' "those confused, restless minds," those characters who stick their noses in everyone's business? By what right do they dare try to transform Paris and to inscribe their mediocre signatures on this great city, as shopkeepers in the rue St. Denis put their names on their boutiques? Yes, by what right? This is the question asked by Victor Hugo, indignant at seeing "these masons" disfiguring the city. The novelist's inspiration, that of the poet, their need to create, never takes up more space than the corner of a library, even when he is named Hugo. But who is this individual, believing himself to have genius when all he really has is audacity and supporters, who thinks he owns the banks of the Seine and has the right to say what he pleases about it? Who is he? Where does he come from? Who are these "restless characters" who are called to public affairs "neither by birth nor fortune. . . ." Descartes, we see, does not mince words; only birth and fortune could justify such pretensions. Here too the Cartesian tradition is clear, well anchored in Parisian beliefs (too well anchored), from then till now, when business advertising tries to manipulate us, point us in another direction, convince us that it must be worthy of respect. There is enormous defiance among Parisians toward those not wellborn, for those unsupported by some king, some god, or better yet some queen or goddess—by what Descartes called fortune. Voltaire thought as did Descartes, and doubted the zeal and the taste of municipal magistrates when no king was there to guide their hand. "O Parisians," Mercier cries, "think how your city will flounder in a sewer without the hand that has broken your worst habits! Be still, bourgeois, and let your princes build beautiful monuments for you." But where have the bourgeoisie of Florence gone? Balzac asks himself, ridiculing the bad taste in architecture of the Paris bourgeoisie. And Giraudoux as well, who conceals his words with subtlety in order not to shock the notables and not to insult democracy too openly. This is what one hears in the Municipal Council itself, from the mouth of Victor Bucaille, mocking the official architecture, at least when it is that of the state interfering in Paris. When it comes from the Municipal Council it is no better. It is true that in the years immediately before 1958 things changed sharply. What I have here dubbed Cartesianism in order better to understand its workings and also, I admit it, to give it a kind of patent of nobility (of which it had great need), played an important role in this change.

The Loins and the Hearts

A plan came out of these sessions. Let us concentrate on the men involved, for the text is not that important. Some plans have never been and will never be anything but paper. The administrative files are full of them, and so too are the archives. These plans are sacrosanct, untouchable, unalterable, and never risk being abused. Then there are plans of another species, less numerous to be sure but which have played a role (and continue to do so), which live with those who have built from them and continue to work from them, those who incessantly modify them to produce a project that bears no relationship to the first proposal. Indeed, the first version, if one took it out of its drawer to show them, would surprise them and so too would what they had originally said of the plan. The plan for the organization of Paris is one such. At least that is how I see it.

I am a bit embarrassed to describe the men involved. What do I know about them? And even if I knew a great deal how would I say it? Here again is the problem of history and the novel, or rather of that indeter-

minate territory that lies between the two, a problem already encountered in these pages. It is not only unclaimed land, it is unsurveyed.
Individuals, their nature, their careers, their interests, their passions, their
worries, everything that is done and undone by them and around them,
in a word their lives—history hesitates to get involved in such a subject
although it holds the key to its secret. History is fascinated by the ease
and ambiguity of the novel, which creates character by small borrowings,
petty thefts, fragments and bits and pieces, thus making reality from ar-
tifice and truth out of error and lies—or rather its version of the truth.
But history loathes this very ambiguity, especially when it has to describe
people who appear more and more difficult to judge as more and more is
known about them.

   This is my situation. If at some last judgment a heavenly judge should
question me, as a witness or a defendant—does one ever know which?—
I would be hard put to say what I saw and heard, what I read (indeed the
prose was unreadable), what I understood, what I knew. I would direct
the inquisitor to that other life, to one of those persons I have already
introduced you to in the prefect's waiting room, to one of those great
administrators of the city who knows everything about construction in
Paris. He was present, fortunately. He was the serious one, the strength
of the group, the conscience and the expert on what was possible and
desirable and what was not. Then there were the others, the rest, whose
oversimplifying psychology I have described. The architects and the urbanists, the architects who wanted to be urbanists and the urbanists who
didn't want to be architects. Then there were the engineers, my exemplary Cartesians; and the architects and urbanists who pretended to be
engineers, while the engineers who were neither architects nor urbanists
lumped both types together (along with me). Figure it out! In truth I have
not even begun to do so. I contemplate it without understanding it. Having read Valéry through the eyes of Alain and being an admirer of *Eupalinos,* I well knew what an architect was, yet it was astonishing to me
that Valéry's Eupalinos was modeled after Auguste Perret, who was not
an architect but an engineer, and whose work, in addition, froze my soul.
Besides, what is an engineer? As for the urbanists, whose very name at
this time was enigmatic, they remained for me a religious congregation
of women—even though the urbanists I had contact with had beards
and smoked pipes—who took their name from Pope Urban VIII, who
recognized their order.[3] We are a long way from figuring it out. Then

3. The pope (1623–44) who transformed Rome by extensive building projects.

there are the promoters, and no longer those promoters off in the distance. They were probably under the table, maybe even (here and there)
sitting next to me, although I was unaware of it. Ignoring "urbanism,"
how would I have had the faintest idea of what the word "promoter"
really meant? It had such a nice ring to it, so useful, so attractive, or
maybe so anodyne. As for the greatest lords, the superstars, the bank
financiers, the kings of business or politics—and what an adventure politics was in those uncertain days!—had they been present I would not
have recognized them, and had I recognized them I would have found
them charming, well-mannered, even ornamental. I judged by the standards of La Bruyère and Montesquieu. My reading made me myopic
rather than penetrating.

For the rest, what difference does it make? What matters is that a
group of men so different yet very remarkable (at least they thought they
were), for the most part young (let us say those in their forties, who were
given to see nothing but decay in those in their late fifties), hesitant
about nothing, especially not about themselves, were involved in this
great enterprise. Not only did they sketch the general contours, the
general program, map it out to insure its success, but they identified
themselves with the task and fixed—for themselves and for all those dependent upon them—the point of departure for more than fifteen years
of stunning success. Not so much in politics or administration. Administrative careers have continued to be, for the greater glory of the Parisian
administration, what they have always been. The change has been in construction. The great projects quite naturally become the fiefs of those who
launched them or contributed most to get them built. To some a large
slice of the pie, to others a small slice, and nothing at all to skeptical
architects or nay-sayers. To some, monstrous projects, that is to say ten
years of work and the possibility—monsters loving each other and pro-
ducing other monsters—of spawning enormous business from nothing.
Some barons of reinforced concrete have amassed great fortunes in two
or three years. Obviously, this is more time than Montesquieu's lackeys
needed. They got rich in a single night.[4] Still it is fast and relatively novel
in the history of Parisian enrichment, which has known some remarkable
cases over the centuries: for some the high-rises of whatever size; for
others a skimpy public housing project, a grade school, or underground
public toilets, or better yet, since they pride themselves on having taste

4. The reference is to the scandalous financial manipulations of John Law in the 1720s
(satirized by Montesquieu in *Lettres persanes*).

and being so vigilant in preserving the old, the impossible task of restoring some old building amidst the proliferation of new ones.

The plan is one thing: the men are different, some completely honest, some only in it for the money, some serving Paris, others using Paris as if it were any other city; some men adhering to the written plan, others more interested in its manipulation, in extending it, using it as an introduction for what they want it to say or what they can make it say, rather than for what it actually says.

The dove might believe that it could fly even better in the void.

Kant

A ND what does the plan say? The question needs asking, for the prose is often confusing, sometimes metaphorical and heavy-handed, à la Claudel, rather than with the light touch of Giraudoux; sometimes studded, in order to complicate matters, with American words. The United States, in any case, provides the model and the vocabulary, the new goal and the necessary neologisms, just as one finds in the catalogues put out by the big department stores the tools one needs, their names, their prices and what they are to be used for; one shouldn't confuse an expressway with a turnpike, a shopping center with a supermarket. But what about the familiar drugstores, which are ten or fifteen years old, what exactly are they? There is an additional difficulty to be included, a certain use of the French language that is simultaneously pompous and frivolous, clear and opaque—I don't want to say chiaroscuro—which a pursuit could not help laughing at. In the organization of things as in the realm of ideas, in treating of cities or philosophy, imprecision of language only expresses the impossibility of putting into words what does not exist and whose final form is unknown. One resorts to images, phrases, paraphrases, assertions, exclamations, questions which work as well for the contrary case. But do the philosophers do otherwise? What a splendid subject for our young researchers interested in such things: the obscurity of administrative language. The more they concentrated on the prose of officialdom the less time they would have to pulverize Racine.

This is what I thought at the time and I continue to think as I read one of the principal documents of this plan for Paris, dated 1956. "It is easy to have grandiose ideas, to cut Paris into slices with highways, to raze the center of the city and put up skyscrapers. It is easy to have ideas, but much more difficult to realize them." What does this say? This "it is easy," these "grandiose ideas," are they condemnation or ill-disguised approval, irony or enthusiasm, apology or criticism, fish or fowl, for or against? Maybe he wouldn't even have understood the question, if there had been a question. Those who might have asked such a question were rare at that time. Even I, to whom these words now seem surprising, at the distance of twenty years, didn't think they posed any specific danger to the city at the time. They seemed only a wave of thought, understandable in the circumstances and perfectly excusable, the result of a certain laxity of style. Yet was not this central Paris razed, replaced by skyscrapers, and all the rest? Was this not the announcement of what was to become of Paris? And the speaker had no awareness of this, anymore than his auditors. If they had, they would have fled in horror. Some of them are now horrified and will never forgive themselves for not having understood, for having applauded, for having let things happen, for having participated. They dream about it at night, they have nightmares. Rather than look each morning at the scene they helped to create (while others work with pride and sing the praises of their high-rises), they prefer to live elsewhere, spurning these creations, much like the old Ford that Dos Passos described, ending its days far from the highways, far from other cars, in some isolated spot one gets to in a cart driven along a rural path. To comfort an old friend who blamed himself for one of these horrors that assault us, I explained that he is not at fault. The authors of these projects, or most of them, could not have understood where they were going, what they were doing, what they said. Beyond the responsibility of men—and this was doubtless more important—there was that of the projects themselves. Once launched, they had a force of their own and went faster and farther than anyone imagined, or thought, or wanted. In a word, I explained to him what I have set forth in the first section of this book.

My words were not uttered out of selfless charity. Contrary to what many think, *consolatio,* in which Seneca excels, is not necessarily a false genre, a kind of amiable insincerity. Even beyond the circumstances I have described elsewhere, I am convinced that with the best good will in the world and the greatest respect for Paris, "the renovation of neighborhoods" brought us closer and closer to what we now have, by a series of destructions and constructions which, obviously, are not over. Unless some terrible check intervenes, it will continue, until we have "la plaine des Sablons."

We must not, however, put excessive emphasis on circumstances. It is a question of the concrete situation, but above all it is a question of the men, certain of whom played key roles and knew perfectly how to exploit the situation and present it in the light most favorable to their interests. This is how it was for the builder—was he architect or engineer?—my cowboy presented in an earlier chapter, who seems to me to have been the evil genius of this whole business. When it comes to the exploitation of Paris, I find him the incarnation of evil. He died a few years ago, and I had nothing to do with his death. He was unable to contemplate the extent of his work. I had no need to console him for it. He was not the kind of man one consoled. The city that was destroyed and remade, and which will probably continue to be remade along the same lines, is more or less the city he envisioned. He directed the first steps in the process, took them in such a way that they were irreversible, marked off, with broad pencil strokes and without much careful consideration, the zones to be "renovated," over which he had control.

These were the areas to be demolished, or what they hypocritically called renovated. From the Porte d'Italie, where they were already chomping at the bit, to the Porte de Clichy, an army of bulldozers leveled everything in their path. Only the beautiful west side of Paris was spared, but there would later be other plans for the west. The delimited zone thus corresponded to all the neighborhoods on the circumference of Paris, a zone they called, with a happy turn of phrase, "the Paris croissant." A croissant is, as everyone in the world knows who salivates just thinking of one, a crusty and flaky butter roll that the fortunate Parisians eat with their coffee. This is a deplorable expression for a plan that literally sought to chew up the city. One cannot help thinking of the Perrault talk about the grandmother. On the land thus cleared they would build so that a far greater number of people could now live there. This work went well beyond the highly ironic wish of the municipal spokesman: "All that we ask of you is to build." Build, do what you have to, "money is the least problem." What was profitable for the builders, now fully reassured that their work would pay off? To have more people living in Paris. As a result, traffic was denser and this demanded further destruction and additional building, not only in the outer arrondissements but in the very heart of the city, which seemed to have escaped the massacre but which they were quick to gut, the force of circumstance and destiny also playing a role.

Thus it was revealed that the man who builds and the man who has charge of traffic are really one and the same. To live, to work, to circulate:

we had hardly asked ourselves which of these would be dealt with first
when I was surprised to see the builder fight tooth and nail for traffic
flow and even offer his own services to develop a plan for circulation.
What disinterestedness! The expressways we encountered at this point
led me quickly to understand the real reasons for this disinterestedness
and also what exactly these expressways were. They were not urban
superhighways, however much they resembled them. I was going to
be made to understand what they were by seeing sprung upon us in
1959 the project drawn up in 1958. This called for opening one of these
streets, baptized an expressway or superhighway or some such (it doesn't
really matter), right in the heart of the city, from the Place du Châtelet
to the gare de l'Est, and maybe even farther, on both sides of the boulevard Sébastopol and the boulevard Magenta, obliterating les Halles
from the map, along with two or three churches, a few theaters, some
"green spaces" which could be rebuilt just as well somewhere else, in
the northern suburbs for example (and other pleasantries of the same
kind). A highway, or rather (and more correctly in this case) "la plaine
des Sablons." And as places from which to contemplate this nothingness,
from one end to the other of this void, enormous buildings were put
up. Here reenters our builder and we are now better able to appreciate
his zeal.

He is the overseer of renovation and circulation, the man in charge of
the Parisian croissant, Molière's "maître Jacques" for this entire banquet.
And with him, curiously, is a man who represents I don't know what
expertise lacking in France, but he is a figure America very generously
loaned, or rather subleased to France, every time it was a question of
setting up in some overseas territory a plan of action magnificently elabo-
rated and wholly impractical: superhighways in the desert or through
virgin forests connecting hypothetical mining to deep-water ports that
one would find some way of dredging from the sand. This character had
been in Madagascar, where I heard about him. Having pronounced some
boastful words and made an expensive report, he departed. Now he was
in Paris, charged with exercising his talents on the city. By what miracle?
I don't know. And to think that they accuse Balzac of exaggeration when
he recounts such careers and such extravagant itineraries! Things had to
be done quickly. The project caused an uproar. It was rejected, but many
feared the moment when it would be adopted. Perhaps it would have
been had its authors shown themselves more prudent and had they not
so prematurely cried victory. Let's not forget we are talking about 1959.

Two or three years later and the project would have been in the bag. But in 1959, despite much progress, minds were perhaps not quite ripe. Despite some audacious decisions the habit of approving things without reason or justice was not yet commonplace. In addition, this highway project was tied into the project to move les Halles, about which some were deeply upset.

The Conversion to Monster Buildings

I N this story it is public opinion that is most interesting and important to examine, more than the plan of development and its role, more than the action of some individuals. Those who will one day write the history of these years will have numerous documents at their disposal, and principally the polls, which will clarify things in the period that immediately follows. In the 1960s pollsters started to ask Parisians what they thought about what was happening to their city, that is, about the projects already completed whose first effects they could see, or the new projects which were more or less guided by the same goals. Most often, and in stunning percentages, they thought the worst of them. The powers that be were careful to submit to the public the results of these polls which, in a good many cases, they had themselves called for. This made no difference. There was no point in hiding from public opinion facts so obvious that it was clear everyone knew about them without being told or without having them put down in black and white. In addition to the polls, and in order to flesh out these numbers, future historians will have literature, the theater, the cinema, song, the music hall, which were no more enthusiastic. And they will even have this book . . .

I don't believe that in the period we are discussing, the years before 1958, such questions would have been asked were it not for the topic of les Halles—we shall see in a moment why—and the subject of circulation, even though public opinion did not make the least connection between the measures taken to improve traffic and some possible danger for Paris. When it occurred to the newspapers (whose ardor was awakened by the Paris commissariat), to tell its readers of the marvels of the plan for the city, public opinion clearly did not understand what this meant, having no idea of what it should prepare for and what the results might be. They fixed on circulation, but failed completely to see that the proposed projects, envisioned to ease traffic flow, would in fact result in the gutting of the city. Yet there it was in black and white. We should not be astonished when it is clear that even the most ardent defenders of Paris did not foresee this. A few were vaguely disconcerted and mildly criticized the plan or concentrated their fire on some isolated aspect of minor importance—an ill-conceived building which was excessively ugly, a facade marked for destruction. Others, with Jules Romains, went so far as to applaud. At last something was going to be done—there had been nothing since the Second Empire—and we should not miss the opportunity. Only Pierre Gaxotte expressed astonishment, in an article entitled "Paris to be rebuilt": "When an architect writes me that three-quarters of Paris is to be rebuilt, I think him overly generous: half seems to me a just proportion. But what I am up in arms about is that they never attack the half that needs rebuilding, only the half that should be preserved." In a word public opinion did not understand the degree of danger, and because of this they readily got used to it. They let little things get by and gradually accepted big changes. One of the first critical appraisals of the whole was that of Claude Bourdet in *Le Monde* (October 22, 1959), which attacked "this strange urbanism" that wanted to build a highway through the Parc Monceau.

The reaction to the high-rises makes clearer how slow public opinion was in grasping the issue as it unfolded. In the old thinking about Paris, about France, about Europe, towers meant chateaux or churches. They signified power or prayer, which was itself a manifestation of power. They also meant danger, insecurity, fear, refuge. Anyway, towers were not thought of as dwellings (except for lovers and madmen). Towers as places to live were an American invention, always regarded by Europeans, who looked at them through European eyes, as reminders of an earlier Europe intruding on their field of vision. Colette wrote of "a romantic vision of New York in the fog," recounting the first voyage of the luxury liner *Normandie*, "like those towns thrusting pointed towers . . . in the dreams of Gustave Doré and Victor Hugo."

Between the wars the first towers, those of Perret for example, caused hostility, anger. After 1950, the first buildings to be called towers provoked similar responses, aside from the marvelous reaction of the Marseillaise to "the madman's house" (an early tower built in Marseille). I note especially that these responses expressed the survival of the old fears. Albert Mousset wrote in *Le Monde* (February 14, 1956): "What they are building in the suburbs is so frightening that one cannot imagine such things could possibly be built in Paris." Frightening and dangerous. "Paris lacks the bedrock geological foundations which support the gigantic buildings of New York. The equilibrium of our most recent monuments is already compromised: the Sorbonne has sizeable cracks, the Petit Palais needs overhauling, and I am not sure that the architect of the medical school is not concerned about the foundations of this building!" There was a similar reaction in the Municipal Council on December 14, 1955, in a discussion of the projects involved in the "reconquest of Paris." We have to build everywhere where there is land. But the substrata are a problem, especially in the Fifteenth arrondissement where there are cave-ins. "A woman taking a bath got out of the tub to answer the phone. Two minutes later the section of her apartment containing the bathtub collapsed."

Nevertheless it seems that prefect Sudreau had no difficulty reassuring the lawyer for the woman whose bathtub disappeared or the people of Paris that the towers were stable. Only one tower in Paris could elicit fear: the tower of John the Fearless.[5] At least this was true for the moment. Fifteen years later, as I write these lines, fear, the old fear has again fixed on the towers. In the first months of 1976 towers have cracked, have burned, have had to be evacuated because of the heat of this brutal summer, these stupid glass towers that stupid experts have built, having thought of everything, calculated everything, foreseen everything, except the essential. Concerning these towers which drive people away, and many of which, dismayingly, stand empty, the articles in the newspapers are so extensive, so well known, that it is best to save them for history without any additional commentary. But in the years I am describing, if the old fears still existed, lodged in the soul, those who feared only asked that mistakes be recognized and they could forget about it. A shrug of the shoulders from the young themselves and their calculations were enough to assuage the fears.

The projects for the development of Paris—or rather the plunder—were well-received. This fact seems to me to reflect the meeting at which those in charge—my cowboy—presented the plan. This took place at the Hôtel de Sens. André Siegfried was there, whom I had asked if I could attend and who saw nothing amiss. His works best express the importance of Paris at this time since Paris scarcely appears in them—with the exception of a *Géographie pittoresque* which is a kind of amusing diversion, the sort of thing one does with someone one knows and loves. The absence of Paris is not because it is forgotten, but from the certitude of finding it again, exactly as it was, after returning from a voyage to the other side of the world. His certitude was not in any way upset by the

5. Louis d'Orléans was assassinated (November 20, 1407), on the order of Jean Sans Peur, duke of Burgundy, in the tower here mentioned.

presentation that followed, with supporting maps, whose program I shall now present.

The Presentation in the Temple

I T was a program that still had to be accepted by the Parisian assembly, receive a favorable decision, which was no easy matter. The intrusion of the state in Parisian affairs, more pronounced than ever before, caused suspicion. Then there was the pretention of these newcomers, expressed in everything they said, to solve all the problems that the city departments and assemblies understood better than they, problems they had wrestled with for years; and this finally angered these departments, who saw a bunch of know-it-alls telling them how to run Paris. The Municipal Council was especially angered to hear that they had done nothing or that what they had done was worthless. At the beginning the Council was treated with consideration. But soon, once the first steps had been taken, one constantly heard harsh words from the smooth-talking young prefect. On the problem of the "unhealthy quarters" Sudreau said: "As you know, the first prefectorial memoir on the problem was in July 1893. It has been discussed since, and this is why . . . my generation is some- times severe." My generation, always my generation! The old councilors couldn't suppress a bitter smile. They were no more taken in now than at the beginning, before the severe rhetoric, when they were still treated with charm. In the beginning it was not pompous youth that reproached them but invincible youth that seduced them: "Jeune trainant tous les coeurs après soi/Tel qu'on dépeint nos dieux ou tel que je vous vois!" But councilor Bucaille heard nothing of the sort, he did not want to play Phèdre and Sudreau was no Hippolyte. The analogy works: the charming Hippolyte at the beginning of the play—Hippolyte and his no less ag- gressively impatient companions—and the critical Hippolyte, almost in- solent after his first victories, if one can speak of victories in the context of Paris, continued to be watched by those, indifferent to a winning smile and engaging words, to politeness or impoliteness, who knew only the facts: I am here speaking of the interventions of the Communists, about which historians will find, year by year, all the evidence they could want on construction in Paris, for both big and small projects. The general issues emerge from specific examples that one would have difficulty find- ing elsewhere and which are quite different from the troubles of the woman who left her bath to answer the telephone.

Little by little there was an evolution, one that can be traced in the

Bulletin municipal, not just in the debates over the important projects whose arguments change over the years, but in the words themselves. The words commonly used around 1955 are no longer those of 1958, and the language of 1958 would have seemed scandalous in 1955. From this point of view the municipal discourse could provide a new subject for the linguistic structuralism of our young people, so given to the study of discourse, to the scrutiny of the word seen as a thing. One could say that some words are nothing more than glacial deposits whose significance is no longer understood, or rather whose original meaning has been lost. Little by little the numerous references still made in the recent past to beauty, to taste, to the tradition of Paris, to the Parisian cityscape, to what was appropriate or inappropriate for Paris, disappear or seem frivolous when they are uttered by some orator who has not yet conformed to current taste. At the beginning of 1958 some of these words still survived. After 1958, once and for all, they would be purged from a discourse that would become functional, technocratic, operational, and administrative; as attractive, rich in nuance, and as capable of inspiring as a wall of reinforced concrete. Only André Malraux, as will become apparent, could permit himself to use extravagant and old-fashioned words. Otherwise the discourse about the city will reflect the city. To understand the city most precisely, those in a hurry, those bored by the city, will no longer need to see it for themselves. It will be enough to read the discourse of those who talk about it. The urbanization plan presented in 1965 said more about the city after 1958 than the city itself could have; less by the projects and analysis presented there than by the arguments, the language, the words. One saw immediately that this text concerned a Paris where one will not enjoy oneself. But this is only a linguistic introduction to the study of Paris, or as one would speak these days, of anticipation, perspectives, futurology. Let's look at the facts.

The important fact is that in those years an idea of Paris that was hitherto inconceivable, incomprehensible, indescribable, began to creep, little by little, into men's thoughts and into their language, or rather first into their language and then, by habit and the effect of words, into their minds. More slowly and much later it entered the visual realm. If such things had been mixed into images of Paris, if some vision of what the Paris of tomorrow would look like had been produced (the Paris of today), some premonition, some dream conjured up, it is likely that there would have been no more projects, or discourse, or words, and the Paris of the year 2000 would have returned to the nothingness that it would be best if it had never left. There were, of course, models, and they were even exposed to public outcry. The Grand Palais could not have held them all. But just as it is a long way from the model to the realization of what it prefigures, so it is a long way from a picture of the model to what it will look like in reality. The visitors to the Grand Palais seemed pleased, even enthusiastic. A few years later the same people would scream bloody murder. The organizers of the display would have accused them of ingratitude! "Cruel one, what have I done to you?" Advertising, the declarations in the newspapers, Paris front-page news as it had never been before, exaggerated publicity, all focus on the planned city. After having angered the Municipal Council, then amused it, this publicity had finally gotten the better of the Council, which was quite a feat. Then even the most skeptical, the most acrimonious, or the most hostile to all political persuasions had to recognize,—construction having begun again—that the clarion call "the reconquest of Paris" was not mere words.

At first the "unhealthy quarters," beginning with Belleville, were attacked, but at the same time several other places where low building densities made high-rise apartments feasible, for example, around the Place Daumesnil, were also targeted. Obviously, the housing problem had still to be solved and if housing was stimulated so too would be speculation. As *Figaro* put it: "When one canters the other gallops." Yet things momentarily seemed to get better, or at least evil had taken on a new face. During 1956 and 1957, in the Communist interpolations in the debates, the people being defended increasingly become those who have had their lodgings destroyed and whom the planners want to send to the far suburbs, worlds away from their work, their friends, their daily lives, worlds away from Paris. Their other choice was to move into the unfinished or badly built apartment houses with their paper-thin walls which made these exiles from the rue Belleville miss the discomfort of the rue du Pressoir.

The buildings went up, the accounting was positive. From year to year there were an increasing number. Sudreau thought it useful, once again, to remind us about "the mistakes accumulated over generations which cannot be eradicated in a few months." Then he would say, turning to the special seats reserved for city officials: "It is because we work hard, despite enormous difficulties, that we can say to you, with our head held high. . . . " It would have been difficult to recall Sudreau to some sense of modesty or to put him in his place as "a presumptuous upstart," but this did not prevent us from thinking that this youth was a bit hard to take, with his head (however charming) held high, and that it was hard to see what relationship there could be between his comparisons of generations and the building of apartments. But the relationship was quite obvious.

It was revealed for the first time at the session of March 25, 1957, when Sudreau alluded to "a project in the Montparnasse quarter under study . . . which will result in more than a thousand additional apartments." This recalls my point, or rather my problem, for which this example offers the beginning of a solution: how did a new image of Paris emerge? It happened gradually, people were not on their guard, they gradually became accustomed to seeing the finished work (or work in progress), which served both as an argument and a pretext for a new Paris. In the end what relationship is there between a simple "renovation" of a neighborhood, an inoffensive operation (like that of the château des Rentiers or the îlot Bièvre), and the Montparnasse project, which were proposed in the same speech? One made passage of the other easy. You couldn't actually talk about a ruse. The Montparnasse project was altogether too large to be kept hidden for very long. Who in the assembly did not know about it or had not at least heard it spoken of? Had there been discord the opponents would have united and there would have been a cry of scandal. What happened was that everyone got used to it. In a few years, almost in a few seasons, people took seriously what had previously made them indignant. They accepted with resignation, or rather with a kind of passivity bordering on indifference, what they had battled or would have battled in the past.

Baptism: The Heights

So it was that between 1955 and 1958 the Municipal Council pronounced favorably (and without understanding very clearly what it was voting), on most of the projects that were going to contribute most directly in the following years (and would continue to do so up to our own day) to disfiguring Paris, to giving the city another face, the nondescript face of cities everywhere, the mask of American beauty: clear skin, no superfluous facial hair, capped teeth, wide-eyed, forbidden to smile for fear of causing wrinkles, forbidden to kiss, assuming one even felt the urge.

Everything began in those years, those months, everything or almost everything that would be unanimously condemned ten or fifteen years later. Thus was this rejuvenated, burdensome, and costly carcass, which it is too late to dispose of properly, created. Aging American movie stars who have nothing to lose can get a face lift when the time comes. But when it is a question of La Défense—what a charming name—or Maine-

Montparnasse, or the Front de Seine, the only way to get rid of it is to move someplace else. This is what more and more Parisians are doing. Let me keep the list short and concentrate on what is essential. In March 1956, the old regulation against building higher than 31 meters was revoked. Several years before this, special permits had been issued, particularly in the better quarters of the city, so the builders could make money: "We cannot ask them to be philanthropists," we read in the minutes of the June 30, 1955, meeting of the assembly. Several times, in the years preceding the revocation, councilors had questioned the height restriction, and some of them were the staunchest defenders of Paris. Apparently they didn't watch what they stepped in. Thanking the assembly for its vote of revocation, and perhaps astonished at how easily it had been achieved, Sudreau said on March 22, 1956: "We have thus transcended the politics of vertical centimeters." It is indeed centimeters that would henceforth be paramount.

In the evolution of Paris this date is historic. No one realized what the consequence of the vote would be. Those who had voted for revocation had done so having become gradually accustomed to the idea of taller buildings, just as those who had put it on the agenda, who, I am convinced, did not at the time want this Manhattanization. Their vote had made it possible, but they hesitated for a long time; even after 1958 they refrained from using the revocation on a massive scale, without scruples, as if such buildings were the most natural thing in the world. I can still hear Pompidou asking, while having a glass of wine with some friends at the Hôtel Mantignon [the residence of the Prime Minister], almost timidly, almost hesitantly, if they could build a little higher, in the Belleville quarter, for example: "There is plenty of room there and the buildings are not very beautiful." I guess that one of his assistants had shown him, just as they were about to sit down to dinner, some project that, at the time, could still shock him. Questioning his friends (or seeming to do so) he questioned himself and perhaps even more Baudelaire, who lived deep inside of him and for whom "these hideous suburbs" had so much charm. So had they for me, especially Belleville, which I loved tenderly. I had suggested that if they absolutely had to build high-rises, it would be preferable to put them around the Place d'Italie or in the Fifteenth arrondissement. I did this not as a malicious act or some weakness I might accuse myself of, if I thought I had had influence in the matter, but as a momentary aberration. I did it because, like most men of the period, I could not imagine how far high-rise building would go and what it could do to Paris. The neighborhood from the Place d'Italie to the Porte d'Italie, for example, is today considered throughout the world (or at least the civilized world), as an example of the worst that can be done, an example to future architects of what to avoid, like those degraded Spartan slaves who were used to make wine-drinking repulsive to children. What a revelation for foreigners arriving at Orly and entering Paris from the airport! After Orly comes Rungis and after Rungis—this accumulation of huge boxes and empty crates that seem to have been dumped along the road in no order by those who drive the big rigs to the Rungis market. Then, before arriving at the gare des Invalides, the visitors have to pass by Montparnasse. What a shock is in store for them if, before landing, they had already been surprised to see this monstrous building from the sky. They had expected the delicate Eiffel Tower, and there was this enormity. When I myself returned from the United States, I experienced this disturbing discovery. A few charming elderly women, thinking they were rediscovering Paris, having visited between the wars, were aboard. When the cabin door was opened they cried out: "Vive la France, vive Paris!" I could have hugged them, but I was ashamed.

The history of the Maine-Montparnasse tower, of "Maine-Montparnasse" as they say, is a paradigm for the history of all the great projects (termed "operations"), even those that should be considered first if we were to follow a careful chronological order—La Défense, for example, which by itself is worth a book but which I shall not linger over. It is not that La Defense is not as important, maybe even more important, for the city's evolution. It is not that what was sacrificed was insignificant: it goes beyond anything we might imagine. Rather it is that the deliberations concerning Montparnasse took place in full public view. The texts that support my presentation are accessible and they cast light on the majority of the Paris projects. La Défense, on the contrary, has a hidden history of which I know nothing more than what prefect Pelletier told me and what he says in his *Mémoires*.

Baptism: La Défense

THE idea of using "the great artery that runs from the Arc de Triomphe to the *rond-point* of La Défense to Courbevoie" is an old one. A good starting point is the 1932 competition organized by the Municipal Council. Then, in 1954, the project, proposed by a manufacturer's organization, to build, on land at La Défense bought a few years earlier (thanks to the collaboration of some banks), an "industrial palace." In fact, this palace was only the thin end of the wedge for a much larger project which was to include the communes of Puteaux, Courbevoie, and Nanterre. They planned to build a commercial park, or more precisely office buildings for important companies. But this new complex could not be developed, could not succeed, except at the expense of other business quarters of the city, which explains the lack of enthusiasm among municipal councilors, representatives of the threatened quarters, and especially a councilor from the Fifteenth arrondissement who insisted that this "industrial palace" would compete with the exhibition halls at the Porte de Versailles. To these reservations were added those of businessmen themselves. "We had to attract to the project the headquarters of several important corporations," writes Pelletier, "and this was begun when a great petroleum corporation decided to concentrate here its offices that were scattered in the center of Paris, most particularly along the Champs-Elysées. Their example was followed, feebly it must be said, and unfortunately not by any public or official organization, such as the ORTF (French national radio and television), any government ministries, or any international organizations." Thus there was only a trickle. This place of exile did not attract many people. It is far from Paris, it is not Paris, it will never be Paris.

The request for a construction permit for the huge CNIT [Centre des nouvelles industries et techniques] at Puteaux and the creation of a construction site in 1957 marked the beginning of the operation. As for the size and height of the buildings, "they had decided on the towers," Pelletier writes, "but for a height less than what would be built." These words foreshadow the difficult sailing from 1960 on, particularly ten years later, with the frenzy of high-rise building. There was an outcry when the Parisians saw a few high-rises already mounting to the sky, upon returning from vacation, the traditional time for bad surprises. There was also an outcry from the finance minister, Giscard d'Estaing, which echoed public opinion. All the newspapers covered the clamor. The headlines were uniformly strident: "M. Giscard d'Estaing wants to lower the towers of La Défense." *Le Point* for September 25 wrote: "One fine day in April 1972 a young technical expert at the Ministry of Cultural Affairs, M. Antoine de Clermont-Tonnerre, returning to his apartment [from vacation?] suddenly saw, at the end of the historic perspective leading from the Arc de Triomphe, the eventual 170-meter shaft of the GAN Building [Groupement des assurances nationales]. He warned the prime minister, Jacques Chaban-Delmas. In June his successor, Messmer, set up a working committee to examine the terms of the financing in order to see if they could "amputate" [couper] the towers a bit. . . . " At the beginning of September Messmer got an answer from Giscard. It came as a great surprise: despite the terms of financing, the severe chief financial officer of the nation chose the most radical solution. He too, he explained, had been literally shocked when he drove to his office in the Louvre, by "this monumental mistake." If I accept the story it is not "he too" that they should have written, but that he was "among the first" (including the author of this book) who wrote in protest to the president of the Republic—a letter which will doubtless be found in his correspondence, if he didn't simply throw it in the wastebasket. I therein wrote, among other pleasantries, that the lion when he gets old ought to wear glasses. But the lion, being the lion, knows what to do, not on account of his humble correspondent, who should not have so inflated a sense of his own importance to think his message was considered, but because of the weight of opinion against the project which he ought to have felt—even though he was cloistered in the Elysée Palace.

The reply of the lion was a statement to *Le Monde,* published October 17, 1972, under the title: "The President of the Republic clarifies his views concerning art and architecture. M. Pompidou responds to questions about the Beaubourg and the La Défense skyscrapers." In regard to La Défense it was a true lion-like message—as I understand La Fontaine's lion—that is, a monument to bad faith. This leads me to believe (and without the least vanity) that my note may have had something to do with this response. Contrary to what the vain usually think, the language of mendacity is often used on friends, an enormity that one saves exclusively for them. Insincerity pushed to an extreme is only a kind of wounded sincerity, just as harsh criticism (as can be seen in my own words here) is only a manifestation of affection to which might be added a strong dose of rough sarcasm. Mendacity, insincerity, sarcasm, call it what you will, one must recognize that it is necessary to be a lion, annoyed by fleas, in order to utter, at least on the subject of La Défense, the enormities that Pompidou did to *Le Monde.*

He had the nerve to say, and without the slightest shame, that he had never considered the perspective of the Champs-Elysées. More precisely, pretending to believe that the problem posed was the perspective from the Arc de Triomphe *to* La Défense, he answered a question that had not been posed while trying to appear to be responding to a question that the entire Parisian public put to him: Does "La Défense, as it is, compromise the perspective in question?" For his imperturbable response, the whole text must be cited: "There never was a perspective from the Carousel to the Arc de Triomphe. Beyond the Arc there was nothing, a broad avenue but without any closure, either architectural or aesthetic. No one ever paused beneath the Arc de Triomphe to contemplate the avenue de la Grande-Armée, l'avenue de Neuilly, and the wretched buildings that occupied the site of La Défense. From the Carousel and the Tuileries one contemplated the Champs-Elysées and the perspective was closed by the Arc de Triomphe. There is the truth of the matter." *Quia nominor leo.*

Was there or wasn't there a perspective and what, in "truth," is a perspective? The truth is not what the lion says it is, it is what public opinion says. The perspective is up the Champs-Elysées, to the Arc de Triomphe and then to the sky beyond, the sky and nothing else. To assert the contrary is to deny the evidence of our senses, it is to disregard some famous pages that have become the property of all, which celebrate precisely this open sky, this remarkable emptiness. This emptiness is the immensity that astonished Hugo more than once: "July 24, 1830. Today at 8 in the evening, as a magnificent sun set behind the Etoile. . . . " Or his description of Napoleon's funeral procession in 1840: "We saw in the distance, through the mist and the sunlight, against the gray and the russet of the trees of the Champs-Elysées. . . . " The arch of the Etoile, and space, glory, and Victor Hugo as well, whose image blends with these images of grandeur. "They have aptly defined the Arc de Triomphe at midday as "a door to infinity," writes Barrès, recounting (in *les Déracinés*) Hugo's funeral with his catafalque set under the central arch. "That night it was a door opening on nothingness and mystery. But like all the rituals of death this funeral exalted life." On one side was the infinite sky, on the other the immense city. It is here that the two meet. It is here that Paris confronts the historian and history confronts Paris. "From this pedestal, Clemenceau, whom I salute as I walk past, has the appearance of coming to walk at our side" (de Gaulle, *Mémoires de Guerre*).

The fact is all the more astonishing, for no other spot in the city would have made the statue so eloquent. Daniel Halévy said it in his *Pays parisiens:* "The rue de la Chapelle ought to be the triumphal route since it leads to the frontier, but the French of the nineteenth century . . . were given to pomposity and one of their most singular pomposities, both architectural and topographical, has been to use for returning armies an avenue and a triumphal entry to the city that turns its back on Europe. The avenue of the Grande-Armée leads right to the ocean. Nevertheless Marshal Foch marched his troops into the city by this route, and if ever Red Cossacks take Paris (history is a pandemonium where one can expect to see everything), you can be sure they will not march up the rue de la Chapelle or through the faubourg St. Antoine, which is poor Paris. All revolutionaries are snobs. They will follow the example of the tsar in

1895, entering the Champs-Elysées, where their ancestors camped in 1815 after defeating Napoleon." Speaking of the Red Cossacks . . . But let us not reproach historians with improvising on history, as they predict or recount. I feel the same seeing the deliberate desecration of the Champs-Elysées and its glorious sky in the decision of President Giscard d'Estaing to change the route of the July 14, 1975, parade. Such grandiose parades could no longer be set against this now chaotic backdrop of La Défense.

Maine-Montparnasse

I F the history of La Défense, as with all sacrileges, is still full of mystery, at least for me, Maine-Montparnasse best reveals the way such things are born, how they have been received, approved, voted. What they have subsequently become each can see for himself. It is the beginning, which is already half-forgotten, that matters. Consequences oppress, beginnings surprise.

For years the prefecture had a file "Montparnasse," not for the quarter, which was healthy, but for the railroad station. For picturesqueness the railroad stations, each one different, held an important place. The gare Montparnasse was special, not only because it was the least picturesque of all, but also (and especially) because its characteristics were probably the best known to Parisians. The gare du Nord and the gare de l'Est were lumped together. The gare de l'Est meant the Battle of the Marne for all those who had their memories reawakened by Jean Mistler's *Gare de l'Est* in 1975. But for the young there were no differences between the two stations. The gare St.-Lazare is a peculiar monster, the largest of all the stations and yet the most deceiving: most of those using it are not long-distance travelers but Parisians who don't even have the illusion of leaving Paris when they entrain for the suburbs. Rather than a furlough they have an overnight pass. The gare d'Austerlitz is enigmatic, astride several regions. Only the gare de Lyon says something, and with an accent: the land of sun. So too in miniature, does the gare de la Bastille which hums the tune hummed in the nearby rue de Lappe: "Au bord de la Marne à Nogent."[6]

Then there is the gare Montparnasse, the railroad station of the Bretons, which means the travelers are Bretons and consequently well known to Paris, whose population includes a large number of Bretons. This also means those who work in the station are Bretons and that the neighbor-

---

6. A popular song celebrating the dances at popular cafés which attracted large Sunday crowds to the town of Nogent-sur-Marne.

hood around the station is Breton. Lastly and most important—and here we are back to the above-mentioned Montparnasse file—this Breton railroad station is neglected by the powers that be, as is everything Breton. The station is unloved as the province is unloved. This at least is what the Bretons think, for whom love is more important than it is for others. "General de Gaulle loves Brittany," my Breton students (who helped me write the chapter on Bretons in Paris in *Les Parisiens* [1967]) told me around 1960. Maybe they were right. Whatever the case, the gare Montparnasse was one of the most uncomfortable in Paris. When the weather was nasty the unfortunate travelers boarded the trains or got off them in the wind with the rain beating down as if they had been in some unsheltered barren field or on the bleak coast of the Pointe Penmarch in Brittany. And there were other unpleasantnesses. Not the risk of having their baggage stolen or their pocket picked, which happened at the gare de Lyon, or suffering an assault, which might happen in the stations crowded with rough provincials. On the contrary, the gare Montparnasse was charitable, warmhearted, always ready to carry your bags, to aid elderly women, to provide information, to love. But the deterioration and the dilapidated state of the equipment, the decay—in a word, the neglect by the authorities—sometimes led to strange and spectacular accidents. Once a locomotive went mad, left the tracks, and smashed into the façade of the station; there it remained trapped, suspended, piercing the wall, as a kind of living symbol of the crumbling station.

So there was a file on the gare Montparnasse. Periodically they would look at it, the councilors being indignant and insistent things could not continue thus. A debate would follow, identical to the one the previous year, and everything would remain as it was until the next year. Aware of the inconveniences of the place, the directors of the railroad system had for a long time made clear their intention of rebuilding the station and replacing the tracks. Agreements between the city and the railroad had even been signed. But these agreements were old and remained a dead letter.

How and why was this file opened again and how did it become something different: no longer a file on equipment but a project of urban renewal? I don't know precisely. I suppose everything was done in the utmost secrecy. The *Bulletin municipal* seems to indicate that it took a long time for the Assembly to find out and that they did so only in bits and pieces, getting morsels of information that didn't fit together and gave no idea of the whole project. As I have said it was at the session of March 29, 1957, concerned with housing, that Sudreau alluded, incidentally and after having spoken about other matters, to "another project already known to certain of my colleagues, in the quarter of Montparnasse, that is being studied. It will give us more than a thousand additional apartments." What could be more reassuring?

I was myself very surprised to receive a letter one day from some young painters living in Montparnasse. They invited me to a lecture on "The Montparnasse of Tomorrow." It would be given by someone that I had seen at certain meetings in the Hôtel de Sens, and I was completely unaware that he was so interested in minor painters and avant-garde painting. I went to the meeting which, it seems to me, was held in a local brasserie or in an artist's studio. This at least was my recollection when I came across this charming letter in my papers, two or three years ago. The memory, it is true, sometimes plays tricks, but even when it deceives us it never fails to tell us a kind of truth by underlining (and contrasting with the present) some enormity, by provoking some surprise. For me the surprise was to see again, some years later, an idyllic fraternal meeting where they painted before our eyes a good-natured picture of a future Montparnasse which would truly be a paradise for artists. Everything would turn on the construction of studios. Knowing the outcome and knowing as well that the great friend of painting, the great protector of painters was one of those who initiated the project that was going to make painting disappear from Montparnasse forever, it seems to me—the tricks of memory!—that I saw the sheep gathered to listen to the wicked wolf whose silhouette was confounded in my mind's eye with the Montparnasse tower itself, which seemed to me to have donned his pelt, taken on his somber color. The color of Montparnasse will later be criticized, even by its greatest enthusiasts. Why didn't they chose a gayer color, one less somber, less sepulchral? The less enthusiastic answered that the tint showed only too well the builders' true colors.

But here it is a question of color, of young painters and of painting. Even a question of the station and the railroad! Even of a completely inoffensive project to build apartments! Taken out of the files where it slumbered, the project became a dominant and unexpected part of the general "urban renewal," the "ice-breaking project that would facilitate others," according to the expression of the boss of the SNCF [the national railroad system], which Pelletier reported to us. He added that "this important urban project" was "a kind of balancing operation, geographically related to La Défense." La Défense on one side, Maine-Montparnasse on the other. On the question of equilibrium one might ask oneself how in the future the center would hold, the true center, the city itself, assuming anything was left of it. I don't know if this essential problem was considered, or even if it entered anyone's mind at the time, or only in retrospect. It is the old Parisian theme of balancing the various orientations of the city, especially the privileged west and the disadvantaged east. "Peaceful West Paris, punctuated with trees, with fine well-kept buildings whose iron shutters let sweetness and light through their slats, security and wealth." Oh, Aragon! Historically it is the rue St. Denis that is the frontier: on one side are the lovely boutiques, on the other the workshops. But the rue St. Denis solidly unites the two sides. Despite all the pressure the center has held. But this time wouldn't the centrifugal forces be overwhelming?

Around this time there was a clown, glittering in the spotlight, at Medrano. He sang a story, perched on a stepladder which monsieur Loyal and his frightful accomplice Paillasse were tugging in opposite directions. In the end the clown found himself on his backside. Where would Paris find itself? Who would have asked the question, assuming they had even thought of it? Had I asked it myself in those years when I described the center of the center? Great was our confidence in Paris and its enduring center, in its resistance, in the solidity of this invisible seam of St. Denis, well known to all those who continue to cross from one side of the street to the other, in these two pieces of the urban fabric that the people of les Halles hold together.

"Business has to move quickly," Pelletier writes, "and the Municipal Council before which I have several times intervened, took up the issues. . . . A committee to study the question was established. . . . It did its work quickly and soon plans were drawn and models constructed which had a 150-meter apartment-tower where, in theory, all the offices of Air France would be housed. The commission on sites . . . was not unanimous. . . . Jules Romains mounted a vigorous opposition. The project later evolved, in the course of its execution, and the number of floors in the apartment-tower was increased which, doubtless, would not have been done had the perspectives of the place been studied." These sentences sum up the whole situation. These austere lines expressing the prefect's discretion and reserve allow us to read between (and beyond) the scenes, the people, the chief actors, the spectators, and this impetuous rhythm which, at a distance of nearly twenty years, is doubtless the most remarkable aspect, the most incomprehensible, the most deserving of historical inquiry.

The commission on sites? I notice that in describing these years I have hardly mentioned it.[7] Is this an oversight on my part? But doesn't this oversight itself make sense? It doesn't matter what it used to be or what the commission on sites still is, officially. All I know about it is what I have myself seen. I was appointed to the commission in 1959 by Pelletier's successor as prefect, Benedetti, of whom I have already spoken. I had the pleasure of encountering there Claude Charpentier, whose presence, at the time, reassured me. I had the displeasure of finding on the commission the cowboy, the architect-engineer-builder and I don't know what else, who, I have already said, incarnated for me the demolition of Paris. He was there as he was everywhere, preparing everything, organizing everything, intriguing everywhere, the living programmer of every meeting, a flesh-and-blood computer. He covered the walls with sketches, he was completely in his element. When it was a question of one of his own projects he left the room, turning the meeting over to some accomplice to whom he would do a similar favor some day. I always had the impression he had not gone very far, and that if one had opened the door one would have found him looking through the keyhole. He was everywhere at once, from the kitchen to the attic, but most often in the kitchen. When something important was in the oven and he thought he needed help, he called in his aides. Then we saw men at the commission on sites we had never seen before and who guaranteed a majority vote for the project in question. This happened for his own projects and the projects of the administration, which usually were one and the same. As for his opponents, at least when they understood the true nature of things, what was really going on, when they were able to see clearly and make a judgment—Jules Romains, for example—what could they do? Sometimes they made themselves heard on small matters—an overly large building, a controversial facade, an ill-placed chimney. What else? A roof, a balcony, some other insignificant trouble we never failed to cause the landlords. When it came to important matters that involved massive sums, everything had been arranged in advance and there was nothing to be done except to ask oneself, and to ask publicly, what the commission was all about: his majesty's loyal (and powerless) opposition? This opposition might have been troubling if the powers that be had not thought it necessary to pay attention, occasionally even to express some concern at the

7. Nor have I spoken of the Society for the Protection of Parks and Parisian Beauty [Société pour la protection des paysages et de l'esthétique parisienne], headed by J.-S. de Sacy and his friends, who are also my friends—Author.

end of a meeting, to offer some vague condolences, some kind of commiseration: How can we ignore your pain, for at bottom you are right? At least this is how it was under Prefect Pelletier, "a man of good will," when Paris was the Paris of Jules Romains, and so too under Prefect Benedetti, who appointed me although he knew full well what my ideas were.

His successor was less solicitous. I stopped attending meetings as the result of an incident. This is probably why, unconsciously, I have failed to speak in this book about the commission on sites. The incident calls to mind the presentation of Prefect Pelletier and evokes Jules Romains, who was habitually silent, voicing his opposition to Maine-Montparnasse. In fact, the commission that played and continues to play the principal role, the only commission whose opinion has had and can have any impact, is not the commission on sites, but the commission of old Paris, independent, objective, competent, informed, respected.

I was not yet a member of the commission on sites at the time of this story. I know only from hearsay about the session in which Maine-Montparnasse was discussed. As for the meetings of the Municipal Council, the *Bulletin officiel* contains a sufficiently eloquent account, especially of the July 8–9, 1957, meetings at the end of which the project was approved by an overwhelming majority. This was the meeting that discussed the question of the proposed height of the building, which differed from the height of the one eventually built. The official text resurrects these days for us. It ceases to be a meeting of the Municipal Council and becomes the night of August 4 [1789], the fête de la Fédération [1790], a general reconciliation, an embrace, a concert of praise, a vision of the future, a great lyrical moment of love. As during the great days of the French Revolution each faction, each order in society, chose its best orator to express their joy. Arms were open, olive branches were waved, these were the symbols of victory. One has only to cite, without altering anything, phrases worthy of being engraved in gold on some cornice— and why not on the Montparnasse tower, which could only gain from it—just as some lines from Paul Valéry were inscribed on the Palais de Chaillot (which they scarcely improved). In this case the great inspirers were the councilors themselves. What did they say? They said "this is the true reconquest of Paris," which doubtless filled Sudreau with joy. He said that "we have to thank the administration for a project that towers over the city of Paris." The word "towers" is here, clearly the happiest choice. There will be apartments, offices, businesses. Marvelous! There will be a hotel with "telephones in the rooms" I scrupulously quote my text, "a moving sidewalk, indoor parking," and I don't know what else.

So many marvels, I forget some! Studios for artists, those adorable creatures, "because Montparnasse without artists is not Montparnasse. . . . I especially think," the orator adds (and we are indebted for the precision) "of the sculptors and painters." But since he thought about them a bit too late, when there was no room left, "we will put the sculptors on the ground floor and the painters on the higher floors." What a strange distinction, what a singular idea. What would they have to do to have a drink together? What about Michelangelo, who was both sculptor and painter; he would have to run from the ground floor to the top floor, spending more time in the elevator than in his studio, at least until he decided, if he were truly Michelangelo, to demolish Montparnasse and build something else.

Amidst this unanimity, this delusion, there was one reservation. It was purely formal, almost nothing, a couple of words, but there it is to tweak the administration over the minutiae of language. Sometimes one has to be a purist, and this was a perfect time. Victor Bucaille was the one who did it. "Why should we misuse the word 'prestigious,' reserved almost by fiat for the Champs-Elysées, and apply it, as we will, to La Défense? And these 'exhaustive solutions,' which contain nothing of value, and this urbanistic, which hurts my feelings?" *Sic incipit Cato.*

The Schismatic Markets

THE offensive against les Halles was less successful. The Fourth Republic collapsed without completing the attack. The old problem of les Halles, a problem posed annually for years before the Second World War, had, from the end of the war to 1958, been an incessant and pressing matter. The recommendation of the Economic Council (June 8, 1944), reiterated regularly, was that "a complete and rational reorganization of les Halles ought to be carried out without delay, in a place and under conditions that would assure: (1) a fixed time and place for offering the foodstuffs for sale which would create a regulated market; (2) easy access, a more rapid turnover, and less expense in moving the foodstuffs; and (3) basic hygienic conditions. . . . "

There is no doubt that les Halles had problems. They were evident in 1944 and they soon intensified. How could the markets, given their restricted space, continue to assure the provisioning of the metropolitan area and handle a constant increase in traffic? "How long do you think we can continue to ignore the evidence?" a municipal councilor declared. "Let me present it. Nothing will change the fact that the sheds at les Halles have a limited capacity, and we cannot undertake in this neighborhood the massive project completed by the Germans in the Old Port of Marseille." Nevertheless, people began to imagine an undertaking on the same scale, without expressing it openly, without then putting it into writing, but rather revealing it in incidental demands which slipped out, disguised by heavy irony: "If only the Germans had destroyed Paris," or "Londoners don't know how lucky they are." Here is the style of my cowboy. Certainly the project of using the departure of les Halles to transform and transfigure the heart of Paris did not appear undisguised until around 1960, only announcing itself shamelessly a bit later. "In a recent article," councilor Minot said on November 18, 1963, "a master of modern architecture who assures us he is not beholden to history, deplores, in no uncertain terms, that Paris did not have the misfortune to be destroyed. . . . This is doubtless unfortunate, but we must resign ourselves to it: Paris has not been the victim of an atomic bomb and it is not Brasilia." But in the postwar years this project to transform the center of Paris can be discerned in the debates about the reorganization of the markets. It is this subject that animates the indictment in which most join, even those who, in all good faith, want only to ameliorate the crisis and are the most deeply attached to keeping les Halles where it is. An indictment? Rather we should think of an apocalyptic mural which was painted with broad brush strokes during these years, in the municipal debates for example, in violent, disorganized images, often incoherent which, twenty years later, would make one laugh if this extraordinary neighborhood had not been the victim, sometimes inadvertently, of those who most loved it.

The main argument was the traffic jams, which around les Halles were stupefying; yet people involved in them, the truck drivers, coped amazingly well and were the last to complain. Then there were the traffic jams of the entire municipal area for which the market traffic was invariably held responsible, even though in the early morning hours on the boulevard Sébastopol (without parked cars because of street-cleaning) traffic moved well, which, paradoxically, was no longer the case once les Halles was moved. But at that time there was not a taxi driver philosophizing with his fare, not a secretary, not a salesgirl or a husband arriving home late who did not blame les Halles.

No less astonishing was the economic argument. "The laws of supply and demand," declares a sacrosanct text, "cannot work in perfectly normal conditions in les Halles because the merchandise cannot be presented at the opening of the market and also, since the goods are not arranged and displayed by category, the buyers cannot make a quick survey of the available quantities." I suggest, timidly, that the telephone exists and one can know at any instant the price of wool in Melbourne or cod in Newfoundland. But it seems this was not possible at les Halles. The economic argument, no doubt because it was the most mysterious and the most obscure, as is everything connected to economic science, was most often invoked. Then there was hygiene, the legendary filth of les Halles. The foodstuffs left out in all seasons, exposed to the heat and cold, in sunshine and rain, in dust and mud, sitting on the sidewalks or the walkways, in the gutters, near sewer openings. Of course, I cite in no particular order the accusations as I find them in the speeches, without attempting to categorize them, arrange them as they do the produce at les Halles, the beans in elaborate careful piles which, in the dramatic artificial light, exude order, beauty, taste, and, of course, cleanliness. They are so fresh, so clean that it even seemed unnecessary to wash them. But filth got everyone's attention. It suggested disease and threatened public health. The fear is hardly credible if one is to judge from the robust appearance of those who worked at les Halles. Curiously, the hygiene argument, flung about by the enemies of les Halles and the partisans of a "definitive solution," had been one of the arguments of those who, beyond shame, had the effrontery to defend the destruction of the Old Port of Marseille. It too was an extraordinary neighborhood, similar in so many ways to les Halles by its destiny, by the unforgettable impression it made upon those, from every corner of the world, who saw it, and above all the themes of the indictment, both neighborhoods being thought a danger to public health: we laughed till our sides ached. Beyond the specific filthiness of les Halles there was the filth of Paris, of which les Halles was the recipient. As for filthiness, those who worked at les Halles were adapted to the imagined unhealthiness of the markets, that is, their own uncleanliness, which they were used to and even appreciated. They breathed the smell with pleasure, a smell which was no more than the good odors of meat and cheese, of the country and the barn; the less welcome smell of the day's catch, which forced the fish sellers to spend an excessive time under the shower so as not to offend their women. "It's incredible how much they can wash," their employers said. If the workers at les Halles so carefully washed their dirty linen in public, they would have found it intolerable that their neighborhood was the dump where Parisians threw everything they no longer wanted, knowing that every day an armada of garbage trucks collected the trash, at les Halles as elsewhere. One found the strangest things, transported from who knows what part of Paris, thrown in the streets around the markets. Councilor Legaret had his office in the rue des Prouvaires, at the remarkable intersection of the rue Saint-Honoré and the rue du Roule.[8] In his office, on certain evenings the "Club des Prouvaires" met; historians will find here important sources on most Parisian subjects, and here still the rich life of les Halles. Legaret recounted in a municipal debate: "You sometimes find old iron safes in the middle of the street, I'm not kidding. I even found one in front of my door. Empty, unfortunately! The counsel of the Republic of San Marino, my neighbor, a diplomat, sometimes would stop by to tell me to look in front of my door. There would be a pile of discarded junk that had not come from les Halles." I don't know how he could know. Fortunately, there was no diplomatic incident to be feared from the Republic of San Marino.

To make it more dramatic, they invoked the rats. The old medieval fear of rats. "An army of rats," the word "army" making the danger more obvious. "In addition to what everyone can see," said a councilor, "there is what cannot be seen, this army of rats infesting the basements of dozens of city blocks." Even though no one had heard of any of the workers at les Halles battling rats as Hugo's fishermen in *Les Travailleurs de la mer* are described fighting the giant octopus, those who heard about the rats or read about them in the newspapers got goose bumps. When les Halles was finally demolished they said the rats had gone elsewhere: this, alas, was the last the press wrote on the subject. The rats of les Halles were no longer to be feared.

If it had only been a question of rats! But there was also the danger of fire. The argument was curious. Since Baltard's pavilions were built of iron the speaker explained rather obscurely, they rested upon wooden piles which were "particularly combustible since over the years they had caught fire and had not been repaired." Here was a medieval vision of an army of rats attacking citizens in the lurid light of fires, a veritable apocalypse of epidemic! To complete this scene worthy of Gustave Doré, were the huge prostitutes of Villon, shameless of course, some of whom displayed their charms on the very steps of St. Eustache. Finally, there were the satyrs and clochards who were lumped together and of whom it was said, according to certain speakers who specialized in such things, that they joined and mated in a witch's Sabbath. This was especially so in certain places: "Around Beaubourg, where a disreputable population hangs out, given over to the most immoral displays" (session of June 24,

---

8. "Coin de Paris, L'îlot de la rue du Roule et ses abords," has been studied by André Chastel and his collaborators. See *Paris et Ile de France* (1967).—Author.

1954). Hieronymus Bosch at Beaubourg! This was a place predestined
for art.

These were the old arguments, but now repeated with a greater violence than ever, even by some with a hatred that many could not help but
find suspect. Those who knew les Halles were not deceived, and reproached the defenders of the place with sometimes falling into the trap.
There were those who did not know les Halles but wanted to or thought
they should have an idea about it. This was the case with the prefect. It
was under Pelletier's administration that the problem was posed, developed, and most sharply, quickly, and intensely transformed. Of the many
problems that needed resolution this was the one he found the most difficult to resolve, in all justice, for the greatest good of the city, which was
his especial concern. Truth, loyalty, altruism, he had everything needed
to decide or delay. His department heads overlooked nothing pertaining
to les Halles. They were as competent as their information was useless,
from the point of view of which course to follow. They themselves would
have been embarrassed to make a choice had they been forced to do so.

Those prefabricated and omniscient technicians I have described already, who were equally at home in the prefecture of the Seine or the
Quartermaster's Corps or the Ministry of Culture, or any ministry, for
they are all equally useful, had not yet descended upon the prefecture, or
there were too few of them to be truly dangerous. Consequently, the prefect went to see for himself, sometimes at inconvenient hours, which was
the best time. Early one winter morning I saw him on the boulevard
Sébastopol, in the glare of those feeble lights used by the merchants to
illuminate their high stools from which they survey the constantly changing scene, doing their accounts, paying out and receiving, supervising.
We had a coffee in that café of cafés aptly called "les Halles." It is still
there. Sometimes I stop by to have a drink to what used to be there. I
think I am not the only one who does so. Perhaps it was this chance
encounter with Pelletier that led me to concern myself particularly with
les Halles. From the "working and dangerous classes"[9] to les Halles,
where the working classes, though working, were not in the least dangerous, was only a step. Still it was necessary to understand this. The technocrats had failed to do so or would have looked at me wide-eyed, like
the fish staring at one on the slabs in the seafood pavilion. Prefect Pelletier didn't need to be told twice. Here was the evidence itself.

9. A play on the title of Chevalier's most famous book: *Classes laborieuses et classes
dangereuses* (1958).

I didn't have a lot to say to him about the problem except that it was more serious than he imagined and more serious than anyone in his entourage imagined. Above all it was of another genre: it was not a neighborhood problem but a city-wide problem. By studying the ancient site of the markets and their evolution over the centuries one would understand the fabric of Paris. Just as the original location of the markets had inclined the city in a certain direction, a new location would abruptly reverse this direction. To change the location of the markets, even to alter the markets, was to run a great risk. To tamper with les Halles was to tamper with Paris.

I don't know if this opinion carried any weight. I don't think so. It had no influence some years later when Louis Vallon, no less hostile than I to moving the markets, in a critical debate cited as evidence what I wrote in *Les Parisiens* of the importance of what I called, not the center, but the center of other centers. The group of quarters that touch on les Halles, that branch off from the markets, that draw some of their life from the markets make up—from Châtelet to the gare de l'Est, from the Marais to the Place de la Concorde—the essential Paris. Was I completely sure this contention was true? If nothing else, what eventually happened would prove that I was right: the decrepitude of some of these neighborhoods a few years after the markets disappeared is the best evidence of what the destruction of les Halles meant.

More important than my opinion, more important than any opinion, than the files or the advice of experts, than arguments or statistics, I believe in the very existence of les Halles near the Hôtel de Ville, vibrantly alive and not having the least indication of dying. Gathered to discuss les Halles, the councilors always had the impression of doing so with the markets looking on. Many of them had walked among the market people that very morning, among the cries and the press of the crowd, and others had walked to experience the spectacle, to take in the vivaciousness and also to chat familiarly, to be called "Monsieur Councilor," sometimes even to have a cup of coffee in one of the cafés where in a few minutes you can catch up on all the gossip, some of which may prove useful. Listening to a councilor tell me about his morning walk I said to myself that in fact Cardinal de Retz, not far from this very spot a few centuries earlier, had done the same thing.

Given all this, how could the Council see the problem of the markets in the same light in which they saw one of those problems that the majority only knew about from official reports or hearsay? La Défense, for example, far from the city's center in a place where most had never set foot, or even Maine-Montparnasse, both of them the concern of technical experts or of some colleague particularly interested in the matter and in whose hands they would gladly leave it. Les Halles was something different than discussing what did not now exist and probably never would, something different than building castles in Spain and taking them for reality. This was true for many councilors, for many functionaries attached to the prefecture, some of whom had their offices in the very heart of the market district, in the midst of the vegetable sellers. For Pelletier himself, especially for him, les Halles meant faces, people one knew, friendships, people who were going to ask you: "What's happening with the markets? Is it starting again?" and "It's a joke! You're not going to do anything so stupid! You'll be the first to kick yourself if you do it." Which brings us back to my original view.

This contagious conviction of the people of les Halles carried all before it. Les Halles was there for good. However irrational it was, or corroded, who would dare touch it? The price of produce, the filth, the rats, these were things to make jokes about. . . . As for the prostitutes, this too was no accident. . . . Everything worked at les Halles for the greater good of Paris and everything would continue to go well in Paris as long as everything went well at les Halles. But if something happened to the markets we could fear the worst for Paris. At the end of the Fourth Republic the situation was little different from what it had been ten years earlier and there were no serious reasons to imagine any change for a long time. With a few additions, notably an important investigation of the Institut français d'opinion publique in 1958, the file remained essentially unchanged.

The Fifth Republic would see and do things differently. On July 7, 1958, a councilor declared that the time had finally come "to put an end to" les Halles, as well as other matters: "At last it is going to be possible to make important decisions. The law of June 3, 1958, which gives us full powers, gives us the right, for six months, to dictate laws on the order of things." The affair will take some time and the coup de grâce, expressed in the language of the lurid killer or the butcher—this brutal "to put an end to"—was still in the future. The city itself would benefit from this reprieve. But before describing this period of grace—the last years of the wonderful city—let us try to understand how it was put to an end.

Chapter Nine

"En finir . . ."

Although Rome, the most gigantic Empire that ever existed, is no more, it is yet with us, a living source of activity and inspiration. . . . What is admirable is that it has suffered no loss of character, of soul, of appearance, in this rapid transition. . . . It is for this reason that Rome once again teaches us. It says, not with Septimius Severus as he lay dying: "I have been everything and it is nothing." But rather: "I have been everything and I am life."

De Gaulle, *Discours au Capitole* (June 1959)

How did it all end? A single question needs answering: how can we explain that this coup de grâce of Paris was delivered under General de Gaulle, that this inglorious act was done during a time of grandeur, that the capital of the kingdom was given to the highest bidder under the reign of its last king? And done with the advice of the greatest writer of his generation? And with the co-operation of the one minister who could best feel and cherish the ir-replaceable beauty of the city? De Gaulle and Paris, that is also to say Malraux and Paris, Pompidou and Paris. There is the singular subject which will occupy me here, as is apparent from all that has preceded. In the first two parts of this work, in effect, I knew nothing more than what anyone could know, divine, or figure out. And since "de Gaulle and Paris" and "Malraux and Paris" are only ancillary questions marginal to more important issues, the former important for history, the latter for literature, "Pompidou and Paris" is a major problem that is self-contained both for Pompidou himself and his relationship with Paris.

Let it be said in passing: how beautiful is our old Paris
rejuvenated.

De Gaulle, televised speech from the Elysée Palace
(December 31, 1963)

To describe how de Gaulle saw Paris one should, doubtless, begin by
describing (assuming it is necessary) how he saw France and history.
He *was* France, that is to say he elevated to historical dignity, by his very
presence, the place he was in, assuming the place was not completely
ridiculous or inappropriate, not to say incongruous (which he was on the
verge of thinking about the Elysée Palace that he considered deserting for
Vincennes, in February 1959). This was a grandiose project which he
rejected for security reasons and also to spare people constant moving—not his ministers, who, after all, could be moved,—but the lesser
folk—commissioners, messengers, secretaries—whom he did not want
to burden even more. He was also totally indifferent to place: royal was
the place where the king was, sacred the place where the Holy Eucharist
was exposed. The most humble office became a tabernacle, the most dubious palace—the Elysée for example, occupied by such questionable
characters from the beginning to the end of its history—became Mount
Olympus. Yet at the opposite end of the spectrum, opposed to this universal vision, was a curious attention to material details, to matters of
decoration, perhaps less on his part than on that of his entourage. What
armchair to choose, what color for the walls? Was this Gobelin tapestry
perhaps a bit too pagan? What kind of cloth for the council table? Green
smacked too much of a subprefecture. Malraux resolved the problem: a
varnished table with a cloth of the same color, wasn't it obvious? Another
problem, the General wanted to have a film shown. Which one? Not a
Brigitte Bardot film, but *La Princesse de Clèves.*

These are all insignificant details. For the age of de Gaulle as for that
of Louis XIV the retailing of anecdotes can begin only after the reign.
There are, however, those recounted by gossipy people, those who cannot wait. Those concerning Paris are rare, or doubtful, or without significance. One phrase struck me. De Gaulle had said, perhaps remembering
something from his youth: "A capital needs two opera houses . . . look
at Vienna." Vienna where Napoleon's captive son dreamed of the chestnut trees of the Champs-Elysées. If only they had remembered this dictum
when they closed the Opéra-Comique!

Anyhow, what is the value of anecdotes and asides? As Malraux writes,
asking himself what he knew about de Gaulle: "The most profound
memory is not necessarily of conversation." Even less does one get an

idea of what de Gaulle thought of the capital from trivial talk. Over the years the Parisians would never have associated de Gaulle with demolition and building, the wheeling and dealing in the city. He had other things on his mind. The idea Parisians had of his grandeur did not fit with the building deals even if he began his reign by inaugurating a building that was erected by the previous regime and that he seemed to approve of—probably because he thought it unimportant. I do not know what photographic trick was used to show the General contemplating, from his great height, the CNIT, in a photo which appeared on the front page of certain newspapers at the time and gave the impression that he was presiding over the sand-castle contest sponsored by *Le Figaro*. People were even more convinced that de Gaulle was not involved in such matters if there was the slightest hint of a shady deal. Not being any better informed than the general public and finding this popular argument sufficiently convincing, I am close to making the opinion of the Parisians about de Gaulle my own.

> For Malraux China is only a historical incident. What interests him is not the city of Shanghai. . . . It is not a book [*La condition humaine*] about the revolution, not about an epoch . . . it is an intimate journal, the stenographic record of the discussions, the dialogues he has with himself, an X ray of himself projected onto the heroes of the novel.
>
> Ilya Ehrenbourg, review of *La condition humaine*, in *Izvestia*
> (May 1933)

D E Gaulle left everything concerning Paris to others. For what was most important, at least for a king, everything that concerned the adornment and presentation of the reign, he left to Malraux. Why Malraux? "Who is our greatest writer," Louis XIV had asked Molière. "Boileau," the playwright responded. "I wouldn't have thought so, but you know better than I. . . ." Let's get Boileau, I mean Malraux. Malraux had the responsibility for a few matters that were personally given to him by de Gaulle, for example, looking after the Trianon at Versailles. He was also to answer all the questions about Paris that de Gaulle asked or others put to him. "Ask Malraux. Malraux knows."

But what did Malraux know about Paris, and about all the other things one must know in order to deal with Paris? I looked in his books. Paris is hardly mentioned. "I have known the sparrows waiting for the horses of the Palais-Royal omnibus and the timid and charming John Glenn, who returned from space, and the Tartar city of Moscow. . . ." The sparrows of the Palais Royal pecking at the horse droppings: in his sprawling *Antimémoires* this is almost the only mention of the city and it is mixed up with cosmic images and visions of Tatary. Although personally more apt to turn to books than to people, even (or especially) if the books are mute and their voices "the voices of silence," I decided to question a friend whose name appears in these very *Antimémoires* (written in 1975). He has already appeared, several times, in my book. What he had to say is particularly valuable because he is an exact man, indifferent to the pathos that the very name Malraux unleashes, like those promontories in the *Aeneid* which nourish tempests and gather the clouds, "monstrous prodigies." I asked him the tough questions, which contrary to general opinion are the only questions worth asking: "Does Malraux love Paris?" The answer was that Malraux has no sentimental feelings. He has passions, which is not the same thing. Most men don't have passions, they have sentiments. Malraux throws himself impetuously at things. Above all he understands, but without knowing much about anything. He lacks culture. I thought, listening to these words, of the many obvious gaffes scattered throughout his books that so amuse those specialists who lack genius. He knows nothing but he understands everything. Reading his first novels one is amazed, as one is in reading Shakespeare. One wonders how a man so young has been able to understand all that his books contain.

But where is Paris in all this? An anecdote from the *Antimémoires* sums it up. Having gone to Versailles to supervise the work on the Trianon, in the store rooms, surrounded by cobwebs and dust, he came upon an old yoke for horses. "We have been looking for that at Les Invalides for fifty years," said the curator. "It's from Napoleon's hearse." The anecdote is used in Malraux's account of his visit to the pyramids: "In this corridor that leads straight through the night, so close to the Pyramids where Napoleon fought. . . ." Passing through a deathly corridor from one image of death to another. Paris in the care of a funeral orator, a man who makes funeral arrangements, who sees to the transmigration of souls, the city in the hands of Malraux, a kind of Orpheus: this does not bode well for Paris.

Let us begin with the picturesque, everything that evokes the history of the Trianon and Napoleon's hearse, and let us not forget we are talking about a hearse. We may be sure that Malraux would have easily turned the coronation vehicle itself, with Josephine and Marie-Louise seated on cushions, into a funeral hearse. The picturesque? We should speak also of the bizarre, not out of nastiness, but rather as it pertains to the many decisions Malraux made about Paris and what he himself said of his curious cast of mind—which did not seem to worry him overmuch, indeed, he even prided himself on it, as he did everything about himself: "I love bizarre museums because they gamble with eternity." Without any scruple we can incorporate this bizarre metaphysics, or more simply the bizarre itself, in considering everything Malraux did to Paris.

In this catalogue of Malrauviana, so to speak, this museum without walls, we can already walk through several rooms. Consider the robust maidens of the Tuileries Gardens, the milkmaids of Maillol, called "nymphs," one of which, we learn (December 29, 1974), was even led away. A suitor, desirous of cashing in on her bronze charms, having kidnapped her in the dead of night, had to recognize that he had overestimated his strength and eventually abandoned her on a sidewalk in the suburbs. What about the Opéra ceiling, and the Louvre moat—"no Roman palace," wrote Voltaire, "has an entrance comparable to that of the Louvre, for which we are indebted to this very Perrault whom Boileau dared ridicule." Not to mention the very arrangement of the Louvre museum: "I love bizarre museums." What about his idea, no less bizarre, of building a museum of the museum in plaster, on the metro platform. How can one explain the stupidity of this idea? The technocrats of culture, described in an earlier chapter, found it so appealing that we will soon see, it appears, a phony museum of the Beaubourg museum at the nearby metro. A box of nails will do the trick, and they can be bought almost next door, at the Bazar de l'Hôtel de Ville,[1] which specializes in these items.

There were so many other innovations! The most detestable, because the most costly and useless, and doubtless the most dangerous, was to whiten Paris, beginning with the monuments. How many monuments could have been saved in Paris and elsewhere, how many churches and even cathedrals could have been saved with the money spent on the most famous Parisian facades, particularly that of Notre Dame, which has probably not yet recovered from the effects, not to mention the enormous sums consumed that had been set aside for repairing the foundations. As for the "whitening" of the Paris monuments, Mercier already said terrible things in his *Tableau de Paris*. So too has Charles Garnier. Writing

---

1. A department store across the street from the Hôtel de Ville, famous for its hardware department.

on June 27, 1883, to the prefect of the Seine to ask him, after authorization from the president of the Council, for "the suppression of the abominable edict that prescribed an artistic assault, the periodic scrapping of houses." He concludes: "If, as I hope, you are opposed to this perpetual vandalism, the artists will have you to thank for bringing it to an end. If, alas, you share M. Rambuteau's ideas I will continue to make this appeal until my complaints are heard." Neither Garnier nor Mercier explain, they assert, declare, and even threaten. How true it is that in such matters explanation serves no purpose. It is useless to explain: Insult is the appropriate language. It too accomplished nothing, but at least it gives pleasure to its author, and perhaps to a few others.

Whence came this idea to sandblast Paris and who put it into Malraux's head? From what I was told I long thought it was his chauffeur. "Everything is dirty, black, M. le Ministre," his chauffeur said one day. "A good scrubbing can't hurt. If I were you, I would clean Paris." Since I take delight in the comic and popular dimensions of history, partly because they remind me of stories of Old Paris when a chambermaid or a lackey had some impact on events, I was tempted to include this story in my own history, but not without having asked a few of my former students, now young technocrats in Malraux's entourage, to verify this with their boss. I should add that none of them was willing to do so. My request was received with disbelief: "Ask Malraux if his driver . . . you cannot be serious!" I realized that, instead of giving an answer, Malraux would have looked daggers at the audacious one who had dared assume that things happened in this way. A bit later I learned, incidentally, that the idea came from a successor of Prefect Pelletier, Prefect Benedetti, or rather from his wife who, full of feeling and love for Paris, was the originator of several such happy decisions. Is it necessary to say that when she thought about "whitening" she did not have only Notre Dame in mind. Trying to imagine how it came about I picture a brilliant councilor's wife arriving late to a meeting of the commission on sites, presided over by the prefect, and offering her excuses. She had been caught in a traffic jam in the Place de la Concorde. She had time to admire the whiteness of the facades, and she thought it might be extended to the entire city. Suddenly, inspired, she said: "It will recall for us the age when the cathedrals were new!" To which her companion, no less brilliant, responded: "Speak for yourself—I'm too young to remember that, my dear!"

This is Paris considered from the point of view of the bizarre and from the point of view of death, and I would not be surprised if the city were identified by him with the bizarre; but the almost total absence of Paris from Malraux's work prevents me from verifying my hypothesis. Why should Paris be made an exception? It is the only living city to be loved by him among so many dead ones, which were the only ones that excited him and that he thought of as living. The ruins of Nineveh, "its bricks crumbling in the clay they were made from," the ruins of Mareth, the ruins of Egypt, the ruined Mayan temples, why not the ruins of Paris? "There will be nothing left of these palaces that saw Michelangelo, exasperated by Raphael, storm off, nor of the small Paris cafés where Renoir sat with Cézanne, or Van Gogh with Gauguin." Nor will there be Brasilia, about which he pronounced, in August 1959 before the Brazilian authorities, a speech which more resembled a funeral oration than an appreciation: "Under the immense indifference of the clouds. . . ."

Under the immense indifference of Malraux. I don't know what Brazilian ears heard any more than I know what the Parisian authorities understood who came to the meetings in the Elysée Palace to ask Malraux (Malraux who knew), his opinion about the future Brasilias in Paris. How many times have I heard it certified, while standing before some model which by comparison made poor Brasilia look like a Parthenon, "Malraux has seen it, he is enthusiastic!" Or, "Malraux wants it." "Maine-Montparnasse was desired by André Malraux. It is not useless to remember this fact. What a conclusion to the *Voices of Silence*," said André Fermigier (*Le Monde*, August 20, 1974). "I have the weakness of believing myself useful," Malraux wrote somewhere. He therefore welcomed, at least so I imagine, the would-be architect of an extraordinary project. The more extraordinary the project and the more unexpected the design the better the chance of attracting the attention of a great writer; this, at least, was how the visitor saw Malraux. A high-rise builder, for example, explained that since the seventeenth century, Paris had only built horizontally. One had to go back to the Middle Ages to find towers. One could make the observation that the tower of the faculty of science or the Montparnasse tower were not the same thing as the military tower of Nesle. But Malraux could only be interested in these historical somersaults, assuming he listened and looked. What is certain is that he talked and, from the "immensity" of what he said—and his speech at Brasilia gives us some idea of that—the visitors, the would-be architects of towers, could always conclude that Malraux agreed with them. Was he in agreement or wasn't he? "Under the immense indifference of the clouds . . ." But if Malraux was in agreement that meant the Elysée Palace was in agreement.

Pompidou

POMPIDOU, on the other hand, played a different role because of his responsibilities and how long they lasted. "Because of what I am and what he is," de Gaulle writes in his *Mémoires,* "I appointed Pompidou in order that he might assist me for a specific period of time. Circumstances were such that I kept him with me for longer than any head of government had kept a minister for over a century!" It is clear that the important issue is not de Gaulle and Paris, or Malraux and Paris, but Pompidou and Paris. When one speaks of de Gaulle and Paris, what this means, with regard to the facts, choices made, and results, is Pompidou and Paris. This is a difficult subject. If Malraux spoke a great deal—I dare not say "wrote a great deal," which would be merely irrelevant— Pompidou hardly wrote at all and spoke little, usually to dissimulate his thoughts rather than to reveal them. I have read somewhere that in his last years he confided to some specialist in what is called contemporary history that, all things considered, he had been wrong about Paris. Asked to explain the towers, he would have told his visitor about a green-shuttered cottage in the same way that years ago they used to show slides. Often he said something, or amused himself by saying something, in order to set others wondering about exactly what it was he had said. This was a kind of private joke he made by inserting literary quotations in a long speech. He used the most banal quotations, the most familiar, and hence the least known to those who were listening to him; they needed to identify the quotations for their articles and had to scurry to the Bibliothèque Nationale to look up the sources. After certain press conferences there were a lot of journalists at the library in the rue de Richelieu. Had he said "Rodrique as-tu du coeur?" which he would not dare say, or "Mignonne allons voir si la rose," he would have caused just as much perplexity and created just as many searchers of dictionaries of quotations. It became necessary to ask *Le Figaro* to stop their contest to identify these quotations—and I no longer remember the year—because the newspaper's readers, though an elite, constantly pestered the librarians to find the answers. The librarians added that if Pompidou himself didn't stop this habit of quotation, their lives would be an absolute hell.

This is why, instead of cobbling together a *Pompidou and Paris* from words reported or heard, I would rather imagine understanding the problem as some sort of school exercise, an amusement, the kind of intellectual game one plays with some historical personage, well known from authentic, signed texts or inscriptions, but for whom the information is fragmentary. This is how the Roman historian Jérôme Carcopino constructed his book *Sylla où la monarchie manquée* or, even better, his *Caesar*.

I would entitle my first exercise "marbles." One of our friends who was poetically inclined had the habit of giving Pompidou each year, on the anniversary of his appointment, a marble in a small leather sack, somewhat, I imagine, as in Augustan Rome the poet Virgil, or some lesser versifier, gave Augustus a precious relic unearthed in the poet's fields. Why a marble? we had asked him. "Don't you think it appropriate?" he answered. Seeing in this ritual some antique mystery, we were in agreement. Then one year, on a particularly solemn anniversary, he wanted to replace the marble or give it along with another present: an original letter of Baudelaire's that we had bought in a special shop on the quay Conti. Pompidou expressed his admiration during the dinner, much more for the letter's style than its touching sentiments.

Baudelaire. Here we are at the heart of the matter. How do you explain that, loving Baudelaire, Pompidou could . . . We talked about it with friends who were as familiar with him (or as unfamiliar) as I. The problem was that the Baudelaire Pompidou loved was not the poet of Paris, the poet of "murky corners of old capitals / Where everything, even horror, is magical," or with even more reason the poet of the "suburb shaken by heavy tombs," "through the old suburb, among wretched hovels / Whose shutters hide secret appetites" the poet of this old crumbling decor which the distracted vagabonds of the inner boulevards seem to be looking for. It is not even the Baudelaire of *La Seine rose et verte,* certainly not this Baudelaire. Had Pompidou loved this Baudelaire, could he have so cold-bloodedly destroyed the quays? No, his Baudelaire was not as Parisian as this, despite the title, *Rêve parisien.* These are the verses which, far from Paris, sing of Paris with distaste: "the enthralling monotony / of metal, stone, water / . . . unimaginable gems . . . Immense mirrors made dizzy / By all they reflected." A scene of stone, metal, and glass, animated by a fountain: "a water jet that sprayed without cease / quiet neither night nor day," in a word a foreshadowing of La Défense. "For myself," Pompidou told *Le Monde* "I would welcome either a sculptural work at La Défense, very tall and very narrow, or an enormous fountain which would close the perspective up the Champs-Elysées." A Baudelarian vision, but not of the Baudelaire who loved the Parisians. His Baudelaire was not the feeling Baudelaire whose song became a part of the song of the poets of Paris, a part of a music that hardly changed from Villon to Hugo to Carco. "A fog descended on the quai de Béthune." "Will it lift tomorrow?" I asked Pompidou, who himself lived on the quai de Béthune, if he had read the column in *Figaro* in which Serge Groussard recalled that Carco had written these lines, which I personally find deeply moving, on the evening of his death. He answered me, with a touch of mockery, that they said absolutely nothing to him. "A fog descended on the quai de Béthune . . ." With what sadness I recited these verses to myself, some years later, surrounded by Parisians in tears looking at a window where the lights had just gone out, "on the quai de Béthune."

Pompidou's Baudelaire was not the poet of feeling and music, but of forms, of this beauty of form which is no more concerned with Paris, and probably a good deal less, then it is with any other place. Let me evoke the oldest memories. The culture of the students of our generation preparing for the examinations for the rue d'Ulm was exclusively a literary culture, and our taste was equally literary. Pompidou—I don't know exactly how it happened—expressed an early taste for painting. He was the first to tell *Le Monde*, "I have always bought only the works of contemporary artists. I began, at age eighteen, by purchasing Max Ernst's *La Femme cent têtes*. Why? Because I could never afford the old masters, at least those that were not either mediocre or of dubious provenance. Simply put, without a great personal fortune one can never buy any recognized artist, but one can always purchase an artist still unknown or relatively unknown." These are words that would perplex more than one of us.

In 1929 Ernst was already celebrated. *Le Rendez-vous des amis* dated from 1922. He had participated, in 1926, in the first surrealist exposition in Paris, organized by Eluard and Desnos. To be able to buy an Ernst painting at age eighteen! Young man, you were clearly living beyond your means! Henri Lemaître, an expert on Baudelaire, whose words are scattered throughout this book, explained. *La Femme cent têtes* is not a painting, but a novel, published in 1929 by Editions du Carrefour: 150 collages by Ernst with a text by André Breton. This, nevertheless, is still a surprising purchase for a Khâgneux. He would have done better to concentrate on his studies. It is true that he took the first prize in Greek translation in the general exams, along with some less significant awards. He had a head start and could indulge unusual tastes and waste his time.

Waste his time? This is a manner of speaking, insisted one of us, an attentive reader of *Le Monde*, underlining the fact that this taste for painting was not completely aesthetic. But can it ever be? Literary culture is aesthetic. To buy a used copy of Racine from a bookseller along the quais is not an investment. But is this strictly true? Let me cite de Gaulle's portrait of Pompidou: "Of course his intelligence and his culture made him familiar and at ease with ideas, while by nature he always considered the practical side of things." Why shouldn't this apply to literary culture itself? After all, it can be said, he prepared for the Ecole Normale Supérieure and ended up reading Thucydides as a textbook, like those sons of judges described by Richelieu, who learned theology to become bishops and cardinals, and ended up sometimes holding even higher positions. It is true that along the way a few become enthralled by theology and became, sincerely and unreservedly, great theologians, sometimes even saints. It was perfectly clear from the very beginning that Pompidou would never become a great theologian or a great saint. A university man by fortune, in the sense that he was the companion of those with whom he had to share board and lodging because there was no other inn on the road. The inn on his road at the time was the Ecole Normale Supérieure. There are those who respond that only chance explains why Pompidou abandoned a university life. There were extraordinary chances in his life, but so continually extraordinary that it is hard to speak of luck or the extraordinary. Everyone has his own opinion about this. The theme of the start of a career is one of the great themes of literature and history but it boils down to the commonest curiosity that leads us to want to know about others. "How did Rastignac get started?" And others less important than Rastignac. To which can be added some apparently disconnected words, gleaned here and there from conversations, which may hold the secret of how Pompidou first saw Paris.

To return to life's chances, there are those who think, and not without reason, that the *métier* of professor was the one Pompidou most loved. He derived great pleasure from teaching, at Sciences-Po for example, even when he was not obliged to teach. The same was true of those activities which he could easily have been able to dispense with but which are a part of a professor's life, no less (and perhaps more) than the actual teaching. He prepared editions of the classics in the series directed for Hachette by his friend Maillard, the organizer of our dinners in the rue Hautefeuille already mentioned: *Britannicus,* some selections from Taine and even from Malraux. He was a professor in his bones, and more than a professor, more than a literate man. Not that others were illiterate, but they were not literate in the same way, with the sometimes cruel refinement that put him ahead of others.

Pompidou was formidable. When he had been a member of the jury for the agrégation oral exams the students had had a hard time. An anecdote recounted to me by one of his later victims will suffice. One May General de Gaulle, having to deliver a speech at the racecourse in the Bois de Boulogne, didn't know how to begin, which was surprising. He turned to Pompidou. Pompidou had two verses of Racine running through his mind that he could not place. These were not verses from one of the tragedies that everyone knows by heart. French theater audiences prompt the actors when they have a memory lapse. These were obscure verses, verses from some poetry that expressed a commonplace. But what verses? Not finding the poems of Jean Racine in the Rothschild Bank, where he was director, Pompidou asked one of his learned comrades, possessed of a formidable normalien's culture, who said he did not know. After being harshly reproached for his ignorance, he discovered the two verses in question in the complete works of Racine, part of a poem entitled "Plaintes d'un chrétien sur les contrarietés qu'il éprouve en dedans de lui-même." This allowed the General, majestically, with his arms outspread in a typical gesture, to begin his speech: "My God, what a cruel war / I have two men within myself."

Was the calling of teacher the vocation of his dreams? I don't believe it for a moment. On the other hand I do not believe, contrary to what many think, that the "vocation of his dreams" was politics. Absolutely not. Between teaching and politics there was a life that he could have led, a "previous existence" in the sense Baudelaire described: "In a rapture of repose I lived there / Amidst the blue, the waves, the glories / and the naked perfumed slaves. . . ." To put at ease those who never understand anything, let us leave the naked slaves with Baudelaire. As for the rest, who can deny that it better fits his temperament, his tastes, his way of looking at life, his culture, classical culture itself which makes the enjoyment of life supreme, than does politics with its perpetual and often long stretches of mediocrity and boredom. The prison of the Elysée Palace, the renunciation of everything he loved, and the people he had to deal with! "When you think that he had to closet himself there for the last months he had to live," said one of his closest comrades, walking by chance (and with great sadness) on the rue du Faubourg St. Honoré, near the Elysée. Judging from the words heard on the quay de Béthune on the night of his death, many Parisians were aware of the sacrifice he made. He did not choose politics. He was pushed into it, constrained, especially by those who wanted to block his path or whom he thought wanted to do so. In politics as in Greek translation he could not stand not being first. Circumstances having made the decision, he devoted himself to his vocation, loyalty, conscientiously, courageously, until his final moment, always thinking of his country before himself.

Why ask ourselves about man's character, about what he loved and didn't love, about his reasoning and his comportment and the choices he made, when he himself explained it all, and lucidly, when "he revealed himself, delivering up the secret of what touched him"? The phrase is his, taken from the preface to his *Anthologie de la poésie française*. What an accomplishment this anthology was and one that nobody much commented upon! What glosses could have been written about it! For once we can thank the general lack of culture. How could this man, so secret, so impenetrable on all subjects (and especially about himself), this man whom everyone knew chose not to hear indiscreet questions, how could he thus "reveal" himself? He never responded to journalists, to politicians, to any political persons (whom he held in low esteem, whatever their affiliations) about almost anything. Terrible judgments did sometimes slip out and history will probably one day report them. May it be soon, before all is forgotten!

He never responded to those he did not respect. But he responded to poets, through the mouths of poets. He responded as a poet convinced, and with good reason that only a poet could understand this special language or would have the necessary curiosity to penetrate it. Who better would read this collection attentively than the youth of France, whom he knew well from having himself explicated these poems for them, with this freedom, confidence, and ease that was the natural climate of an epoch when the teacher was a friend, not a suspect instantly put in the dock?

Here then, in beautiful verse, often the most familiar in our language, are the answers to the questions we put to ourselves. "Your memory, equal to uncertain fables / Rests suspended in my haughty rhymes." One could apply to the compiler of this anthology these verses of Baudelaire which he chose (only a single verse on his origins and the beginning of his career, but one perfectly appropriate, sweeping all before it, explaining everything: the man, his career, his way of judging others, his self-assurance, his considerable scorn for the powerful, his capacity for friendship, his faithfulness to his origins).

A simple verse of Villon: "Poor, I am from my youth / Of poor and humble origins . . ." That's enough. As for politics (discreet, indirect, hidden, allusive), it is there because it has to be, because one would be astonished if it were absent. Politics speaks through the mouth of Corneille: "And as he sees in us uncommon souls / Out of the common order, he makes our fortunes." "This sad and proud honor agitates me without exciting me" (*Horace*). There is also: "You want to assassinate me tomorrow on the capitol." I leave it to the reader to interpret as he will. Finally, from Racine, a certain "My astonished genius trembles before your own" which must have amused de Gaulle. There is not great prominence given to politics. It is there and cannot be ignored, "but it doesn't matter. One must follow one's star." The line is from Molière, from *The Misanthrope,* but not in a light mood.

"I love recreation, love, books, music, the town and the countryside, in a word everything. . . ." Here is what matters and it comes from La Fontaine. Life, but what is beautiful and touched by beauty, which is the same for Baudelaire as for Malherbe: "Beauty, my lovely obsession!" Life joyously and vigorously lived, not whined about. There are not many verses here about death. It's a peasant's healthy way of looking at death by not speaking much about it. With an almost joyous tone he one day told us, at lunch, about his father's death: "It was a fine death!" Proudhon spoke thus of his own father, an old kindling carrier in the forests of the ancien régime. "An old woodcutter completely covered in twigs and branches . . ." La Fontaine's *La Mort et le bûcheron.* On the question of death, as well as all else, it is La Fontaine who has the most to say. "Death is a cure for everything / But let's avoid it as long as we can: Suffer rather than die / That is the motto proper to man." And God knows, when it came to suffering, Pompidou had more than his share. "As for myself, I am doing an apprenticeship in illness," he wrote in a letter to one of us who was concerned about his health. In contrast, we have all the jeremiads of Malraux, this endless funeral oration even delivered over the healthy cradle of Brasilia, about the death of civilizations, the death of cities, pure hogwash: "These stories interfere with our appetites but they don't prevent him from digging in." Even more than this ridiculous and useless meditation on death, there is the practical side of life. As always, and under all the embroidery, there is La Fontaine. Not a Machiavellian, as Siegfried sees him, but full of good sense. In *La Laitière et le pot au lait,* there is wisdom: "Who doesn't roam in the country / Who doesn't build castles in Spain? . . . Each has fantasies . . . should something happen to return me to reality / I am John the Clodhopper as before." In a word, the common sense that de Gaulle paid homage to and which, more than anything, explains the way Pompidou saw Paris.

No doubt "a city's form, alas, changes faster than the human heart." The meaning turns on the weight given to the "alas." This verse of Baudelaire's has an appropriate application. In the deliberations of the Municipal Council one finds all the possible variations, and they are also in the official speeches. The administrative repertoire contains all manner of appropriate quotations, for every circumstance and ceremony, just as in venerable families there is an accumulation of social formulas to telegraph for any occasion: "Bravo, a thousand times bravo" is highly recommended when a friend's horse wins the Grand Prix. "My heart is with you" serves equally well for a wedding or a funeral. Clearly "a city's form" is used more and more frequently as the form is called into question. I am absolutely persuaded that the phrase came from official lips when the Right Bank expressway was baptized, on February 9, 1976, "The Georges-Pompidou Expressway," or rather "Georges-Pompidou Way." Many friends of Paris wondered about this, those nostalgic about the quays of the Seine as well as friends of Pompidou. A strange thing to name after him! How should one pronounce this "alas"? Not having seen the new road I cannot say. What I am sure about is that had Pompidou pronounced this "alas" he would have wanted to say: it is very unfortunate but nothing can be done about it.

He himself thus explained it in *Le Noeud Gordien*, the book he began writing after he left the Matignon Palace and whose rewriting was interrupted by the April 27, 1969, referendum and the presidential election. The chapter in question is entitled "Toward an Economic Policy." Need I say that there is no question in this regard, even for a moment, of Paris. But in this chapter we find Pompidou's angle of vision and what he would like for Paris, or rather what he would let those do who see Paris in a certain way and want to transform it. It is obvious that this is a work of circumstance. We read between the lines allusions to recent events and also, in careful language, a settling of accounts, a complete history cast in an extraordinarily depersonalized, almost neutral language, or almost administrative. Or perhaps only the language of extreme prudence, a language that looks to the future and wants to give offense to no one. The preface to his anthology has a completely different tone. Many, myself included, have regretted that *Le Noeud Gordien* had been published so quickly. It would have been better had it appeared later and with numerous notes. The contrast between these pages and Pompidou himself appears both painful and singular. Popular feeling saw the distinction and discovered it on the very eve of his death, a distinction he left to the future. History will have to take into account this kind of deathbed revelation, this metamorphosis, this consecration of a man; it is not the first time the Paris populace has had to make up its mind about a man.

Whatever he was, Pompidou describes his economic choices in this book. I would be out of my element and it would be, in addition, of little interest to explicate them here. A single sentence sums it up: "France has chosen to compete on an international level and has therefore accepted the risks and laws involved." The harshness and even the cynicism of the words used by him in this chapter are more revealing than a long speech. It is the words, the tone, that matters, not the intention. His way of speaking about "the transfer of farmer's sons to industry"—this "transfer" from the pen of a virtuoso of the language! He also wrote that "French individualism in this field (the size of industrial undertakings), as in so many others, is tied to a dislike of trusts" and opposes them. He also praised "management and marketing which in all the most prosperous enterprises are considered essential." In sum, it is the law of profit— "what are prosperity, the possibility of investments, productivity in a word, if not profit, to use unambiguous language." What I reproach you with, you and other academics, he told his friends, is not being straightforward. In this book he certainly was.

Actually it is not very important, or rather it will be the task of history, to fix his place in the transformation of Paris. Much has been made of a letter sent November 30, 1964, by the prime minister (signed Pompidou) to the prefect of the Seine, with a covering note from the minister of the interior (who had read it first). It is a terrible letter that has as its theme surgical procedures whose ramifications I have described, dating from the Fourth Republic: rezoning, the north-south axis, cutting streets on a grid, the construction of high-rises in the zones outside the center of the city, beyond the so-called "sacred perimeter." This fig leaf of a letter hid nothing of the most monstrous schemes. There is no need to reread this letter of four or five pages. It is enough to look over the cityscape. Let me, however, single out a few lines. "In order to encourage the construction of buildings for residential use, it is important to build them in zones of sufficient space so that all kinds of constraints would be limited." Or "Each of these plans will have to determine the density of building and the height of the constructions which can courageously go beyond the actual norms fixed by regulation." Courageously! All you who are audacious, march onward! I see again, as I read this letter, my cowboy flare his nostrils. Does he even have to read a text he already knows, probably better than anyone? I don't know anything about it. What I do know is that this letter, signed Pompidou, was not written by him, or even by one of his assistants. Maybe he didn't even read it. But what does it matter? It is clear he agreed with it and that he shared this angle of vision.

Whether he played a role, gave his opinion about this or that operation, whether it was a role more or less important at different times, whether he played this role during his wandering in the wilderness—that great biblical and historical wandering and his own smaller one, inflicted upon him by General de Gaulle—it will be up to the historians of these years, concerned about matters great and small, to determine. Malraux has pointed the way, from a distance, from on high, or better, he has opened the way; more prosaically, he has furnished some words for the journey, one of those pompous texts one inscribes as an epigraph: "For de Gaulle," he wrote in 1965, "Pompidou was General Berthier. Napoleon won all his battles when Berthier was with him. Berthier was the tactician who complemented and inspired strategy. He was the man who never got bogged down in numbers, who was not easily fooled, who remained untouched by false rumors, who knew exactly where the grenadiers were or the lancers of the 14th brigade." He was also the man who knew—and this was especially important I presume—how things were administered. He used the old-fashioned word "intendance"[2] on good days, and much less sonorous words on bad days. This is a flattering eulogy coming, as it does, from a connoisseur, a familiar of the gods. The man thus dubbed Berthier ought to feel himself flattered, even amused to find himself given a uniform and endowed with some other characteristics that, of course, the author of the *Museums without Walls* knew absolutely nothing about.

That didn't prevent him from seeing the Napoleonic campaign differently. In the last conversation Malraux had with de Gaulle and which he recounts in *Fallen Oaks*, the General said to him: "Historians imagine that one can do what one wants when in power," which would seem to indicate that de Gaulle was in agreement with Bossuet, which was not bad company. "Louis XIV complained of not being obeyed in the Auvergne," Pompidou's province. "Napoleon complained he had had to go to Orleans to be obeyed there. And I could not have built useful buildings at les Halles. Everything was corrupt—in May 1968 and even long before. This was because everything went off course, even before the reelection of 1965, when I brought in Pompidou." Malraux, citing these words, saw in them "a cold, impenetrable allusion to something indescribable."

2. The word for the public charge of administration. In the last century of the ancien régime the Intendant was appointed by the King to administer one of the thirteen provinces of France. This official was directly responsible to the monarch.

We should see in a conversation between Malraux and de Gaulle or Mao, as reported by Malraux, that it is essentially about Malraux (which is in itself important). We can say that the "indescribable" something, in which each will see what he wants to see but where Malraux is most concerned, there probably lies this confused field of politics and economics which the historians will have to investigate. How did de Gaulle see the economy? What did he know, or rather what had he learned, and from whom? But above all what did he think of men? Cruel words are often cited. But one does not accomplish things politically, much less economically, with choir boys and philanthropists, and especially not with economists. These things were Pompidou's concern, at least in theory. This was more true when things turned sour, when projects were stalled, when some particularly embarrassing scandal was uncovered. The historians will nuance all this, but I have the clear impression that during the happy years of de Gaulle's reign, if Pompidou had ultimate authority over the economy, if he was Berthier, some subalterns (to use military language) had access to the Elysée and could themselves authorize this or that project, because they had the favor of the prince. Even though Pompidou was completely informed and most of the time in agreement, I would say he was detached. It is no accident that he used as an epigraph for the *Noeud Gordien* these words of Valéry: "this curious inaction/so full of power." This certainly describes the temporary lethargy of the spring of 1969 which he was impatient to see pass. But it signifies even more. For me it sums up his very particular, very curious responsibility for this disfiguration of Paris: here and there he was active, although I know nothing about this, but in general he played a significant role by the way he saw Paris, by his consent, by "this curious inaction/so full of power."

He was in agreement. More, he was in harmony with circumstances, with these forces I have described, which he knew or understood better than anyone and in which he took pleasure: "That's what profit is all about." During these years, his years in power, things irresistibly developed to make this period the golden age of real estate and building, or rather the golden age of the great facilitators, the banks, from beginning to end, almost without interruption. From 1963 on, especially, when the building consortia came into being, that is to say when the banks formed such consortia, they needed government support immediately. The banks intervened directly with the prime minister and obtained regulations that would permit them to function regally and that would open Paris to exploitation. After the slight slowdown of 1967–68, the crisis of 1968 itself would seem to have been the signal, once the great fear was passed, for new and more audacious undertakings, as if the victory over the revolution could be considered as the justification for a system that the good-for-nothings and the filthy demonstrators of May 1968 had wanted to reject. The gods agreed. From now on everything would be allowed, everything would be possible, especially during the months that separated Pompidou's departure from his return to power. When he was elected president he himself would observe that in his absence some had lost no time. His style was not to stand in the way of such doings. He was determined to imitate de Gaulle, to hold himself aloof, even if administration had been his special preserve for many years. Henceforth, he would be more concerned with foreign affairs, he would confirm or ignore the decisions that were made, he would not interfere with some astonishing appointments. These days were unique for the lords of building and for all those I have described. In the full light of public scrutiny and awareness, without any dissimulation, even with jubilation, the president of an important commercial bank will speak, without the slightest embarrassment, in the pages of the revue *L'Expansion,* of this "complex net of influences that work in a double sense in which human relations, memories, habits, and interest play a role it is difficult to assay." The same bank will pride itself, in its house organ, on having, "a unique and secret record of the parcels of land and a map of the various banking fees paid in the Paris region." To best realize its potential, the bank created a special department whose job consisted of "coordinating the acquisition of land in order to reduce the annoyances due to internal overlapping." Annoyances! Ah, what gallant language . . .

Clearing the Building Site

So we see that Paris, the place chosen for exploitation, was weak. The obstacles that could have been used to defend the city were no longer in place by the end of the Fourth Republic. At the beginning of the new regime, just waiting for his job to disappear, the prefect of the Seine was present at the demise of his authority. It was a great sight to behold how the councilors treated prefect Benedetti at the sessions of the Municipal Council: with sympathy and kindness, with all the affection with which one surrounds the gravely ill, those who haven't long to live. As for the Council itself, they could only acknowledge that all their business was done elsewhere. When others bothered to consult the Council it was only a formality and often the projects submitted for approval were already underway. The Council didn't know, in 1961, if they were to be suppressed. They learned, from *France-Soir,* that a commission had been created to decide their fate. With what sauce would they be eaten? It is appropriate to speak of sauce here. As one councilor observed, France decolonized the Third World while colonizing Paris, appointing as head of the commission charged with making decisions about the capital functionaries who had made careers in Black Africa or in Asia. They had the unconditional support of some and the equally unconditional opposition of others, positions equally useless to all government projects, which are usually only the simple expression of these contradictory forces. It remains to be noted about these opposed forces that the several meetings on the fate of Paris, influenced by personal accusations, presented a spectacle of confrontation which made the most acrimonious meetings during the Fourth Republic nothing more than conversations.

Thus did the liquidation of Paris take place under the aegis of good business. We have come a long way from yesterday's argument: housing and traffic control. What is good for La Défense is good for all France, and Pompidou's statement sums it up: "The idea of creating a business sector, a center where all the headquarters of the great corporations would be located, was an idea integral to the general effort to make France a major economic power and Paris a great commercial capital." As if Paris was not already a great commercial center and as if the new business center, not to mention the other centers which were no less desired, no less zealous to play their part, could not have developed in any other way but by ruining the old center, the center of centers, that is, the city itself, the only living part, the only part worthy of interest! Provocation, repression, revolution. In sum, as a Marxist student told me, the tactics of capitulation applied to Paris imitated the tactics of the Left, and even its dialectic: the construction of a new center, completely useless and half dead and the destruction of the old center that was perfectly useful and marvelously living. This, rather than the revitalization of the old center, or as they say, its renovation. Construction, destruction, construction: every phase makes money. Only Paris loses.

From about 1963 all the interrupted or suspended projects were approved and relaunched in a brisk wind. Projects previously approved—and the majority were in this group—were amplified. The first buildings of Maine-Montparnasse and the new railroad station were erected between 1960 and 1968, and in the project approved in March 1959 the tower was to be 170 meters high. In November 1965 the Municipal Council voted "on a proposition that said no building in the Maine-Montparnasse complex could exceed a height making it visible from the

Esplanade of Les Invalides." In 1967 the responsible commissions voted to carry the tower to 200 meters. The Right Bank expressway was voted in 1964, the project for the neighborhood of the Place d'Italie in 1966, the building of the Porte Maillot in 1966. I almost forgot the Front de Seine. Planned between 1958 and 1961 and approved in the latter year, it was, according to a happy official expression, "backed up" by public opinion at the exposition "Tomorrow's Paris" at the Grand Palais. "Backed down" would have been better. I have doubtless missed some projects that killed the cityscape. My picture is incomplete and my dates not absolutely precise, maybe even inexact. But this is not what is important.

The Last Day of les Halles

WHAT is important, astonishing, and—if I were superstitious, as they are in a certain Parisian tradition—inexplicable, is the resistance of les Halles, the old markets, the center of Paris, facing their destiny. If all the dossiers of the "powerless" Fourth Republic had not been able to get anything done, the Fifth Republic, "all powerful," took the longest time in dealing with the markets. What an offensive they mounted! How much money was at stake! Construction, destruction, construction: see the dialectic at work.

This leaves out of account a supplementary benefit, a mass move that had never been seen in the entire history of Paris, except as the result of a great disaster. Only the rats would move, without baggage, under their own steam, uncertain of where they were going. And they were not alone. Where would they put the markets, in whole or in part, if they succeeded in driving them out? This essential question set in motion the debate, often pitiless, which highlighted the immense financial interests involved. This became clear from the moment the Rungis location was proposed. In the spring of 1962 a Communist councilor stripped bare the question. His exposé, which demands quotation, calls for no commentary. It provoked none when it was made:

> It is clear that with this important project we are confronted by a formidable capitalist operation with many complexities and ramifications. Around the company of the Rungis market, a kind of mixed economy, there are going to be related companies, such as the trucking corporations, for which are envisioned the building of a commercial center next to Rungis, without even speaking of what will be created to exploit the void in the center of Paris created by the transfer of les

Halles. Good opportunities for capital investment will not
be lacking as a result of this important operation which will
be created by the market at Rungis. Knowing, as we do, the
orientation and the assumptions of the political economy of
the present government no one can doubt that the national
market at Rungis will be a means of favoring particularly
the development and the domination of conglomerates and
large companies and to eliminate a number of smaller independent competitors who cannot accommodate themselves
to the new circumstances created by the disappearance of
the central markets of Paris. (*Bulletin municipal officiel,*
March 30, 1962)

Succinctly put, the consumer society earlier described is lying in wait (not
merely the builders) for a piece of business which goes beyond the quarter
of les Halles and the center of Paris and concerns all of Paris. This is the
vanguard of a ferocious offensive against Paris compared to which the
assaults of the last years of the Fourth Republic were only skirmishes.
Beyond the traffic jams, the cost of living, the hygiene, and even the prostitution, beyond these infamous butchers accused of buying councilors
drinks at the "Pied de Cochon," beyond those old accusations which
were never forgotten, a louder voice was heard which spoke of "national
disgrace," of "decay," of a "place that brings shame upon us."

Nevertheless les Halles, publicly decried, dragged to a public place,
stripped, beaten, pelted, continued to fight back. At first she fought, for
reasons both clear and complicated, which historians will elucidate in
time from published and nonpublished documents. With the exception of
those who directed the game, the wire-pullers—though even they argued
among themselves about the future placement of the markets—most of
those involved were not in agreement, neither the authorities nor the
professionals. In addition the positions of both changed over the years.

Let us look only at the beginning of the Fifth Republic. Among those
most concerned with the question, the minister of construction, Pierre
Sudreau, was more interested in questions of urbanism than of economy,
was the man most deeply committed to solutions called "dictatorial" by
some; the technocrats of the treasury [caisse des dépôts] were obviously
(and by inclination) fierce partisans of radical administrative solutions,
the best solution being the one that made most obvious the power of the
administration; and the *Direction générale des prix* was most favorable
to moving the markets, fearful of the damaging consequences to the economic indicators. The more one heard about les Halles, in fact, got to

know it better, the more hesitant one became. This was true at the Prefecture of Police itself, despite the admitted problem of traffic flow, but it was especially true at the Prefecture of the Seine where prefect Benedetti was as sensitive as his predecessor, Pelletier, to the concerns of the professionals. As for his assistants, I still see the inspector of les Halles whose office was alongside one of the sheds, who showed me the green beans stacked in mountains in front of St. Eustache—"from the height of these Pyramids" to echo Napoleon—and guided me through the fantastic tumult of early morning to show me the perfect order of the markets: I was already converted.

Even the wholesale merchants of the markets themselves could not agree. If, to speak the language of les Halles, the sellers of fruits and vegetables were less systematically opposed to the transfer than those who sold dairy products or meat, the eighty middlemen (licensed by the Tribunal de Commerce), themselves often of little importance, were attached to what they called their "privileges" and had more than four hundred merchants supporting them. Even among the middlemen themselves and among the merchants, their choices varied individually, with their interests, their financial resources, the way they ran their businesses, and according to the advantages and commodities of their businesses. The pleasure they found in working at les Halles, their life-style, and their age also counted. It was pointless to ask the owner of the "Pied de Cochon," a meat middleman, if he wanted to see the meat market moved, or to ask some merchant who, in addition to his stand had real estate around les Halles, including some fully rented hotels, whether he was enthusiastic about the renovation of the quarter. It was total confusion, capable of discouraging the technocrats if anything could discourage them. This was a reflection of life, the very proof of life. It also had the advantage of delaying a decision. It made for a multiplication of reports that usually were contradictory and many of which were concerned with finding arguments for those who had commissioned the reports and paid for them. As if the respected work of the IFOP, established under prefect Pelletier, was not enough! In place of this quantitative sociology of les Halles, in place of this attempt to measure, through direct contact with practical matters and on the level of familiarity with people, they now turned, happily, for this was the era of the technocrats, to higher mathematics. This was applied not to people who refuse to sit still for such analysis and whose opinions really don't matter, but to the economy, that is to say to merchandise, to transportation, to costs, to whatever supported elegant hypotheses, always satisfying, convincing, reassuring.

They had only to be sure they made no errors in calculation. This had sometimes happened and so glaringly that even those who knew nothing about mathematics could see it and the technocrats had to start all over again. In the end they didn't understand things any better.

Above all they were afraid. Leaving aside these overly simple explanations or trying to discover what they hid, I would stick with the Parisian mythology of the inexplicable, for it goes so deep and is respected by the wisest, and because it probably contained some truth. They were afraid to tamper with les Halles. There were obvious reasons which everyone knew or felt; the fear that such tampering would injure other quarters, other activities that had nothing to do with fruits, vegetables, or cheese, but with the 300,000 people who, directly or indirectly, made their living from the markets. Despite all the inquiries, or maybe because of them, no one knew very clearly what the removal of les Halles might mean. The most convinced opponents of les Halles themselves were apprehensive of the consequences. Some of them came to long for the "international survey" they had asked for, a report whose conclusions were known in advance. Having decided the fate of les Halles, as if it were Madagascar (or anywhere else), the fortunate author of the survey could, after collecting his fee, take himself in peace to some other part of the world and wash his hands of les Halles. He was gone in an instant. Less fortunate were those who remained. They would have to be present at the spectacle of destruction, watching from the box seats. One of these men confessed to me he had nightmares. This did not, however, despite his sleepless night, keep the fellow from redoubling his hatred against this Satanic quarter which had found another way of preventing honest men from getting a good night's sleep.

Whether or not it was Satan, it must be noted that there was something about the resistance of les Halles, something about the place itself, something mysterious. There are places in Paris which, having once been the victims or witnesses to some horrible act, a now forgotten sacrilege—a church destroyed, a palace sacked, a part of a banner thrown to the dogs—have become whispered about, shunned. Here's a fine subject for a book! I don't know what will become of the soul of les Halles. As a good citizen I hope they will eventually build something beautiful there, which will, however, never replace what has vanished. If I judge from what happened at Beaubourg, the adjunct to les Halles, this happy road will not be the one followed. If something of its old soul remains, something overlooked, in the abyss, today completely sterilized, where its roots penetrated, where its strength lay hidden, may les Halles never be able to revenge itself for what was done! There was the visible, joyous les Halles, scintillating at night, simultaneously hard-working and easy-going. Then there was the subterranean les Halles, secret, shadowy, capable of the highest good and the greatest evil, able to bring abundance or famine, order or disorder, the joy of life or epidemic. This was the real market, les Halles at its most profound, literally and figuratively. Parisians never doubted the existence of this subterranean les Halles, if one is to judge from so many historical and literary documents, from the archives of the French Revolution, for example, full of descriptions of cellars, hideouts where plots were hatched, from which raids were launched. In an even more astonishing way we still find alive, in inquiries dating from the 1960s, a belief in some kind of lurking and powerful monster.[3]

Despite their desire to get it over with and despite their accumulation of the necessary means, the enemies of les Halles had much more difficulty and spent much more time than they expected in accomplishing even part of what they thought had been already accomplished. An ordinance, published in the *Journal officiel* in January 1959, made possible "the transfer of all the operations of les Halles to a market national in scope," and at the same time another ordinance designated the wholesale market at La Villette as a national market. Meat would be distributed from La Villette, the other products from another site to be chosen, whether at Valenton (a few kilometers from the Porte de Charenton) or Rungis (which they then considered less likely). But from this moment until 1966, the date planned for the move, a great many things could happen.

Rereading the newspapers for the second week of January, 1959, for example, I note that the journalists sent to les Halles to see the impact of this unbelievable news, wrote that those involved took it philosophically. "There would still be lots of nights to have a cup of spiked coffee and a bowl of onion soup," wrote Jean Fayard in *Le Figaro* (January 9). Less upbeat than Fayard, or not knowing how to make myself so, I seem to remember that those I talked to about the move hadn't heard anything about it—"You don't say!" I thought myself a bit ridiculous. I could think of nothing better than to laugh at myself. This all happened around 10 P.M. on the rue des Prouvaires side of les Halles in a café on the

---

3. In the file dealing with this phenomenon I find, in 1974, information about the danger of a sudden collapse of the church of St. Eustache, and in October 1976 information about a sudden and inexplicable accumulation of water in the cellars of the area. The experts said that the water table was 15 meters below this level.—Author.

ground floor of a building that was Molière's house and where Wagner reports that he himself lived. In the very heart of les Halles, one January evening in 1959, soon after the holiday celebrations, at a time when nights in les Halles, as one year became another, were a perpetual New Year's party: how could anyone have other fish to fry!

There was a new alert in the spring of 1960. This time it was official, the fate of les Halles had been decided. As foreseen, the meat market would go to La Villette and everything else to Rungis. The same indifference reigned, and it sometimes seemed like provocation! In March 1960 the motorized porters and those who used hand trucks found a way of getting into a confrontation with the traffic cops by using the one-way streets to avoid, so they said, the traffic jams. This happened at the very moment when the old argument about traffic jams resurfaced, augmented by additional insults and accompanied, as always, for reasons of some necessity or linguistic reflex, by the argument against prostitution. Then the whores of les Halles, she-devils even worse than the porters, rather than shrinking from publicity, being discreet, started talking to the newspapers, telling the authorities what was in their hearts—here was the height of provocation! The merchants' wives along the boulevard Sébastopol did not fail to report this to their neighbors in the rue Quincampoix. I was never sure why they remained out on the sidewalk through the night, muffled up in corduroys and sweaters. Was it to help their husbands or to keep an eye on them! Les Halles would thus make its exit. This is what they said in the newspapers, which must make it true! But they had said it for so long and always in the same terms, that the more they affirmed it the less one believed it. Then, in December 1961, the decision was made official. The Municipal Council discussed it on December 4. The opponents of the project, among whom were the representatives of les Halles district, had no difficulty in pointing out the vagueness of the governmental text. Approved for the first time by political adversaries, the Communist representatives proposed, should the market be moved, the installation of another market of retail and mixed retail-wholesale establishments. This, I continue to think, was the best solution. There was a discussion, like so many previous discussions and doubtless like so many future discussions, peppered with insults. One speaker suggested, for example, that should les Halles be moved "they vote to replace it with the Santé Prison, which would prove indisputably attractive to certain of our colleagues who enjoy walking in the neighborhood, because it would warn them of their ultimate destination." "Smiles everywhere," the stenographic record of the session indicates.

In fall 1963, the project for moving les Halles was given form. A corporation was created to study the organization of the markets and adjacent areas. The enemies of les Halles were too grandiose. Their idea of destroying, root and branch, what they called "the Right Bank center of Paris," then appeared so extreme that people who worked in les Halles and their supporters took it as an occasion, despite the inherent danger, for continued optimism. "How could a de Gaulle, a Pompidou, let such a thing happen?" was heard everywhere. I don't know what de Gaulle thought about les Halles or what he knew beyond what he had learned, as I had myself, from Cardinal de Retz, who remains an excellent informer. One of de Gaulle's faithful followers, a deputy, a municipal councilor, and a great defender of les Halles, told me, around this time, that the kings of France had always loved les Halles and found there faithful subjects who loved them. They also found some opponents who were not very manageable: all the more reason to sustain the place. January 1, following royal tradition, de Gaulle accepted, very regally, on the steps of the Elysée, a bouquet of lilies of the valley, whiter than calla lilies, and the porters of les Halles saluted him, with their caps on, like the grandees of Spain. How could he betray his supporters?

As for Pompidou, who knew my affection for this quarter and ribbed me about it, he never disclosed to me the slightest confidence about les Halles. I suppose the matter, seemingly interminable, appeared to him thorny and without urgency. To see the popularity of this child of the Auvergne in the cafés of les Halles, three-quarters of which were owned by Auvergnats, led me to believe, despite official reports, that he was not indifferent to what they said around the rue St. Flour. If he later may have changed his mind or decided upon a policy of laissez-faire (and I don't know anything about it) he did choose to erect at Beaubourg the museum which, alas and doubly alas, he could not foresee would one day bear his name. Beaubourg was the old dump of the market area where the trucks parked, where all the night people came to hire hands and sometimes to fire them, in the feeble light of dawn, far from the brightly lit pavilions, like actors preparing in the wings before going on stage, engaged in indescribable activities, much like those one would see in the future museum which was then unimaginable. Beaubourg was still a part of les Halles, the center of the city. Not knowing what would become of the marketplace one could hope, and one can still hope today, that the presidential choice, even if it fixed upon a museum of contemporary art—thin fare—would have left to the neighboring quarters something of the old life that the vanished markets had radiated far beyond their

borders, even if the aesthetes and their delicate hangers-on cannot pretend to replace the butcher-boys—"the butchers who live with blood,
have helpers the color of blood who wait for them, seated at the edge of
the market"—O, Mercier![4]

Thus, les Halles, for a few more years, repelled all assaults, survived
and even lived, as if the prospect of disappearing, more and more real
after 1964, meant, at least for the young, a hatred of life. "Let's live while
we may, it's not at Rungis that we'll be able to laugh about things." Such
was the caption for an elaborate cartoon by Moisan in *Le Canard*. Rungis! It is as if one had said the Big Bad Wolf. But soon, even at les Halles,
there wasn't much laughing. From 1968, as far as young people were
concerned, there was hardly any—certainly not in May 1968—except
for some stragglers from the Latin Quarter preaching revolution to some
poor prostitutes waiting to hook a client. "We will miss les Halles!" they
said in my bistro in Molière's old house. They already missed it, obliged
to serve (and with some disdain), God knows what drinks made with
mineral water, even whiskey, to the antique dealers who were now their
clients. Here where only yesterday Silenus was pouring red wine for the
young gods of Olympus.

When the last night came, the last night of les Halles, the evening of
the day long-dreaded, Thursday, February 27, 1969, the evacuation and
the transportation by truck to Rungis of the fruits and vegetables, of the

---

4. Concerning the monument itself, this pile of metal which is painted red, blue, and
green, seen in the gray splendor of a Parisian sky, the general opinion is so uniform that
there is no need to insist upon it. As for some works of propaganda, some reiterated theory
insisting that Beaubourg is a masterpiece, the historians who describe our time will only
have to read the newspapers for the first months of 1976. I offer these words from October
1976, chosen from among many others: "It's like a shotgun blast, both barrels." As for
Pompidou's responsibility, I share unequivocally the views of his chief assistant for Parisian
matters, René Galy-Dejean, writing in the *Figaro* of October 6, 1976, on the controversies
ignited by the jury's selection: "What can be said about this, it seems to me, is that it was
impossible for France, being honor-bound by the rules of the competition, to oppose the
outcome, whatever it might be. Was President Pompidou satisfied? He revealed his thoughts
to no one, as far as I know. My feeling is that he was quite surprised and that he hadn't
imagined that a competition of this kind might choose a piece of architecture such as they
did." I myself remember asking him if he was pleased, if this is what he hoped for. He didn't
answer and began speaking of something else. Whatever might be the case, knowing from
the Parisian past the influence that place names have in fixing in the minds of people the
image they have of historical personages whose names are connected with this or that place,
I cannot bear to think that Pompidou will find himself associated, in men's minds, with this
building, even if he played no important role (or even if he did) in its erection. One day a
historian writing his life will put things in perspective. Why not baptize it "The Beaubourg
Museum" or remove the "beau," which it does not deserve.—Author.

cheese and flowers—"here are the flowers, here the fruits . . ."—there was hardly anyone to contemplate the scene, a few nocturnal creatures, a few nostalgia seekers, a few poets, a few clochards. In fact, there wasn't anything left to see. At the moment les Halles disappeared, the old gare Montparnasse would come under the wrecker's ball.

CONCLUSION
"Une Ville Merveilleuse . . ."

They will speak of the capital of a great kingdom where there were
neither public places nor baths, fountains nor ampitheaters, galleries nor promenades, but which was nevertheless a marvelous
city.

La Bruyère, *Discours sur Théophraste*

WITH les Halles gone, Paris is gone. How is it we are surprised
when some immediately reach this conclusion? This is almost
exactly what Richard Cobb, the great English historian of the
French Revolution, wrote to me around this time: "Les Halles are no
longer there, which makes Paris less tempting for me"—unless he had
to consult the archives of the Revolution in the Archives nationales,
then in the Hôtel de Soubise. One used to reach the Hôtel de Soubise
only after walking through vegetable crates in the market. Then at noon,
to restore one's energy before tackling another box of manuscripts, to
revive oneself between two accounts of revolutionary famine, to regain
one's equilibrium between executions during the Revolution, in a word
to live in the flesh among the people one left behind in the archives, one
went to one of those overcrowded little restaurants that the hateful Beaubourg has crushed under tons of sadness along with everything else (without anything to replace them); they were bulldozed and, in one clear
night that I can still see in my mind's eye, set on fire. Thus it was for
Cobb and for the historians who worked in the Archives nationales at
this uncertain and shifting frontier between les Halles and the Marais. So
it was, for example, for Cobb's friend, Jean Meuvret, who knew everything about the ancien régime. Les Halles was les Halles; and les Halles
was Paris.

Paris, that is to say people from all walks of life and all classes, people
of all sorts, from high society, from the middling sort, from no society at
all. Let's begin with those in high society since that's the accepted order,
and we will take them in small doses. We don't have to go so far as to

guillotine them, as we historians in the restaurants in the rue Rambuteau used to do. What is most tiresome about these "former" aristocrats is that however little one lets them do, they immediately believe themselves the masters. Give them an inch and they take a mile. In the old popular neighborhood from which all the bums have been removed, one now meets only countless copies of the mink-coated woman walking her dog. Thank God, the dogs at least are not all of the same species!

As for the bums, as one might expect, I put among them, without hesitation, those cherished children of Parisian historians; those who prefer calm periods to the troubled revolutionary waters, those who don't make jokes about morality, and dedicate the product of their explorations in the darkest corners of the past to their chaste spouses—"To my faithful wife, from her faithful husband, this history of Grosse Margot [Queen Margot]." Among the bums I include, to speak the language of Mercier, those male and especially female bums "whose bums are more often bare than their feet." This is the way Cobb sees it: getting at Paris through les Halles, which he sees as did Mercier. This is what I myself did describing "the populace of the nineteenth century" when I was living through these final years of Parisian history. This is what numerous other historians of Paris did and will continue to do, with the blessing of the father of us all, Michelet, who has given, once and for all to his parishioners, "with a full heart" and to spare them hurt (and their lovers as well), a general absolution.

All this world was at les Halles. These people lived together during the nighttime hours when one lives two lives, part taken from the day, the rest from the night, which consumes the strength, beauty, health, life itself. It is thus that les Halles was the image of Paris, by these entwined destinies, this intense life that reveals or lets one discover the most important character and the pleasures offered by the whole city which have been sung forever by the poets, described by the novelists, analyzed by the sociologists. It is the collective existence by which individual existence (whatever it might be at any given moment), when one strolls, or works, or amuses oneself, eats or sleeps, feels, finds itself transformed, exalted. The new generation of sociologists, I am told, no longer believes in this collective existence, about which one of their masters, Halbwachs, wrote a masterpiece. It is probably because, among other reasons, in order to believe in it Halbwachs had only to look around him and into himself, to look at Paris or at Chicago, something his successors no longer are able to do, at least not Paris. Clearly, a study of the collective existence of Parly 2, or of one of the new cities, would reveal complete

248 Conclusion

alienation. This is what I guess, having never visited one of these places. What about the collective existence of La Défense, a quarter consecrated to business about which one would not dare say, as Zola said of the old business quarters, such as the Bourse, "this feverish quarter"? What about the Front de Seine? And Maine-Montparnasse, about which *Le Journal du Dimanche,* as I write these lines, affirms on its front page, in huge letters (April 13, 1975), that to live there provides "a foretaste of hell." It is indeed true that hell is but another kind of collective existence.

Collective existence in Paris? About fifteen years ago I tried myself to nail down the causes, the character, the effects of this existence at the very time when the evolution and decline I am here recording was underway, although I was ignorant of it. "Good God, how we were free and how we lived then!" Almost contemporaneous with my book, these few words of Lawrence Durrell sum up my thought. Liberty, life, and along with life a psychology, a quality of intelligence, a spirit that is the essence of the word intelligence—perspicacious, lucid, comic. His book received little attention. Mine only described what everyone knew. What was the use of that? It had an unimaginative title: *The Parisians.* In retrospect, this neglect of my book seems to me a kind of homage.

> Where everything, even horror, turns into enchantments.
>
> Baudelaire

M Y book was missing a chapter, perhaps the most important chapter, one that summed up everything and proved it. It is not because I forgot it but because I saw no point in writing it. One problem was not then apparent, which recent events have revealed in obscure outline, like a black diamond in shadow, wrapping in mystery what only yesterday was clear: the influence of collective life on creation in all fields, but above all in what one did not yet call culture, unless one was a pedant. Let us call it beauty, beauty in a thousand different forms, this unique beauty that is the glory of Paris. "Beauty, my great solace." The city did not have to worry about what so tormented the women of Paris. Beauty emanated from the place in great waves. It was everywhere, especially where it was least expected. It was in the streets, often the most destitute streets, in those debased quarters, in the most barren faubourgs. Beauty was in the air. Michelangelo praised the atmosphere of Florence. "The Atmosphere of Paris" (*L'Air de Paris*) is the title of a film in which Marcel Carné presents, in a dilapidated shed in les Halles, on the rue du faubourg St. Denis, the habitués of boxing pressed around the ring where two fighters are squaring off—the reigning champ and an up-and-coming challenger—their faces bloody, their muscles, built up by work in les Halles, glistening—"these muscle-bound torsos" described by Aragon. The atmosphere of Florence and that of Paris? The sculptor of the *David* and of the *Battle of Cascina* would be the last to be annoyed by the comparison. The atmosphere of Paris was in the central shed at les Halles which smelled of sweat and dust. It was like the Cirque Médrano[1] which smelled of sawdust and horses, and, during the afternoon performances for children, of orange and lemon drinks. So many scenes today vanished, stored in the attic of history. Their disappearance helps us understand better than would a long speech how these small pleasures—and the city was not stingy with its small pleasures—were created and how it did not take a treasure hunt to find them. All of the places just mentioned, and they are only a sample of many others—theaters, streets, alleys, passageways, intersections, cafés, the quays of the Seine and those of the St. Martin Canal, Donogoo's Canal, the Hôtel du Nord of Dabit's novels, and Carné's film *L'Hôtel du Nord,* set along the St. Martin Canal—each of these places (and many even more ordinary ones), had its place in some important chapter of the history of literature, of theater, of art, of beauty. This is not so much because beauty was born here, as it might have been born somewhere else, but because it could not have been born elsewhere, especially not in those places set aside for beauty, where they tried to create it. At least this was true in yesterday's Paris as it was true in the Paris of long ago. The "pensoir" [inspiration] was not there.

"Pensoir" is not in the dictionary: one finds only "pensum," punishment, in the form of additional work, inflicted on a bad student. Inspiration is not found on the American campus either, where you can't escape the students, who are always underfoot. It is more trying than enduring tea with colleagues, which is enough to push even the Americans to murder, however thick-skinned they may be, if one can judge from some classics of detective literature. Inspiration is not found in the symbolic mountain where Hugo would have us believe he went to seek it, while he tells us frankly, in *Choses vues,* how he found his ideas by chance, in the streets, often through unexpected encounters, not hesitating to rescue some girl in distress. He is speaking in *Les Misérables* of the unexpected in the Paris streets, of encounters that are not hallucinatory in his novel precisely because these streets are themselves the origin of these hallucinations.

Inspiration was thus born in the city, the city of yesterday which in

1. The celebrated circus of Montmartre, now demolished.

numerous places (and despite Haussmann) was still the city of *Les Mi-sérables*. This came about naturally, spontaneously, as a supplementary grace that no one could have imagined they would one day have to ask for, beg for, seek; something that no power would have imagined it would one day have to finance. To pay people from city funds to encour-age them to have ideas or, as they say today, to exercise their "right to create,"—to finance culture—would still have seemed, a few years ago, a mad scheme. To borrow money to create was to admit a lack of crea-tivity. To rough it has been the Golden Rule that the history of Paris verifies and that present-day Paris confirms. But I'm treading on sensitive territory. Moreover, it is not a question of today but of yesterday. In two words, the city was an inspiration. Les Halles proves this; les Halles for me *was* the city.

Maecenas in a Work Shirt

I don't want to disavow the fellow who falls on hard times but it is difficult to speak of falling on hard times when talking about les Halles, where they were charitable. They have always reached into their pockets and so have those along the commercial streets which are nearby. "The genius of the rue St. Denis," and Balzac's definitive description re-veals an enduring truth: the street was not only commercial, it was also a street for literature, theater, dance, all those expensive diversions that benefit from business and are willing to take their chances in such a place. The entire range of French literature proves this truth. Sometimes one sees it in the guise of aristocratic sentiments, or romantic passions, or religious elation, or altruism, or scorn for inherited wealth, or even when a would-be noble practices wearing court dress. This literary tradition puts in bold relief the origins of these two orders of genius, those who pay and those who consume, or rather those who pay so others can cre-ate. If, since the middle of the nineteenth century the more prosperous quarters of the city have taken over the role of Maecenas from the rue St. Denis, les Halles, on the contrary, has increased its giving. From the pe-riod between the two world wars to our own day it has glittered. Les Halles has been the mundane aspect of Paris's illustrious history, the pol-len of glory, the small change of anecdotal history (most of it well known to the habitués of the markets), celebrated by them on important occa-sions or anniversaries. Everyone knows, for example (and without fol-lowing the ballet closely) that of our two great choreographers and directors of troupes, both of whom had been themselves dancers under

Lifar when they were young, one is the son of a distinguished philosopher and the other grew up in one of the bistros of les Halles. It is not difficult to discern in the ballets of the former a hint of the philosophical quest of his father, a kind of intellectual (and somewhat artificial) concern for the future, or, if one distrusts one's own judgment, it is enough to read the reviews of the ballets of the latter and find, even in the choice of words, an echo of the celebrations of les Halles. For example, "Roland Petit," writes Claude Baignières in *Le Figaro* about a recent celebration at the Porte St. Martin, "returns in 1975 with the carefree, bubbly, lightheartedly popular, deeply tender ballet about a unmistakably Parisian occasion that was among the glories of the 1950s." The reviews of the 1950s were even more explicit: popular light-heartedness was the high-spirited people, bubbly champagne was a glass of table red. I even think I remember that a ballet was cut into sections, like slices of sausage.

A memory of the rue d'Ulm sums up this creative manner for me. It concerns a "tapir," which I have previously explained is a pleasant, complacent student. In this case my "tapir" was an important merchant who provided Paris with I no longer remember what commodity. He loved the theater to the point of renting one, and one of the most prestigious, for the current up-and-coming actress, Célimène on stage, Célimène in the city, but more fit for the city than the stage.[2] This beauty having expressed the desire of changing her image and performing in an English piece then playing to rave reviews in London, myself and a friend were given the task by the merchant in question of putting a bad translation into good French. Then circumstances having changed, Célimène having a new whim or the world economic crisis affecting our Maecenas, the project was abandoned, forgotten. He even forgot to pay us! The bounty of les Halles was no longer ours.

When I spoke about my disappointment to the great lady whom, as I have already explained, found time to learn some history between races at Auteuil, she burst out: "The bitch hasn't paid you? I swear to you she will pay you." The war between women is a war without pity, in which I became a weapon. The lawyers went to work, so well that the celebrated actress was trapped and asked me to come to the theater one evening for an interview one would die for. She was waiting for me in her dressing room, at the intermission, rather than going somewhere backstage. This was an enormous favor for which some had paid with their fortunes and

2. Célimène, a back-biting flirt, is a character in Molière's *Le Misanthrope*.

one even with his life. I have forgotten what she was appearing in: Marivaux, Musset? I only saw an athletic Pierre Brasseur in the moonlight, taking the greatest care not to break this porcelain marquise in his arms. I followed the marquise. She explained things to me, she begged me, she supplicated, I even believe that having to change costume she did so behind a flimsy screen. I remained adamant. I had some help. The Célimène in question was not, to remove any doubt, she who for half a century was called, out of affection, our national Célimène, Cécile Sorel.

I did worse. Clearly this is not a moral tale. Not only did I reject the advances of a beautiful woman (which were not made) but I took advantage of the intermission and stole, yes I stole. In the company of my friend who had come to see what had happened and to snatch me, if need be, from those famous claws, I furtively picked up a handful of visiting cards strewn on a table, not those of the actress, of course, cards with insufficient funds behind them, so to speak. I took the cards of a businessman who was worth a lot of money. So it was that night, a Mardi Gras night, ensconced in a famous brasserie in the Place Blanche frequented by actors looking for an engagement, we were able to listen to them during the night and pass out the precious purloined cards with hints of a future meeting. It was not as tranquil as usual the following morning around a certain office in les Halles

A merchant offering a theater and Pierre Brasseur into the bargain, the future Frédérick Lemaître[3] forced to coo: this is obviously an exceptional story. The people of les Halles, from all walks of life and whatever might be their tastes, find it easy to get provisions right there, with choice morsels: they point out, hanging around St. Eustache, if beautiful women come to do their shopping themselves at les Halles, carrying a grocery sack, they are probably not doing it only because they are interested in saving some money.

More a tale with a moral than an anecdote, this memory sums up not only the role of the markets, but even more that of Parisian wealth in the abundance of Parisian pleasures, a luster unique in the world, shining in a crown whose principal jewel was the theater. The theater, the pleasure of public performance. But les Halles was also the meeting place for other pleasures, first of all the beauty of women. In the quarrel that began in January 1956, caused by André Roussin's attempt to set curtain times at 9 P.M. or 8 P.M., or even 7:30 (as they do in England), an inquiry of

---

3. A famous actor in the nineteenth century. He is one of the characters in Marcel Carné's film, *Les Enfants du Paradis*, where he is played by Pierre Brasseur.

great importance for the history of Paris was launched at the forty-five city theaters and revealed that the majority of the public wanted to retain the status quo. To hell with the suburbs, which no one cared about! What was important was that Parisian women could look their best: "A 9 P.M. curtain time," said the owner of a luggage shop near the Madeleine, "gives me time to return to my apartment and freshen up." An industrialist, whose statement should not be seen as typical, went even further and wanted a 10 P.M. curtain: "In France a theatergoer is more favorably disposed after he has eaten." He surely had in mind a fine meal, which is to say at one of the better restaurants, which was the necessary accompaniment, the antechamber, the prologue to the theater. Finally, after the theater lights came the city lights, the glow of Paris against a night sky. Soon after the departure of les Halles the Parisian night would begin to darken, with the exception of St. Germain-des-Prés, the Champs-Elysées, Pigalle, isolated and blinking patches of light which, by contrast, made the rest even darker. So that Christmas in 1967, Christmas in the city, might not look too lugubrious, they put up official lights, lamps, candelabra, hanging lamps, Venetian lamps, decorations for amusement parks which in the rain, in the cold, the wind, the solitude, made Paris even more lugubrious. The Pont Neuf and the Concorde made one think of the title chosen by Baudelaire for a poem that he never wrote: "Festival in a Deserted City"! From around 1960 the theaters, especially those of the boulevards, began to have difficulties, although they had not been touched by the preceding crisis. In November 1956, for example, box-office receipts unmistakably showed that the political situation, everyday concerns, gas shortages caused by the Suez Canal crisis had not affected attendance. The theaters took in as much money as in the previous year. We should remember it was in March 1961 that Alain Delon invested money earned in movies to make his stage debut at the Théâtre de Paris in the Elvire Popesco production of John Ford's 'Tis Pity She's a Whore, directed by Visconti. There were sixty-six actors in the production, among them Valentine Tessier, Daniel Sorano, Romy Schneider! Such a production would be unthinkable a few years later.

We get an idea of what the decline of the theaters meant by comparing celebrations for the end of the year 1957–58, which hinted at the future, with those of 1964–65, which saw the end of an era, the decline of restaurants, brasseries with live orchestras, shops, and, in a word, the boulevards themselves. The restaurants became shabby, fine dining was replaced by fast-food establishments or pizzerias, the store became a bargain basement ("get that one off the rack for me"), a shop out of business was replaced by a bank. The neighborhood metamorphosed into a kind of sub-Pigalle, the real Pigalle of the period not having much in common with the nightlife kingdom in the decade following the war, when six theaters (even in 1957) continued to thrive, and they were the most celebrated in Paris. This is without counting the music halls and the Médrano Circus where, in January 1955, Aristophanes' *The Birds* was playing.

Movie houses held on longer, or rather evolved differently. They are more independent of the ups and downs of the Parisian economy than other forms of entertainment. Those factors which have a direct effect on the theater do not act in the same way upon movie houses. Even more to the point, movies are more independent of the history of Paris, perhaps even more independent of the places and the scenes of Paris. Among the pleasures of Paris, movies introduce another kind of pleasure which is not specifically Parisian, which one finds elsewhere as well as in Paris. The theater is Parisian, the cinema is in Paris. This does not prevent the incorrigible Parisian from choosing a movie house according to its quarter, its public, the route leading to it; or for other, more obscure reasons, from going to the other end of town to see a film which is playing in his own neighborhood. Obviously when the day comes that all the quarters of Paris resemble each other, far from having the itch to get out, the Parisian will stay in his neighborhood, maybe even at home.

Despite the relative independence of movie houses from the evolution of the city, from its prosperity and its splendors, from its pleasures, from this mixture that forms a whole and effects the other spectacles, the cinema too, here and there, began to show the first signs of decline. These appeared earliest and were most apparent in those parts of the city which first felt the consequences of the disappearance of les Halles, around the intersection Strasbourg-St. Denis, for example. This is an extraordinary intersection, still fascinating in the years here under consideration as it was when I studied there *Classes laborieuses et dangereuses*. It is as vibrant, as important for Paris as it was in the first half of the nineteenth century, whose aspects I found still existing around me, amplified by what had happened since. It was changed in appearance but not in its essence. Here, in what has been called the crossroads of the city, people from the rich neighborhoods of the west, the working-class neighborhoods of the east and north, and especially from the boulevard Sébastopol and the rue St. Denis, from les Halles, all met and mixed and sometimes confronted each other, as they always had. What was concentrated here, between the two monumental arches and in the surrounding streets, extending on one side to the edges of the Place de la République and on the other almost to the intersection of the rue de Richelieu and the rue Drouot, and stretching as far as one could see in the direction of les Halles, was an intensity of life which no other part of Paris—and probably no place in the world—could match. Compared to Strasbourg-St. Denis, the fever of Times Square was only a crowd and Broadway was, according to Henry Miller, "without fire or heat, a bazaar of lit-up shops, a paradise for hucksters." All of Paris was at Strasbourg-St. Denis, except the high society, of course, who were not missed. To explain the city, but above all to feel it, there was no need to look further. It was enough to station oneself here, for example in the enormous café, the "Tout va bien," which has disappeared and about which one could write a book, and from this vantage to watch and listen.

The working classes were there, parents and their offspring, and also, well represented, the dangerous classes or rather those who could become dangerous. These latter emphasized better than did the others—the common run of mankind which history neglected—the determining role the intersection played in the lives of both groups. The criminality of Strasbourg-St. Denis was not that of Montmartre, not the settling of accounts between Corsicans over the rackets or prostitution—pistol shots at the corner of the rue Victor-Massé and Place Pigalle, or better yet some domestic massacre, complete with unbelievable details. Take the January 1956 shooting in the rue Tardieu in Montmartre: two men and a woman found naked in a room, their bodies riddled with bullets. The woman's corpse was on the bed, and clutched in her hand was a crime novel, *Les Durs de Barbès*. Nor was it the sudden disorder of les Halles, a moment of madness, revenge against a boss or a fellow worker, a woman killed without really knowing why following a sleepless night spent unloading vegetables and drinking. Nor was it the crime of some wretched suburb, a crime committed by ragpickers heavily fortified with cheap red wine, while singing the *Légionnaire* in some wooden shack built near a junkyard full of automobile carcasses and broken bedsprings. Nor was it the crime of Belleville, the sad story of a steady young man who lived with his parents and was well thought of in the machine shop where he worked, but who ruined everything by killing a rival as they left a dance. One should rather talk of an accumulation of risks, of bad luck, of chance, in a specific place, in cafés, in alleyways, in a movie house, in the corridors of the metro, on the sidewalk, during shopping, which can as easily lead to the scaffold as to behind a counter, or on the assembly line at Renault, or even in the city hall of the Tenth arrondissement, by entering into matrimony with the daughter of a successful merchant from the Sentier neighborhood whose eye you had caught.[4]

What if the Parisian's clairvoyants and card readers write their memoirs! They were, at least in the period I am talking about, specialized according to quarter. A fortune-teller of Strasbourg-St. Denis, from whom I have these anecdotes, excelled in the sorrows of love. She counseled, she consoled, she sometimes made matches. Beautiful love stories, successful business careers, spectacular careers in crime were made here. Only the last of these are well-known. The same is true of musical careers, so celebrated, so impressive in number, that one could conclude that, during a certain period, it was better to go walking near the St. Denis arch than to practice for the National Conservatory. It was while delivering hats or dresses in the boulevard Bonne-Nouvelle, not far from the theaters where she would one day triumph, that Gaby Morlay had her first role offered to her, by a director charmed by her childlike face and her crystalline laughter.

I have been drawn to this spectacle and have never tired of it. The street scene is inseparable from the other sights I have been discussing, for here work and play mingle, complement each other, sustain each other, so that the decline of one precipitates that of the other: that of the theater affects the cinema, despite its staying power.

Around 1964 a man who had played an important role in the evolution of the cinema in Paris, Sammy Siritzky, asked me what I thought of a movie house near Strasbourg-St. Denis he intended to buy. Before becoming a movie house it had been a famous music hall. All the great vaudeville artists had made their debuts here. The hall still had handsome vestiges of its past. As late as 1958 it was showing films to full houses that today are the chief attractions in art houses and rerun theaters. Yet, four or five years later, with the departure of les Halles, with the decrepitude of the boulevard Sébastopol and of all the neighborhood separating the markets and the boulevards, one might think that setting up a movie house in an area in the process of becoming a skid row—a movie house, not one of the rat traps they throw together today, but a handsome and comfortable theater, the kind Sam Siritzky usually opened—was a waste of time and money.

---

4. Each of the twenty arrondissements into which Paris is politically divided has a mayor and a city hall where civil weddings are traditionally performed on Saturdays.

I want to speak about Paris and I find myself recounting my life.

Daniel Halévy

I T was a question of money! Several times, between 1955 and 1960, passing by Strasbourg-St. Denis in early afternoon, I happened to run into Merleau-Ponty, whose courses at the Collège de France everyone in St. Germain-des-Prés attended (wearing the regulation existential outfit: a ponytail, dirty fingernails, and a thick volume of Sartre under one's arm). What was he doing there? What I myself often did. He hoped to find in this purposeful crowd which was not in the least philosophical, ideas for a class he was dissatisfied with, some last-minute inspiration. The place could be inspiring, as could the entire city. Lawrence Durrell wrote in 1957 to Henry Miller, whose most recent book, *The Rosy Crucifixion*, had disappointed him, that he should leave America to come to look for ideas in old Europe, especially Paris. In an expression that today awakens a painful nostalgia in us, he cried: "What a city!"

Twenty years earlier it was Miller himself that I might have run into, and precisely at this intersection, although at a later hour, it must be said. Anaïs Nin tells how he loved, in going from Montmartre to Montrouge with friends, to make a long stop at 32 rue Blondel, in a house of prostitution he liked. The rue Blondel ran parallel to the boulevard. One reached it, or better disappeared into it, from the rue Ste. Apolline, its companion, by walking through the backyards of blocks of flats. This was "the street of joy" of Damia:[5] "It is in the Street of Joy, it is in the rue Blondel." In another title of another realistic song it is the essence of a street, quite simply "the street." "The deafening street shouting at me." The verse is Baudelaire's! "The street draws me in spite of myself." Perhaps it's from Damia, or Fréhel, or some great Parisian lyricist, perhaps Marguerite Monnot, who died in 1961. That is, my memory may be accurate after all; in some way or other, the verse is from Baudelaire. "The street screams and cries, tempest, injury." It was the street of popular unrest. Evoking the days following February 6, Daniel Halévy recounted that he loved to walk around the area. "You see," he wrote, "the café at the corner of a small neglected street and the boulevard Sébastopol. Seated at their small tables, zinc painted green, were the girls. They had an expression that said 'But where are all the guys today?' " This was also a street of crime. But above all, incorporating all else, this was, as the song says, "the Street of Joy, the street of pleasure, the rue Blondel." Then

5. A famous female singer of "chanson réaliste" in the 1920s and 1930s.

ignorant of Henry Miller's itineraries, it was of Baudelaire and Damia that I thought, while dining one evening with some American students, including the future historian, Rudolf Binion, in a room in the above-mentioned house, "dans les étages" as they said during the Belle Epoque.

The houses of prostitution had been suppressed as the result of a law due to Marthe Richard, who had moved from serving France to the service of virtue, which was always a way of serving France. They had lodged students in what had once been a notorious address, because they couldn't think of what else to do with it. Not Parisian students, who would have had a number of wicked ideas on the subject, but Americans, who were in the 1950s thought to be very puritanical, and even a little prudish—"Hurons" as Voltaire said.[6] I am sure our talk was very intellectual. It was all about historical questions and literature, and good books we would write. But Henry Miller and his friends, what had they spoken about? One would have to be obsessed or, to use a word much loved by Descartes, completely devious to imagine one went there for any but the obvious reason.

When Miller left this notorious address he passed les Halles, and so shall we with him. But by what route can we pass it? However one went, no matter from where one came, whether one knew Paris intellectually or by the feel of it, in the Paris of Miller's time as in that of yesteryear, in the itineraries of Balzac's *Comédie humaine* or Hugo's *Les Misérables*, in those of Jerphanion as in those of Aragon ("Instinct led him to les Halles however much the narrow streets beckoned him . . ."), in those of Daniel Halévy regaining the quai de l'Horloge or in those of the young Pierre Gaxotte returning at night from the printing house of Action française, in the rue du Croissant, one had to pass by les Halles! That's how the streets were laid out; even more, that is what each one wanted, and each let himself be convinced that he would find there what he loved. Most important were the faces: "I love the faces," are the simple words of *Pays parisiens*. Faces, not things. Halévy was also sure of finding ideas there.

In the same vein, "to live in Paris was to exist, in the absolute sense of the word." To live in Paris was to find what one had failed to find elsewhere. A particular building proves this proposition to me, the one said to be Molière's house, on the ground floor of which was the café where we have already stopped, earlier in this book, at the end of the day, to listen to the tumult of the markets. I don't know if Molière lived here, despite his bust on the facade of the building and a painting of men in

6. The heroes of Voltaire's tale *L'Ingénu*.

perukes carrying candles, with a kind of Tartuffe character, the reasons for whose presence in the picture are obscure. Be that as it may, Richard Wagner did live here. He recounts in his *Journal* that a few steps from the building, making his way to the Palais Royal by the rue de Rivoli one January night in 1862, borne along by the Paris crowd, "by this human wave," he found "by a sudden inspiration the melody of the lines on the Reformation versified by Hans Sachs, the tune with which the people, in the last act, greet their beloved master." The inspiration for the great protest of the German people, the hymn to Germany's glory, to her hardworking folk, her virtuous women, whose French models, if we are to believe Balzac, were rare in this neighborhood.

To find inspiration on the rue de Rivoli, even to make less grand creative discoveries, there is an example, much less exceptional than Wagner's inspiration for *Die Meistersinger*. After all, Wagner also found inspiration elsewhere. In its very banality, with this happy ordinariness that is so intimately connected to a description of Paris, it sums up these pages and brings this work to an end.

The example comes from certain movies, as with those great books one reads and rereads over the years . . . But let me tell the story. I admired, when it was released, *On The Beach* (1959). Everyone knows the story: After an atomic war, a radioactive cloud floats over the planet, destroying all life. The beach in question is in Australia, where people are waiting to die. The Cold War and the fear of nuclear weapons made this film a classic for the history of the decade after World War II. I saw it when it came out, and its anticipation of the Apocalypse was real if we can judge from the profound silence of the youthful audience amidst whom I sat (the only one of my generation there). I saw it again recently in a small art and rerun house near the Place de la République, at the bottom of the rue du Faubourg du Temple, which is one of those fragments of streets marvelously alive of which a few remain, here and there. Fifteen years later it is not this apocalyptic vision that struck me, but a sentence I had not understood the first time I heard it, a sentence that this time I was probably alone, in the entire audience, in understanding. It reduced me almost to tears. The beautiful Ava Gardner was explaining what she would have loved to do before dying. She would have loved to go and buy a pair of gloves on the rue de Rivoli: "Because it is in Paris, on the rue de Rivoli, that they have the best gloves." This was still self-evident in 1959. Today it seems unimaginable. Paradise lost.

EPILOGUE

Twenty Years Later

"**W**HERE the author of *The Assassination of Paris,* Louis Chevalier, is surely correct," writes Julien Gracq in his *Carnets du Grand Chemin,* "is seeing in the 'trou des Halles' [the enormous open pit left when the markets were destroyed] the surgical removal of the secret heart of the city. It was certainly a heart filled with much that was repugnant, from which there emanated, in the early hours of the morning, a heady, bloody smell of low-life, a smell from whose essences was made a most original perfume. This was the intimate smell of a city that gathered around an inextricable group of stinking streets, having for a medieval core its streets of butcher shops and triperies from whence violence incessantly spilled, even before blood-red arms began their work. There was at the center of the city this undeniably ignoble viscera, so attached to its living substance by nerve and ligaments, vessels and veins, that the long-term consequences of radical surgery remain problematic." The following pages are a response to these remarks.

Overview

TO understand and to relive Old Paris it sufficed to make a tour of les Halles. To grasp and to understand what has happened to Paris it suffices, if one has the stomach for it and no sense of the past, to go and see what has replaced les Halles. On one side was the esplande where the truckers parked their rigs and sought secret pleasures, which has now been baptized the Pompidou Center after my unfortunate comrade whom I cannot bring myself to believe was personally responsible for this horrible thing. On the other side were the market "pavilions" whose replacement some minister, doubtless ignorant of Latin, has baptized the "Forum," unaware that a Forum means open air, light, bird-song. The misnamed Forum des Halles has no other purpose than to concentrate in a deep, fetid underground all that Paris has to show and offer as high-class merchandise, all that one found in the shops along the great boulevards and elsewhere, without counting those of the rue de Rivoli where poor Ava Gardner wanted to buy gloves for one last time. On one side Beaubourg and the Pompidou Center, that frightful jumble of pipes and conduits and ducts that they have dubbed the gas works or the refinery. On the other side the so-called Forum des Halles which doubly offends me; by the removal of the original les Halles and by its replacement with this.

For crowds of youth who never tire of either place and who cannot distinguish between them, and also for myself who is using these pages to take a last look at what has become of les Halles and Paris, the dreadful blow delivered against the markets, whose consequences can be seen in the last twenty years, sums up, in every way, the fatal wound that some had, for a long time, secretly proposed inflicting on Paris, not hesitating to cut into its body. After having done so, out of complete ignorance and indifference to what was for the whole world "the queen of cities," building the ugliest structures in the name of some imagined culture, they did not hesitate to resort to extravagance or buffoonery. Then there are those who lined their pockets from these disasters, who collected the eternal "argent" of Zola.

Even if what has happened is forgotten, les Halles was, and will always be, central to the fate of Paris. This is why, before looking at what has become of Paris, we turn to the starting point, les Halles, which everyone today still calls les Halles, or Beaubourg, without ever mentioning the Forum and almost never, except when wanting to make a distinction or follow the guidebooks, the Pompidou Center. "Excuse me, monsieur, how do I get to les Halles?" The question, still heard in the streets, is in itself an opinion poll and expresses what I want to discuss.

les Halles

L ET'S look first at les Halles. . . . I first had occasion to do so, to go and see for myself despite my long estrangement and distaste, when I was studying the first signs of decline in Montmartre, thinking about a book which should be titled *The Ruins of Subure,* the name of the most wicked and celebrated neighborhood in ancient Rome. This was between 1975 and 1980, in winter. I boarded the metro at Place Pigalle and a bunch of youths, extravagantly dressed and with hairdos even more bizarre than what one might see in Pigalle, invaded the car I was riding in. I was curious to see where they were going and so followed them. I had only to listen to what they were saying. They were bored with Montmartre. They were going to Beaubourg. Not to the library or the museum, not to the cultural shrine in the Pompidou clutter of pipes and vents and ducts, where they all would have been completely lost and about which this text will not speak, but to the well-heated depths of the so-called Forum, full of little shops—a Forum they never spoke about, identifying it lightheartedly with les Halles or Beaubourg.

There they mingled with an enormous crowd of other young people from the suburbs who filled the place, not knowing where else to go. Out of work and without hope, fleeing with horror the hideous cities where they were warehoused or where others hoped to confine them, hurrying back and forth each day on the metro, they came for refuge to the Forum, in its early sumptuous days, which had not been built for them and from which the business owners tried vainly to exclude them; a stunning series of robberies quickly discouraged some of the important names in Parisian commerce who had originally believed it a good idea to open stores here. They descended in droves on these once forbidden places, with all their belongings, with their musical instruments, their accoutrements, their strange haircuts, with their work and their diversions, with their innocent amusements and those that were not innocent—drug addicts in corners and their suppliers observing them from the shadows.

With the good weather, from the first years of this story, this sinister and subterranean spectacle where everything began was repeated at Beaubourg, on the old esplanade of the truckers, in a completely different kind of amusement which would change the character of what was happening underground. Meandering ceaselessly from the Forum to Beaubourg, and then back again, to pass the time, an enormous crowd made up almost exclusively of young people—the largest crowd in Paris—came, from all over, to see what was going on. It was a scene of fire eaters, dancers, wrestlers, musicians with every kind of instrument, singers—one was reminded of the acrobats on the Pont Neuf in the days of Louis XIV—who found here a public their own age, always ready to applaud. Perhaps more important was the spectacle of themselves leading a kind of exalted existence, surprising, that these young people, sometimes desperate, offered themselves to each other in a kind of shared theater. To the Parisian youth, those from the suburbs, those of France, were rapidly added the young from other countries, who filled out the bulk, a bit standoffish and mocking, having come, in the first wave, from England. Recently one of my former students who has kept me informed was surprised to hear German spoken there. It was a group of young East Germans, not having had any other desire after the fall of the Berlin Wall but to come to this fabled Beaubourg. There they were, sitting on the ground before a rapt public, telling of, or rather miming, their exceptional journey.

The epic of Beaubourg, of this *cour des miracles* so to speak, whose history will one day be written—and I am surprised that no novelist has yet used it—did not pass through these last twenty years without misadventures and drama. Beyond the robberies—by 1980 two-thirds of the shops at the Forum had been burgled—beyond the destruction wrought by drugs and an occasional struggle (on one occasion hundreds of youths tried to prevent the arrest of a street merchant), beyond the rapes and the pornographic displays which, late at night are part of the street scene, beyond the rage of the neighborhood at the noise, beyond various kinds of violence, there were deaths, these too of various kinds.

From the deaths I would choose that which seems to me the most significant for this carnival of illusions, this masquerade which is often only a disguise for despair: suicide. As I have noted a number of times in writing about the history of Paris, the most famous Parisian monuments (and the highest) have always attracted suicides. First, there is the Eiffel Tower that holds the record with 364 suicides. Then come the Arc de Triomphe and Notre Dame. August 19, 1977, is a macabre historical date. A twenty-three-year old man, one of these young men I have been describing, threw himself from the top of the Beaubourg Center at 9:50 P.M., ten minutes before it closed. It was the director of a small circus performing in the cement space below, seeing a body fall, who called the police.

When will the first suicide take place from the monumental arch at La Défense? I swear such a suicide would astonish me, despite the relationship, today forgotten, that links La Défense (and other buildings like it) to the Pompidou Center. Evidently this common ancestry somehow means the buildings are not well maintained. For ten years the rust has gone unchecked and some even ask themselves if the center might not one day collapse. Still, this is where it all began.

Sacrileges and Extravagances

FOR the last twenty years and especially for the last ten, when the pace of everything seems to have accelerated, those who adore and flatter power have spoken of the Golden Age of architecture, whereas I would be more prone to speak of the Age of Iron, assuming the "golden" here is not understood in the sense of money, for in that case I would be in agreement. Everywhere, but especially in the west of Paris where the land is worth more, the buildings multiply; the Paris skyline is now crenelated with towers, each more extravagant, higher, and especially more profitable than its rivals. Promoters, development groups, French and more and more often foreign, are enriching themselves to satiety. They want to make Paris, or at least what they still call Paris, one of the office capitals of Europe, if not the world. The periphery of Paris now being built up (or it soon will be), they have turned their attentions on the city itself, where the steel and glass towers are thrusting upward even in the central parts of the city and on the Left Bank of the Seine, where they replace old buildings from the Haussmann era and even townhouses dating from the eighteenth century that have been allowed to decay quietly. The English are fortunate in having Prince Charles to defend London! Here it is the president of the Republic himself who sets the worst example, with what are pompously called "the president's work sites" set up in the heart of the city. Doubtless there is now a mayor of Paris worthy of the name ensconced in the old office in the Hôtel de Ville which had belonged to Haussmann and which I know well. Theoretically the mayor is the protector of the patrimony of Paris. But in most cases the president and the mayor—a two-headed Janus—seem in agreement and even seek to outdo each other in a competition which I, obviously, condemn, and most older Parisians with me. The present mayor in his younger days had been one of Pompidou's assistants: I recall having noticed him in the hallways. How could he be expected to condemn what, after all, is insignificant next to a Pompidou building, the chief horror of the genre, the Beaubourg, from which all the others have descended? This is the ultimate character of what is built around Paris and, with increasing frequency, in Paris. It is a question for those one hesitates to call architects—where are you Paul Valéry?—of being original at any price, of abandoning themselves to the worst gestures, of fleeing from what is now called pastiche, which is, in fact, an architecture that makes a city beautiful and creates unity. "It is important to me in everything," the poet says to his Eupalinos, "to realize what is going to be, and that it answer, in all the vigor of its newness, to the reasonable requirements of what has been." This paints in broad strokes what deserves the most careful drawing, sustained by numerous examples.[1] I prefer to flip through my notes to find one of those daily logs in its natural state which, generally not

---

1. The documents on these matters and contemporary Paris have been deposited in the manuscript collections of Yale University Library.—Author.

overly indulgent, is of the kind often kept by those who walked about Paris.[2]

The attacks on the historic patrimony, under the pretext of enrichment and in the name of a culture that those who use the word do not know much about, destroy that patrimony. The projects already completed or nearing completion—others would speak of sacrilege—are scattered throughout the city. Following the chance logic of my walks, I came first upon the Bastille Opera, built at the expense of Garnier's Opéra, universally thought the most beautiful in the world. A child led me to discover and judge it. Going to look at the rue de Lappe, the scene of the *bals musettes* of my youth, but also an important background for the literature of the first half of the twentieth century, I took a bus which twice crosses the Seine before ending up on the rue du Faubourg–St. Antoine that the old revolutionaries insisted upon called rue "Antoine" (without the Saint). An old woman sat facing me, with a small child, about twelve years old. When we crossed the Seine the boy cried, excitedly, "Boats, boats!" An elderly man said to the woman: "It's clear that he loves beautiful things, your boy." Suddenly the child, terrified, threw himself on his grandmother's bosom and cried out, "No, no." The grandmother explained: "He was operated on six months ago and he was afraid I was taking him back to the hospital." Need I add that he had just seen the Bastille Opera?

Another scene observed: a newspaper announced that the minister responsible for the new Opera had decided, to soften the facade, to install a fountain with three water sprays—one blue, one white, and one red, of course. Two passerby seeing the headline exclaimed: "I hope it's not contagious!" Clearly the images of a hospital, and in the second case a pissoir, cling to this building. So much for the exterior. As to the interior, a famous American singer passing through Paris whom they would have very much liked to engage for a performance, came to see the hall. After trying a few passages and vocalizations she made a horrible grimace. The hall was abominable, the acoustics detestable. But there was something even worse, something unexpected, the unbearable odor of cooking. The ducts were incorrectly connected and the smells came from a restaurant on the first floor that the architect had thought a good idea. "I guess," said the American singer, "that when you stage Wagner you cook sauerkraut and when you stage Verdi it's macaroni!"

2. For example *Journal d'un bourgeois de Paris au XVIII siècle, ou le Journal d'un bourgeois de Paris sous le règne de Louis XV*, by E. J. F. Barbier.—Author.

But let us leave this ill-conceived Opera to its sad destiny. Besides, it may never open. There are already those asking what better use it could be put to. Why not a hospital? Truth from out of the mouths of babes. The story of this Opera would be comic but for the blow it delivered against Garnier's Opéra, which has had its revenge. One has only to see the crowds of young people who gather at the end of the week on its steps and around the building while the Place de la Bastille and its Opera remain desperately empty. Garnier's Opéra continues to fascinate and attract. The Bastille Opera repels and instills fear.

But among these attacks against what has always represented the splendor and glory of Paris, there is worse. Rather than consult my notebooks, since my visits to these sacked places are rare, I would rather reproduce a letter recently written to me by my old Balzacian friend, Suzanne Bérard, born into a family of distinguished classicists.[3] "Returning from Italy," she writes, "where the monuments and artistic treasures are preserved with a scrupulous piety, one is even more struck to see what strange procedures are followed in France. It seems they have done everything to deceive the public and prevent it from seeing the problem in its proper context." And, referring to the columns designed by a certain Buren and installed in the courtyard of the Palais Royal: "M. Buren's columns are not a *horror*. They are, if not genial, at least nice enough. They would make an excellent effect elsewhere . . . in the park of St. Cloud, for example, in some open place with trees and no architecture." Why not at the public dump, I would add? "As for the rest," Suzanne Bérard goes on, "the pyramid of Pei at the Louvre is, in itself, lovely. M. Pei should have been able to understand that the environment of the Louvre would do him a serious injustice. The juxtaposition of the pyramid and the Louvre is perfectly wrong. There is nothing transparent, nothing pointed in the architecture, which is, it goes without saying, not the work of Palladio or Michelangelo, but which does have unity of style. The airy charm of the pyramid in no way complements the monument it quite simply encumbers. There is no point in stressing that what the pyramid does could have been done equally well under any other style of architecture . . . a simple stone slab if one wanted something less visible." I would add, as a parenthesis to this letter, that on the issue of "services" there is something new. In March 1990 the opening of a restaurant and

---

3. Her most celebrated work is *La genèse d'un roman de Balzac: "Illusions Perdues"* [1837], (1961).

a cafeteria—as at the Bastille Opera, as if alimentation was a necessary accompaniment to art—and a museum shop which, when it was announced, made the souvenir shops and leather workers of Barbès and elsewhere fear for their livelihood. The pyramid so attracted and diverted visitors that most didn't have time to see the galleries. Evidence of this is something I saw in the metro, which made me sit up: "For sandals at a reasonable price, you have to go to the museum shop of the Louvre."

Going to the heart of the problem and disregarding this endless complaining of the Paris pedestrian, these "things seen" (and heard) that Victor Hugo himself did not disregard, Suzanne Bérard continues. "What is it all about? First, it is a cultural phenomenon. In order to convince the citizen to adapt himself to a world of progress and renewal, it is essential to undermine his traditional culture, to convince him that the masterpieces that have nourished his appreciation of art and in some measure formed his aesthetic judgments, are neither as moving as he thought them nor, more importantly, irreplaceable. This is a clever way to 'smash' them. Drawing a beard on the Mona Lisa worked for our forebears. Putting Buren's columns in the Palais Royal, that marvel of taste and harmony, or erecting Pei's pyramid in the courtyard of the Louvre (certainly less lovely than the Palais Royal, but more frequented), is assuredly a good way to carry out this work. It is an insolent and melancholy enterprise, but in truth it succeeds. And let them not say that numerous buildings had been similarly mistreated in the past, that many a renaissance porch has disfigured many a Gothic church. This is true but it is regrettable. At least our forebears could plead naiveté. It is not today through innocence that these things are done. There is a hidden side to these projects that the public never sees—to wrap the Pont-Neuf in fabric, to set up Buren's columns, to build the pyramid—people in the art world are paid and handsomely paid. They are obviously enthralled as the most insignificant nobleman was enthralled when called to share the manna. Every man celebrates his benefactors lavishly, from the highest to the lowest, in whatever occupation. Everyone wants a commission. Thus have our charlatans become popular"—like those of the Pompidou Center. And to close her letter, these lines on the center in which the dominant theme—but one usually neglected—of my epilogue appears: "I only regret that Pompidou, no doubt tormented, as are many at the end of their lives, by the desire to appear 'young' had opened the way to these indecent projects. Chagall is a charming artist, however limited in his inspiration, but why suspend him from the ceiling of the Opéra? Imitating such a high example the acrobats have rushed in. (But perhaps I do the acrobats, who are often dedicated artists, a disservice.) The next victim could be Versailles. Let us pray! . . ."

While waiting for the possible assault on Versailles, and having been absolved from their mortal sins, even celebrated for having committed them, those I am tempted henceforth to call acrobats are unleashed in the city, some going to the west—it is more lucrative—others to the east, and already, since there is not much space left, setting up their cranes, erecting their construction fences, in the middle of the city.

Let's begin with the west, with La Défense, whose long, unhappy story may one day be told by historians. The image of continual adversity seems to capture its essence, and I heard it from a prostitute at Pigalle as I was working on my *Montmartre du plaisir et du crime*. She and a few of her colleagues had considered moving their charms to this new quarter. She had returned disgusted after seeing the place: "It's a bit much when you can't even defend yourself at La Défense," she said! Then, as circumstances, especially international circumstances, changed, this quarter which seemed permanently moribund, came to life. In a few years a bouquet of steel and glass towers with thousands of offices sought to make Paris the business capital of Europe. To top it off—while waiting for a new road that was already announced and dubbed, quite simply "historical axis"—a monumental arch, itself containing office space, had been built to line up with the Arch de Triomphe, destroying forever "the door opening on infinity" that Barrès had celebrated.

A monstrous structure this arch—I am tempted to write "diabolical"—so built that although I have tried a number of times to visit it (by metro, by bus, by car, and even, very foolishly I have been told, on foot) I have never succeeded in reaching my goal. I have asked myself, wandering in this glass-walled labyrinth as among hostile cliffs, if I would ever find my way back to Paris, back to the land of men. There is a curious impression of nothingness, of death, and above all of fear created by these towers, which, they tell us, are full of people. I am not alone in having this feeling, just as I am not alone in not having been able to reach the monument that is already called "the arch of failed rendez-vous." In his article "Impressions de Paris" the young writer Christian Denis, recounting his exploration of La Défense, which was as painful and almost as desperate as my own, writes: "Behind the [Grand] Arch is an unrestricted view over a cemetery. In the final analysis wouldn't those in the cemetery who looked at the Arch have the same view?" A view of death. This is also the theme of Patrick Grainville's *Les Fortresses noires*.

It is doubtless to counteract this sinister aspect and to dissipate this impression that the light-shows visible from Paris, the fireworks, the laser beams, the projections on enormous screens, and other such inventions of illusion are used on certain solemn occasions. It was done for the Bicentennial of the Declaration of the Rights of Man and Citizen. Hasn't the Arch itself been baptized the Arch of Fraternity? Following the same pattern, an extravagant costume parade marched down the Champs Elysées in honor of the bicentennial of the Revolution. It would seem, said a proud political figure, that the event attracted an enormous crowd from all over the world, as much for the light show at La Défense as the bicentennial parade (or as some might say the masquerade). A letter from my friend, Rudolph Binion, made clear how the spectacle was seen abroad: "Find the time to write me, between two carmagnoles."[4]

La Défense is only the highest achievement of what has been built around Paris in the last ten years, and more and more often in Paris. Rather than decry this, instance by instance (with what sympathy is already obvious), let us rather see what has happened to the remnants of Paris, stabbed in the heart twenty years ago, assassinated.

Parenthesis

BEFORE describing, or rather penetrating to what seems to me essential, before confronting the mystery of so many inexplicable survivals, I have to underline an important fact which is now inseparable from all descriptions, not only of the suburbs but of most of the quarters of Paris. I am speaking of the development, especially in the last ten years, of a kind of immigration which, quantitatively and qualitatively, is completely different from what I have previously described.[5] This immigration has come essentially from North Africa, from sub-Saharan Africa, but also from the Near East. It has spread virtually everywhere on the Right Bank: the Left Bank has been a bit less affected. There is a general predominance of North Africans, but most striking in certain places, principally Barbès, there is a mixture of all the races. This has brought changes, increasing from year to year, which are most apparent in the appearance of North African bazaars, the prevalence of foreign dress, the way women dress and behave in public, the ardor of mosque attendance. I have described the irresistible Arab penetration of Montmartre in my

---

4. One of the more frenzied popular dances of the revolutionary period.
5. See my *Documents sur l'immigration* (1947), *La formation de la population parisienne* (1950), and finally *Les Parisiens* (1967).—Author.

"les ruines de Subure." One could describe in the same way the implantation of blacks at Strasbourg-St. Denis, despite the hostility with which certain café owners treat them, as well as that of those from the Near East, Turks, Armenians, Lebanese, and Greeks, who fill the neighboring streets.

In contrast to this ethnic mixing and a phenomenon that runs contrary to the old Parisian tradition that had no ghettos, where all the neighborhoods were open, which was as true when Daniel Halévy published *Les Pays parisiens* (1932) as when I published *Les Parisiens* (1967), is what has happened in the high-rises near the Place d'Italie between 1975 and 1980. This became a closed, mysterious neighborhood called "Chinatown": Indo-Chinese refugees, largely of Chinese origin by way of Cambodia, who were fleeing the Khmer Rouge, above all young men who had no intention of serving in the army of Lon Nol. More recently arrived Chinese from Hong Kong, less numerous than their predecessors but distrusted by them, were suspected of organizing the rackets, preying on the businessmen and restaurant owners from Cambodia. Chinatown is almost a place apart in the Parisian landscape.

This invasion creates great difficulties for one who wants to describe or record, day by day in his notebooks, what endures and (more often) what disappears in Paris. Language is paramount. Balzac tells how he would dress like a workingman in order to eavesdrop on conversations and listen to what the workers were saying: This or that episode in *Scenes from Parisian Life* were thus born. For one not knowing Arabic (not to mention the other languages), not knowing the market, not having the right physique or face, any such research is impossible, except by some unexpected chance. Such was the discovery, in the middle of the Barbès quarter, the Arab quarter par excellence, of a tiny bookstore called L'Abencérage—named after a lovely story by Chateaubriand, "les aventures du dernier Abencérage." I was so taken aback that I spoke to the owner, a Tunisian, and thanks to him I was able to explore the quarter, to understand what before had only been some kind of shadow theater. In the same way the existence, not far from Strasbourg-St. Denis, of the oldest pharmacy in Paris, which opened there in the years just before the French Revolution in a house where Napoleon Bonaparte lived on the second floor, allowed me, thanks to the distant successor of the original apothecary (so they were then called), to make sense of the ethnic confusion of the quarter, the center of centers of the city, even after twenty years, still the great intersection Haussmann had wanted. Today it is the necessary point of contact, or rather of friction, between groups who detest each other and sometimes kill each other, even more so when their countries of origin are at war. The Gulf Crisis—I am writing these lines in 1990—has sharpened these animosities.

Survivals

DESPITE this new population, despite these construction projects (more numerous and destructive than ever), despite the intrusions of men and things, what still endures, here and there, of the Old City, unchanged and miraculously preserved, always has a strange fascination for me. It is the very mystery of Paris I am speaking of, that I feel so strongly and that others feel, a feeling I always try to analyze, as have those in the past, trying to account for this feeling that is stronger in Paris than in any other city. This "nostalgia for Paris" about which Carco wrote a book in 1941, or this "melancholy" about which the young novelist Claude Dubois wrote that it is "an emanation of Paris" since "entire quarters of the City exude a vague melancholy."

It would be to betray this feeling, to lie to oneself about it, to denature it, if I were to see in it as men of my age, who have known the old Paris for nearly a century have often done, mere nostalgia for one's own past. "The Journal of the Catacombs" was the title I imagined giving, for a number of years, to the diary of my Parisian wanderings. To stroll in Paris was for me and those like me a stroll in the past, as through a dark tunnel now and then suddenly lit up. Some unexpected apparition emerges, often very moving, of some detail, some fragment, that expresses in itself and recalls large parts of the city which have today vanished, and brings back the still ardent memory of an experience lived there. The simple signs of shops which, one shudders to think, are exposed to be obliterated or ripped by the wind. For instance the sign for "La Blouse des Halles," a long way from the former markets, which is the only witness to the vast area dominated by les Halles. Or again a café in the rue St. Denis named "les deux Saules"—a corruption or "deux sols" or "deux sous," which was the price of a drink under the ancien régime—which was entirely decorated with china of many colors which depicted les Halles in full swing, completely alive. One could multiply the examples.

Then there are the men much younger than myself who have not known, as I did, this now vanished Paris. They struggle desperately to save as much of it as still remains, but are sure to fail because one cannot win against the rich promoters. They angrily scream their rage. Now we come close to getting at, or is it augmenting, the mystery of Paris. "You don't appear to be very old," one of Claude Dubois's readers wrote to him. "Where did you get this taste for Paris that you elaborate in your ballads?" Why are some so ardent to stop this imminent, inevitable destruction: the Hôtel du Nord (scene of the action in a Marcel Carné film) on the banks of the St. Martin Canal; the dance hall Petit Jardin on the avenue de Clichy (inseparable from the history of the quarter and an important place in my *Montmartre du plaisir et du crime*); the Petit Balcon, a place where *bals musettes* were held, near the rue de Lappe, which is near the Bastille Opera and directly threatened by the development frenzy set in motion by the new Opera throughout the quarter. Yes, why? Claude Dubois, who with other young men is obviously my friend, explains it from his own childhood memories, from the walks with his father, who told him about Paris. Dubois goes on to explain so many futile battles for these seemingly insignificant remnants by the existence of many distinguished literary works which not only describe them but owe their very existence to these remnants of Paris—which will never be true of what they build these days; despite all the fireworks displays, the drum-beating, and the costume parades, nothing worth reading has yet appeared and will doubtless never appear.

An old wall they want to destroy is all that remains of the rue Pagevin where *Ferragus,* a celebrated Balzac novel, begins: "In Paris there are certain streets dishonored in the same way a man is who had done infamous deeds. At 8:30 in the evening the rue Pagevin . . ." In the same vein, to attack Montmartre is to attack those who have written of the quarter, from Carco to Miller, in whose work about the Butte Montmartre you would certainly find this bit of ground planted with wretched trees and covered with weeds, called the maquis, in whose defense as I write these lines, the entire neighborhood is mobilized against the authorities to save the spot from being turned into a parking lot. Probably these courageous people who are holding off the tree cutters have not read Carco or Miller, or any of the others, but they know, perhaps better yet they feel, that their corner of the Butte is famous, or rather venerated, throughout the world, that it is sacred.

How many survivals like this are there in Parisian literature! One of the oldest and most dramatic examples—made even more so because the house in question still exists—is given by Chateaubriand at the beginning of his *Mémoires d'Outre-Tombe.* Having come to Paris from Brittany on the eve of the Revolution, to be presented at court by his father, he loved to walk, especially at night "through the desert of the crowd." One particular place drew him, a poor house near les Halles where a curious incident, recounted by Marshall de Bassompierre, had taken place in 1606.

Much given to the pleasures of the flesh, as was his friend King Henri IV, Bassompierre had a rendezvous with a beautiful woman he had met by chance and had told to wait for him between ten and midnight "and even later" on the second floor of a house in the rue du Bourg l'Abbé. This was near the rue St. Martin, not far from a bathhouse where, still in my time, everyone from the markets came to bathe. When Bassompierre arrived, the second floor was aglow. Climbing the stairs he discovered that "this glow was the bed-straw burning, and there were two naked bodies laid out on the table." What had happened? "Had the plague (for there was plague in Paris) or jealousy arrived in the rue du Bourg l'Abbé before love? One's imagination can play with such a subject. Mix the poet's inventions with the popular chorus, the burial detail arriving, Bassompierre drawing his sword, a superb melodrama will unfold from these events." When I recently went to see this house, three young gentlemen were there, furnished with notebooks, tape measures, and all the paraphernalia of the perfect "restorer." I fear the worst.

"One's imagination can play with such a subject. . . ." Here we are at the heart of the mystery of Paris: the secret attraction exercised by so many apparently insignificant remnants of the past. Chateaubriand saw it. Two recent texts analyze it or rather give an account of it that allows me to dispense with a more extensive development of the theme. The first is by Jean Plumyène, who died in 1986.[6] His admirable book, *Trajets parisiens,* published in 1984 and which, for obvious reasons—the power of real-estate interests are enormous and its ramifications numberless—had no success.

Plumyène sums up at the outset what I myself have described throughout these pages: "The sadness and even the sense of despair at seeing disappear dead-end streets, historic restaurants, immemorial facades that made up one's memory. The enchantment of finding spared from all manner of destroyers, as if by a miracle, the old-fashioned bakery, the fountain in the center of a courtyard, the end of a sidewalk where one played as a child, the permanently open brasserie. This soul of the place, formed from the time of the July Monarchy"—and long before, as Chateaubriand shows us—"crystallized under the Second Empire when Baron

---

6. The eulogy of Jean Plumyène and the most important work of this already-forgotten author have been published by Alain Besançon in the review *Commentaries* (1986).—Author.

Haussmann, cutting into the living flesh of Paris made his rational boulevards." In our own day, and more than ever, the sensitive Parisian
groans under the devastating effects of urbanization, then, turning the
corner of a street, marvels to rediscover, intact and even renovated, facades from before Haussmann. "The explanation is that the Paris stroller
is an engaged stroller. His steps follow history, I mean a literary history
which, for the last two centuries of modern times"—and long before, I
would add—"provided nourishment for his sensations, his emotions, his
reflections, occupying him as reader, critic, writer. Contemplate these
gray facades, these discolored metal shades, these inaccessible mansard
roofs, lament that a wood- and coal-seller has been replaced by a pizze-
ria, stand on the corner of some bleak street: you are a part of literature.
The City of Paris is writing its memoirs in which you are a paragraph, a
word, a punctuation mark. Here is something mysterious."

In *Paris*, published in the 1980s, Julian Green writes: "In my eyes Paris
will remain the setting for a novel that no one will ever write. How many
times have I returned from long walks through the old streets, my heart
heavy with all the inexpressible things I have seen! Is it an illusion? I don't
think so. Often I stop suddenly in front of some large window with artificial lace curtains, deep in an old part of the city, and daydream endlessly about what unknown destinies had unfolded behind these dark
windows." But Balzac wrote of nothing else, and the Parisian chapters of
his *Comédie humaine* should bear sufficient witness to the fact that he
wrote what the city dictated to him; he felt that he was transcribing its
dictation, as the city has made others feel and still makes many feel
today.

This is the secret that one might discover from the many remnants of
Old Paris that have miraculously escaped the demolishers; this is the attraction, or rather the fascination, they still hold for so many.